Sojou

South Carolina, 1865–1947

Sojourns in Charleston, South Carolina, 1865–1947

From the Ruins of War to the Rise of Tourism

EDITED BY

Jennie Holton Fant

THE UNIVERSITY OF
SOUTH CAROLINA PRESS

© 2019 University of South Carolina

Published by the University of South Carolina Press
Columbia, South Carolina 29208

www.sc.edu/uscpress

Manufactured in the United States of America

28 27 26 25 24 23 22 21 20 19
10 9 8 7 6 5 4 3 2 1

The Library of Congress Cataloging-in-Publication data
can be found at http://catalog.loc.gov/.

ISBN 978-1-61117-939-2 (cloth)
ISBN 978-1-61117-940-8 (ebook)

Contents

Illustrations

Acknowledgments

In the research and preparation of this anthology, I have incurred many debts of gratitude. I owe my appreciation to the descendants of Owen Wister, via Alice E. Stokes, for permission to publish an excerpt from *Roosevelt, Story of A Friendship*. My thanks to the Norman Rockwell Family Agency for permission to reprint "The Battle of Charleston 1918" from Rockwell's autobiography, *Norman Rockwell, My Adventures as an Illustrator*. My gratitude to the heirs of Schuyler Livingston Parsons, Stephanie Wharton Holbrook and Lena Pless, for permission to reprint the Charleston portion from Parson's autobiography, *Untold Friendships*. My appreciation to Mark De Wolfe Howe descendant Fanny Howe for permission to reprint the article "The Song of Charleston." Credit is owed to the Archives of American Art at the Smithsonian Institution for the account of Holger Cahill, excerpted from the Rockefeller report in the Holger Cahill papers. My thanks to Russell & Volkening, literary agents for the May Sarton Estate, for permission to reprint Sarton's poem "Charleston Plantations." My appreciation to Jerry Rosco, literary executor of the Glenway Wescott estate and coeditor of Wescott's journals, *Continual Lessons,* for permission to reprint excerpts regarding Wescott's visits with Somerset Maugham at Yemassee, South Carolina. I am further indebted to Mr. Rosco for the photograph of Wescott.

My gratitude to the National Gallery of Canada for rights to the artwork of Charles Henry White. My appreciation to Houghton Library at Harvard University for the reproduction of Amy Lowell; and to Albert and Shirley Small Special Collections at the University of Virginia Library for the reproduction of Emily Clark Balch. My thanks to the Abby Aldrich Rockefeller Folk Art Museum at Colonial Williamsburg for rights and reproduction of the paintings *Legareville* and *Old Plantation*. My appreciation to the Thomas Cooper Library at the University of South Carolina for reproductions of the artwork of J. Champney Wells, and Mrs. T. P. O'Connor. As well, I am indebted for illustrations garnered from the collections of the Library of Congress Prints and Photographs and the New York Public Library.

Finally, my gratitude to James Wood, the incomparable genius with technology, and to friends and family who have tolerated my decades-long obsession with Charleston history, which has taken up *all* my time.

Introduction

noun pa·limp·sest \ˈpa-ləm(p)-ˌsest, pə-ˈlim(p)-\: a manuscript in which later writing has been superimposed on earlier (effaced) writing; something that has many obvious stages or levels of meaning, development, or history; a multilayered record.

"Here, four years ago, the first fortifications of the war were thrown up. Here the dashing young cavaliers, the haughty Southrons . . . determined to have a country and a history for themselves, rushed madly into the war as into a picnic. Here the boats from Charleston landed every day cases of champagne, pâtés innumerable, casks of claret, thousands of Havana cigars, for the use of the luxurious young Captains and Lieutenants and their friends among the privates. . . Here, with feasting, and dancing, and love making, with music improvised from the ballroom, and enthusiasm fed to madness by well-ripened old Madeira, the free-handed, free-mannered young men who had ruled "society" at Newport and Saratoga . . . dashed into revolution as they would into a waltz. Not one of them doubted that, only a few months later, he should make his accustomed visit to the Northern watering places, and be received with the distinction due a hero of Southern independence. Long before these fortifications, thus begun, were abandoned, they saw their enterprise in far different lights, and conducted it in a far soberer and less luxurious way."—Whitelaw Reid from *After the War: A Southern Tour,* 1866.

"And the story depicted in the irregular weave is of a place extravagant in its beauty, reckless in its fecundity, terrible in its indifference, and dark with memories."—Sally Mann, *Hold Still*

"There is properly no history, only biography."—Ralph Waldo Emerson

"Five years ago Charleston sat like a queen living upon the waters," writes Farley Peck, among the northern journalists who herded south in 1865 to report on the defeated Confederacy. "Its fine society has been dissipated if not completely destroyed." Journalist Whitelaw Reid notes: "We steamed into Charleston Harbor early in the morning; and one by one, Sumter, Moultrie, Pinckney, and at last the City of Desolation itself rose from the smooth expanse of water." Correspondent Sidney Andrews observes, "A City of ruins, of desolation, of vacant houses, of widowed women, of rotting wharves, of deserted warehouses, of weed-wild gardens, of miles of grass-grown streets, of acres of pitiful and voiceful barrenness,—that is Charleston."

The queen of the South before the Civil War, Charleston fell to Federal forces on February 17, 1865. Approximately 12,992 South Carolina men had died as soldiers, leaving young boys, old men, women and girls to pull the pieces together. The fire in December of 1861, which destroyed one hundred and forty-five acres of the peninsula, and northern bombardment of the city for eighteen months left Charleston in shambles—a wreck that would remain apparent until well after World War I. Martial law was declared, lands were confiscated by the government, and citizens were ordered to take an oath of allegiance if they wanted their houses returned, passes for mobility, or any favor whatsoever. Reconstruction ensued, and for the next eleven years federal troops were garrisoned in the state.

To present an anthology of "travel accounts" of Charleston from the Civil War into the twentieth century is to see history unfold in an ever-shifting landscape. Further, even in the decades before the war, any standard genre of travel accounts and travel books that had dominated in earlier antebellum times had ended. After the war, travel documentation of the region becomes less orthodox and more American. Progressively, travel was no longer predictable, with the rise of faster steamships, hundreds of thousands of miles of railroad tracks, the automobile, and air travel. New travelers were increasingly middle class, who began touring in droves. Unlike antebellum travelers, whose American travels had lasted sometimes one or two years and included stays in private homes, new middleclass travelers took shorter trips and stayed in hotels. Another notable difference is the writers themselves, who—although from today's perspective are not as diverse as one would wish—gradually become more diverse than earlier chroniclers.

My focus has remained to explore the history of the Charleston region through the documentary testimony of its travelers and tourists. Taken from a variety of resources and written in a variety of styles, including poetry, these "travel accounts" increasingly follow no general pattern—yet trace a travelers' history of Charleston and the region. My intent has been to collect eyewitness accounts and see the region through the eyes of outsiders, to see where these observers take us, and what and who we can uncover in unraveling a history. Therefore, in an overlay of narratives, superimposed through time and multiple memories and viewpoints, this is a search for a palimpsestic truth. Taken all together, we are left with an "irregular weave" of recorded evidence of life in the region over these decades.

As Northern war journalists arrived to describe postwar conditions in reportage, Farley Peck was among the first. He had been in Charleston when the first shots of the Civil War were fired in 1861, was there during the war, and was returning to experience the aftermath—all of which he documented for *Harper's New Monthly*. In "Four Years Under Fire," he recalls: "There are events in a man's life which he never forgets; there are scenes which never fade from his sight, and sounds which are ever fresh in his hearing, though he attain a century of years." Peck best sums up the war and its aftereffects on the city.

Whitelaw Reid, a twenty-four-year-old correspondent, had gained national renown as a talented journalist in the war. As the war was ending in 1865, he joined US Chief Justice Salmon Chase on the U.S.R.C. *Wayanda*, a United States steam revenue cutter, for a tour of the defeated southern states. From the South, Reid sent dispatches north for publication. In 1866, he overhauled his dispatches and published them as *After the War: A Southern Tour*. Described as a masterpiece of journalism, it was said to answer every question that the North was raising. Reid concluded that southerners remained "arrogant and defiant, still nursing the embers of 'rebellion' and cherishing its ashes." In fact, fifteen years later, he was still bemoaning conditions in the South in newsprint. Reid documents the early occupation of Charleston in "City of Desolation."

In "The Dead Body of Charleston" from his book, *The South Since the War*, journalist Sidney Andrews disparages "the widespread lack of education and culture in the South, undemocratic caste system, festering racial tensions, and the entrenched anti-Union sentiment." Like most northerners, Andrews resented the aristocratic hierarchy, whom he felt had long controlled government to their benefit before the war—yet after the war seemed to lack the "recuperative power" to resurrect itself without northern intervention. In Charleston, he opines, "If Northern capital and Northern energy do not come here, the ruin, they say, must remain a ruin; and if this time five years, finds here a handsome and thriving city, it will be the creation of New England." He predicts, "The Charleston of 1875 will doubtless be proud in wealth and intellect and rich in grace and culture. Let favoring years bring forward such fruitage!"

Among northern newspapermen, it was John T. Trowbridge, who in his investigation of the postwar Confederacy first wrote, "The ruins of Charleston are the most picturesque of any I saw in the South."[*] Although his account is not included here, he was the first to style the city's ruin as "picturesque." After

---

[*] Trowbridge, *A Picture of the Desolated States and the Work of Restoration*, 515.

1870, this would become the term most often used in depictions of the region. As reformist accounts ebbed, local color narratives began to take hold.

In the post–Civil War years, production and sales of newspapers, magazines, and books began to flourish at a prodigious rate due to the faster speed, lower costs, efficient and more rapid distribution by railroad, and the growth of advertising. The public was curious about the American landscape and touring in search of the "picturesque," a convention of the time. Although the former states of the Confederacy were considered backward and morally corrupt, the South had begun to recover enough to attract travelers and travel writers. Northerners had become intensely curious about the South and its "mysterious" southerners, and the reading public was interested in knowing "what was *different* down there." As early as 1866, *Harper's Weekly* introduced a series of woodcuts of Southern life with the remark, "To us the late Slave States seem almost like a newly discovered country."[*]

In 1869, the periodical *Appletons' Journal* led the way when they began publishing articles about American cities by travel writers accompanied by traveling artists who provided on-the-spot high-quality illustrations. Thus began a concerted effort by *Appletons'*, followed by *Scribner's Monthly*, to reintroduce northerners to the South and encourage reconciliation, as well as promote investment. In an effort to attract northerners to the region, it was D. Appleton & Co. editor and author Oliver Bell Bunce who, influenced by his artist, Henry Fenn, first so vividly portrays Charleston in sweet semitropical decay, its "time-tinted mansions" in "the hush of venerable repose," coupled with the "sweetness and beauty of the scene" and the "transition to a terrestrial paradise." In "Charleston and its Suburbs," published in *Appletons'* in 1871, Bunce writes of "a fine bit of dilapidation, a ruin with a vine clambering over it, a hut all awry, with a group of negroes in their flaring turbans set against the gaping walls, old chimneys and old roofs." His symbolic and colorful style of rendering Charleston would endure. Soon after, he more widely promoted a picturesque, exotic paradise and gothic South. Before long travel writers were flocking to Florida, Virginia, and Louisiana, the particularly "swampy" regions of the South, to exaggerate elements and enhance an "eerie and grotesque" beauty. Author Rebecca McIntyre has written that because of the flurry of articles and illustrations that followed, northern readers began to find the South increasingly amusing but, what was more important, they found it reassuring. These images solidified a growing assumption that the North was "normal," representative of the best

[*] Garrett Epps, "The Undiscovered Country," 411–28.

in the nation, while the South remained simply an exotic "other."* Nonetheless, the exotic other was intriguing and alluring, and Charleston was particularly so. The city would be portrayed as picturesque and exotic for a very long time—as would the region's blacks.

In competition with *Appletons'*, a few years later *Scribner's* sent Edward King on an extensive tour through the South and southwest during 1873 and the spring and summer of 1874, with his own illustrator, J. Wells Champney. King's fifteen illustrated articles on the South appeared in *Scribner's Monthly* and were so popular in both the United States and Britain that he revised and published them as *The Great South* in 1875. In "Charleston, South Carolina. The Venice of America," he touches on the picturesque but more fully concentrates on the political and financial state of Reconstruction, something Bunce fails to mention. King sees a city ripe for commercial development and applauds the "vigorous enterprise of arriviste investors" but finds the true condition as one of "fierce Southern honor pitched against Northern appetites." However, as King was more sympathetic and conciliatory to the South than were earlier northern journalists, his account signifies a slight change in northern attitude.

As northerners gave up hope of "colonization" and returned north, there was a growing curiosity about political and social conditions of blacks in the South. In 1878, Sir George Campbell, Irish M.P. for the United Kingdom, took an extended trip through the South to investigate unsettled racial relations, which he documented in his book, *White and Black* (1879). He arrived in "The Petrel State" at Columbia just after the displacement of the "carpetbaggers" and during the November 1878 reelection of Wade Hampton III for governor. Campbell took stock of the political situation before he traveled on to Charleston to describe conditions there. He encountered blacks and whites in the region and witnessed the rise of the "New South."

Two years later, author Eliza Houston Barr journeyed to John's Island to perform mission work among ex-slaves for the American Missionary Society. While living at Headquarters Plantation, also known as Fenwick Hall, she penned "Inside Southern Cabins" for *Harper's Weekly*, in which she describes social conditions, work, religious practices, and the customs of blacks living in the outlying island regions and in Charleston. Soon after, Lady Duffus Hardy, a popular British novelist and travel writer, tours the city that "seems to have stood still during the last century," a place with "a character peculiarly its own." Hardy uncovers the dire conditions, destitute aristocrats, idle blacks, and the

* McIntyre, "Promoting the Gothic South," 33–61.

proud shabbiness of Charleston in those years in "A Ghost of Dead Days" from her book *Down South* (1883).

From the 1880s Ward McAllister, a Savannah native who became arbiter of New York City society from the 1860s and created the "Four Hundred" families' plutocracy, fashioned a fascination with southern life and southern ancestors among the upper-class of New York and Newport. Soon wealthy northerners began to frequent the region in search of southern roots, mild weather, outdoor sports, and the quaint charm of Charleston, reminiscent of European towns. Impoverished Charleston aristocrats opened their rooms to lodgers and "courted the Yankees," who eventually bought property and participated in civic and cultural affairs. Beginning around 1892 and lingering into the 1940s, rich northerners purchased plantations as winter residences, acquiring lowcountry acreage and whole islands. Buying, building, restoring, decorating, and staffing these plantation properties contributed to employment regionally for both blacks and whites. Further, this northern descent coincided with the genesis of Charleston preservation efforts and the creation of a mythology from the past envisaged by the descendants of old Charleston families. The romance of a fallen aristocracy fascinated visitors, and this was a first glimmer of a financial future for Charleston, which would be tourism.

Charleston experienced a major cyclone in late August of 1885, and the next year (August 31, 1886) the city was nearly destroyed by the largest earthquake ever recorded in the southeastern United States. One hundred people died and hundreds of buildings were destroyed. In *A Short Sketch of Charleston*, published just after the earthquake, an anonymous author observed, "The brave old city will survive this shock, too, though by far the severest blow to its prosperity and well-being it has ever received. The indomitable spirit and energy of its people will, in the future as in the past, maintain it in its accustomed rank among the cities of the world in spite of all obstacles, and Charleston will continue as heretofore, on account of its excellent harbor, beautiful location and historical interest to attract business men, pleasure seekers and students alike."[*]

Indeed, over time the charm of Charleston was becoming well-known, and travelers were venturing to the city, a few documenting their stay. Some wrote articles for publication, others included their experiences in a larger work. Owen Wister and his wife first discovered the city on their honeymoon in 1898 and were "enchanted." They returned on a subsequent visit during the South Carolina Interstate and West Indian Exposition, a regional trade exposition held in Charleston (December 1, 1901, to June 20, 1903), which attracted 700,000 people

---

[*] Anonymous, *Short Sketch of Charleston, S.C.*, 37.

from around the nation to Hampton Park. At the same time, Wister's friend, President Theodore Roosevelt, attended the Exposition amid much controversy, which Wister reveals in an excerpt from *Roosevelt, The Story of a Friendship*. He describes the city, politics, and the poor but proud Charlestonians at the turn of the century. In 1905, his enchantment would result in his novel, *Lady Baltimore*, set in a Charleston renamed Kings Port.

In 1907, artist Charles Henry White both wrote and illustrated a travel article for *Harper's Monthly,* depicting a Charleston "still shunned by the artist" and "only beginning to be discovered by the tourists." As a result of the article, White planted the first seeds of the Charleston Renaissance, a flowering of the arts and cultural institutions in the city in the next decades. His rendering of the region attracted northern artists, who ventured to town to create artwork that was widely distributed, bringing national attention to the city.

In 1912, Edward Hungerford, an author and railroad enthusiast in search of material for his *Personality of American Cities,* was urged to include Charleston in his book. In "Where Romance and Courtesy Do Not Forget," he travels by railroad from New York to experience the "modern" city which he finds not so up to date. He opines, "Charleston society is never democratic—no matter how Charleston politics may run. Its great houses, behind the exclusion of those high and forbidding walls, are tightly closed to such strangers as come without the right marks of identification. From without you may breathe the hints of old mahogany, of fine silver and china, of impeccable linen, of well-trained servants, but your imagination must meet the every test as to the details. Gentility does not flaunt herself. And if the younger girls of Charleston society *do* drive their motor cars pleasant mornings through the crowded shopping district of King Street, that does not mean that Charleston, the Charleston of the barouche and the closed coupé, will ever approve." Soon after, Mrs. T. P. O'Connor, unwell in London and longing for the South of her youth to revive her, tours "Hospitable Charleston," which she documented in her book, *My Beloved South* (1913). O'Connor rambles all over town and, well-connected socially, attends a St. Cecilia ball.

Author William Dean Howells visited for ten days in April of 1915. In his travel sketch for *Harper's Monthly,* he discovers "the sense of something Venetian" in "a city imagined from a civic consciousness quite as intense as that of any of the famed cities of the world." Nevertheless, he writes, "If I speak here of the rude wooden balcony overhanging the pavement of a certain Charleston Street where men, women, and children used to stand and be bidden off at auction by the buyers underneath, it is not to twit the present with the past in a city apparently unconscious of it."

Artist Norman Rockwell, stationed at the Charleston Naval Base during World War I, left a record of this assignment in his autobiography, *My Adventures as an Illustrator*. Rockwell describes his short stay in the region, and provides a comic glimpse of the goings on at the Charleston Navy Yard in "The Battle of Charleston 1918."

After World War I, with leisure travel in Europe no longer viable, tourism increased in America. Between 1916 and 1925, the number of automobiles purchased in the country tripled, causing a boom of road travel and bringing middle-class American travelers to Charleston. As cars flooded in, with them came wide streets, gas stations and the razing of mansions to make room for them, damage to old structures from exhaust—and commerce. Charleston began to teeter a fine line between preservation and the commercialism necessary for a tourist industry. Yet having failed to attract industry, tourism remained imperative, being one of the only means of raising city revenues.

Of course, the real wealth in the lowcountry for locals remained the antiquated city, a rich geography, and the pleasurable lifestyle created therein. The threads of rivers, creeks and marshes provided shrimp, crab, oysters and sea turtle. Sweet salt breezes carried the calls of the shrimp and vegetable vendors as they peddled their wares through town. Like clockwork, the Mosquito Fleet left the harbor before dawn and returned at sunset trawling nets full of fish, crowned with flocks of sea gulls following in their wake. This was the natural wealth of Charleston. According to one turn-of-the-century transplant, a Charleston gentleman remarked, "Why does anybody want to live out of Charleston who can live in it? Here he can have his shrimp and hominy for breakfast, his okra soup for dinner, a good hair mattress to sleep on at night, and everybody knows who he is."* Native poet and author Josephine Pinckney wrote, "Luckily the climate is ameliorating; the struggle for subsistence is less hardening than in colder temperatures." She described the South in these decades as she saw it from Charleston, and the southerner as "still rather ritualistic towards his dinner-table; his breakfast of roe-herring and batter bread demanding a half hour or more of his time. The big meal is at two o'clock in the afternoon, a light supper well after dark followed by a stroll on the Battery in the cool of the evening. The absence of huge cities, the large percentage of townspeople lately recruited from the plantation and the farm, make for simplicity in human intercourse. You have neighbors for better or worse, and you drop in to see them and take them some hot rolls when the cook bakes especially well. The South is not yet speeded up to the American tempo, and this results in a leisure time that allows for small

* Breaux, *Autobiography of a Chameleon*, 89.

courtesies."* The larger truth is that most locals were impoverished during these decades, yet poverty had become fashionable in Charleston, with a strict code of courtesy, gentility, and good manners, regardless of hard times. What persisted has remained legendary in the life of the region—tradition.

The cultural institutions founded during the 1920s had an impact on the city. The Society for the Preservation of Old Dwellings was founded in 1920, and the Joseph Manigault House was opened as Charleston's first museum house. (In 1928, a second museum house, the Heyward-Washington House opened to visitors.) The Poetry Society of South Carolina was founded in 1921, attracting well-known poets, authors, and the literary to town. Among those who came to lecture the Poetry Society was Boston poet Amy Lowell, whose visit and travel poems are included here as "And the Garden Was a Fire of Magenta." Ultimately this literary exposure on the national scene, as well as the regional poems, articles, and books being published by members of the Poetry Society, further enhanced the city as a travel destination. The most notable book among members was DuBose Heyward's *Porgy,* published in 1925. The novel brought Charleston a great deal of attention, as would composer George Gershwin in 1934, when he arrived to research and compose *Porgy and Bess,* transposing Heyward's novel into the first American opera.

With the rise of cotton mills that provided industry to upstate South Carolina, and freight rates favoring inland regions, age-old agricultural traditionalism remained manifest in Charleston as industrial development largely passed the city by. Regardless of attempts made in the 1880s and 1890s to participate in the New South—whose advocates espoused a willingness to work hard for economic renewal and advocated for sectional reconciliation and racial harmony—an ultimate lack of new industry and new construction "allowed" Charleston to "lay in splendid isolation." In 1922, Ludwig Lewisohn, contributing editor to *The Nation,* was accused of libel for his comments on both Charleston and the state in "South Carolina: A Lingering Fragrance." Lewisohn immigrated to the state with his family as a child and, being Jewish, remained an outsider in Charleston. In his article, he reveals his love-hate relationship with Charleston, grieves the New South men in power in the state, and laments the loss of the cultivation of the Charleston gentry of earlier times, shedding light on the city's literary past.

In the outside world, both Europe and America experienced a cultural schism in the 1920s. "The world broke in two in 1922 or thereabouts," author Willa Cather wrote of the years in America between the traditionalism of the past and

* Pinckney, "Bulwarks against Change," 47.

modernism. Tourists to Charleston came in a steady stream after 1923, when the New York City musical *Runnin' Wild* introduced the dance, "The Charleston," which became a worldwide craze. When the Prince of Wales took to the dance floor in London in 1925 to skillfully perform the Charleston, the public wanted to see the town where the dance originated. However, Charlestonians of this era had a civilization to which to cling, and, after a brief flirtation with the more superficial times of the Jazz Age, locals remained where they were, cementing long-standing traditions and nurturing the myth of Charleston. As cultural renewal enveloped the city, focus remained on restoring old neighborhoods. In 1931, the planning and zoning ordinance established the "Old and Historic District" to protect twenty-three blocks and four hundred buildings, the first such legislation in the country supported by government. At the same time, the Board of Architectural Review, sponsored by the City, was created to regulate exteriors in the Historic District.

Meanwhile in 1928, Schuyler Livingston Parsons, heir to a New York fortune, was sent to convalesce in Charleston. He first rented Josephine Pinckney's mansion at 21 King Street, and was wintering in town when the stock market crashed in 1929. Over the prior decade, antique dealers had increasingly descended on a destitute Charleston. Whole rooms were stripped, sold, and carted off by wealthy visitors and museum directors who sought to purchase the city's architectural elements—mantels, balconies, moldings, gates, paneling, and anything redolent of Old South souvenirs. Parsons, who dabbled in antiques, began to sell off family heirlooms for locals bankrupted in the crash. Although Charlestonians did not consider this a respectable way to produce income, they sold out of dire need and with "quick, quiet reluctance." Yet Parsons, who knew all the well-off socialites of his day, socializes more than he works. In "Mr. Parson's Mansion" from his autobiography, *Untold Friendships,* Parsons recounts his experiences in town during his seasonal migrations.

Travelers in the 1930s provide a record of more of the city's ongoing cultural institutions. The Society for the Preservation of Spirituals, founded in 1922, was exclusive to white Charlestonians born or brought up on plantations "or within the tradition." Members sought to preserve and perform the songs they had heard in their youths from nurses, maids, and other blacks in the region. Still in existence, the group continues to perform a white version of black spirituals. In 1930, Mark De Wolfe Howe traveled from Boston to attend a Society concert and wrote an article for the *Atlantic Monthly* titled "The Song of Charleston." That same year, Emily Clark, founder of *The Reviewer* in Richmond, Virginia, published an article for *The Virginia Quarterly Review* on her literary relationship with DuBose Heyward, in which she chronicles "Supper at the Goose Creek

Club," an event she attended on a plantation outside of Charleston. From there, she takes a retrospective look back to her literary association with the Charleston author who had become famous, and to the origins of the Poetry Society.

In the years following World War I, as increasing emphasis was placed on technology and mass production, a national fascination with regionalism, folklore, Americana, and Afro-American culture gained strength. Folk art became relevant to the national consciousness as nostalgic reminders of simpler times. By the 1930s, weathervanes, portraits, decoys, hooked rugs, needlepoint, theorem paintings, and other forms of folk art were being displayed in major art museums. This culminated in the establishment of museums such as the Abby Aldrich Rockefeller Folk Art Museum in Colonial Williamsburg in Virginia, and the American Folk Art Museum in New York City. In 1935, Holger Cahill—soon to be appointed national director of the Federal Art Project of the New Deal's Works Progress Administration—traveled to South Carolina to scout for folk art for Abby Rockefeller's Williamsburg museum. Cahill left a record of his searches in the South, known as the Rockefeller report. He devoted the second half of the report to the four days he spent on the hunt in South Carolina. In "Scouting for Folk Art," he describes his searches in Charleston, Orangeburg, and Columbia, and his purchase of items including notable South Carolina paintings.

In 1940, Richard Coleman incensed Charlestonians with "Charleston: The Great Myth," published in *The Forum* under the pseudonym "Edward Twig." In the article, Coleman writes of "a legendary Charleston that exists only in the minds of the self-deluded." May Sarton was a young poet in the 1940s when she drove her Mercury convertible to Charleston, and loved it. However, she soon discovered deeper complexities. In her poem, "Charleston Plantation," she notices her reflection in a cypress-blackened pond, seeing a "face too white," and perceives a Charleston century as "embalmed as Egypt."

One visitor to the outlying region was famous British author Somerset Maugham. He was living on the French Riviera when in 1940, the collapse of France and its occupation by the German Third Reich forced him to take refuge in this country. He spent four years of the World War II–era in Yemassee, sixty miles south of Charleston, courtesy of his publisher, Nelson Doubleday, who owned Bonny Hall Plantation nearby. During these years in Yemassee, when Maugham worked on his novel, *The Razor's Edge,* and other projects, his young friend, author Glenway Wescott, visited him twice. Wescott documented these visits in his journal, *Continual Lessons* (1991). "With Maugham at Yemassee" is an intriguing account of the famous author in the lowcountry in the 1940s.

Over these decades, visitors often remarked that the atmosphere of the region owed much of its charm to the region's blacks and their Gullah culture. Yet reality went beyond these superficial typecasts in the mythology of old Charleston. Shortly after the Civil War, rural blacks migrated to Charleston in large numbers hoping for economic advantages they did not find and increasing the city's black population, a clear majority over Charleston whites. Poverty was rampant for whites but moreso for blacks, many who were living in back alleys and under bridges. The worldwide depression in the 1870s further devastated the city's weak economy. Fifty-three hundred blacks (and two hundred whites) lost their modest savings in 1874 when the Freedman's Bank failed, along with thirty-eight Charleston firms. Once the Radical Republicans were driven from political power in 1876, the pace of discrimination and enforced separation of the races quickened in Charleston.* During the 1880s, African Americans were all but excluded from the political life of the state, due to systematic disenfranchisement of black voters after Reconstruction. Economically, by the turn of the century the majority of southern blacks were reduced from the promises of financial freedom and fair wages to other forms of monetary dependency, and a return to work in the fields as tenant farmers and sharecroppers. From 1900 to World War I, there was a huge migration of African Americans to the North due to the demise of contract labor, crop failures, lynchings in the South, and Jim Crow laws, coupled with an increase in job opportunities in the North. In Charleston, after 1936 New Deal agencies commenced slum clearance projects and the building of public housing, which contributed to dividing the city by race. Beginning in 1938, the destruction of an African American neighborhood bordering the city's Historic District to build an all-white public housing project, Robert Mills Manor, displaced blacks and considerably altered the demographics of the downtown landscape.

Many African Americans are encountered in these narratives, and I have identified many, yet accounts by black visitors to Charleston are hard to find. However, when Vashti Maxwell Grayson, an African American poet and Ph.D. from Baltimore, married William Henry Grayson Jr., the descendant of a leading black Charleston family, she lived in town for a number of years. In 1945 she published a poem about Charleston in *Phylon,* a journal founded by W. E. B. Du Bois, leaving a unique glimpse of the city into the World War II era from her perspective.

In 1947, on a four-month lecture tour through the country, French writer Simone de Beauvoir visited Charleston, which she refers to as "these aristocratic paradises" in *America Day by Day.* De Beauvoir provides a glance at Charleston tourism in the late 1940s. However, she writes, "To create private paradises as

---

* Jenkins, *Seizing the New Day,* 159, 161.

extravagant as the Alhambra, it took the immense wealth of the planters and the hell of slavery; the delicate petals of the azaleas and the camellias were tinged with blood." At the same time, she privately wrote Jean Paul Sartre of the inherent racial tensions she observed in the South. After witnessing the segregation of facilities, water fountains, restaurants, and buses, she wrote elsewhere in her journal: "It is our own skin that became heavy and stifling: its color making us burn. We are the enemy despite ourselves, responsible for the color of our skin and all that implies."

De Beauvoir's perceptions on segregation set the stage for the ensuing years. A few years later, Thurgood Marshall—who would become the first African American appointed to the United States Supreme Court—would lead a team of lawyers in filing a lawsuit against the school district of Clarendon County, South Carolina, challenging public school segregation and declaring desegregation illegal. Though they would lose the case, the dissent of Charlestonian Judge Waites Waring (1880–1968) in *Briggs vs. Elliott* would form the legal foundation for the Supreme Court overturning the "separate but equal" doctrine in the *1954 Brown v. Board of Education* decision, inciting whites and setting off a tumultuous civil rights struggle that would envelope the city, state, and nation in the next decades.

Meanwhile, by 1947 Charleston was headed to its ultimate future as a major tourist destination, focusing on its past. Today Charleston is one of the most visited of American cities. Paradoxically, it remains provocative as a major antebellum center of slavery.

To me, this centuries-old city—in all its complexities—remains one of the most fascinating places on earth. Its history is a vast tome of stories, biographies, and intrigue. This is foremost the exploration of a geography, physical and human, black and white and a journey through the region's multi-layered history from the tragedy of the Civil War.

So let me take you back. It is 1865 and the Civil War has just ended.

Notes on Text

The British English variant of some accounts has been retained, therefore irregular spelling, grammar, punctuation, and quotations remain as they appear in the original text.

Innumerable visitors describe the same Charleston attractions, such as St. Philip's, St. Michael's, the Huguenot Church, the Old Market (which some incorrectly refer to as the Slave Market), Magnolia Cemetery, Magnolia Gardens, Drayton Hall, and so forth. Some of these duplications have been retained, as one visitor's observation may contribute to the validity of another's, offer an alternative view, or provide additional information. Further, facts stated by these travelers—dates, people encountered, situations, or events—have been researched to validate fact and probability, and identities, corrections, clarifications (and amplifications) are provided in extensive footnotes, which are important to the texts.

Disparaging remarks made about African Americans in these accounts, even by abolitionists, in no way reflect my views or those of our more enlightened times. Contributors were limited by the times in which they lived, by racism, classism, a lack of women's' rights, and such of their day.

Charleston, South Carolina. Ruins, 1865. Library of Congress

W. F. G. Peck (1865)

"Four Years Under Fire"

W. F. G. Peck, "Four Years Under Fire" from *Harper's New Monthly*
31:183 (August, 1865): 358–66.

William Farley Peck (1840–1908) was a lawyer, journalist, and historian from Rochester, New York. His father, Everard Peck, was a printer, publisher, banker, and a founder of the University of Rochester, who served as a trustee. Farley Peck attended boarding schools and spent a year at the University, before he transferred to Williams College in Williamstown, Massachusetts, graduating in 1861. He afterward received a law degree from the State Law School at Albany, New York, and spent a short time working for a law firm before he became a journalist, which brought him to Charleston at the beginning, during, and at the end of the Civil War. In 1865, he published an article of these experiences in *Harper's New Monthly*.

Before the war, the village of Rochester had been a center of antislavery sentiment and played an important role as a station on the Underground Railroad. Peck's half-brother, Henry Everard Peck, a Congregationalist minister and professor, was an abolitionist involved in activities of the Underground Railroad, piloting fugitive slaves from Ohio to Canada via Rochester. His cousin, Samuel Drummond Porter, also worked for the Underground Railroad and assisted his close friend Frederick Douglass by hiding fugitive slaves and helping them escape to Canada. It is less clear whether Farley Peck was involved in these activities, although it is easy to assume he shared the sentiment.

From 1868, Peck was an editor of two Rochester newspapers, the *Democrat* and the *Chronicle,* and other newspapers. He afterward wrote articles and historical books about the Rochester region.

In the following article, Peck, witness to events in Charleston at the start of the war, returned to summarize the war and its immediate aftereffects for *Harper's*.

SOURCES

Leonard, John, ed. *Who's Who in America*. Chicago: A. N. Marquis Co., 1901.
Peck Family Papers (1824–1965). Rush Rhees Library. University of Rochester. Accessed Jan. 4, 2016. http://rbscp.lib.rochester.edu/1079.

Peck, William Farley. *History of Rochester and Monroe County, New York: From the Earliest Historic Times to the Beginning of 1907.* Vol. 1. Chicago: Pioneer Publishing Co., 1908.

Porter Family Papers. Rush Rhees Library, University of Rochester. Accessed Dec. 14, 2015. http://rbscp.lib.rochester.edu/1094.

Snodgrass, Mary Ellen. *Underground Railroad: An Encyclopedia of People, Places, and Operations.* London: Routledge Co., 2015.

"Four Years Under Fire"

Five years ago Charleston sat like a queen living upon the waters. With the Ashley on the west and the Cooper on the east, her broad and beautiful bay covered with the sails of every nation, and her great article of export affording employment to thousands of looms, there was no city in the broad South whose present was more prosperous or whose future seemed more propitious. Added to its commercial advantages were those of a highly-cultivated society. There was no city in the United States that enjoyed a higher reputation for intellectual culture than the metropolis of South Carolina. With this high intellectual culture were associated a refinement of taste, an elegance of manner, and a respect for high and noble lineage which made Charleston to appear more like some aristocratic European city than the metropolis of an American State. Combined with the English cavalier element which originally peopled the State, there has always been a strong admixture of the descendants of the old Huguenot families, who fled to this part of the world upon the revocation of the edict of Nantes. Some of these families, tracing their descent even back to a prior emigration from Italy into France, claim as their ancestor one of the Doges of Venice. The Huguenot element has always been evinced in the society of Charleston, not only in peculiarity of taste and of feature but likewise in ecclesiastical organization. The present Huguenot Church is the third which has stood upon the site—the first organization of the congregation occurring about 1690—and is distinguished by a liturgy which for beauty of expression and simplicity of style is unsurpassed by that of any other religious body.

The general appearance of the city was in keeping with the historical precedents of the people. Its churches, especially those of the Episcopal denomination, were of the old English style of building, grand and spacious but devoid of tinsel and useless ornament. Its libraries, orphan asylums, and halls of public gathering were solidly constructed, well finished, and unique as specimens of architecture. Its dwellings combined elegance with comfort, simplicity with taste. The antique appearance of the city and its European character was the remark of almost everyone who visited it.

But all this is now changed. Except to an occasional blockade-runner the beautiful harbor of Charleston has been sealed for four long years; its fine society has been dissipated if not completely destroyed, while its noblest edifices have become a prey to the great conflagration of 1861, or have crumbled beneath the effect of the most continuous and terrific bombardment that has ever been concentrated upon a city.

The act that ushered in this momentous change was the passage of the ordinance of secession on the 20th December, 1860. No one living in Charleston at the time that event occurred can ever forget the scenes by which it was accompanied. No sooner had the bells of St. Michael's announced the fact than the wildest frenzy seemed to seize the whole population. The air was rent with huzzas; the national ensign was everywhere supplanted by the emblem of State sovereignty; palmetto branches were borne in triumph along the streets; bales of cotton were suspended on ropes stretched from house to house, on one of which was inscribed in large letters, "THE WORLD WANTS IT"; while the stirring notes of the *Marseillaise,* afterward exchanged for those of Dixie, met the ear at every corner. When the night had set in the sky was lurid with the glare of bonfires, and the ground fairly shook beneath the double-quick of all the young men of the city under arms and apparently eager for the fray.

Some there were who viewed all this with tearful eye and deep though suppressed emotion. Notwithstanding the confident assertion of Mr. Rhett, of the *Mercury,* that he would drink all the blood that would be shed,* they saw the future lurid with all the horrors of civil strife. Among these was the venerable Judge Pettigrew.† Walking along the streets of Columbia when the secession furor was at its height, and being accosted by a stranger with the inquiry "Where the insane asylum" was to be found? His reply was, "My friend, look around you; the whole State is one vast insane asylum."

The first overt act of hostility which followed the passage of the ordinance of secession was the firing upon the *Star of the West.* It is true that, previous to

*Robert Barnwell Rhett Sr. (1800–1876), a leading advocate of secession and a "Fire-Eater" before the war, owned the *Charleston Mercury,* a newspaper he acquired in 1857 and would own until 1868. It was edited by his son Barnwell Rhett Jr. (1828–1905). However, it was James Chesnut who had boasted he would drink all the blood shed as a result of secession, after which the elder Rhett claimed he would join the feast by eating all the bodies of those slain, so confident was he that no war would result from secession.
† James Louis Petigru (1789–1863), a Charleston lawyer and judge who had been the state's most prominent Unionist before the war, had died during the war.

this, Major Anderson* had been compelled through threats of violence to evacuate Fort Moultrie, and that it had been taken possession of by the South Carolina Militia; but no gun had yet been fired, no act had been committed which
might be regarded as a direct and open defiance of the United States Government. This was reserved for the following 9th of January. The resident in the
lower part of the city, looking out of his window that morning, at first saw
nothing particularly noticeable in the bright blue bay which lay stretched out
before him, flanked by the low, shelving shores of Sullivan's and Morris Islands,
and embracing the grim, gray walls of Sumter. Soon, however, the top-masts of
a vessel were seen to rise slowly above the horizon. As it approached every eye
was strained to catch its form, and every ear opened to hear the reception which
its arrival might evoke. Soon a white puff of smoke was seen arising over the
gray sands of Morris Island, and the ear caught the faint report of a gun. Another, and then another, till the far-sighted of us could see the balls ricocheting
over the waves in the direction from which the steamer was approaching.[†] Had
it kept on its course Sumter, whose ramparts were now glistening with bayonets,
and whose shotted guns were protruding from every port, might have made the
attempt to protect her, and there would have been enacted, though doubtless
with greater honor to the United States Government, the combat which occurred
three months later. But the *Star of the West* turned its prow and sped back to
the open sea whence it came.

There is a little incident connected with the discharge of that first gun of the
war which I have upon the testimony of one of the first ladies of the city. When
ordered to fire, the cadet who held the lanyard of the gun was seen to hesitate.
"How can I," he exclaimed, "fire upon that flag which I have been taught to respect and reverence from my youth? But a stern duty compels me"; and with that
the iron messenger went speeding on its course.

Just three months after the firing upon the *Star of the West* occurred the
attack upon Fort Sumter. The whole previous night the people of Charleston
had spent in anxious expectation. It had been rumored that the opening of the
contest would take place within the next twenty-four hours, but whether it
would occur at midnight or at the early dawn it was impossible to conjecture.
At just four o'clock in the morning, before the gray light had begun to break in
the east, we were all aroused by the report of a heavy gun fired from one of the

---

* Major Robert Anderson (1805–1871), a former slave owner from Kentucky who remained
loyal to the Union, was the commanding officer of US Army forces in Charleston.
† A detachment of Citadel cadets manning a battery on Morris Island fired on the *Star
of the West*, a civilian supply ship trying to reinforce Anderson and his men on Fort
Sumter.

adjoining islands. It was the signal to open, and in five minutes the air was filled with the whizzing of shot and the explosion of shell. The famous iron battery on Cumming's Point, constructed by Stevens, the cashier of one of the city banks,* belched forth flame and smoke at an interval of every three minutes, and sent its shot crashing against the very walls of the defiant fort. This was continued till the day broke, and the sun was up before Major Anderson saw fit to make any reply. Having, like a discreet commander, first refreshed his men and put everything about the fort in fighting trim, he opened alike from *barbette* and port batteries. There was not a man who witnessed that scene who was not struck with admiration at the regularity and precision of Sumter's fire. Gun for gun and volley for volley, the heroic Major paid the rebels back in their own coin. Had the fort contained a supply of mortars as well as cannon, and a full complement of men, well provided with the necessaries of life, the strife might have continued for weeks instead of days, and the fort never passed into other hands than those of its rightful owners. But the hostile mortar-batteries, inaccessible to mere shot, first drove the Union soldiers from the use of the *barbette* guns, then set the fort on fire and compelled its surrender. Let me here state positively that in this combat there was not a single rebel, as there was not a single Union soldier, killed. The only destruction of life which occurred took place at the bursting of the gun with which Anderson saluted his flag upon the evacuation of the fort. It was the remark of Judge Huger, made in my hearing, that "Providence seemed determined to accomplish his decrees in regard to the South without the shedding of a single drop of blood."[†]

When the old State flag, riddled with shot, was brought from the Stevens battery up to the city and carried through the streets, the excitement was tremendous. Church-bells rang out their peals of joy; handkerchiefs waved from every window; friend embraced friend in a wild delirium of delight; while the whole mass of the population, believing that the North must yield to such a display of Southern valor, pressed upon the heels of the horseman and actually did homage to the ensign which he bore aloft.

---

*Clement Hoffman Stevens (1821–1864), who worked for the Planters and Mechanics Bank, was a colonel in the South Carolina Militia before the war. In early 1861, he designed and constructed an iron-plated vessel on Morris Island known as The Floating Battery of Charleston Harbor. A marvel to Charlestonians, it was used in the bombardment of Fort Sumter on April 12 and April 13, 1861, making it the first floating battery to engage in hostilities during the Civil War. Stevens, wounded several times in the war, was promoted to brigadier general in 1864. He died in action the same year.

[†] Peck confuses Sen. Alfred Huger (1788–1872) with Judge Daniel Elliott Huger, who died in 1854. Alfred Huger, an ex-state senator and longtime postmaster who was a Unionist before the war, made the statement.

Let us now pass over the time which intervened till the occupation of Morris
Island by the Union troops. It was a time of varied sorrow and gladness. Now
the news of some victory, like that of Bull Run,* would stir the whole heart of
the city, and cause it to beat high with hope. Then some defeat, like that of Port
Royal,† would equally depress it. But, upon the whole, there was the most confident reassurance in regard to the result. "Whatever drawbacks we may meet
with," remarked one of the first citizens of the State, "there is not the least
doubt in my mind about our eventual success." "We may have reverses," said the
Rev. Dr. Palmer,‡ "but the policy of Providence from the time of the dispersion
at the Tower of Babel has been the disintegration of nations. He allows them
to grow large and unwieldy, as this nation has grown, and then, to promote the
interests of civilization and of His kingdom, he breaks them asunder, as He will
eventually break asunder this mighty people."

The dread of the Monitors, which made their appearance about this time,
was very general throughout the city. None had seen one except at a great distance, but everyone had heard the most fabulous accounts of their formidable-
ness and power.§ So lively was the apprehension created by them that batteries
went up like magic on the shores around the bay. Sullivan's Island became one
vast line of earthworks, the most formidable of which was Battery Bee, on its
extreme western point. Earthworks were also thrown up along the shores of
James Island. Fort Sumter was immensely strengthened. Castle Pinckney received

* The First Battle of Bull Run near Manassas Junction, Virginia, which began on July 21,
  1861, was the first major land battle of the Civil War. The Confederate victory gave the
  South a surge of confidence and shocked many in the North, who realized the war would
  not be won as easily as they had hoped.
† Given the Union's plan to win the war was (in part) by a blockade of the South, they
  needed a base along the southern coast from which to resupply their coal-burning ships.
  The obvious choice was Port Royal Sound, close to both Charleston and Savannah. On
  Nov. 7, 1861, a large Union flotilla led by Capt. Samuel Dupont (1803–1865) had blasted
  Confederate fortifications at the mouth of Port Royal Sound, routing the outgunned
  defenders, and more than 12,000 Union infantry occupied Hilton Head, the surrounding sea islands, and the town of Beaufort.
‡ Rev. Benjamin Morgan Palmer (1818–1902), Charleston native and Presbyterian theo-
  logian.
§ In May of 1861, in response to news the Confederates were refitting a scuttled US steam
  frigate as an ironclad warship, Congress approved a million and a half dollars for ironclad construction for the Union Navy, the building of which was highly publicized. Navy
  Department officials in Washington hoped for a success that would validate a new form
  of warfare, armored warships mounting heavy guns that would reduce forts to rubble.
  The original ironclad was the U.S.S *Monitor*. Under the command of Rear Adm. Samuel Dupont, on April 7, 1863, a fleet of nine of these ironclad warships attacked the
  Confederate defenses near the entrance to Charleston Harbor.

a new armament. Fort Ripley, an entirely new fort, was constructed of palmetto logs in the center of the bay. The beautiful Battery walk, the favorite promenade of the Charleston ladies and gentlemen, was partially torn up, and bristled with heavy guns. Then followed the submersion of torpedoes in the harbor and the organization of a company of men called "Tigers," who, in spite of shot and shell, were to board the Monitors as they came up the bay, and planting ladders against their smoke-stacks, to throw bags of powder and other explosive compounds into the furnaces beneath. So numerous were the preparations for defense that it was certain no vessel could come up to the city without running the gauntlet of at least three concentric circles of fire.

Some time after all these vast preparations to the enemy had been completed, on a bright sunny day, about the hour of noon, Colonel Rhett* telegraphed from Fort Sumter that *"The turrets are coming!"* and over the low flat land of Morris Island we could see the smoke-stacks of the Monitors moving slowly along. One after another they came in solemn file, followed by the long black hulk of the *New Ironsides,*† and took their stations near the fort. Then followed discharge after discharge from the neighborhood of the southern extremity of the heaviest guns which had ever been brought into naval warfare, answered by long, reverberating peals from the batteries on Sullivan, James and Morris islands. The very earth and sea shook under the terrific din. At one time the *Ironsides* floated directly over a submarine torpedo, and must inevitably have been blown up, had not the apparatus by which it was to be fired failed to elicit the necessary spark. After some hours the Monitors withdrew, having made but a slight impression upon the walls of the fort.‡ The result of this combat inspired the Charlestonians with great hope. It relieved them of those fearful apprehensions which they had entertained in regard to the Monitors, and convinced them that they were by no means irresistible.

In anticipation of a conflict with the Monitors, great numbers of military men had flocked to the city from all parts of the South. As a consequence, the hotels and public promenades were crowded with officers, and the greatest dissipation prevailed. Balls and parties followed each other in rapid succession; gambling saloons were opened and drove a thriving business; loose women frequented

---

* Col. Alfred Rhett (1829–1889), son of Sen. Robert Barnwell Rhett, was in command of Fort Sumter.

† The U.S.S. *New Ironsides,* a wooden-hulled broadside ironclad built for the Navy.

‡ Unable to navigate in the obstructed channels leading to the harbor, Dupont's ships were caught in a crossfire and he withdrew them before nightfall. Five of his nine ironclads were disabled in the failed attack, and one more subsequently sank. The battle became known as the First Battle of Charleston Harbor.

the streets, impudently accosted passers-by, and filled the hotels with their presence. Nor were these evil influences encouraged and promoted by officers of
inferior rank alone. Military men, high in station, and regarded as the principal
supports of "the Confederacy," by their immoral bearing succeeded in bringing
themselves into disgrace, and tainting with suspicion the character of heretofore
reputable women. At no time during the war have those high moral influences
which have been brought to bear upon the Union soldiers, by means of the Christian Commission and other religious associations, pervaded the armies of the
South. Both officers and men were swept away by the same current of dissolute-
ness and vice, till in many cases whole armies became pest-houses of immorality
and irreligion.

The Charlestonians at this time also began to experience trouble with their
slaves. Many were induced to follow the example of Robert Smalls,* and in small
boats running the gauntlet of the rebel batteries, to join the enemy. So frequent
did this become that negroes were finally forbidden to occupy boats in certain
parts of the harbor for fishing purposes, and the inhabitants of the city were
deprived of one of their principal articles of diet. These runaway servants, it was
well known, carried with them to the enemy much valuable information which
would be made use of in case of an attack on the city.

Thus affairs went on till the early part of July, 1863, when just at daybreak
one morning the people who lived on the Battery were aroused by a sharp, rapid
fire of musketry. So sudden was it and so in contrast with the quiet of the preceding days that it took everyone by surprise. It was soon discovered to proceed
from the neighborhood of the southern extremity of Morris Island, and later
information developed the fact that the Union troops had opened a masked battery on Folly Island and seemed determined to force their way across the narrow strait which separates it from Morris Island. How they contrived to elude
the rebel generals in the erection of this battery was a mystery.† The surprise,

---

* Robert Smalls (1839–1915) freed himself, his crew, and their families from slavery in
1862, when he commandeered a Confederate transport ship, the C.S.S. *Planter*, in
Charleston Harbor and sailed beyond the federal blockade to freedom.
† Gen. Quincy Adams Gillmore (1825–1888), the federal field commander assigned to plan
and carry out operations against Fort Sumter, Charleston, and Morris Island in 1863,
afterward claimed that secrecy was "an essential element in the preparations" when
between mid-June and July 6, ordnance and ordnance stores were quietly accumulated
on Folly Island. Armaments were placed on the north end, masked from Confederate
view by sand-ridges and undergrowth. Work on the batteries, and all the transportation
to them, was accomplished at night, and in silence. According to Gillmore, "One fortunate circumstance favored these operations. A blockade-runner had been chased
ashore just south of the entrance to Light-house Inlet, within point-blank range of our

however, was complete. The solitary company of artillerymen which had been stationed there were soon driven back, and thus an entrance effected through the only door by which an approach to Charleston could have been made. In vain had an attempt been essayed over James Island; in vain had the Union gunboats endeavored to force the Stono; in vain had Sumter been assailed by the powerful armament of the Monitors. The Charlestonians began to exult over their secure and impregnable position, and avow their belief that all the armies of the world could not force their way to their metropolis, when the action of the 10th of July suddenly convinced them of their error and filled them with the gravest apprehension. There was no one so blind but could perceive that the charge of great negligence must be laid at the door of some one of their generals; but whether Beauregard, who had supreme command, or Ripley, who acted as his subordinate and was entrusted with the particular supervision of the batteries, should be arraigned was long a matter of dispute.* The feeling of recrimination eventually ran so high between the two generals that Ripley was forced to resign, and the Charlestonians were thus deprived of the services of one of the best artillerists in the Southern army.

It may not be amiss just here to relate the impressions formed in regard to the character of Beauregard, who during most of this eventful period held command in the city. By all the Charlestonians he was held in high respect, even admiration. He was gentlemanly in his bearing, fluent and affable in conversation, remarkable in his military capacities as an engineer (as the fortifications around Charleston testify), and versed as a strategist. But he was greatly deficient in moral courage, and in the power to enforce discipline among his troops. This was manifest in the battle of Shiloh where, after virtually achieving a great victory, he lost its results in the dispersion of his soldiers to secure the plunder which the Northern troops had left behind them. It was also exhibited in the shameful and execrable conduct of many of the soldiers under his command

batteries, and while the enemy on Morris Island were industriously engaged in wrecking this vessel by night and day (an operation which we could easily have prevented), our batteries were quietly and rapidly pushed forward to completion. They were ready to open fire on the 6th of July. The fact that forty-seven pieces of artillery, with two hundred rounds of ammunition for each gun, and provided with suitable parapets, splinter-proof shelters, and magazines were secretly placed in battery in a position within speaking-distance of the enemy's pickets, exposed to a flank and reverse view from their tall observatories on James Island, and to a flank view at pistol-range from the wreck, furnishes by no means the least interesting and instructive incident of this campaign."
* Gen. Pierre Toutant Beauregard (1818–1893), in command of Confederate defenses in Charleston, and Gen. Roswell Sabin Ripley (1823–1887) assigned army command of the Department of South Carolina and its coastal defenses.

which were stationed within the precincts of the city. All the disasters which he experienced may apparently be traced to this deficiency. But Beauregard likewise labored under great disadvantages from the inveterate prejudice which existed in the mind of Jefferson Davis against him.* So strong was this prejudice that it was exhibited even in the most trivial military arrangements, and served to increase that sentiment of hostility toward Davis which began to be evinced in the minds of the people of Charleston soon after the commencement of the war. Beauregard had the malignity and power of the administration pitted against him.

Having obtained a foothold on Morris Island, the Union troops slowly advanced by a system of parallels till they arrived within gun-shot of batteries Wagner and Gregg, which the rebel troops had erected on the extreme northern point of the island, and nearest to the city. With their Parrott guns† they could even command the walls of Sumter. And now commenced that long artillery contest which will make the siege of Charleston eventful in all subsequent years. Night and day the air was filled with shrieking shell and whizzing shot. Standing on the Battery promenade in the darkness of the evening, I have counted no less than eight bombs in the air at one time. This bombardment was almost daily participated in by some portion or by all of the Union fleet, and then the thunder of artillery would be so great that every house in the lower part of the city trembled to its base.‡ It was interesting also to witness the effect of the Parrott

---

* Jefferson F. Davis (1807–1889), president of the Confederacy, did not like Beauregard's "Napoleonic pretensions." The two quarreled for much of the war, as well as postwar. See Drury Wellford, "G. T. Beauregard (1818–1893), at http://www.encyclopediavirginia .org/Beauregard_G_T_1818-1893, accessed Dec. 22, 2016.

† The Parrott rifle, a muzzle-loading artillery weapon patented in 1861 and used extensively by both sides by the end of the war.

‡ The bombardment was commanded by Gen. Gillmore, who had succeeded in capturing or destroying numerous fortifications during July, August, and September, and now from Morris Island commenced the punishing 545-day bombardment of Charleston. John Trowbridge wrote, "The greatest panic occurred immediately after the occupation of Morris Island by General Gillmore. The first shells set the whole town in commotion. It looked like everybody was skedaddling. Some loaded up their goods, and left nothing but their empty houses. Others just packed up a few things in trunks and boxes, and abandoned the rest. The poor people and negroes took what they could carry on their backs or heads, or in their arms, and put for dear life. Some women put on all their dresses, to save them. For a while the streets were crowded with runaways—hurrying, hustling, driving—on horseback, in wagons, and on foot—white folks, dogs, and [negroes]. But when it was found the shells only fell down town, the people got over their scare; and many who went away came back again. Every once in a while, however, the Yankees would appear to mount a new gun, or get a new gunner; and the shells would fall higher up. That would start the skedaddling once more. One shell would be enough to depopulate a whole neighborhood." Trowbridge, *A Picture of the Desolated States and the Work of Restoration*, 515.

guns upon the walls of Sumter. They accomplished with ease what the heavy eight, ten, and even fifteen-inch balls of the Monitors had in vain essayed. Every shot sent the brick and beams and mortar high into mid-air, and in some cases went through and through the solid walls. Soon one could see the light shining through its grim, dark ramparts. Then followed great breaches; then fragments would topple down into the water below. The Southerners worked incessantly to repair these damages. Vessel-loads of sand and other materials were nightly sent down, and large forces of negroes were kept constantly at work. At one time a portion of the wall fell, burying beneath it a number of the garrison. At another time a Federal shell caused the explosion of a quantity of ammunition, and destroyed many valuable lives. Captain Harleston, a very promising young officer,* who was entrusted with the command, was struck down while inspecting the injuries done to the fort, a loss which was felt to be irreparable.

But notwithstanding these apparent calamities, it was eventually ascertained that the enemy's guns, so far from materially injuring the work as a fortification, were actually making it stronger. The loose debris heaped up afforded a far more efficient protection against solid shot than the massive brick walls. It was only necessary that the soldiers should be protected from the fragments of shells which were continually bursting over the fort, and this was accomplished by erecting vast "rat-holes," or bomb-proofs, and by excavating long subterranean passages which connected one part of the fort with another. When the signal was given by the sentinel on the look-out of the discharge of a gun, it was amusing to see how the area of the fort, just before filled with men, would suddenly become as solitary as if never trodden by a human foot.

The superiority of a fortification of debris or sand over brick and stone, as opposed to heavy artillery, was particularly conspicuous in the instance of Battery Wagner. Day after day, and week after week, that simple sand-work withstood the whole Union fleet and all the land batteries which could be erected against it, and fell only through the close approach of the Federal parallels, whereby their sharp-shooters effectually prevented the Confederates from using their guns.†

---

* Capt. Francis Huger Harleston (1839–1863), who had recently graduated from The Citadel with first honors, was serving duty with the First South Carolina Artillery on Fort Sumter when he was hit by enemy fire.

† Gillmore claimed, "Fort Wagner was found to be a work of the most formidable character—far more so, indeed, than the most exaggerated statements of prisoners had led us to expect. Its bomb-proof shelter, capable of containing from 1500 to 1600 men, remained intact after one of the most severe bombardments to which any earth-work was ever exposed. The attempt to form an opening into the bomb-proof by breaching failed from want of time. The heavy projectiles were slowly eating their way into it,

The successful defense of Wagner and of other points of attack about the city was also owing to the possession by the Confederates of the Union code of signals. From the walls of the city they could decipher with ease every communication which passed between the army and the fleet, and thus became cognizant of intended movements on the part of the Northern troops in time effectually to resist them.

Just previous to the bloody assault on Wagner I was sitting upon one of the seats of the Battery promenade in the city when a colonel passed by who had been in command of a battery on James Island. Upon inquiring of him the news, he informed me that an assault on Wagner would be attempted at a certain time, and that the Southern generals were making busy preparations to meet it. When I asked him how the information was obtained, he confidentially told me of the possession of the Union code of signals by the Confederate officers. Upon further inquiry as to how the Southerners were fortunate enough to obtain this code, he said that some days previous a Union signal-master had been captured on the beach, and when he had been locked up in prison the services of a clever fellow were secured, who was to array himself in Federal uniform and feign himself a captured Union officer. He was then to be surrounded by a guard, marched to the jail, and confined in the same cell with the signal-officer, where it was understood he was to obtain his confidence, and elicit from him the desired information. The device succeeded beyond the most sanguine anticipation!

The Union soldiers wounded and captured at the bloody assault on Wagner were brought up to the city on boats, and placed in a large brick warehouse in Queen Street, near to Church Street. It was in the month of July, when the heat is more intense than during any month in the year. The locality was close and confined, and the consequence was that they died by scores. I am not prepared to say that no other locality could have been obtained for them. I fear that the military authorities of Charleston will find it difficult, in this instance at least, to acquit themselves of the charge of a want of due consideration toward a prostrate and wounded foe. The high sense of magnanimity and honor, on the possession of which they were accustomed to pride themselves, was at this time entirely absorbed in feelings of resentment and vindictiveness.

There are events in a man's life which he never forgets; there are scenes which never fade from his sight, and sounds which are ever fresh in his hearing, though

---

although their effect was astonishingly slight. Indeed the penetration of ride projectiles, fired into a sand parapet standing at the natural slope, or approximately so, is but trifling. They are almost invariably deflected along the line of least resistance, or one departing slightly from it, scooping out in their progress a small hollow, the contents of which are scattered but a short distance."

he attain a century of years. I can never forget, and there are many others who can never forget, the impression which the sound of the first shell thrown into Charleston made upon the mind. It was near midnight, and, with the exception of a few of the more wakeful ones, the whole city was buried in slumber. Suddenly, and without the least premonition, a whizzing, shrieking sound was heard above the roofs of the houses, which was conjectured by some to be a rocket sent up from one of the signal-stations in the lower part of the city. A few moments served to convince them of their error, for the sound was repeated, communication which passed between the army and this time with such unmistakable distinctness as to remove all doubt from the mind of even the most dubious. It was also noticed that the sound was each time preceded by the faint flash and reverberation of a gun located apparently on the southeastern extremity of James Island. The fact then became evident, and was soon corroborated by the shouts of the people in the streets, that the Federals were shelling the city. Had the advent of the final judgment been announced it could not have created greater surprise and consternation. The sidewalks were soon filled with flying women and children hurrying to secure in the upper part of the town a refuge beyond the reach of the deadly missiles. The excitement was increased by the breaking out of a fire reported to have originated by the explosion of one of the shells. These first shells, it was subsequently ascertained, were thrown from the Swamp Angel Battery, located in a marsh to the southeast of James Island, the erection of which had escaped the observation of the Southern generals.* This marsh, it was calculated, was four miles from the nearest point of the city, and the shells were consequently thrown a distance of four miles and a half. And yet this was by no means equal to what the Union artillerists subsequently attained, for when they had taken possession of Battery Wagner they sent their shells three or four blocks above Citadel Green—a distance approximating to five and a half or six miles. The great difficulty which has always been experienced in throwing shells to such enormous distances consists in the great elevation which must thereby be given to the gun. When a horizontal shot is fired the retrograde motion of the gun caused by reaction is comparatively easy. It slides along the rail on which it rests until the force is spent, without the least injury to itself. But it is not so when the gun is elevated to a great angle. Then the concussion, instead of expending itself horizontally, drives the gun almost perpendicularly into the ground, and unless carefully guarded against will be certain to disable it. This was illustrated in the first attempts of the Union army to shell the city at such enormous

---

* Gillmore implanted a massive Parrott rifle nicknamed the "Swamp Angel," which fired two-hundred-pound shots into the city of Charleston itself.

distances. The guns at first almost invariably became disabled, and it required a considerable time to attain the perfection which they subsequently exhibited in the demonstrations made from Forts Gregg and Wagner.

Again, it is a well-known fact that a new gun will fire to a much greater distance than one that has been subjected to much use. This owing to the grooves of the gun being sharp and unworn, whereby the shell fits the more compactly, and the whole blast of the powder is made available. We always knew in Charleston when a new gun had been mounted, by its length of range, and, however great the distance which it attained, always comforted ourselves with the reflection that the next shot would be sure to fall short.

There was a great rush and crowd the next morning after the first shells were thrown into the city to see where they fell and the effect which they had produced. The fragments of one were discovered in the neighborhood of the store of G. W. Williams and Co.,* to the rear of the Charleston Hotel. It had shattered the building, and buried itself in the street just in front. Another had attained the distance of a square farther to the north, and fell at the corner of Anson and Hasell streets, scattering its fragments far and wide. It was soon positively ascertained that a residence in the lower part of the city was no longer safe. Even should the Confederate batteries succeed in silencing the "Swamp Angel," the energy and enterprise of the Northerners would soon command another station, where they might repeat the experiment, and perhaps with greater success. Houses in the upper part of the city, therefore, began to be in demand, and that exodus commenced which, upon the establishment of the Union batteries upon Morris Island, left the lower districts of the town a complete solitude.

It was ascertained when the Union troops had obtained possession of Morris Island that they trained their guns on the city by the tall, massive steeple of St. Michael's. About no one church of the numerous churches of Charleston do such interesting associations cluster as about this time-honored edifice. It is reputed to have been built after a design furnished by Sir Christopher Wren, the architect of St. Paul's, London. Its organ was played at the coronation of one of the Georges; its chime of bells, by far the sweetest in the land, was originally brought from England, whither they were taken back upon the capture of the city in the Revolutionary war by the British. Here they were put up at auction, and bought in by a wealthy Englishman, who, after the war, returned them to the church. It was just in front of this church, at the corner of Broad and Meeting streets, that a statue of William Pitt used to stand, which was struck by a ball

---

* This was the wholesale grocery firm of George Walton Williams (1820–1903) at 1 Hayne Street.

from the British batteries erected during the Revolution on James Island, and which threw their shot right into the streets of the city. The mutilated statue may still be seen standing in the grounds of the Orphan House.* During the whole of this present war the steeple of St. Michael's has been converted into an observatory. Near its top a room was constructed, fitted up with a stove to keep its occupant warm during cold weather, and furnished with a powerful telescope, through which all the movements of the Union army could be easily distinguished. Night and day the observer was kept at his post, transmitting not only frequent records of the various maneuvers of the enemy to the quarters of the general in command, but also making note of every shot fired at the city. There was imminent danger lest some one of these shot might strike the steeple and choke up the narrow passage by which alone a descent could be effected, and so a rope ladder was stretched on the outside from the observatory above to the ground beneath, by which, in case of such accident, an escape might be made. Strange to say, though the shells fell like a rain of iron all around, striking the guard-house opposite, riddling the City Hall on the north, plowing up the graveyard on the south, and almost demolishing the Mansion House in the rear,† yet this steeple was not once struck, nor was the body of the edifice injured till a short time previous to the evacuation of the city.

It was interesting to notice the varied effects of the shells in their descent into the city. Certainly one half failed to explode, the percussion shell being so arranged that it must fall at a particular angle in order to crush the cap which ignites the combustible material within. Failing to explode, they would simply drive a hole through the wall or roof against which they struck and bury themselves in the ground below. Many accidents occurred from digging up these unexploded missiles and attempting to extract the fuse. When a shell exploded, on striking the noise was equal to that of a good-sized piece of artillery, and it

* The Charleston Orphan House (c. 1790), the nation's first municipal orphanage, at 160 Calhoun Street. The building was razed in the 1950s. The statue of William Pitt (1708–1778), first Earl of Chatham, which has stood in Charleston since 1770, now stands inside the Charleston County Judicial Center at the corner of Broad and Meeting streets.
† The Mansion House at 71 Broad Street, was first operated after 1815 as Jones Hotel, a popular hotel for whites owned by free black Jehu Jones. The name Jones Hotel stayed with the property until 1852 when Mrs. Jane Davis, proprietor of The Mansion House at the corner of Meeting and Queen streets, relocated her establishment to the building. She rented the property and renamed it The Mansion House. After the Civil War the structure became a boardinghouse. It was dismantled in 1928. In 1930 the Schachte Building was built on the site, which now serves as the parish office of St. Michael's Episcopal Church. Simons and Simons, "The William Burrows House of Charleston," 155–76; Schweninger, *Black Property Owners in the South,* 132; Myers, *Forging Freedom,* 99.

was certain to produce the greatest destruction for many roads around. I have
seen almost the whole front of a two-story building torn off by a single shell. A
large shell entered the loft of a warehouse on East Bay Street, and striking the
joists of the roof at a particular angle, caused the whole roof to slide off to one
side. A 30-pound Parrott exploded between the roof and ceiling of one of the
churches of the city, made fifteen apertures of different sizes in the ceiling, demolished a bronze chandelier over the pulpit, broke the reading-desk, split the
communion-table, partially demolished two or three pews, and made several
rents in the floor beneath—all the effect of a 30-pound Parrott, the fragments
of which were afterward collected and fitted together. Another shell tore open a
Bible upon the pulpit-desk of a church, leaving a leaf upon which were conspicuous the words, *"An enemy hath done this."* A large two-hundred pounder
struck the Second Presbyterian Church in Charlotte Street just in the rear of the
portico, and so seriously injured it that it was apprehended that the whole front
of the church would fall in. But the percussion shells, though more destructive
to property, were not so destructive of human life as the time fuse shells which
were thrown comparatively late in the siege. The fragment of a shell one day
entered a barber's saloon and took off the head of a negro while engaged in his
work. Another negro walking along one of the principal streets of the city, and
hearing the approach of a shell ran into an alley to get clear of it, and crouched
behind a door. The shell entered the alley, struck the door and killed the negro.
A couple newly married were found one morning lying dead in each other's
arms. A shell had struck the house during the night, penetrated to the chamber
in which they were, and extinguished the life of both at the same instant. In a
house in Queen Street a woman was sleeping in her bed when a shell penetrated
the roof of the building, passed through the bed, just grazing her outstretched
arm, and then sank through the floor into the cellar beneath.

Yet notwithstanding the occurrence of so many casualties, people soon became hardened to the idea of danger, and would not hesitate to take their walks
in the lower part of the city even when the shells were passing overhead. One
of the most amusing incidents of the bombardment was the eagerness exhibited
by the boys of the city to obtain possession of the shells. The sound of the approach of one would no sooner be heard than a troop of them would be seen
dashing through the streets to the spot where it was likely to fall. Arrived at the
place they would immediately commence to excavate it with such instruments
as they could command. The fragments of the shells they would sell for old iron
and obtain a very good price for them, but the copper ring which banded the
shell was especially valuable from the great scarcity of copper in the arsenals
of the Confederacy. An unexploded shell was picked up one day near the bridge

at the head of Rutledge Avenue, on which had been inscribed by the Unionists, "Find your way to the arsenal, old fellow!" When we reflect that the arsenal was only two squares distant, and lying directly in the line which the shell was pursuing when it fell, we must give to the Union artillerists the credit of having been remarkably good shots. The accuracy of fire which was continually exhibited astonished the people of Charleston more than anything else. I had frequent occasion to notice this accuracy. A fire would break out in the lower part of the city and the Federals would train their guns with such exactness that the shells would fall directly into the flames. Upon one occasion one of the fire engines was struck while it was being worked, and some of the firemen severely injured. Recalling the fact that these shells were thrown from a distance of over four miles, the accuracy of aim will appear astonishing indeed.

More particularly was this accuracy of fire exhibited when directed to the blockade-runners that were unfortunate enough to get aground in running into or out of the harbor. They were generally discovered at daylight, and in the course of a few hours hardly a vestige of them would remain.

During those long wearisome days and weeks when the city was under fire almost the only event of joy which would occur would be the arrival of some one of these blockade-runners. The business was finally reduced to a science. Even in the darkest night the cunning craft would work their way in or out through the tortuous channels of the harbor. When outward-bound the captain generally went down to Sullivan's Island upon the evening of sailing to learn the disposition of the Union fleet and plan the course of his exit. Lights also were always prearranged along the shores of the island, or suspended from boats in the harbor, in order to indicate the channel. The most dangerous point, and that which demanded the exercise of the greatest skill to avoid, was a narrow tongue of land which ran out from Sullivan's Island just opposite Sumter, and which was known as the Breakwater Jetty. Here the channel is not only very narrow but takes a sudden turn, and it was in making this turn that the vessel was in danger of getting aground. The Union artillerists after a while learned many of the cunning arts of the blockade-runner, and whenever they saw a light from the opposite shore of Morris Island, which they supposed was intended for the guidance of a vessel, they would immediately open fire. They had a way too of sending out picket-boats which would quietly allow the vessel to pass till it had rounded the jetty and return became impossible, and then by means of rockets would signalize the fleet outside.

The chase of a blockade-runner was the most exciting thing imaginable. Like a hunted deer it would speed through the water, its fierce avenger after it, every beam from stem to stern quivering through the violent pulsations of its

great iron heart, and the dash of the paddles as in their lightning-like revolu-
tions they would strike the water. Sometimes not only was one half of the cargo
thrown overboard, but every combustible thing that could be laid hold of crowded
into the furnaces to increase the steam. Some of these blockade-runners were
very successful. I knew of one which had run the gauntlet no less than nineteen
times, and had consequently proved a mine of wealth to its owners. When a
vessel had once run the blockade it was considered to have paid for itself, and
every subsequent trip was consequently clear gain. The captain generally cleared
on each round trip ten thousand dollars in gold, and the pilot and mate in
proportion.

To be at all connected with or interested in a blockade-runner was in those
days esteemed in Charleston a signal piece of good fortune. It insured at least a
partial supply of the comforts and luxuries of life; for the ladies an occasional
new silk dress, the envy and admiration of the streets; for the gentlemen a good
supply of Bourbon—a box or two of cigars, or a larder filled with Stilton cheese
or West India fruits. By-and-by came an edict from Richmond forbidding the
importation of luxuries of this kind, and restricting the cargo of a vessel entirely
to those articles which the country needed in its military operations, or which
contributed to the supply of the actual necessities of the people. One half of the
cargo of the vessel going out was also required to be devoted to government account, and one half of the cargo of the vessel coming in. This, of course, greatly
curtailed the profits of the owners, but still immense fortunes continued to be
made on both sides of the water.

It was about this time that a large number of Union prisoners were brought
into Charleston from various parts of the South. They were sent here partly for
security against the Federal raids, which were becoming very frequent through
the land, and partly on account of the scarcity of provisions, which compelled
their distribution through the various cities and towns of the country. The officers at first were crowded in with the men, and both were placed under fire in
the lower part of the city. Upon a remonstrance, however, sent up from General
Gillmore, on Morris Island and a threat to retaliate, which was actually carried
out, these prisoners were removed to a place of comparative security. Among the
officers who were confined in Charleston at that time was General Seymour,*

*Gen. Truman Seymour (1824–1891), chief of staff to Gen. Gillmore until early 1863,
when he was given command of the Second Division, Tenth Army Corps. His division,
with the famed black 54th Massachusetts Infantry, had led the attack on Battery Wagner. Captured in Virginia in 1864, Seymour was sent to Charleston as a prisoner of war
and held captive while the city was being besieged by Union gunboats. He spent a nervous summer in Charleston until he was released in mid-August.

whose frank and gentlemanly bearing won for him the high respect and admiration even of his enemies. Upon one day he sent for the Rev. Toomer Porter, rector of the church of the Holy Communion,* with whom he had had a slight acquaintance before the war to come and see him. Mr. Porter accordingly went, and in course of conversation the General remarked that he had sent for him to inquire whether arrangements could not be made whereby himself and his fellow-officers could enjoy the privileges of religious worship. If so, he was desirous that Mr. Porter himself should come the following Sabbath and preach to them. In reply to the General's request Mr. Porter immediately remarked that he "thought there would be no objection made to his coming, but that he would feel himself obligated to perform the whole service of his Church." "Certainly," replied the General, not at first comprehending his meaning; "I am sure that there is no service which will be more acceptable to myself, having been educated in your Church—and perhaps I may say to my fellow-officers." "But you do not understand me, General," continued the clergy-man. "I mean to say that there is in our service a prayer for the President of the Confederate States, which I could not deem myself at liberty to omit." "As for that," replied the General, "I myself care nothing. There is no one whom I consider so greatly to stand in need of being prayed for as Mr. Davis. However, I cannot answer for the sentiments of my brother officers, and I will consult them and let you know our determination by the approaching Sabbath." The other officers were accordingly consulted, and the result was that Mr. Porter received a note from General Seymour, the following Sabbath, stating that upon the whole, it would not be agreeable that the services should be performed under such conditions. A clergyman, however, was found who, though of the same denomination, consented to respect the scruples of the Union officers and to omit the prayer.

Every day, as the war continued, the currency became more and more depreciated. Four months before the evacuation of the city gold was selling as high as seventy for one. This, of course, greatly increased the price of provisions, and rendered living to those who were dependent upon annuities or salaries a serious matter. A piece of roast beef, adequate for a family of three or four, cost forty dollars; sweet potatoes, a natural product of the soil, one dollar each; a barrel of flour five hundred dollars, and other things in proportion. A family of four could hardly live on rice and the ordinary cow-pea soup under one hundred dollars a week. Butter, coffee, sugar, and tea were among those luxuries about which the least that was said the better.

---

* Rev. Dr. Anthony Toomer Porter (1828–1902), Episcopal clergyman who in 1867 would found Holy Communion Church Institute (Porter Military Academy).

The effect of this low diet, combined with the great anxiety attendant upon the support of a family and the political state of the country, soon became apparent in the countenances of the people. Never have I seen men grow old so fast as the inhabitants of Charleston, from the time the shelling of the city commenced down to its occupation by the Union troops. Heads which were of raven blackness became silvered with gray during the interval of only a few months. Faces which were as smooth as an infant's became seamed and furrowed with wrinkles. Boys looked like old men, and old men speedily dropped away and died. Never has there been such mortality among old people as among the old people of Charleston since the commencement of this war. The anxiety, change of diet, and circumstance, were more than advanced years could endure, and they went down by scores to the grave.

Among the calamities which befell the city not the least was the conduct of the troops who had been quartered in the city for its protection. One or two companies of them were stationed on the Battery, and of all the thieves, burglars, and highwaymen who were ever brought together, I may not hesitate to affirm these were the worst. They roamed through the lower part of the city perfectly unrestrained. There was not a house which they did not enter, plundering it of furniture, of carpets, of books, of everything upon which they could lay their rapacious hands. Leaden pipes were dug up; copper pumps were carried off; even the locks and keys of doors were abstracted, sent out of the city, and sold. By-and-by the lives of people who ventured into this part of the city to look after their abandoned property were not considered safe. The marauders prowled the streets, gun in hand, ready both to rob and murder anyone who ventured within their power. For a season no one ventured out after nightfall, in any part of the city, without secreting a revolver about his person.

The lower portions of the city, thus given up to be a prey and plunder, soon began to evince the most unmistakable appearance of dreariness and desolation. Some of the streets became so covered with grass as to conceal the cobblestones beneath. I have seen cows and goats quietly pasturing where for years the highway had been worn by the corrosion of passing vehicles; I have seen the crow and the owl roosting where for years the tramp of horses and the rattle of cartwheels were almost the only sounds to be heard; I have seen rank weeds springing from the gutters of streets which were once busy with the tide of passing men, to such a height as almost to exclude from view the opposite sidewalk. The highways of Herculaneum and Pompeii never filled one with such a feeling of utter loneliness and desolation as some of the streets of the lower part of the city of Charleston.

At last the climax of all this misery and suffering approached. It became evident to the far-sighted that by the march of Sherman through the State the city must of necessity be evacuated. Military men, however, persistently refused to acknowledge this necessity; they refused to acknowledge it even while they were secretly transporting the large supplies of ordnance which the town contained. Finally, the truth was made apparent to all by the violent explosion of ammunition which it was found impossible to carry away. Then followed the heavy tramp of the retreating soldiery, and the bursting out on every side of the city of vast sheets of flame and clouds of smoke. The order from the commander was, as I know from unquestionable authority, that every building should be laid in ashes. Thanks to a merciful Providence, the iniquitous and barbarous edict was only partially consummated when the Union troops marched in and saved the city. The apprehension, tumult, and horror of that day will never be effaced from the mind, and can only be compared with the exceeding joy arising from the sense of relief produced by the entrance of the Union troops.

Whitelaw Reid [between 1870 and 1880]. Library of Congress.

WHITELAW REID (1865)

"City of Desolation"

Whitelaw Reid, "City of Desolation," in *After the War: A Southern Tour,
May 1, 1865, to May 1, 1866* (London: Sampson Low, Son, & Marston),
1866.

Whitelaw Reid (1837–1912), journalist, diplomat, and politician, was a native of
Ohio. He graduated from Miami University in 1856 and was a young newspaper-
man writing for three Ohio papers when the Civil War broke out. Although he
had forebodings of it from his college days, he was incredulous at the actual
onset of war. According to his biographer: "The first news from Charleston Harbor on the fateful April 12th could not persuade him. He thought the dispatches
were bogus! All Columbus was of much the same opinion—for a few hours. The
crisis was unbelievable. In the legislature military appropriations were blocked
by Democrats whose minds were not merely clouded by party feeling but subject, like all others, to the hallucination that what had happened simply could
not happen. As the storm fell and there was no mistaking its import; every man
in the town had to remake his world overnight. The old story which is the story
of cities and towns all over the North—of incredulity; stunned emotions; hur-
ried, confused preparation; and, amongst individuals, of heart-stirring choice—
was unfolded before Reid's eyes." Reid signed on as war correspondent for the
Cincinnati Gazette and as aide-de-camp to Union generals Thomas A. Morris
and William S. Rosecrans. He was present at both the battles of Shiloh and
Gettysburg and became famous for his war accounts written under his penname,
"Agate." From 1862 he was Washington (D.C.) correspondent for the *Gazette*.
During the war an avid public read his "earnest and patriotic presentation" of
news from Washington and the front as he became known as one of the North's
greatest war reporters.

    Claude Bowers wrote in *The Tragic Era*, "The smoke had scarcely ceased to
curl around the smouldering ruins of the South, and Lincoln had not yet been
buried, when [U.S.] Chief Justice Salmon P. Chase set forth into the stricken

region, accompanied by journalists, on a political mission."* Just as the war was
ending in 1865, the U.S.R.C. *Wayanda,* a steam revenue cutter built during the
war for the U.S. Revenue Cutter Service, was placed at Chase's disposal for a
tour of the defeated southern states. Chase, as secretary of the Treasury, had
managed the nation's finances during the massive Union war effort, and he was
appointed chief justice of the Supreme Court at the end of 1864. As he would
oversee cases connected to Reconstruction, he set off on the *Wayanda* on a
fact-finding mission—although critics saw it as Chase "electioneering" and promoting immediate "negro suffrage." (A strong supporter of black civil rights,
during the voyage Chase would utilize his observations to lobby President Andrew Johnson for southern black suffrage. Johnson rejected Chase's proposals.)
Whitelaw Reid, as an eager young journalist as well as a friend of Chase, joined
the *Wayanda* at Norfolk, Virginia, in May of 1865 for the mission of six weeks.
From Fort Monroe, they voyaged around the Atlantic and Gulf coast to New
Orleans and the Mississippi before arriving in Charleston.

At the end of the tour, Reid returned to the South, overhauled his notes from
the voyage, and in 1866 published *After the War* in London and the United
States. The book elevated him to the top of his profession.

Reid was later hired to write editorial by Horace Greely, founder and editor
of the *New York Tribune,* the powerful newspaper that had played an important
role in the social and political movements surrounding the Civil War. By 1869
Reid was managing editor. In 1872, he purchased the *New York Tribune* from
Greeley and was publisher until his death, making the *Tribune* the most influential newspaper in the United States during much of that period. He continued
to write and publish on the ongoing debacle of Reconstruction in South Carolina. As late as 1879, Reid was writing in the *Tribune,* "Fifteen years have gone
over the South, and she still sits crushed, wretched, busy displaying and bemoaning her wounds."

Reid was a famous voice of the Republican Party. In 1881, he married Elizabeth Mills, the daughter of Darius Ogden Mills, a California millionaire,
increasing his power. He was minister to France from 1889 to 1892, and was
ambassador to Great Britain from 1905 to 1912. He published six books subsequent to *After the War,* including *Ohio in the War* (1868).

In the following excerpt from *After the War,* Reid describes a defeated
Charleston.

---

*Claude G. Bowers, *The Tragic Era: The Revolution after Lincoln* (Boston: Houghton
  Mifflin Company, 1929), 45.

SOURCES

Buck, Paul H. *Road to Reunion 1865–1900*. Boston: Little, Brown, 1937.
Cortissoz, Royal. *Life of Whitelaw Reid*. New York: Charles Scribner's & Sons, 1921.
Woodward, Vann. *Origins of the New South, 1877–1913*. Baton Rouge: Louisiana
     State University Press, 1951; reprint, 1971.

"City of Desolation"

We steamed into Charleston Harbor early in the morning; and one by one, Sumter, Moultrie, Pinckney, and at last the City of Desolation itself rose from the smooth expanse of water, as the masts of ships rise from the ocean when you approach them. Where, four years ago, before the fatal attack on this now shapeless heap of sand and mortar, the flags of all nations fluttered, and the wharves were crowded with a commerce that successfully rivaled Savannah, Mobile and every other Southern city save New Orleans, and even aspired to compete with New York in the Southern markets, only transports and Quartermasters' vessels were now to be seen, with here and there a passenger steamer, plying to and from New York for the accommodation of Yankee officers and their wives! The harbor itself was dotted with insignificant-looking iron clads, mingled with an occasional old ship of the line, and, in ampler supply, the modern "Yankee gunboats," of the double-ender type, which formed so potent a cause for alarm in the councils of the privates in the Rebel armies.

   The elegant residences along the battery front retained the aristocratic seclusion of their embowering shrubbery, creepers and flowering plants; but even through these gracious concealments which Nature cast over them, the scars from the "Swamp Angel" could everywhere be seen. Pavements had been torn up from the principal business streets, to build the batteries that lined the shore; and great embankments, crowned with Tredegar guns, shut out the prospect from many an aristocratic window. The unfinished Custom House was among the most conspicuous buildings, the white marble blocks lying scattered about it, as they were left by the workmen four years ago. "We'll never finish it," the fervid revolutionists said, as they began the war. "We've paid Yankee tariffs long enough; now, hurrah for free trade with our friends of France and Great Britain!" But the Custom House stands, and next winter Mr. Fessenden will be reporting to the Senate an item in the military appropriation bill for its completion.*

---

* Construction on the US Custom House, which began in 1853, was interrupted in 1859
    due to costs and the possibility of secession. After the war, William Pitt Fessenden
    (1806–1869), former treasury secretary under Abraham Lincoln, returned to the Senate
    and was chair of the Joint Committee on Reconstruction. Construction on the Custom
    House would be restarted in 1870. The building was completed in 1879.

Admiral Dahlgren and Fleet Captain Bradford came alongside in the Admiral's gig,* soon after our arrival; and while our boatswain was piping his whistle as the Admiral came over the ship's side, the guns of the *Pawnee* began a salute for the Chief Justice. The Treasury Agent and some other officials soon followed, and the Admiral took the party under his charge, transferred us to a comfortable and speedy little harbor steamer, and started toward that first goal of every man's curiosity—Sumter.

The rebellion has left its marks on the pale, thoughtful features of the Admiral, not less than upon the harbor he has been assailing. The terrible death of noble young Ulric Dahlgren, a martyr to the barbarism of slavery, might well grave deep traces on a father's face;† but the climate here, and the labors of the past have also been very trying, and one can readily believe, what used to be rather sarcastically urged by the Admiral's enemies, that his health did not permit him to keep up in gunnery with General Gillmore.

We passed a little sailing vessel manned by blacks. The Admiral told us that they had brought it down one of the rivers, the other day, and he had allowed them to keep it. They earn a livelihood bringing wood to the city. Recently there have been a number of outrages perpetrated on the blacks inland, by their late masters and some of the returning Rebel soldiers. Greatly infuriated, the blacks came to him begging for arms. "I have never before doubted their orderly disposition," he said, "and I am not sure that anybody would remain orderly under those circumstances."

The Charleston city negroes were represented as unexpectedly intelligent. "Out of two hundred and seventy-four laborers at work on the streets," said one of the city officials who had joined us, "one hundred and seventy-four are negroes—the rest whites. Of the negroes, over a hundred (or over four-sevenths)

---

* US Navy Adm. John Dahlgren (1809–1870) had replaced Adm. Samuel Du Pont as commander of the South Atlantic Blockading Squadron fleet (whose principal mission was the capture of Charleston), after Du Pont was "sacrificed" for the failures of the ironclads in attacking Charleston. Dahlgren proved to be a great commander in directing naval activities in Charleston Harbor. He helped Sherman secure Savannah in December of 1864 and the following February had moved his vessels to an evacuated Charleston. He greeted the *Wayanda* party in his flagship, the U.S.S *Pawnee*, which had participated prominently in the war. Lt. Cmdr. Joseph M. Bradford (1824–1872) was Navy fleet captain under Dahlgren in the South Atlantic Squadron.

† Dahlgren's son, Col. Ulric Dahlgren (1842–1864) was killed in a failed raid on Confederate headquarters in Richmond. There were papers found on him with orders for an assassination plot against Jefferson Davis and the Confederate cabinet. The discovery and subsequent publication of the "Dahlgren Papers" sparked controversy in the South and was disavowed by some as a forgery in the North. It is suspected this alleged attempt may have inspired John Wilkes Booth in the assassination of Lincoln.

can read, while scarcely one-seventh of the whites have made the same advancement!"*

A little before the time of this visit, James Redpath, acting as Superintendent of the schools,† reported nine public day and five night schools, under the superintendence of his bureau, with the following average attendance:

At Normal School, 620
At St. Philip School, 1,100
At Morris Street School, 822
At Ashley Street School, 305
At King Street School (boys), 306
At Meeting Street School (boys), 256
At Chalmers Street School (girls), 161
At St. Michael's School (boys), 100
Night Schools for adults contain, 500

Captain Bradford gave a significant illustration of the progress of some ideas among the less intelligent negroes of the country. They had again and again asked him, he said, what good it did them to make them free, unless they were to own the land on which they had been working, and which they had made productive and valuable. "Gib us our own land and we take care ourselves; but widout land, de ole massas can hire us or starve us, as dey please."

A huge mass of iron was pointed out as we passed. It was one of the Rebel iron clads, sunk just before the evacuation of the city. They had injured it very little, and our authorities are confident of making it one of the best iron clads in the service. Enforced self-reliance had, indeed, gone far toward making the South a nation; for here were fine engines, worthy of our most extensive Northern shops, which had been manufactured in Georgia within a year. Before the war, such an undertaking as making engines for a great steamer, in the South, was scarcely dreamed of. Near the iron clad lay some of the cigar-shaped torpedo boats—an invention never very successful, and now, let us hope, with its occupation, wholly gone.

The obstructions in the harbor, which so long kept the iron clads under Dupont and Dahlgren at bay, still stretched in a long line, unbroken in parts, across from Sumter toward the land on either side. Plenty of torpedoes were supposed

* Reid's note: "The ignorance of the poor whites in South Carolina is proverbial. But, as a negro acutely pointed out, 'Dey haven't learned, because dey don't care; we, because dey wouldn't let us.'"
† James Redpath (1833–1891), agent of the New England Freedman's Aid Society of Boston, was designated superintendent of public instruction in March of 1865.

to be still in the harbor—Captain Bradford himself had been blown up not long
ago by one of them, to the serious discomposure of his personal effects, in cabin
and state-room, but without actual physical injury.

But for two things, a stranger might have supposed Sumter a mere pile of
mortar, stones and sand, which only culpable lack of enterprise left to block up
the harbor. From the center of the rubbish rose a flagstaff, with the stars and
stripes floating at the top; and near the water's edge, uninjured casements still
stood among the debris, with black muzzles peeping out, as from the lower deck
of an old ship of the line. Closer inspection showed, also, some little howitzers
and other light pieces, placed on what was once the parapet. The sun fairly par-
boiled us, and, coming into this tropical heat so suddenly—for the night before,
on the deck of the *Wayanda,* at sea, we were wearing overcoats. It was so op-
pressive as to produce a sickening faintness on some of the party; but we patiently followed everywhere, clambered over the shapeless sea wall, inspected the
sand gabions, worked our way into the snugly-protected little out-looks for the
sharp-shooters. We ran down the inside of what had been the walls, and dived
into the subterranean regions where the casemate guns stood all the time of the
bombardment, uninjured, but not deigning to waste their ammunition in useless
replies. The contracted but comparatively comfortable quarters here remain
almost as the Rebels left them. A long, damp hall, with a few cots still standing
in it, was the place for the garrison, where they slept in comparative indifference
to the explosion of shells overhead; a rather more airy hall still contained the old,
split-bottom arm-chairs, which the officers had collected; on another side were
the hospitals, and—ghastly sight—there, on a shelf, were half a dozen coffins,
which had been all ready for the reception of the next victims to Gillmore's shells!

It was one of the strange personal complications of this war, that the regular
Rebel officer who had command of Sumter when our terrific bombardment
began, had no faith in its defensibility, and had been replaced by a young nephew
of the very Dominie of our party, who has been walking with us over the ruins.
The Doctor is as glad as any of us that the fort is reduced, but his eye kindled
as Admiral Dahlgren gave the tribute of honest admiration to the splendid bravery and tenacity of his Rebel nephew.*

* Reid later identifies "Dominie." He was Rev. Dr. Richard Fuller (1804–1876), a native
  of Beaufort, a founder of the Southern Baptist movement, and pastor of Seventh Baptist Church in Baltimore from 1847. Fuller's nephew, Capt. George Barnwell Cuthbert,
  had been commander of the Palmetto Guards, the first Confederate garrison of Fort
  Sumter. On the night of Robert Anderson's surrender of Fort Sumter in 1861, Cuthbert
  and his Palmetto Guards allegedly sent the first shot into the fort. In 1863, Cuthbert was
  mortally wounded at Chancellorsville.

From Sumter we steamed off to Sullivan's Island, and in a few moments were clambering among the mazes of the Rebel works. Here, four years ago, the first fortifications of the war were thrown up. Here the dashing young cavaliers, the haughty Southrons who scorned the Yankee scum and were determined to have a country and a history for themselves, rushed madly into the war as into a picnic. Here the boats from Charleston landed every day cases of champagne, pâtés innumerable, casks of claret, thousands of Havana cigars, for the use of the luxurious young Captains and Lieutenants and their friends among the privates. Here were the first camps of the war, inscribed, as the newspapers of those days tell us, with such names of companies as "The Live Tigers," "The Palmetto Guards," "The Marion Scorpions," "The Yankee Smashers." Here, with feasting, and dancing, and love making, with music improvised from the ballroom, and enthusiasm fed to madness by well-ripened old Madeira, the free-handed, free-mannered young men who had ruled "society" at Newport and Saratoga, and whose advent North had always been waited for as the opening of the season, dashed into revolution as they would into a waltz. Not one of them doubted that, only a few months later, he should make his accustomed visit to the Northern watering places, and be received with the distinction due a hero of Southern independence. Long before these fortifications, thus begun, were abandoned, they saw their enterprise in far different lights, and conducted it in a far soberer and less luxurious way.

The works stretched along the sandy shore of Sullivan's Island almost as far as the eye can reach. They consist of huge embankments of sand, revetted with palmetto logs, and were evidently planned throughout by a skillful engineer. Coupling these with the works on the other side of the harbor, and with Sumter, one readily believes them to constitute the strongest system of harbor defenses on the coast. Strolling around one of the works, we came upon a little slab, near a palmetto tree, under the shade of the embankment, "To Osceola, Patriot and Warrior." It is the grave of one of the last of the Florida chieftains, who died here in confinement,* and for whom some white enemy but admirer, had done these last tender honors. Shall the latest warriors of this island ever find similar admirers?

After our fatiguing trip, the Admiral spread out, on our return to the flagship, a lunch of oranges, bananas, pine-apples, and other tropical fruits, brought over from Havana. At the end of his table hung the only Union flag, or trace of

---

* Osceola (1804–1838), leader of the Seminole Indians, buried near the entrance of Fort Moultrie. Seized in 1837 and imprisoned with members of his tribe at Fort Moultrie, he died of a throat infection, possibly malaria.

anything resembling it, which the naval officers have been able to find anywhere in South Carolina or Georgia—a long, narrow strip of coarse bunting, containing two stripes, red and white, and few stars in a ground of blue—taken from a deserted cabin near Savannah.

New York papers, only five days old, had just arrived. In the midst of the wonders which the war had wrought here, it was scarcely surprising to see even the *New York Herald* out vigorously for negro suffrage!

Charleston, Now and Four Years Ago

In the afternoon, the General commanding the post was waiting with carriages for the party, at the wharf, when Admiral Dahlgren set us ashore. The wheels cut deep into the sand, throwing it into our faces and filling the carriage with it, till we began to realize what it meant to have taken up the pavements to get stone for the fortifications.

"Shall we go first to the statue of Calhoun?" asked the General. "It is scarcely necessary—here is his monument," said someone, pointing around the destroyed parts of the city.

A foreigner, who visited Charleston in May, 1861, spoke of these streets as "looking like Paris in the revolution—crowds of armed men singing and promenading the streets; the battle blood running through their veins; that hot oxygen, which is called 'the flush of victory,' on the cheek; restaurants full; reveling in bar rooms, club rooms crowded, orgies and carousings in taverns or private houses, in tap rooms, down narrow alleys, in the broad highways." This is the anniversary of that mad era; but the streets look widely different. There are crowds of armed men in the streets, but they move under the strictest discipline and their color is black. No battle blood mantles the faces of the haggard and listless Charlestonians one meets—it is rather blood born of low diet and water gruel. For the flush of victory we have utter despondency. The restaurants are closed and the shutters are up; the occupants of the club rooms are dead, or in prison, or in exile; there is still carousing in taverns, but it is only by the flushed and spendthrift Yankee officers who are willing to pay seventy-five cents for a cobbler.

Of the leaders of those days, scarcely one remains to receive the curses which, even in the midst of their hatred of the Yankees, the people pour out upon the men who converted their prosperity into desolation. Then they were singing:

"With mortar, paixhan and petard,
We send Old Abe our Beauregard."

But Beauregard is a prisoner, given leave, by "Old Abe's" parole, to humbly enter his home at New Orleans, from which the loving wife, whom he deserted for secession, has gone out forever.* Huger is dead. Barnwell Rhett is in exile, and the very journal by which he fed and nurtured the germs of the Rebellion, has passed absolutely out of existence—no new editor daring to revive so ill-omened a thing as the Charleston *Mercury*.†

Governor Pickens, who announced in one of his early proclamations that he was born insensible to fear, has lived to learn his mistake, and has vanished into the dim unknown of "the interior."‡ Governor Aiken, who, (like that political eunuch, Alexander H. Stephens), weakly yielded his convictions and eased his conscience by blockade running, instead of fighting, has, for some unknown reason, been arrested and sent to Washington.§ Governor Manning,** Porcher Miles,††

---

* Beauregard's second wife, Marguerite Caroline Deslonde, had died in 1864 in New Orleans, when that city was under Union occupation.
† Reid's note: "A proposition has since been made to re-establish it, as an organ of the freedmen—to be edited by negroes!"
‡ Francis W. Pickens (1805–1869) was governor when South Carolina seceded. He died in Edgefield.
§ At the start of the war, ex-Gov. William Aiken Jr. (1806–1887) had chosen not to side with his state "nor take an active part against her." After the surrender of Fort Sumter, he was invited by the federal government to the raising of the national flag over the fort, and he declined the invitation. Shortly afterward, his house was looted and he was arrested and sent to Washington under guard. Subsequently President Andrew Johnson, a friend, ordered his release. Alexander Hamilton Stephens (1812–1883), Georgia Whig politician, opposed secession right up to the time it became a fait accompli for Georgia, after which he served as vice president of the Confederate states.
** John L. Manning (1816–1889), ex-governor (1852–1854) and senator representing Clarendon District, was a signer of the Ordinance of Secession. During the war, he was aide-de-camp with the rank of colonel on the staff of Gen. Beauregard. Immediately after the war, he was elected to the US Senate but declined to take the oath of allegiance and was not seated. A planter in South Carolina and Louisiana before the war, he lost his fortune but managed to hold on to hold on to Milford (c. 1839), his plantation near Pinewood, S.C.
†† William Porcher Miles (1822–1899), another of the most ardent of states' rights advocates known as the "Fire-Eaters" before the war, believed that "for any secessionist to return to public office in a reconstructed Union entailed a forfeiture of self-respect, consistency, and honor." He went to work for his father-in-law as a factor in New Orleans, then managed a plantation in Virginia. In 1880, he was appointed president of the newly reopened South Carolina College. After his father-in-law's death in 1882, he took over family business interests in Louisiana, where he managed a dozen plantations. In 1892, he and his son founded Miles Planting and Manufacturing Company in Louisiana.

Senator Chesnut,* Barnwell,† have all vanished into thin air before the Ithuriel touch—nay, rather before the mere approach of negro bayonets. The merchants, too, whom Southern independence was to make the cotton factors of the world, have long before the politicians had given it up, these men were hopelessly ruined. Trenholm, indeed, pushed a precarious but lucrative trade in blockade running, and succeeded better in managing his own funds than he did those of the Rebel Treasury Department; but he is now an absconding member of the Jeff. Davis Cabinet, and will be fortunate if he escapes arrest.‡ Rose and Minor are gone.§

---

* Sen. James Chesnut Jr. (1815–1885), a Camden lawyer, politician, and planter, had been an aide-de-camp to Beauregard when in the spring of 1861, he was sent to demand the surrender of Fort Sumter. When Maj. Anderson declined, Chesnut gave the orders for Fort Johnson to open fire. A colonel in the Confederate army, he was later aide to Jefferson Davis. He was promoted to brigadier general in command of state reserve forces in 1864. After the war, Chesnut returned to practice law in Camden and struggled financially. A delegate to the national Democratic convention in 1868, he took an active part in Reconstruction.

† Robert Woodward Barnwell (1801–1882), law partner (and second cousin) of Robert Barnwell Rhett, was a representative and senator from Beaufort and past president of South Carolina College (1833–1841). A secessionist delegate to the convention of seceding states in Montgomery, Alabama, he cast the deciding vote in the South Carolina delegation which carried the state for Jefferson Davis and made him president of the Confederacy. After the war, Barnwell returned to South Carolina College as an instructor. He was the chairman of the faculty from 1866 until 1873, when he retired and conducted a private girls' school in Columbia.

‡ George A. Trenholm (1807–1876) of Fraser, Trenholm and Company, with a branch of the firm in Liverpool, arranged cotton sales and financed his own fleet of blockade runners during the war. By the end of the war, he was the South's most successful blockade runner. In 1864, he replaced Christopher Memminger as secretary of the treasury of the Confederacy and kept "the South's crumbling war machine" financed and many fed and clothed, but ultimately found rescuing the South's failed economy impossible. As a function of the treasury, gold and jewels had been entrusted to Trenholm by banks and private citizens. When these assets disappeared, many believed he had stolen them. At the war's end, he fled Richmond with the Confederate cabinet and was apprehended and arrested. The federal government held him prisoner until October of 1865, when he used his influence to secure a pardon. He afterward fought the federal government in lengthy lawsuits over the claim that he and his partners had illegally converted "several hundreds of millions of dollars" in Confederate assets and were in procession of the funds. Trenholm appeared before numerous boards of inquiry before the government ultimately confiscated over a hundred parcels of his real estate. Phillips, *City of the Silent*, 170–71; Nepveux, *George Alfred Trenholm*, 97.

§ Alexander Rose (1839–1863), a Charleston corporal first appointed aide-de-camp to Gen. Beauregard, was serving on Gen. W. M. Gardner's staff when he died of typhoid fever at a hospital in Jackson, M.S. Col. Minor M. Millikin (1834–1862), Whitelaw Reid's college friend, had served in the 1st Ohio Volunteer Cavalry and was killed in battle at Tennessee.

One name, of all that were so prominent in Charleston four years ago, should never be taken on loyal lips save with reverent regard—that of Mr. Petigru. He remained faithful to the last; but his eyes were not permitted to see the old flag waving again, and his wife is today in Charleston, living on Government rations! She has stated her destitution frankly, however, to General Gillmore, command-ing the Department, and some small part of the nation's debt to her husband will yet, it is hoped, be paid in the tenderest care for herself.*

"There are twenty thousand people here in Charleston." said the haughty representative of an ancient Carolinian name, "and only six families among them all!" Judging from what one sees on the streets, one could very readily be-lieve the paradox which, in Carolina lips, becomes no paradox at all. There are plenty of resident Irish on the streets; the poorer class of natives, too, begin to venture out; but, in the course of the whole afternoon's driving about the city, I did not see a single one whom I should have supposed to belong to a leading family. My companion had spent the greater part of his life in Charleston, and, in his own language, knew everybody in the town; but he failed to see one whom he recognized as having ever held any position in politics or society.

The extent of the damage by the bombardment has, I imagine, been gener-ally overrated at the North. The lower part of the city was certainly not an eli-gible location for a quiet residence; but it is an error to suppose that most of the houses, or any considerable number of them, have been destroyed. The shells generally failed to explode, and the marks on the houses are rather scars than serious breaches. Roofs are injured, walls are weakened, windows destroyed and floors more or less ripped up; but still the houses stand, and can, with compar-atively little outlay, be repaired. The General's headquarters are established in the midst of the bombarded district; but the elegant house which he occupies shows no mark whatever. Most of the other officers who have taken houses are in the same quarter, and I observe that they have the same passion, as at Wilming-ton, for getting the very best establishments in a place.

The General drove us through the Arsenal grounds, and past those of the Military Academy, where, of old, the martial spirit of South Carolina had been fostered. The drives and walks had been bordered with spherical case, round shot and shell; and here and there, at the corners, little ornamental effects were produced by the erection of small pillars, made of our long rifle projectiles,

* Gillmore, now in command of Union army troops occupying the captured districts of South Carolina, Georgia, and Florida for the Department of the South. For her hus-band's loyalty to the Union, James Louis Petigru's widow, Jane Amelia Postell Petigru (1795–1868), soon after received the "goods and services" of the federal military and lived far better than most in Charleston.

flanked by a few broken bayonets. It was thus the Charlestonians amused themselves during the progress of the bombardment.

Passing through the shabby suburbs, which would hardly comport with the dignity of a first-class Northern village, we came out upon the track where, of yore, all the beauty and fashion of Charleston was wont to congregate—the Race Course. Of late years it has been used for a different purpose. Here, without shelter, without clothing, and with insufficient food, were confined the Yankee prisoners; and in a little enclosure, back of the judges' stand, may be seen their uncounted graves. Sympathizing hands have cleared away the weeds, and placed over the entrance an inscription that must bring shame to the cheek of every Southern man who passes: "The Martyrs of the Race Course."* Near it was an elegant cemetery, carefully tended, glorious with superb live-oaks, and weeping with the long, pendent trails of the silvery Spanish moss; but into this consecrated ground no Yankee's body could be borne. Negro soldiers were strolling through it as we passed, and some were reading from showy tombstones, to the dusky groups around them, the virtues of the—masters from whom they had run away to enlist!

Occasional vehicles were seen on the road, bringing in black and white refugees. The country is in such confusion that many seek the safe shelter of the cities, solely from the blind instinct that where there is force there must be protection. Such wagons and such horses were surely never seen. Each rivaled the other in corners, in age, in protuberance, and shakiness, and general disposition to tumble down and dissolve. They all bring in saddening stories of destitution in the country. Still I am inclined to think that these stories are exaggerated. There is little evidence of actual suffering in the country; and in the cities none who want have any scruples in calling upon the hireling minions of the tyrannical Washington Government for rations. Next winter is the dead point of danger.

---

* At least 257 Union prisoners of war had been buried in unmarked graves at Washington Race Course. After Union forces occupied Charleston, two associations of Charleston's free black community, the Friends of the Martyrs and the Patriotic Association of Colored Men, with northern whites, prepared a burial ground. The dead were exhumed and reburied with respectful markers. In April 1865, freedmen built a fence around the burial ground with an arch reading "Martyrs of the Race Course." Just before Reid's visit, on May 1, 1865, ten thousand blacks—freed slaves, children, and Union soldiers—made a procession to the cemetery. They laid flowers on the graves, listened to speakers of both races, and picnicked on the grass. This celebration was America's first Memorial Day. In 1871, these Union soldiers were exhumed again for proper military burial in South Carolina's national cemeteries at Beaufort and Florence. Jenkins, *Seizing the New Day*, 35–36; "Washington Race Track 1792–1900," at http://www.halseymap.com/flash /window.asp?HMID=29, accessed October 24, 2015.

There is a smaller breadth of cereals sown in the South this year than in any year since 1861, and by fall the stock on hand is likely to be exhausted. Now the suffering is only individual; then it promises to be too nearly general.

On the other hand, the reports from the North-west, or mountain region of the State, indicate little prospect of suffering. "I tell you," said a South Carolinian, from Greenville, "the South could have continued the war for ten years, if it had had your Northern gift of perseverance. We were neither exhausted of men nor of provisions; it was only that the flame of enthusiasm had burnt out. I have myself traveled, within the past month, through sections of South Carolina, from Greenville to Columbia, and thence north-east and north-west, so as to know accurately the condition of the crops in one-half the State. There is no trouble about starvation. The people are not suffering, except in such isolated cases as you will always find, and there is a larger breadth of grains planted than ever before. With reasonable care there ought to be no starvation this winter."

There was a little party in the evening, in the fine old mansion of a noted Charleston banker, but there were few South Carolinians there, excepting the house servants who had remained to wait on the new occupants. Admiral Dahlgren, Major-General Saxton,* two or three Brigadiers and Brevet Brigadiers, and their wives, made up the bulk of the company; and the talk was of the army and navy and the policy of the Government. A gentleman was introduced as the editor of the Charleston *Courier,* and I was not a little surprised to find that redoubtable Rebel personage greeting me with the warmth of an old acquaintance.[†] He turned out to be a former attaché of a leading New York paper, who had often reported to me in Washington, when I had been in temporary charge of its bureau there. Persons writing from here in the spring of 1861, said there was no feature of the feeling among the leaders more marked than their scarcely disguised hostility to the freedom of the press. I had been reading over some of those letters, of four years ago, in the morning; and it sounded curiously, like a continuation of the old strain, to hear the editor's lamentations over the

---

* Union Army Gen. Rufus Saxton (1824–1908), a fellow cadet of Gen. Gillmore at West Point, had been military governor of the Department of the South (1862–1865). He was now assistant commissioner of the Freedman's Bureau, from which he would be removed by President Andrew Johnson in January, 1866.

[†] When Sherman's troops seized the *Charleston Courier* on February 21, 1865, they turned it over to two Union war correspondents, George Whittemore, a veteran of New York newspapers, and George W. Johnson. They were ordered to publish it as a "loyal Union newspaper." Johnson left after a month, but Whittemore returned the newspaper to its prewar format before he left for New York in November 1865. The *Courier* was afterward published with military restrictions under Charlestonian Thomas Young Simons (1828–1878), a former Confederate officer.

impossibility of making a newspaper where you could express no opinions, and couldn't always even print the news. "Here, yesterday, for example, was a reconstruction meeting. The call for it was sent to me. I published that, and then sent phonographers to make a full report of the proceedings. There was a big row; the whites ordered out the negroes; then the latter got re-enforced, and came back to maintain their ground, whereupon the whites left. The speeches on both sides were racy; there was a good deal of excitement. I had a splendid report of the whole thing, and it was capital news. I had it all in type, when an order came to make no allusion whatever to the meeting. This morning everybody thinks the *Courier* is behind the times, because it didn't know anything about the reconstruction meeting!"

After the party, the Dominie told me of his explorations among his old friends in Charleston.

I ought, perhaps, before this, to have explained that my genial roommate, whom I have been rather irreverently terming the Dominie, is Rev. Dr. Fuller, of Baltimore, now a noted Baptist clergyman, formerly a leading South Carolina lawyer and planter. He still owns large plantations on the sea islands, and, down to the date of the emancipation proclamation, had on them between two hundred and two hundred and fifty slaves, who came to him by inheritance, and whom, under the laws of South Carolina, he was unable either to educate or emancipate. Governor Bradford* said to him once: "Mr. Lincoln's emancipation idea has been an expensive one to you, Doctor. It must have cost you over a hundred and fifty thousand dollars." "Yes, I presume it did; but then, Governor, it took over a hundred and fifty thousand pounds of iron off my conscience!" So great had been the change since he held his public discussion with President Wayland, on the rightfulness of and Scriptural warrant for, slavery!†

All the Doctor's connections were with the South, and nearly all his relations, who have not been killed, are living here. It was his nephew who held Fort Sumter to the last; a near relative of his laid out the fortifications at Fort Fisher; another was the Rebel engineer at Norfolk. Last night he found a granddaughter, of perhaps the most prominent member of the first Congress, living on Government rations! Another, equally destitute, bears a historic name, and is the granddaughter of one of Washington's most confidential friends and intimate advisers in the Revolutionary war.

---

* Augustus Williamson Bradford (1806–1881), governor of Maryland (1862–1866).
† Fuller had preferred to look on slavery "with a calm and impartial judgment" from a border state. His spiritual debate over slavery with Rev. Francis Wayland (1796–1865), president of Brown University and a Baptist pastor in Providence, Rhode Island, was published as *Domestic Slavery Considered as a Scriptural Institution* (1845).

It has been naturally supposed that the bitterest drop in all the bitter cup of humiliation for these haughty South Carolinians, must be the necessity of accepting alms from the Government they had been seeking to overthrow. But the ingenious high priestesses of secession regard the matter in no such light. The Dominie found a number of them living solely on Government rations. He hastened to offer them assistance. Their Northern relatives had already repeatedly volunteered similar offers, but they refused them all, and persisted in living on the bacon and hard bread issued by the United States Commissary. They explained that they preferred to make "the Washington Government" support them. It had robbed them of all they had, and now the very least it could do was to pay their expenses.

Every penny of cost to which they put it was so much got back from the fortunes of which it had robbed them, by waging this wicked war for their subjugation! Doesn't somebody think it a shame that these repentant South Carolinians should be treated with so little magnanimity as the Government is displaying; and that Northern Abolitionists should quit watching them critically, and "mind their own business?" Already, a few of the South Carolinians talk thus; and in a few months, if freedom of expression is allowed them, we shall see much of the old vituperation of the Government and of the North.

"Unionism"—Black and White, in Charleston and Through South Carolina

A very few Union men could be seen. Perhaps it would be more accurate to say, a few could be found less treasonable than the majority of South Carolinians. "To be frank with you," said one of these men, a sallow-faced country lawyer, from the mountain district, "to be frank with you, we were all Rebels. The North has never understood, and I doubt if it ever will understand, the absolute unanimity with which, after the war was begun, we all supported it. While there was any use in it, we resisted secession; but after the State seceded, our district, which was always strongly Union, sent more and better volunteers to the war than any other."

"You mean, then, that after secession was accomplished, the former Unionists became more violent Rebels than the rest; and that, practically, not a soul in the State remained true to the Union, except the negroes?"

"Well, I suspect you're a little mistaken about the negroes. They're very ignorant, and most of them were, and are, governed by their masters' notions."

"What security have we, in restoring political power to a community disposed toward us as yours was, and still feeling as you now represent?"

"Oh, our people are impulsive, and they are always decided, one way or the other!"

"Suppose Representatives should be admitted to Congress, and South Carolina should thus be clothed with all her old power. You who, before secession, were the Union men, will be the only voters now; but in two or three years, of course, everybody will vote again. Will not you original Union men be again outnumbered by the original secessionists?"

"I don't believe we ever were outnumbered. I don't believe there ever was a majority for secession in South Carolina."

"The poll books tell a different story."

"Yes; but remember we had been fighting secession for thirty years, and had got tired of it. Men said these restless spirits will never be quiet until they have tried secession. If we don't let them try it now, they'll keep us in a constant turmoil until we do. It is bound to come some time, and we may as well spare ourselves further trouble and let it come now."

"In other words, then, men said, let the Union be destroyed, with whatever attendant horrors, rather than one should be bothered to keep up this perpetual struggle."

"Well, not exactly that. You must remember there was a tremendous pressure. I myself had my house surrounded by a hundred and fifty armed men, one night, before the election, because they thought I was a Union man. There was no making head against the current."

"By your showing, then, the rebel element was resistless before the passage of the secession ordinance, and universal after it. As you frankly say, you were all rebels. We have incurred an enormous debt in subduing you, and we know that there is a small party at the North openly, and a larger one secretly, desirous of repudiating that debt, in order to shake off the burden of heavy taxation. Now, if South Carolina, and other States occupying her position, are restored to power in the nation, what security have we that all you rebels would continue voting for heavy taxation to pay the debt incurred in whipping you? Would there not be very great danger of your uniting with this minority at the North, and thus securing a national majority in favor of repudiation?"

"Well, our attention has never been called to that subject, and we were not aware that there was likely to be any portion whatever of your people favorable to repudiation. I can't say, however, what our more violent people would do. There has been very little comparison of views; and all our efforts must first be given to getting our civil authority and power restored, without considering what questions may come up back of that."

"With what political party at the North, then, would your people be more likely to affiliate?"

"Of course with the Democratic. We have understood all along that it sympathized more with us than any other; that it was more opposed to the war, more disposed to leave us alone with our slaves, more-ready for favorable terms of peace."

"And if any considerable portion of that party were to propose lightening the taxes by repudiating (in reduction of interest or otherwise) part of the debt incurred in subduing you, you would be very apt to unite with them?"

"I don't know but we would; but I can't say; for, as yet, we are giving no attention to anything excepting re-organization!"

Recurring to his admissions concerning the bitterness of the original secessionists, I asked: "What security will we have, if political power should be fully restored to South Carolina, that the secessionists may not regain control of the State Government, and prove as pestilent as ever, if not in the field, then in Congress, and in the old expedients of obnoxious State legislation?"

"Oh, a barrel of cider never ferments twice."

I asked about the popular feeling toward Jeff Davis, curious to see if the hatred to him, of which we have heard at the North, really exists among any class in South Carolina except the negroes. My Union man replied: "There is a very general feeling of great kindness to him, and great sympathy for his present misfortunes. One party in the South assailed his administration very bitterly; but the feeling was not, to any extent, a personal one. He is greatly admired and loved by our people."

"Was the South exhausted of men when the rebellion broke down? Was it really impossible to re-enforce Lee's army, and, if so, what citizens have you now for re-organizing State government except the rebel soldiers, unless, indeed, you reckon the negroes?"

"The South never was exhausted of men, sir; there were plenty of them everywhere. Disaffection, weariness, indisposition to the long strain of an effort that took more than four years to accomplish its purpose; that was what broke down the Confederacy. There were plenty of men all the time, but they dodged the conscripting officer, or deserted at the first chance they got. Of course, our losses by death and disabling wounds have been terribly great; but the race of arms-bearing men in South Carolina is not extinct."*

On the afternoon of our last day's stay in Charleston, a meeting, in one of the negro churches, afforded me the first opportunity of the trip to see large

---

* Reid's note: "This man now holds an office under the National Government in South Carolina."

masses of negroes together. It was called a week or two ago by General Saxton, who stands in the light of a patron saint to all these people; but it was doubtless swelled by the hope that Chief Justice Chase, whom General Saxton had earnestly invited, might consent to be present. He had emphatically refused, the evening before, and had forbidden any announcement of his name; but had finally said that, if he could go unheralded, he would like to see the negroes together.* The church is of the largest size, and belongs exclusively to the negroes, who have their own negro pastor, occupy pews in the body of the building, and send the poor people to the galleries, very much after the fashion of their white brethren. The pavement in front was crowded, and the steps were almost impassable. A white-wooled old deacon saw my difficulty in forcing my way up the steaming aisle, and, crowding the negroes and negresses aside with little ceremony, led me to a seat almost under the pulpit, where I found, perhaps, a dozen whites, all told. Among them was Colonel Beecher—a brother of Henry Ward Beecher—† and at the table sat the inevitable reporter.

A Major-General, in full uniform, occupied the desk and was addressing the crammed audience of negroes in a plain, nervous, forcible manner. It was an odd sight, but General Saxton certainly adorns the pulpit. Ladies would call him a handsome man; and his black hair and luxurious English whiskers and mustache would be their especial admiration. He looks—to judge of his intellect by his

* Chase consented to address the meeting at Zion Presbyterian Church—which had become a "meeting place and rallying point" for blacks and their northern liberators—after he was much solicited by white citizens. Known for his strong views against Southern slave owners and his conviction that blacks should be given the vote, Charleston whites were anxious to hear future plans. According to the *New York Times*, "Between fifty and sixty of the prominent men of the city, among whom were Mayor Macbeth, John Phillips, Esq., Geo. Williams, Esq., and R. W. Seymour, Esq., called upon Judge Chase, at the residence of Brig. Gen. Hatch, on the day following that of his arrival. The object of the citizens was to get an idea, if possible, of the course the government intends to pursue in the matter of restoration and representation. They were informed that the authorities at Washington would, at the proper time, define the course of procedure which it would be necessary for the people of the State to follow in order to place themselves on a right footing in the Union. That night at Zion Church, Chase gave a 'guarded speech.'" "Our Charleston Correspondence," *New York Times* May 22, 1865:1.
† James Chaplin Beecher (1828–1886), colonel of the 35th US Colored Troops, had heralded the end of the war in March of 1865 when he led his troops into Charleston under a banner designed by his half-sister, Harriet Beecher Stowe, author of *Uncle Tom's Cabin*. A political activist, abolitionist, and editor of religious magazines, his half-brother, Rev. Henry Ward Beecher (1813–1877), the most famous preacher in the country, had delivered the main address when the flag was ceremoniously raised in victory over Fort Sumter on April 14 (the same day Lincoln was assassinated). Applegate, *The Most Famous Man in America*, 9.

face and head—narrow, but intense; not very profound in seeing the right, but energetic in doing it when seen; given to practice, rather than theory; and, withal, good and true. He is the first regular army officer who was found willing to undertake this work of caring for and superintending the freedmen; and he has done it faithfully, under all manner of slights and obloquy from brother officers, who thought his work unworthy of West Point. And yet he undertook it, not from any special love of the negro, but because he was ordered. "I would have preferred being in the field," he said simply, "last night, but I was ordered to do this thing, and I have tried to do it faithfully, till the Government gave me something else to do. I was educated in its school and for its service, and I thought it my business to do whatever it required." The Government has rarely been so fortunate in selecting its agents for tasks that required peculiar adaptability.

The audience was a study. Near the pulpit sat a coal-black negro, in the full uniform of a Major of the army, with an enormous regulation hat—be sure there was no lack of flowing plume, or gilt cord and knots—disposed on the table beside him. At every emphatic sentence in the General's speech he shouted, "Hear, hear," and clapped his hands, with the unction and gravity of an old parliamentarian. Near him were two others in uniform, one a mulatto, the other scarcely more than a quadroon, and both with very intelligent faces, and very modest and graceful in their bearing. One was a First Lieutenant, the other a Major.

Around them was a group of certainly the blackest faces, with the flattest noses and the wooliest heads, I ever saw—the mouths now and then broadening into a grin or breaking out into that low, oily, chuckling gobble of a laugh which no white man can ever imitate. Beyond them ranged all colors and apparently all conditions. Some, black and stalwart, were dressed like quiet farm laborers, and had probably come in from the country, or had been field hands before the war. Others, lighter in color and slighter in build, were dressed in broadcloth, with flashy scarfs and gaudy pins, containing paste, or Cape May diamonds. Others looked like the more intelligent class of city laborers; and there were a few old patriarchs who might recollect the days of Denmark Vesey.* On the other side of the church was a motley, but brilliant army of bright-colored turbans, wound around wooly heads, and tawdry bandanas, and hats of all the shapes that have prevailed within the memory of this generation, and bonnets of last year's styles, with absolutely a few of the coquettish little triangular bits of lace

---

*Denmark Vesey (ca. 1767–1822), a free black carpenter who allegedly led plans for a slave revolt in 1822. The revolt was never acted out; however, thirty-five blacks involved were tried and hanged, including Vesey, and another thirty-two were convicted and sold out of the region.

and flowers which the New York milliners have this year decreed. Some of them wore kid gloves, all were gaudily dressed, and, a few, barring the questionable complexion, had the air and bearing of ladies.

They were all enthusiastic, the women even more than the men. Some of the ancient negresses sat swaying to and fro, with an air of happy resignation, only broken now and then by an emphatic nod of the head, and an exclamation, "Dat's true, for shore." The younger ones laughed and giggled, and when the great cheers went up, clapped with all their might, and looked across to see how the young men were doing, and whether their enthusiasm was observed. Ah, well! Who is there who doesn't want to know whether his world, be it a big one or a little one, is noticing him?

But the noteworthy point in all this enthusiasm was, that it was intelligent. Bulwer makes Richelieu* relent toward a young man who applauded his play at the proper places. General Saxton had equal occasion to be gratified with his auditors. On taking his seat, he was followed by the gorgeous Major (who turned out to be the same negro about whom Lord Brougham raised that beautiful little diplomatic muddle with United States Minister Dallas, at a meeting of the Royal Geographical Society in London).† The Major was not happy in his

---

* Reid refers to Cardinal Richelieu, a character in the historical play *Richelieu* (1839) by English author Sir Edward Lytton Bulwer (1803–1873).

† Maj. Martin R. Delany (1812–1882), a free black physician born in West Virginia, had been the first black field officer in the US Army as well as the highest ranking black Union Army officer at war's end. After Union occupation of the city, he was assigned to the Freedman's Bureau where "he called for black pride, the enforcement of black civil rights, and land for the freedmen." One of the earliest blacks to encourage a return to Africa, Delany had sailed to Liberia in 1859 to investigate the possibility of a new black nation, and signed an agreement with eight chiefs in the Abeokuta region to permit settlers to live on "unused land" in return for using their skills for the community's good. Londoners were much interested in Delany's explorations, which led to many speaking engagements and an invitation in 1860 to attend the International Statistical Congress, a major scientific gathering at London's Somerset House chaired by Queen Victoria's husband, Prince Albert. Among the American delegation was George Mifflin Dallas, minister to the Court of St. James, and Judge Augustus Baldwin Longstreet of Georgia, both outspokenly proslavery. They were seated on the platform when, in opening remarks, Lord Brougham, president of the Congress (but also former chancellor of Great Britain and a pioneer of abolition and antislavery reform), called attention to Delany's presence, remarking, "I call to the attention of Mr. Dallas the fact there is a Negro present, and I hope he will feel no scruples on that account." Delany rose and said, "I rise, your royal Highness, to thank his lordship, the unflinching friend of the negro, for the remarks he has made in reference to me and to assure your royal highness and his lordship that I am a man." Dallas, offended by Brougham's intervention, the reply of Delany, and the applause of the audience, kept his seat; however, the rest of the American delegation, led by Longstreet, walked out of the meeting. The tumult nearly

remarks, and elicited very little applause, till, suddenly, he was astounded by a thundering burst of it. He began acknowledging the compliment, but the tumult burst out louder than ever; and the orator finally discovered that it was not for him, but for Major-General Gillmore, commanding the department, who was advancing up the aisle, escorting Chief Justice Chase. Presently General Saxton introduced the Chief Justice, and the whole audience rose and burst out into cheer after cheer, that continued unintermittently till we had counted at least nine, and possibly one or two more. The negroes may be very ignorant, but it is quite evident that they know, or think they know, who their friends are. The little "talk" that followed was like its author, simple, straightforward and weighty, till, at the close, it rose into a strain of unaffected eloquence that almost carried the excitable audience off their feet. "'It isn't only what he says," whispered an en-thusiastic negro behind me to his neighbor, "but it's de man what says it. He don't talk for nuffin, and his words hab weight."*

After more tumultuous cheering, the audience called for Gillmore, till the great artillerist absolutely blushed in his embarrassment. *His* speeches for Charleston were made from the muzzle of the "Swamp Angel."

I spent the evening in the Charleston *Courier* office. The old library remained, and *Congressional Globes* and arguments on the divine right of slavery stood side by side with Reports of the Confederate Congress, and official accounts of battles, while on the wall was pasted one of the most bombastic proclamations of the runaway Governor. Several of the old attaches of the concern remain, among them a phonographic reporter and the cashier. The circulation of this most flourishing Southern paper in the seaboard States, had dwindled down to less than a thousand. "We wrote our reports," said the phonographer, "on the backs of old grocery bills, and in blank pages torn out of old account books." "We deserved all we got," he continued, "but you ought not to be hard on us now. The sun never shone on a nobler or kinder-hearted people than the

---

caused a diplomatic incident and had taken some time to die down. US Congress, "To The Public," 473–75.

* Reid's note. This was Mr. Chase's single "speech" during the entire trip. Ten minutes, or less, of familiar and fatherly talk to helpless negroes, advising them to industry, economy and good order, telling them he thought they should vote, but didn't know whether the Government would agree with him, and advising that, if the right of suffrage should be refused them, they should behave so well, educate themselves so fast, and become so orderly and prosperous, that the Government should see they deserved it; this was what subsequently became, in certain Northern newspapers, "Chief Justice Chase's endless stump speeches, and shameless intriguing with old political leaders, in his electioneering tour through the South."

South Carolinians, and this was always the nicest town to live in, in the United States."

Encountering a so-called South Carolina Unionist, from the interior, I asked about the relations between the negroes and their old masters.

"In the main, the niggers are working just as they used to, not having made contracts of any sort, because there was no competent officer accessible before whom the contracts could be approved. A few have been hired by the day; and some others have gone to work for a specified share in the crops. In a great many cases the planters have told them to work ahead, get their living out of the crops, and what further share they were entitled to should be determined when the officers to approve contracts came. Then, if they couldn't agree, they could separate."

"Have there been no disturbances between the negroes and their former masters, no refusals to recognize the destruction of slavery?"

"In our part of the State, none. Elsewhere I have heard of them. With us, the death of slavery is recognized, and made a basis of action by everybody. But we don't believe that because the nigger is free he ought to be saucy; and we don't mean to have any such nonsense as letting him vote. He's helpless, and ignorant, and dependent, and the old masters will still control him.

"I have never been a large slaveholder myself—for the last year or two I have had but twelve, little and big," he continued. "Every one of them stays with me, just as before, excepting one, a carpenter. I told him he'd better go off and shift for himself. He comes back, every two or three nights, to tell me how he is getting along; and the other day he told me he hadn't been able to collect anything for his work, and I gave him a quarter's provisions to get started with.

"I had to give him," he significantly added, "a sort of paper—note, of course, pretending to be legal—certifying that he was working for himself, with my consent, in order to enable him to get along without trouble."

There was a World of meaning in the phrase, "To enable him to get along without trouble," though he was as free as the man that gave the paper. I asked what they would do with the negroes, if they got permission to reorganize.

"Well, we want to have them industrious and orderly, and will do all we can to bring it about."

"Will you let any of them vote?"

"That question has not been discussed. Nobody could stand up in the State who should advocate promiscuous negro suffrage. It is possible that a few might be willing to let the intelligent negroes vote—after some years, at any rate, if not now."

"I believe you let the sandhillers vote. Don't you know that these disfranchised negroes of Charleston are infinitely their superiors, in education, industry, wealth and good conduct?"

"Well, they're pretty bad, it's true—those sandhillers—but there isn't the same prejudice against them."

The moon lit up, with a softened effulgence, all the beauties, and hid all the scars of Charleston, as, late at night, I walked, through its desolate streets, and by its glorious shrubbery, to the landing, and hailed the *Wayanda*. A boat shot out of the shadow for me; and before I had joined, below deck, the anchor had been hoisted and the vessel was under way.

Charleston, S.C. View of ruined buildings through porch of the Circular Church (150 Meeting Street). George N. Barnard 1819–1902, photographer, 1865 [April]. Library of Congress.

SIDNEY ANDREWS (1865)

"The Dead Body of Charleston"

Sidney Andrews "The Dead Body of Charleston" from *The South Since the War: As Shown by Fourteen Weeks of Travel and Observation in Georgia and the Carolinas* (Boston: Ticknor and Fields), 1866.

Sidney Andrews (1835–1880), journalist and editor, was born in Sheffield, Massachusetts. He attended the University of Michigan, and served as editor on the staff of the *Daily Courier* in Alton, Illinois, from 1858 to 1861. Andrews then went to Washington where he was an attendant in the US Senate. While acting in that capacity, he became Washington correspondent for the *Boston Daily Advertiser*. His first dispatch, written under the pseudonym "Dixon," appeared in 1864, followed by a series of letters and dispatches concerning the military and political events of the day. He attracted much attention as a representative of the press in Washington.

Five months after the war ended, Andrews set out to take stock of the postwar South. He spent September, October, and November 1865 traveling in South Carolina, North Carolina, and Georgia—attending state reconstruction conventions in Raleigh, Columbia, and Milledgeville, and speaking with people from a variety of backgrounds to report on political, economic, and social conditions following the South's defeat. He wrote more than forty articles on the South, firsthand reports that ran in the *Chicago Tribune*—a Republican newspaper that had competed with Horace Greeley's *New York Tribune* as the leading antislavery paper before the war—and in the even more deeply antislavery *Boston Daily Advertiser*. His articles were so popular with northerners that *The Atlantic* published his "Three Months Among the Reconstructionists" in 1866. Later that same year, Andrews published his experiences in book form as *The South since the War: As Shown by Fourteen Weeks of Travel and Observation in Georgia and the Carolinas*. His powerful and "scathing" assessment of the South proved ammunition to those advocating Congress for a more aggressive northern hand in Reconstruction and influenced the later creation of the New South.

Andrews remained on the *Daily Advertiser* as journalist and editor until 1869 and published *St. Thomas Treaty: A Series of Letters to The Boston Daily Advertiser* (1869). He also wrote for *Every Saturday,* a Boston literary magazine, and several other leading journals. While serving as secretary to Governor William B. Washburn of Massachusetts from 1872 to 1874, he married Sarah Lucretia Washburn, his second wife. He also served as secretary of the Massachusetts Board of State Charites from 1872 until his death. In 2004, a new edition of the *The South Since the War,* abridged by Heather Cox Richardson, was published.

Traveling in the South in 1865, Andrews wrote:

> Personally, I have very little cause of complaint, for my role was rather that of a listener than of a talker; but I met many persons who kindly cautioned me, that at such and such places, and in such and such company, it would be advisable to refrain from conversation on certain topics. Among the better class of people, resident in the cities and large towns, I found a fair degree of liberality of sentiment and courtesy of speech; but in travelling off the main railway-lines, and among the average of the population, any man of Northern opinions must use much circumspection of language; while, in many counties of South Carolina and Georgia, the life of an avowed Northern radical would hardly be worth a straw but for the presence of the military. In Barnwell and Anderson districts, South Carolina, official records show the murder of over a dozen Union men in the months of August and September; and at Atlanta, a man told me, with a quiet chuckle, that in Carroll County, Georgia, there were "four d—n Yankees shot in the month of October." Any Union man, travelling in either of these two States, must expect to hear many very insulting words; and any Northern man is sure to find his principles despised, his people contemned, and himself subjected to much disagreeable contumely. There is everywhere extreme sensitiveness concerning the negro and his relations; and I neither found nor learned of any village, town, or city in which it would be safe for a man to express freely what are here, in the North, called very moderate views on that subject. Of course the war has not taught its full lesson.

However, Andrews claimed his reception was better than that of other northern journalists. "Yet at one town in South Carolina," he wrote, "when I sought accommodations for two or three days at a boarding-house, I was asked by the woman in charge, 'Are you a Yankee or a Southerner?' and when I answered, 'Oh, a Yankee, of course,' she responded, 'No Yankee stops in this house!' and turned her back upon me and walked off. In another town in the same State I learned that I was the first Yankee who had been allowed to stop at the hotel since the close of the war."

In the following excerpt from *The South Since the War,* Andrews depicts the "dead body of Charleston."

SOURCES

Andrews, Sidney. *The South Since the War: As Shown by Fourteen Weeks of Travel and Observation in Georgia and the Carolinas,* ed. Heather Cox Richardson. Baton Rouge: Louisiana State University Press, 2004.

Chase, Theodore Russell. *Michigan University Book, 1844–1880.* Detroit, Michigan: Richmond, Backus Co., 1880: see 1860.

Cushing, William. "Dixon." In *Initials and Pseudonyms: A Dictionary of Literary Disguises.* New York: T. Y. Crowell & Company, 1885.

"The Dead Body of Charleston"
Charleston, September 4, 1865.

A city of ruins, of desolation, of vacant houses, of widowed women, of rotting wharves, of deserted warehouses, of weed-wild gardens, of miles of grass-grown streets, of acres of pitiful and voiceful barrenness,—that is Charleston, wherein Rebellion loftily reared its head five years ago, on whose beautiful promenade the fairest of cultured women gathered with passionate hearts to applaud the assault of ten thousand upon the little garrison of Fort Sumter!

"The mills of the gods grind slow, but they grind exceeding small." Be sure Charleston knows what these words mean. Be sure the pride of the eyes of these men and women has been laid low. Be sure they have eaten wormwood, and their souls have worn sackcloth. "God's ways seem dark, but soon or late they touch the shining hills of day." Henceforth let us rest content in this faith; for here is enough of woe and want and ruin and ravage to satisfy the most insatiate heart,—enough of sore humiliation and bitter overthrow to appease the desire of the most vengeful spirit.

Who kindled the greedy fire of December, 1861, whereby a third of the city was destroyed? No one yet knows. "It was de good Jesus hisself," said an old negro to me when I asked him the question—"it was de Almighty Hand workin' fru de man's hand." Certain it is that the people were never able to discover the agency of the fire; though, so far as I can learn, no one doubts that it was the work of an incendiary—"some man," say the ex-Rebels, "who wanted to do you Federals a good turn."*

---

* On the night of December 11, 1861, Meta Morris Grimball recorded in her diary: "The fire broke out in a sash & blind factory and the difficulty of getting water and the previous drought and a very high wind which drove the flames caused the general destruction.

Recall last winter's daily bulletin about the bombardment—so many shells
and no damage done—so many shells and no damage done—day after day the
same old story, till one almost believed it true. Yet ex-Rebel officers will tell you
now that our aim was so perfect that we killed their sentinels with our Parrott
guns; and go where you will, up and down the streets in almost any portion of
the city, and you find the dumb walls eloquent with praises of our skill.

We never again can have the Charleston of the decade previous to the war.
The beauty and pride of the city are as dead as the glories of Athens. Five millions
of dollars could not restore the ruin of these four past years; and that sum is so
far beyond the command of the city as to seem the boundless measure of immea-
surable wealth. Yet, after all, Charleston was Charleston because of the hearts of
its people. St. Michael's Church, they held, was the centre of the universe; and the
aristocracy of the city were the very elect of God's children on earth. One marks
now how few young men there are, how generally the young women are dressed
in black. The flower of their proud aristocracy is buried on scores of battle-fields.
If it were possible to restore the broad acres of crumbling ruins to their foretime
style and uses, there would even then be but the dead body of Charleston.

The Charleston of 1875 will doubtless be proud in wealth and intellect and
rich in grace and culture. Let favoring years bring forward such fruitage! Yet the
place has not in itself recuperative power for such a result. The material on which
to build that fair structure does not here exist, and, as I am told by dozens,
cannot be found in the State. If Northern capital and Northern energy do not
come here, the ruin, they say, must remain a ruin; and if this time five years, finds
here a handsome and thriving city, it will be the creation of New England,—not
necessarily the pattern of New England, for the influences from thence will be
moulded by and interfused with those now existing here; but yet, in the essential
fact, the creation of New England.

It was noted on the steamship by which I came from New York that, leaving
out the foreign element, our passengers were from Charleston and from Massachusetts. We had nearly as many Boston men as Charleston men. One of the
Charleston merchants said to me that when he went North the passengers were
also almost equally divided between Massachusetts and South Carolina; and he
added, that, in Eastern Massachusetts, where he spent some days, he found many
men who were coming to Charleston.

This fire began at Cooper River and burnt across the City to Ashley River. The fire
burnt from 9 o'clock at night to the afternoon of the next day." Journal of Meta Morris
Grimball, transcript, 51.

Of Massachusetts men, some are already in business here, and others came on to "see the lay of the land," as one of them said. "That's all right," observed an ex-Rebel captain in one of our after-dinner chats—"that's all right; let's have Massachusetts and South Carolina brought together, for they are the only two States that amount to anything."

"I hate all you Yankees most heartily in a general sort of way," remarked another of these Southerners; "but I find you clever enough personally, and I expect it'll be a good thing for us to have you come down here with your money, though it'll go against the grain with us pretty badly."

There are many Northern men here already, though one cannot say that there is much Northern society, for the men are either without families or have left them at home. Walking out yesterday with a former Charlestonian—a man who left here in the first year of the war and returned soon after our occupation of the city—he pointed out to me the various "Northern houses"; and I shall not exaggerate if I say that this classification appeared to include at least half the stores on each of the principal streets. "The presence of these men," said he, "was at first very distasteful to our people, and they are not liked any too well now; but we know they are doing a good work for the city."

I fell into some talk with him concerning the political situation, and found him of bitter spirit toward what he was pleased to denominate "the infernal radicals." When I asked him what should be done, he answered: "You Northern people are making a great mistake in your treatment of the South. We are thoroughly whipped; we give up slavery forever; and now we want you to quit reproaching us. Let us back into the Union, and then come down here and help us build up the country."

Every little variation from the old order of things excites the comment "Yankee notion," in which there is sometimes good-natured querulousness and sometimes a sharp spice of contempt. Stopping a moment this afternoon in a store where were three or four intelligent men, one of them asked me the use of the "thing" I had in my hand. It was one of the handle-and-straps so common in the North for carrying shawls, cloaks, overcoats, &c. Seeing that none of them had any idea what it was, I explained its use. "Well, now, what a Yankee notion!" "Yes," answered another, "but how handy it is."

To bring here the conveniences and comforts of our Northern civilization, no less than the Northern idea of right and wrong, justice and injustice, humanity and inhumanity, is the work ready for the hand of every New England man and woman who stands waiting. There is much prejudice to overcome, and some of it is bitter and aggravating; but the measure of success won by Northern men already in the field is an earnest reward for others. Self-interest is a masterful agent in modern civilization.

Business is reviving slowly, though perhaps the more surely. The resident merchants are mostly at the bottom of the ladder of prosperity. They have idled away the summer in vain regrets for vanished hopes, and most of them are only just now beginning to wake to the new life. Some have already been North for goods, but more are preparing to go; not heeding that, while they vacillate with laggard time, Northern men are springing in with hands swift to catch opportunity. It pains me to see the apathy and indifference that so generally prevails; but the worst feature of the situation is, that so many young men are not only idle, but give no promise of being otherwise in the immediate future.

Many of the stores were more or less injured by the shelling. A few of these have been already repaired, and are now occupied, very likely by Northern men. A couple of dozen, great and small, are now in process of repair; and scores stand with closed shutters or gaping doors and windows. The doubt as to the title of property, and the wise caution of the President in granting pardons, unquestionably has something to do with the stagnation so painfully apparent; but very much of it is due to the hesitating shiftlessness of even the Southern merchant, who forever lets *I dare not* wait upon *I would*. Rents of eligible store-rooms are at least from one fourth to one third higher than before the war, and resident business men say only Northern men who intend staying but a short time can afford to pay present prices. I'm sure I can't see how anyone can afford to pay them, but I know the demand is greater than the supply.

I queried of the returning merchants on the steamship how they were received in the North. An Augusta man complained that he could get no credit, and that there was a disposition to be grinding and exacting. One Charleston man said he asked for sixty days, and got it without a word of objection. Another told me that he asked for four months, was given three, and treated like a gentleman everywhere. Another showed me the receipt for a debt of about fifteen hundred dollars contracted before the war, which he had paid in full; and when he asked for four months on a bill of eight thousand dollars, it was readily given. Still another settled his old indebtedness with one third cash and eight and twelve month's notes for the balance, while he got ninety days on three fourths of his new bill. One man said he had many friends in the North, and they all knew him for a thorough Rebel; he expected some taunts, but tried to carry himself like a gentleman, and was courteously received, "even in Boston."

I judge that such of the merchants as first went North and settled with their creditors made more favorable terms than those who went later. If it be said that those were men who had loved the Union, while these are men who had not; that those were men of keen sense of commercial honor and integrity, while these are men who cared less for an adjustment; that those are men who deserved favors, while these are men who have forfeited all claim to special consideration,—if this be said, the pith of the matter will probably be hit so far as regards most of those who now complain of their reception.

Yet there are men who deserved better than they have received. These are they who, whatever their views on the questions at issue in the war, meant to pay all their debts. Most of them are men who loved the Union and hated secession. That there were such men in all parts of the State is beyond question. When the negroes say any one was a Union man during the war, the fact is established; from their judgment and testimony there is no appeal. These men, having no faith in the Confederacy, put everything they could into cotton or rosin or turpentine—hoping to save something from the general wreck they saw impending—only to find in the end that they are scarcely richer than those who invested everything in Confederate bonds.

It is not clearly understood how thoroughly Sherman's army destroyed everything in its line of march—destroyed it without questioning who suffered by the action. That this wholesale destruction was often without orders, and often against most positive orders, does not change the fact of destruction. The Rebel leaders were, too, in their way, even more wanton, and just as thorough as our army in destroying property. They did not burn houses and barns and fences as we did; but, during the last three months of the war, they burned immense quantities of cotton and rosin.

The action of the two armies put it out of the power of men to pay their debts. The values and the bases of value were nearly all destroyed. Money lost about everything it had saved. Thousands of men who were honest in purpose have lost everything but honor. The cotton with which they meant to pay their debts has been burned, and they are without other means. What is the part of wisdom in respect to such men? It certainly cannot be to strip them of the last remnant. Many of them will pay in whole or in part, if proper consideration be shown them. It is no question of favor to any one as a favor, but a pure question of business—how shall the commercial relations of the two sections be re-established? In determining it, the actual and exceptional condition of the State with respect to property should be constantly borne in mind.

Yet when all this is said in favor of one class of merchants, it must, in good conscience, be added, that by far a larger class is showing itself unworthy of anything but stringent measures. "How do you find the feeling?" said I to a gentleman of national reputation, who is now here settling the affairs of a very large New York house. "Well, there are a good many merchants who don't mean to pay anything more than they are obliged to," said he in reply. I asked of one of the leading merchants this morning, "Are your people generally disposed to settle their accounts?" His answer was, "Those who expect to continue business must of course do so." "How about the others?" I queried. "I'm afraid there isn't so much commercial honor as there should be," he replied. I am told of one firm which represented itself entirely ruined, when subsequent investigation showed that it had five thousand pounds sterling to its credit in Liverpool; and of another which offered only thirty cents on the dollar, when its property in New York alone will cover over seventy cents on the dollar of its entire indebtedness.

That Rebellion sapped the foundations of commercial integrity in the State is beyond question. That much of the Northern indebtedness will never be paid is also beyond question. What is desirable is, that creditors should become cognizant of all the facts in the case before fixing terms. For the rascal there is but one set of terms; for the honest man there should be every possible consideration.

The city is under thorough military rule; but the iron hand rests very lightly. Soldiers do police duty, and there is some nine-o'clock regulation; but, so far as I can learn, anybody goes anywhere at all hours of the night without molestation. "There never was such good order here before," said an old colored man to me. The main street is swept twice a week, and all garbage is removed at sunrise.

"If the Yankees was to stay here always and keep the city so clean, I don't reckon we'd have 'yellow jack' here any more," was a remark I overheard on the street.* "Now is de fust time sence I can'mem'er when brack men was safe in de street af'er nightfall," stated the negro tailor in whose shop I sat an hour yesterday.

On the surface, Charleston is quiet and well behaved; and I do not doubt that the more intelligent citizens are wholly sincere in their expressions of a desire for peace and reunion. The city has been humbled as no other city has been; and I can't see how any man, after spending a few days here, can desire that it shall be further humiliated merely for revenge. Whether it has been humiliated enough for health is another thing. Said one of the Charlestonians on the boat, "You won't see the real sentiment of our people, for we are under military rule; we are whipped, and we are going to make the best of things; but we hate Massachusetts as much as we ever did." This idea of making the best of things is one I have heard from scores of persons. I find very few who hesitate to frankly own that the South has been beaten. "We made the best fight we could,

---

* Yellow fever was called "Yellow Jack," after the flag that was flown from quarantined ships in harbors.

but you were too strong for us, and now we are only anxious to get back into the old Union and live as happily as we can," said a large cotton factor. I find very few who make any special profession of Unionism; but they are almost unanimous in declaring that they have no desire but to live as good and quiet citizens under the laws.

For the first two months of our occupancy of the city scarcely a white woman but those of the poorer classes was seen on the street, and very few were even seen at the windows and doors of the residences. That order of things is now, happily, changed. There doesn't yet appear to be as much freedom of appearance as would be natural; but very many of what are called the "first ladies" are to be seen shopping in the morning and promenading in the evening. They, much more than the men, have contemptuous motions for the negro soldiers; and scorn for Northern men is frequently apparent in the swing of their skirts when passing on the sidewalk.

One doesn't observe so much pleasantness and cheerfulness as would be agreeable; but the general demeanor is quite consonant with the general mourning costume. A stroller at sunset sees not a few pale and pensive-faced young women of exquisite beauty; and a rambler during the evening not unfrequently hears a strain of touching melody from the darkened parlor of some roomy old mansion, with now and then one of the ringing, passionate airs with which the Southern heart has been fired during the war.

Mothers yet teach their children hate of the North, I judge; for when I asked a bright-eyed girl of half a dozen years, with whom I walked on a back street for a block or two, whose girl she was, she promptly answered, "A Rebel mother's girl." Patience, good people who love liberty, patience; this petty woman's spite will bite itself to death in time.

Down in the churchyard of St. Philip's, one of the richest and most aristocratic of churches in this proud city, is a grave which every stranger is curious to see. There are only the four plain panelled brick walls about three feet high, and on them a mottled white marble slab, some nine feet by four in size. At the head of the grave is a single sickly ten-foot-high magnolia tree. At each corner of the foot is a sprawling and tangled damask rose-bush, and about midway on the right there is also a small white rose-bush. All around the little plat is a border of myrtle, sweet in its rich greenness, but untrimmed and broken and goat-eaten. It is the grave of the father of the Rebellion, and on the marble slab there is cut the one word—"CALHOUN."*

---

*Sen. John C. Calhoun (1782–1850), US congressman, secretary of war, seventh vice president, secretary of state, and senator from South Carolina, was the South's acknowledged

This churchyard symbolizes the city of Charleston. Children and goats crawl through a convenient hole in the front wall, and play at will among the sunken graves and broken tombstones. There is everywhere a wealth of offal and garbage and beef-bones. A mangy cur was slinking among the stones, and I found a hole three feet deep which he had dug at the foot of one of the graves. Children were quarrelling for flowers over one of the more recent mounds. The whole yard is grown up to weeds and brush, and the place is desolate and dreary as it well can be; more desolate because cruel hands have broken away the corners of the great marble stab of Calhoun—for mementos, I suppose. Time was when South Carolina guarded this grave as a holy spot. Now it lies in ruin with her chief city. When Northern life shall rebuild and revivify that city, let us pray it may also set chaste and simple beauty around this grave; for there is no need to wish the brave but bad spirit of Calhoun greater punishment than it must have in seeing the woe and waste and mourning which the war has brought the region he loved so well.

---

intellectual and political leader from the 1820s until his death. A champion of states' rights and a staunch defender of slavery, he did not live to see the war.

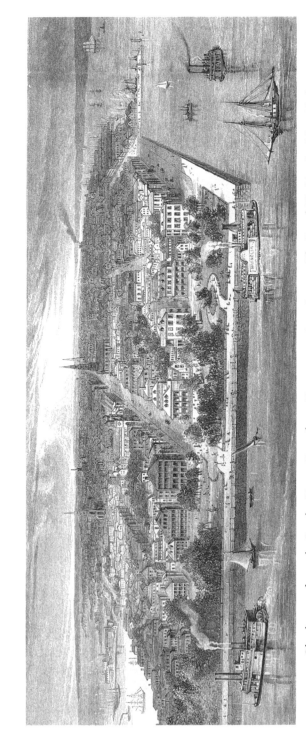

Charleston, from the Bay by Harry Fenn from *Picturesque America; or, The Land We Live In*, New York: D. Appleton & Co., 1872, Vol I. Courtesy of the Irvin Department of Rare Books and Special Collections, University of South Carolina Libraries, Columbia, S.C.

OLIVER BELL BUNCE (1870)

"Charleston and its Suburbs"

Oliver Bell Bunce, "Charleston and its Suburbs" from *Appletons' Journal,*
Vol. 6 (Sat, July 15, 1871): 57–73.

Oliver Bell Bunce (1828–1890), born in New York, never went to college but he
was a prolific writer in his day. As a very young man he wrote plays, one of
which was performed by famous actress Laura Keene. At the age of twenty-five,
Bunce went into publishing and worked successfully for a few publishers before
going to work for D. Appleton & Co., where he remained until his death. He
was literary advisor to the Appleton Co. from 1867, associate editor of *Appletons' Journal* from 1869, and editor from 1872.

Oliver Bunce was among the first to envision the South's postwar cities as
perfect destinations for travelers. Soon after *Appletons' Journal* was launched in
1869, he began a series called "Picturesque America" with articles on Southern
cities. Ignoring the trials of Reconstruction, he sought to publicize the "ruined
South," an exotic and appealing travel destination for a public in search of the
picturesque. By "rendering the strange more understandable," he hoped to promote the South and, at the same time, bring about a cultural reunification of the
country based on an appreciation of art and culture. In hopes of removing the
stigma of southern cities, he presented a stable region in the process of revitalization. The inaugural southern story in *Appletons' Journal* was Bunce's "Charleston and its Suburbs," which proved to be one of the best articles in the series. On
the cover was one of artist Harry Fenn's stunning illustrations of lowcountry
scenery and Gullah blacks. The article was the first to promote the region as picturesque and exotic to a national audience, and it heralded the local color depictions in writing and art that would eventually dominate portrayals of the region.

Bunce and author William Cullen Bryant collaborated as editors on a subsequent book, *Picturesque America; or, the Land We Live in, in Two Volumes*
(1872–74). It became one of the most influential illustrated works of the nineteenth century. Unfortunately, in the new arrangement of the material for the
book, the focus on the South in the original series was lost. Bunce also wrote

and published novels and a book on manners as well as stories, essays, editorials, and plays.

Artist Harry Fenn (1837–1911), illustrator for "Picturesque America" (both series and book), became the most prominent landscape illustrator in the United States from 1870 to 1895. When *Appletons'* first commissioned him to interpret the American landscape for "Picturesque America," he was already well-known for his work. Born in Surrey, England, he had immigrated to the United States, and in 1857 and 1858 he had produced wood engravings for *Frank Leslie's Illustrated Newspaper* and other publishers before going to Italy to study painting. On his return, he completed illustrations for books and magazines for Boston publisher Ticknor and Fields, and various popular periodicals including *Appletons' Journal*. He subsequently produced drawings, prints, and paintings from his extensive travels throughout the world. His best work in black-and-white appears in *Picturesque America, Picturesque Europe,* and *Picturesque Palestine*. In 2013, Sue Rainey and the University of Massachusetts Press published a book about Fenn's work entitled *Creating a World on Paper: Harry Fenn's Career in Art*.

In the following article, Oliver Bunce describes "Charleston and its Suburbs" in the spring of 1870.

SOURCES

"Bunce, Oliver Bell." *The Critic* 13:334 (January–June 1890): 262.
"Obituary. Oliver Bell Bunce." *Publishers Weekly* 37: 955 (May 17, 1890): 649–50.
Rainey, Sue. *Creating Picturesque America: Monument to the Natural and Cultural Landscape*. Nashville: Vanderbilt University Press, 1994.

"Charleston and its Suburbs"

If one go to Charleston from the North, let him go in the springtime. The almost sudden change from wintry landscape and bleak winds to summer suns and summer foliage is a delightful surprise. If it chance with the traveller, as it chanced with the artist, Mr. Fenn, and this writer, that the steamer sail away from the New-York wharf amid the rain and wind of a Northern March, that all the way southward cloud and storm surround and beset the vessel, and then at once come with the longed-for sun, the wished-for harbor, the sudden sweetness and beauty of the scene will seem to him a transition to a terrestrial paradise.

Because Charleston lies low, and seems to rise up out of the waters as one sails up to it, it has been called the American Venice. It may be doubted if one would think of this comparison if the guidebooks did not suggest it. There are charms enough in the American city to please even an experienced traveller, but one would scarcely find his appreciation of them enhanced by recalling the wonders of the Bride of the Adriatic. If in no true sense a Venice, Charleston yet rises with charming effect from the sea. The long, palm-studded shores of the bay, the islands and forts that dot its surface, the mansions that front the waters, and the spires that lift to the skies, all make up a very pretty picture.

The first impression the streets of Charleston give is that of retiring respectability. There are no splendid avenues, no imposing public structures; but a few fine old churches, and many noble private mansions standing in a sort of dingy stateliness amid their embowering magnolias, command your attention. Our New-York custom, derived from our Dutch ancestors, of painting our brick fronts, is not in vogue here, where the houses have the somber but rich toning that age alone can give when its slow pencil lines are never disturbed by the rude intrusion of the painter's brush. The Charleston mansions are nearly always built with gable-end to the street. At one side rises a tier of open verandas, into the lower of which the main entrance to the building is placed. Usually, after the English fashion, a high brick wall encloses the grounds of the house, and it is only through an open gate-way that one catches a glimpse of flowers, and shrubs, and vines, that bloom and expand within the enclosure. But the rich dark green of the magnolia half screens the unsmoothed brick walls far above, and seems to hold the ancient structure in the hush of venerable repose.

It is quite possible the somewhat rude surface and antique color of the brick houses in Charleston would fail to please the taste of Northerners reared amid the supreme newness of our always reconstructing cities. But every one ought to travel in the company of an artist. It is only when associated with one of this instructed class that a man discovers the use of his eyes, and begins to understand fully the beauties, and harmonies, and rich effects that pertain to many things neglected by ordinary observers. These time-tinted mansions of Charleston, to the eye of an artist, have many charms. It was even a revelation sometimes to see him extract a picture out of apparently the most unfavorable material. Nothing, indeed, seemed foreign to him but the merely pretty. Sweet, new houses of a respectable primness have no attraction for his artistic longings. Fresh paint is his abomination. The glare of the new enters like iron into his soul. But a fine bit of dilapidation, a ruin with a vine clambering over it, a hut all awry, with a group of negroes in their flaring turbans set against the gaping walls, old chimneys and old roofs, the dark grays and browns that form into such rich pictures in an old town, these things would be sure to catch his eye and delight his fancy. In these semi-tropical places there are a hundred bits that would be admirable for a sketch in oil or watercolors, that would lose their value in black and white.

The search for the picturesque that would meet the necessities of our purpose was not expeditious. It is only after walking around a place, and surveying

A Glimpse of Charleston and Bay, From Michaels Church, c. 1871 by Harry Fenn from *Picturesque America; or, The Land We Live In*, New York: D. Appleton & Co., 1872, Vol 1. Courtesy of the Irvin Department of Rare Books and Special Collections, University of South Carolina Libraries.

it from different situations, that an artist can settle upon his point of view. We were three days in Charleston 'ere Mr. Fenn discovered the prospect from St. Michael's belfry.

Note the far stretch of sea and the long, low shores; there is Fort Sumter far down the bay, and nearer the famous Castle Pinckney, a fortress that stands guard in the direct approach to the town. The portion of the city which this view commands is its most ancient quarter. Many of the buildings were erected in colonial times, and up to the period of the Revolution this comprised nearly the entire city. The chimneys are of a quaint fashion, and the roofs are mostly of grooved red tiles. The widest street is the Charleston Wall Street,* where congregate all the banks and banking houses, brokers' offices, and law-offices. Here assemble the merchants and brokers; here are effected those transactions in commerce and finance so dear to the heart of the money-making world. The building at the foot of the street is the ancient custom-house,† which during the recent war was rudely hustled by many an irreverent shell, unceremoniously battered

---

*Broad Street.
† The Old Exchange (c. 1767–1771), first built as the Royal Exchange and Custom House.

by ball and petard, and now stands a broken and shattered reminiscence of by-gone belligerency. This structure, which dates back before the independence of the colony, is dear to the Charlestonians. It has always excited their patriotic sympathies, for here during the Revolution the patriot prisoners were confined, and from its portals the heroic martyr Hayne* was led to execution.

The old buildings that the church looks down upon are not more ancient than the church itself. St. Michael's was built in 1752—it is said from designs by a pupil of Sir Christopher Wren. The tower is considered very fine, and the situation of the church makes the spire a conspicuous object far out at sea. During the siege of Charleston in the late war, it was a mark for the Federal artillerymen; but, though persistently shelled, it was struck but a few times, and then only with slight injury.

Another of the ancient churches in Charleston is St. Philip's. This was the first church establishment in Charleston; but the present structure, which is the third erected by the parish, although of venerable age, is yet not quite so old as St. Michael's. The view from the spire is fine; but there is a keener interest in the graveyard than even in the old church itself, for here are met with at every turn those family names that have so long been associated in honor, not only with Charleston, but with the whole country—Gadsden, Rutledge, and Pinck-ney. In the portion of the graveyard that lies across the roadway is the tomb of Calhoun. The remains of the statesman were removed during the war, when Charleston was threatened with capture, under a most misjudged apprehension that the Union soldiers would disturb them. They were replaced in the spring of this year, a few weeks after our visit to the tomb.† St. Philip's, with its embowering

---

* Isaac Hayne (1745–1781), a planter and patriot from Jacksonborough, was imprisoned in the Old Exchange before he was executed by the British after the fall of Charleston in the Revolution.

† At the death of John C. Calhoun in 1850, Henry Gourdin (1803–1879) and Robert Newman Gourdin (1812–1894), bachelor brothers who owned a prosperous local factorage, helped pay off his debts. During the evacuation of Charleston in 1863, the brothers removed Calhoun's body from its grave to avoid its being desecrated. Robert Gourdin wrote to Calhoun's son, Andrew P. Calhoun: "The appearance off this Bar, on Sunday morning last of a fleet of twenty-eight vessels, nine of them Monitors and Iron-clads, determined us to proceed immediately, to remove the remains of your venerated father. We repaired to the Cemetery at 11 o'clock on Sunday night, and at 12 ½ o'clock succeeded in opening the Tomb. This was accomplished with considerable difficulty, owing to the solidity of the masonry. The metallic coffin was transferred to a strong pine case and removed into the Church. Here the remains reposed until tonight. At 8 o'clock in the evening, when every thing was quiet, and it was quite dark, the Sexton of the Church had the grave opened on the spot designated to the East and in the rear of the church, and at 11 o'clock the re-internment took place. The grave is well marked by

trees, its ancient gravestones, its scarred and broken walls, its marks of hostile shells, its surroundings of old buildings, the tiled roofs of which show quaintly through the green of the trees, affords a picture that is picturesque and pleasing.

Charleston has been accused of not having a public park; but the promenade known as the Battery is an enclosure which, if small, has some advantages that very few parks can supply. Like our own New-York Battery, it is on the water's edge; it commands a view of the extensive bay, and is fanned by winds that come laden with the salt odors of the ocean. It is surrounded by fine private mansions, and at early morning, at twilight, or on moonlit nights, is thronged with people seeking rest and recreation.

After one, in Charleston, has promenaded on the Battery; has visited the churches; has seen all the ruins effected by war and by fire; has examined the handsome new custom-house, now erecting; has admired all the stately old residences; has visited the fine military academy; has watched the various aspects of negro character, which in these Southern cities is an endless source of amusement—he must sail down the bay, and he must visit the rich lowland scenery of the suburbs.

Down the bay are many points of historic interest; but Fort Sumter crowns them all. On Sullivan's Island, at the sea-line, is the famous Fort Moultrie of Revolutionary fame. Here, before the war, was the Moultrie House, watering-place resort* for the Charlestonians. On another island is, or was, the Mount

---

adjacent points in the Cemetery, and may be readily identified. It lies to the East of the burial grounds of Capt. James Welsman and immediately at the foot of his Welsmans, his wifes grave; And this is marked by substantial head and foot Stones. Of course, my brother Henry and I were present from the beginning to the Conclusion of this work. On each night we were accompanied by our friend Mr. Edward P. Milliken and on the last by your and our friend Capt. Francis T. Miles, of the Calhoun Guards. The only other persons present at the internment were the two labourers who opened the grave, John Gregg, Sexton of St. Philips and Robert L. Deas, Sexton of the French Protestant Church. The labourers knew nothing of what had occurred the night previous, and the Sextons, free persons of Colour, are entirely reliable and trustworthy. The Masons who opened the tomb supposed that the remains were to be sent into the Country. Should I survive the war, I will make it my duty to restore them to their original place of deposit." Indeed, in 1871 the Gourdin brothers removed Calhoun's body from its secret grave near the church and returned it to its original resting place. Stoney, "Robert N. Gourdin to Robert Anderson, 1861," 10–14; "Calhoun's Remains," *New York Times,* 3; Racine, *Gentlemen Merchants,* 580.

* The Moultrie House (c. 1850), a large hotel on eight acres. Early in the war, military authorities took possession and it was used for a barracks. It was damaged in the war and reestablished afterward for a time, but "never recaptured its former splendor." Pressley, "Extracts from the Diary," 40.

Pleasant Hotel,* where there is good bathing, and also forests that afford fine drives and pleasant rambles. Our own expedition down the bay terminated at Fort Sumter. To this place there is a daily ferry, consisting of a capacious yacht, the commander of which is an Athenian Greek. There was to our minds something of the Mediterranean in the whole aspect of the vessel, crew, and passengers, which a lateen-sail would have rendered complete. The passengers, that came in little groups to the vessel, were motley and picturesque: the buxom and turbaned negro "aunties," the solemn but ragged negro "uncles," the gay and chattering negro young folk, the varied complexions and costumes of poor whites and rich whites—these elements seemed well fitted for the presiding genius of a mariner from the Archipelago.

The wind was brisk, and so we ran down to the fort swiftly. Sumter is a ruin, as all the world knows; but possibly all the world does not know that on the highest point of its walls a light-house has been erected, thus utilizing the historic ground. One experiences something of a sensation, as he picks his way over the broken bricks and stones of this fort, and, if alone, would be apt to drift away into far reaches of meditation. On the piled-up rocks without the walls, amid the debris of masonry, surrounded by remains of cannon, shell, and round shot, we picnicked—a party, one moiety of which represented those who assailed, and the other moiety those who defended, the walls.

After clambering over the ruins, penetrating the dark underground passages, visiting the casemates that still remain, we returned, a high wind giving animation and expedition to the sail.

Perhaps the greatest charm to the Charleston visitor is the lowland scenery of its suburbs. The city is situated at the confluence of the Ashley and Cooper Rivers, and the banks of these streams have all the characteristics of Southern landscapes. Oaks, magnolias, myrtles, and jasmines, give splendor and profusion to the picture, while rice-fields and cotton-fields vary and enrich the scene. Here once resided, during a part of the year, a wealthy aristocracy; but, alas! nearly every mansion is in ruins. The destructive arm of War fell upon this paradise with all its force, nearly every one of the fine old houses having been fired by Sherman's soldiers.

---

* The Mount Pleasant Hotel, which stood near the ferry wharf at Mount Pleasant, was described as "ample, cool and well-kept, with the usual adjuncts of bowling and billiard-saloons." The hotel burned a short time before the war. In 1870, the site remained a vacant grass-grown lot. South Carolina Institute, *Premium List of the South Carolina Institute*, 62.

Our expedition to the Ashley we shall long remember. It was by the invitation of Charleston friends, whose hospitality justified the social reputation of the city. The political elements composing the party were as antagonistic as possible; but, regardless of North or South, the Klu-klux, or the fifteenth amendment, we gathered in peace. There were in our small company a Northerner, who had fought under the Union flag, a descendant of one of the proudest names of Revolutionary fame; a Virginian, also of a family of renown, whose love of daring and danger had led into many a strange adventure under Mosby;* an Englishman, whose enthusiasm for the Confederate cause had brought him all the way from London to do battle under Lee; another Englishman, whose sympathies for the Federal cause had been marked all during the war; a son of a distinguished journalist of New York, whose name has been notably identified with the Republican party; and, lastly, the writer, of whose political complexion it is not necessary to speak. But, in the face of all these elements of difference, the company was supremely harmonious; and the day, ill the estimation of at least some of us, must be marked with a white stone.

The main road from Charleston into the country has been highly praised, and, although some of the fine trees that bordered it have been destroyed, it is still an avenue of singular beauty. The road emerges from Charleston almost immediately into a green wilderness, and for a long distance it is canopied by the boughs of pines and oaks and magnolias with rich effect. There are no signs along the road, as would be the case in our northern section, of the proximity of a great city. No houses or villas line the way; you seem a hundred miles from a town. You meet occasionally a queer, slight cart, drawn by an ox or a donkey; you pass a group of sports men; you encounter now and then on the road-side a group of negroes. Mr. Fenn catches the spirit of the scene with great fidelity. The extemporized covering of boughs shelters a "sweet-'tater" woman, one who dispenses to hungry wayfarers of African hue the edible baked potato of the South.

We reached Ashley River by a sort of by-road. Here a bridge once spanned the stream, but it was destroyed during the war, and now there is a boat propelled by the lusty arms of negro ferrymen. A rope would aid the passage greatly; but our Southern Africans take usually the most troublesome means possible to accomplish their ends. They are proficient in the art of how not to do a thing.

---

* John S. Mosby (1833–1916), a Confederate army cavalry leader from Virginia nicknamed the "Gray Ghost." He commanded the 43rd Battalion, 1st Virginia Cavalry, known as Mosby's Rangers or Mosby's Raiders, noted for lightning quick raids and their ability to elude the Union Army.

*A Road-side Scene near
Charleston*, c. 1872
by Harry Fenn. Still image.
New York Public Library.

When we reached the bank, the boat was on the opposite shore. The current was swift; it took fully half an hour to get the boat over to us, and then the vessel could only accommodate one of our two vehicles. We were nearly two hours getting our forces to the opposite side of the stream.

Once on the opposite side, we were driven through a striking scene—a narrow road winding through a superb Southern forest, where the mammoth live-oak and the tall pine and the princely magnolia (*Magnolia grandiflora*) unite to form vistas of rare beauty.

The live-oak of the Southern lowlands is the most picturesque of trees. The famous California trees are of interest solely on account of their magnitude. Their gigantic proportions impose upon the imagination, it is true; but they lack altogether the quaint, fantastic, and picturesque form of the live-oak. An artist could make a series of studies of these trees in which every one would be essentially peculiar in form. On the banks of the Ashley, there are two of these trees, comparatively small in size, whose trunks stretch out for a distance almost horizontally; a monstrous trunk stands near the Ashley, which in diameter almost rivals the "big trees" of the Pacific, and which in form has far more novelty and beauty. We saw one of these trees, of magnificent proportions and nearly symmetrical in form. We lifted the low branches that nearly swept the ground, and entered what seemed a vast forest cathedral. The quaint trunk was covered with knobbed protuberances, and scarred and seamed as if with the marks of many centuries. Its branches, mammoth trees of themselves, shot out at a low elevation in a nearly horizontal line, extending probably a hundred feet, dipping at their extremities to the ground. The pendent moss from every bough hung in long, sweeping lines, and the sun flickered through the upper branches, touching up moss, bough, and trunk, and relieving the gloom of the interior with bright flashes of light. I would rather, for my part, have that live-oak in our parks than the tallest of the California trees. We were shown an avenue of live-oaks, standing in the very heart of the forest, that would make a superb approach to the finest palace in Europe. But, alas! here it leads only to a ruined waste. A romantic story is connected with this avenue, which some poet should put in verse. The young owner of the estate—this was many years ago—had brought a fair bride from foreign lands. A bridal cavalcade swept out of Charleston to escort groom and bride to the manorial mansion on the Ashley. The proud and eager groom, anxious to show his young wife the charms of her new home, urged her steed ahead of the rest, and, when they reached the avenue of oaks, called upon her to look and admire. Almost as they spoke a cloud of smoke appeared at the other end of the avenue, and instantly flames of fire shot up among the tree-tops. The old manor was in a blaze, and the bride arrived only in time to see the destruction of her promised paradise. The young husband was so cast down by this calamity that he carried his wife abroad, and never returned to his American estate. Trees and bushes have grown up around the old oaks, but the avenue retains all its distinct majesty amid the encroaching growths of the forest.*

Of all the planters' houses that stood along the Ashley, but one remains, and this is abandoned. "Drayton Hall" is a large brick mansion, standing in the centre of grounds of a park-like character. The rooms are wainscoted from floor to ceiling, the fireplaces are lined with old-fashioned colored tiles, and the mantels are richly carved, but the building was never entirely finished. The story goes that it was erected in exact copy of an English mansion, in order to gratify the taste of the lady to whom the owner was betrothed. The wainscot, the tiles, the carved mantels, and marble columns, were all imported from England; but, ere the chivalrous lover had reproduced on the Ashley a full copy of the house which had charmed his betrothed on the Thames, the lady died; and, since then, the unfinished manor, like a broken monumental column, stands in its incompleteness a memorial of his loss. Another story relates that it was saved from the fate of its neighbors, at the time of the Sherman incursion, by the devotion of a negro, who assured the Federal leader that it belonged to a man of Union sentiments. It is now occupied by negroes. Its parlor is a granary. Its wainscot is badly

---

*This was Schieveling Plantation (c. 1785), an estate of the Izard family. According to legend, Ralph Izard Jr. was the groom. In 1826, the Izards sold the 1,056-acre plantation to the Drayton family, owners of the neighboring plantation. It was turned over several times until 1835, when it was purchased by Henry Augustus Middleton. After the war, nature reclaimed the deserted plantation. Hendrix, *Down & Dirty*, 104.

marred, and the rare, colored tiles of its fireplaces have been in part carried off by predatory hands.*

Our destination was the estate known by the name of "Magnolia," on the grounds of which we were to lunch. This place is almost a paradise, but a paradise in ruins. The abundance of magnolias gives it its name, but these are interspersed with immense oaks, and, at the time we were there, under the trees a splendid display of japonicas and azaleas filled the spaces with an array of color such as we had never seen approached. These low-country plantations were not usually occupied by their owners in midsummer; then fevers, heat, and insects, made them far from safe or agreeable, and so the white members of the family went into town or northward to upland habitations. This accounts for the special culture of spring blossoms which we noticed at "Magnolia." The planter had given devoted attention to azaleas, grouping the different shades of color from white to deep scarlet in delicate contrasts; and this flower, blooming on bushes from three to a dozen feet in height, lined all the winding avenues, and flashed under the shadows of the magnolias a tropical splendor of bloom that filled us all with admiration. And all this in the midst of desolation and neglect, with overgrown pathways, unweeded beds, and the blackened walls of the homestead looking down upon the scene!† A few Negroes were in possession, and one tall,

---

* Constance Woolson described it for *Harper's* in 1875: "Drayton Hall was built in 1740 by Thomas Drayton, Esq., and named after the family residence, Drayton Hall, Northamptonshire, England; its cost at that early period being ninety thousand dollars. It is built of brick, the columns of Portland marble, and much of the finer material having been imported from England. Within, the stairway, the mantels, and the wainscot, which extends in a quaint fashion from floor to ceiling, are of solid mahogany, paneled and elaborately carved, the wainscot at a later period having been painted over, probably on account of the daily oiling and polishing which old-time ideas of shining mahogany required. Over the mantels are frames set in the wainscot for pictures or coats of arms, the fire-places are adorned with colored tiles, and the size of the rooms, together with the great kitchens and ovens below, take one back to the old baronial days in England when size was a criterion of grandeur, and everything belonging to great families was great also, from the breadth of their apartments to the bulk of their four-horse coaches. In one of the cellars are to be seen a number of marble columns lying on the ground just as they came from England. These columns have given rise to the story that the old mansion was never entirely finished; but this is an error, the columns having been intended not for the house, but for a gateway outside. The Drayton family occupied the Hall for a number of years. Many persons in Charleston remember the stories told by their fathers and mothers of the dinner parties and other entertainments given at Drayton Hall, when carpets were laid down over the broad flights of steps at both entrances and on to the carriage-ways, that the ladies might alight and enter without endangering the satin of their robes." Woolson, "Up the Ashley and the Cooper," 1–24.
† These were the remains of a plantation house that burned in the Civil War. Soon after Bunce's visit, a Drayton family summer house in Summerville was disassembled, floated

melancholy, gray-haired mulatto, with all the dignity and deportment of the old school, lifted his hat, and said: "Welcome, gentlemen, to Magnolia!" On the border of a small lake within the grounds, shadowed by the moss-hung boughs of the oak, we lunched, and then bade adieu to the place. A pathetic story is told of the ruined proprietor, who comes often to his old favorite grounds, and wanders about them with profound melancholy, or sits for hours with his face in his hands, brooding over his desolated home.

The day after our visit to Ashley River we drove to a very old church on Goose Creek, near Cooper River, and about seventeen miles from Charleston. This church was built in 1711.* It is situated in the very heart of a forest, is approached by a road scarcely better than a bridle-path, and is entirely isolated from habitations of any sort. A deep ditch surrounds the building, dug as a means of protecting the graves—within it from wild animals. This church was saved from destruction by the Tories during the Revolutionary War on account of the British arms that are emblazoned on the wall just above the pulpit. The interior is very odd. Seventeen square pews fill up the ground-floor, which, like all old English churches, is of stone. A gallery at one end has three or four rows of benches, and under this gallery are a few more benches designed for the negro servants. The altar, the reading-desk, and the pulpit, are so small, and crowded in a space so narrow, that they seem almost miniatures of those church fixtures. The monumental tablets on the side of the altar are very oddly ornamented in form, and, what is still more singular, are highly emblazoned in color. Although these tablets have been in their places over one hundred and fifty years, the colors retain apparently all their original brilliancy. The lion and the unicorn over the pulpit also preserve their original tints. These specimens of old-time fresco gave us unexpected proof of the duration of this method of color-painting; and the whole chancel in its gay tints and ornamental carving seemed queerly out of place in the otherwise plain and rude structure. A stone tablet in the floor just before the pulpit is to the memory of Francis Lejau, D. D., of Trinity College, Dublin, who was the first pastor of the church, and who died in 1717. The memorial tablets on the walls are inscribed to Colonel John Gibbes, who died in 1711, and to Jane Gibbes, in 1717. Gibbes, our readers will recall, as one of the honored South-Carolina family names.

---

down by water, and reassembled on the site. This cottage remains the main house at Magnolia Gardens today.

* St. James Goose Creek Church (c. 1713–1719) remains one of the state's oldest surviving buildings, and one of the few extant early Georgian chapels in the country. Built by early planters from Barbados, it was declared a National Historic Landmark in 1970.

Goose-Creek Church was once the centre of flourishing settlements, but, with the decadence that has come over the old Commonwealth—the plantations are forsaken, and this historical vestige stands, in the midst of a wilderness, neglected and almost unknown. Trees and bushes have overgrown and hid the gravestones, and the native forest threatens in time to obscure the very foundations of the building. It is so usual with us to erect churches in the centre of settlements, with the school-house, the parsonage, and other structures near, that this odd edifice, standing so far apart from habitations of any kind, seems singular enough. But the system of the settlement of the South, with large plantations and few towns, partially explains the anomaly.

"Magnolia Cemetery" is one of the places in Charleston to which strangers are directed. It is a new cemetery, and its name is rather derived from what is expected of it than what it exhibits.* So far, very few magnolias adorn it, but there are some live-oaks exceptionally fantastic and queer in form. In this cemetery is a monument to Colonel Washington,† whose exploits in the Revolution are well known; to Hugh Swinton Legare, one of the ripest scholars South Carolina has produced;‡ and in a vault repose the remains of Commodore Vanderhorst,§ whose coffin, shrouded with The Union Jack, may be seen through the latticed door of the tomb.

Our visit to Charleston came only too soon to an end. We parted regretfully from the friends whose hospitality had been so generous, and with a measure of sorrow for the city saddened with so many misfortunes. We could but recall the days when it was at the height of its glory—when it was the centre of a far-extending circle of brilliant homes, and its old mansions echoed to the tread of famous statesmen and renowned women. We recall the report of the noted Elkanah Watson,** who, just after the Revolution, travelled from Providence to

---

* Magnolia Cemetery, dedicated in 1850, was built on the site of Magnolia Umbra Plantation, for which it was named.
† William Washington (1752–1810), Continental army officer in the Revolution.
‡ Hugh Swinton Legare (1797–1843), lawyer, politician, and scholar who founded and edited the *Southern Review* between 1828 and 1832. Legare was appointed chargé d'affaires to Brussels in 1832, and in 1841 was named attorney general of the United States by President John Tyler.
§ Elias Vanderhorst (1825–1850), a fifth-generation member of a prominent family who developed the Vanderhorst House and plantation on Kiawah Island in the late eighteenth century.
**Elkanah Watson (1758–1842), a northern merchant, banker, and agriculturist, had described Charleston in 1777, a visit chronicled in *Men and Times of the Revolution,* published by his son in 1856.

Charleston in a buggy, and whose descriptions of the towns and cities he visited are usually accepted as trustworthy. The wealth and luxury of Charleston surprised the Rhode-Islander, and he speaks of the almost "Asiatic splendor" in which the citizens lived. Charleston was the centre of a somewhat peculiar civilization, and one highly favorable to the cultivation of the few. It was resorted to in summer as a watering-place by the people of the country. The planters brought with them wealth and leisure, and these naturally led to luxurious tastes and habits. We doubt if any community of the same number has produced so many men of distinguished merit. Pinckney, Rutledge, Gadsden, Legare, are but the leading names of a host of worthies who shed bright luster on the place. We may hope yet to see the old plantations on the Cooper and the Ashley attain a prosperity under the new dispensation as brilliant as that they enjoyed under the old; we may trust that the old mansions within the city shall renew the social triumphs of their brilliant past; and we may believe that statesmen and men of letters will not fail to perpetuate that renown the famous city once so fairly won and so fully enjoyed.

The Orphan House—Charleston by James Wells Champney from
Edward King, *The Great South; A Record of Journeys in Louisiana, Texas,
the Indian Territory, Missouri, Arkansas, Mississippi, Alabama, Georgia,
Florida, South Carolina, North Carolina, Kentucky, Tennessee, Virginia,
West Virginia, and Maryland*, Hartford, C.T.: American Publishing Co., 1875.
Courtesy of Thomas Cooper Library, University of South Carolina.

Edward King (1873)

"Charleston, South Carolina. The Venice of America"

Edward King, "Charleston, South Carolina. The Venice of America" from *The Great South; A Record of Journeys in Louisiana, Texas, the Indian Territory, Missouri, Arkansas, Mississippi, Alabama, Georgia, Florida, South Carolina, North Carolina, Kentucky, Tennessee, Virginia, West Virginia, and Maryland* (Hartford, C.T.: American Publishing Co.), 1875.

Edward King (1848–1896), from Middlefield, Massachusetts, published prose and poetry in his teens. At age seventeen (1867) he was sent to Europe as a special correspondent for the *Springfield Republican*, and after his return, he was made literary editor of the newspaper. He returned to Europe in 1869 as correspondent, reporting on the Franco-German War and the Paris Commune. In 1872 King was commissioned by the editors of *Scribner's Monthly* to write a series of articles in order to "present to the public, through the medium of a popular periodical, an account of the material resources, and the present social and political condition, of the people of the States formerly under the domination of Slavery." He was told "to give the reading public a truthful picture of life in a section of the country which has, since the close of a devastating war, been overwhelmed by a variety of misfortunes, but upon which the dawn of a better day is breaking." He began a twenty-five-thousand-mile journey through the post–Civil War South describing conditions, which was published in *Scribner's Monthly* as "The Great South: A Record of Journeys," and appeared in installments from November 1873 to December 1874. Artist J. Wells Champney, who accompanied King on the trip, provided engravings of illustrations, and the overall series proved to be one of *Scribner's* most successful examples of travel writing as well as "an effective factor in sectional reconciliation." In 1875, King published the series in book form as *The Great South*. A second edition was published the next year in England.

King later returned to Europe as Paris correspondent for several American journals. He published subsequent books, but none so successful as *The Great South*.

James Wells "Champ" Champney (1843–1903), born in Boston, attended the Lowell Institute, where he studied drawing and took courses in anatomy under Oliver Wendell Holmes. At the age of sixteen, he was apprenticed to a Boston wood engraver but left in 1862 to serve in the 45th Massachusetts Volunteers during the Civil War. He was at the Battle of Gettysburg, but most of his service was spent on garrison duty in the South, where he contracted malaria. He was discharged and recuperated in Nova Scotia. Champney resolved to be a professional artist and studied in France and at the Royal Academy in Antwerp, Belgium. In 1873 he was commissioned by *Scribner's* to illustrate King's "The Great South" series, which greatly added to its success. He was afterward a successful oil painter of genre scenes, and a foremost pastelist of his day.

In *The Great South*, Edward King describes a South ripe for commercial development but with "fierce Southern honor pitched against Northern appetites." He saw the developing story of Reconstruction as "a near tropical indifference to labor acquiescing to the more vigorous enterprise of arriviste investors, who sought to claim the national Eden that bitter partisans continued to waste."

In Charleston in 1873, King picturesquely refers to Charleston as "The Venice of America," but he pays attention to the political landscape of Reconstruction and the economics of the debt-ridden city. Among his observations, he provides a first glimpse of the phosphate and fertilizer industry that, aided by northern investment, would provide an economic boom in the region for a time.

SOURCES

"Champney, James Wells." In *National Cyclopaedia of American Biography,* Vol. 11. New York: J. T. White Company, 1909.
Colby, Frank Moore, Talcott Williams, eds. "Edward King." In *New International Encyclopedia,* Vol. 13. New York: Dodd, Mead, 1918.
Diffley, Kathleen. *Witness to Reconstruction: Constance Fenimore Woolson and the Postbellum South, 1873–1894.* Jackson: University Press of Mississippi, 2011.
Wilson, James Grant, John Fiske, eds. "Edward King." In *Appletons' Cyclopædia of American Biography,* Vol. 3. New York: D. Appleton, 1888.

"Charleston, South Carolina. The Venice of America"

If we climb into the tower of the stately building known as the "Orphan House," some pleasant evening, when the sunset is beginning to throw the dark walls and picturesque groupings of the sea-girdled city into strong relief, we can get a panoramic glimpse of all the chief features of Charleston's exterior. We shall, perhaps, be too far from the Battery and its adjacent parks to note fully the effect of the gay group promenading the stone parapet against which the tides break gently, or to catch the perfect beauty of the palm-girt shores so distinctly visible beyond the Ashley's current, now that the sunset has given them a blood-red background. The Battery is not crowded with carriages, as in those merry days when the State was still prosperous, or on that famous day when yonder black mass in the harbor was aflame, and when the flag of the nation which floated over it was hauled down. But it is one of the airiest and most elegant promenades possessed by any Southern city, and the streets leading to it are quaint and beautiful. The church spires here and there are noticeable, and that one glistening in the distance was a white mark for many a day for the Federal batteries; yet few shells struck the stately steeple of St. Michael's, the old-fashioned, staid Episcopal house of prayer.

Beyond this church one sees a mass of buildings, whose queer roofs and strangely shapen chimneys remind him of Antwerp or of Amsterdam. These date from colonial times; it is the Charleston of pre-revolutionary days which one sees clustered around St. Michael's. The bells were removed during the siege of Charleston to Columbia; were captured and accidentally cracked; were recovered, sent to England, and recast in the foundry in Whitechapel, from whence they were originally obtained. After the war they were put back in their place in the steeple with great rejoicing amongst the old Charlestonians. Yonder, out of Church Street, arises another spire. It is the tower of St. Philip's, also an Episcopal church. The venerable cemetery is embowered in trees, and hemmed round about by old buildings with tiled roofs.

The formidable ruin, which the sunset-glow throws so sharply upon your vision, is the old cathedral of St. John and St. Finbar, destroyed in the last great fire. On its site, when the Charlestonians were compelled to surrender to the British, occurred a tremendous explosion, occasioned by the rage of the conquered. They were compelled to deposit their arms at the arsenal, which was also a powder magazine, and all coming at once, and hurling down upon the ground hundreds of fire-arms, and explosion took place, igniting twenty thousand pounds of powder and blowing to atoms the adjacent Lunatic Asylum, Poor-House, Guard-House, and Barracks, as well as conquerors and conquered. The city has many other interesting churches, among them the Huguenot, which has on its walls numerous interesting ancient inscriptions. Grace Church (Episcopal)* is the resort of the fashionable worshipers.

There is nothing remarkable in the secular architecture of Charleston; yet this old Orphan House, from whose tower we survey the others, with its lovely garden hedged in from the street, with its statue of William Pitt, which the grateful citizens erected when the "stamp act" was repealed, is imposing. It was

---

* Grace Episcopal Church (c.1846) at 98 Wentworth Street.

founded in 1790, is bountifully endowed, and thousands of orphan boys and girls have been well cared for within its walls. John C. Fremont* and the Carolinian Memminger,† were educated there. There is an institution of the same class for the colored people.‡ Neither the hotels nor the banks are distinguished for architectural excellence. The Charleston Hotel has an immense stone-pillared piazza fronting on Meeting Street, but the Mills House and the Pavilion are simply solid blocks.§

* John Fremont (1813–1890), explorer, soldier and antislavery political leader, was born in Savannah to an unmarried couple after his mother, a married member of an aristocratic Virginia family, ran off with a French tutor hired for her by her husband. Fremont's French father died when he was six, and his mother moved with him to Charleston. He may have spent a few years at the Orphan House, or attended classes there. His friend and mentor was Joel Poinsett (1779–1851).

† Christopher Gustavus Memminger (1803–1888), lawyer, statesman, and first secretary of the Confederate treasury, was born in Württemberg, Germany. His widowed mother immigrated to Charleston, where she died when he was four. He lived at the Orphan House until age eleven, when he was adopted by Charlestonian Thomas Bennett (1781–1865) and reared in "an atmosphere of refinement and opportunity."

‡ In 1865, James Redpath founded Shaw Colored Orphan Asylum in honor of Col. Robert Gould Shaw (1837–1863), killed at Fort Wagner as commander of the 54th Massachusetts Infantry. In May of 1865, a number of destitute black orphans were housed in a deserted building on Mary Street before they were "domiciled in the elegant of a Mrs. Ross on East Bay." After Mrs. Ross took the oath of allegiance and regained her house, the black orphans were moved to the "abandoned" house of "rebel" Christopher Memminger at 150 Wentworth Street. According to a South Carolina Institute publication just prior to 1870: "Adjoining the yard of the Scotch Church, on the south, is a very large mansion, which was formerly the residence of Governor Allston, but is now occupied as a Catholic Colored Orphan Asylum." This was the Nathaniel Russell House on Meeting Street, the house of Gov. R. F. W. Allston (1801–1864). These orphans were possibly there under the auspices of The Sisters of Charity of Our Lady of Mercy, who in 1870 turned the house into a convent school. The orphans were next housed at the "Elliott Mansion on George Street." The Colored Orphan Society was continued until 1875, when it was reorganized as the State Orphan Asylum and moved to Columbia, where it was victim to the graft and embezzlements of Radical Reconstruction and was closed. Freedman's Society, *Freedmen's Record*, 55; South Carolina Institute, *Premium List of the South Carolina Institute*, 55; McKivigan, *Forgotten Firebrand*, 107–8; Fleming, *Documentary History of Reconstruction*, 356; "Annual Report of the New York National Freedman's Relief Association," 165.

§ The Charleston Hotel (c. 1839), grand in antebellum times, stood at 200 Meeting Street between Pinckney and Hayne streets. It would remain one of Charleston's most popular hotels for years to come. It was demolished in 1960. The original Mills House (c.1853) on Meeting Street, later the St. John Hotel, was closed in the 1960s. In 1970, a replica of the original Mills House was built on the site. The Pavilion Hotel, built in the early 1800s, stood at Meeting and Hasell streets, the site of the King Charles Inn since 1958.

The Charleston Club-House is an elegant structure,* and the building of the South Carolina Hall is fine in interior arrangement. The Club-House has become the seat of the Federal courts, and white and black men sit together in juries there. The Court-House and the City Hall are substantial edifices, fronting each other on corners of Broad and Meeting streets. Around them are always lounging crowds of negro men and women, as if they delighted to linger in the atmosphere of government and law, to the powers and responsibilities of which they have lately been introduced. At the Guard-House[†] one may note white and black policemen on terms of amity. Charleston prospers despite the anomalous condition of politics and society in the State. What might she not become if the commonwealth were developed to its utmost? The citizens suffer many trying ills, the most aggravated of which is the small rôle that the present leaders of the majority permit them to play in State politics. The Legislature has out-Napoleoned Napoleon III in measures for the corruption of suffrage, and has enacted an infamous law, which allows Governors of the State to control the ballot-box completely through commissioners appointed virtually by himself. Its vote is swallowed up in the vote of Charleston County, and consequently it is represented only at second-hand in the State Assembly, getting but a meagre and partial hearing through a score of ignorant negroes, sent from the plantations and small towns in the vicinity.

The first election in Charleston after reconstruction was held in 1868, and the Republican candidate for Mayor, Pillsbury,[‡] was elected by a majority of twenty-three in a poll of ten thousand. He remained in office until the summer of 1871, when the Conservatives attempted a fusion, and ran a ticket composed of white and black candidates, against the Republicans, with John A. Wagener, for Mayor,[§] and elected him by 777 majority. This administration had continued to the date of my visit, in 1873, when a new election took place, and exhibited

* The Charleston Club House (c.1853–1854) stood at Meeting and Broad streets on the site of what is now Post Office Park. A handsome brownstone built "by one of the wealthiest clubs in America for their own entertainment," the club lost money, and the property was sold in 1869 to the US government for use as a federal court house. The building was later damaged in the 1886 earthquake and demolished. South Carolina Institute, *Premium List of the South Carolina Institute: 55.*
† The Guard House (c.1838), damaged in the earthquake, stood adjacent to the Charleston Club, now the site of the US Courthouse and Post Office.
‡ Gilbert Pillsbury (d.1893), a Radical Republican from Massachusetts, first came South as an agent of the Freedman's Bureau. He was stationed in Hilton Head before moving to Charleston with his wife in October 1865. In 1872, he returned to live in Massachusetts.
§ John Andreas Wagener (1816–1876), a leading German in Charleston and founder of Walhalla, South Carolina, served one term.

Houses on the Battery by James Wells Champney from Edward King,
The Great South; A Record of Journeys in Louisiana, Texas, the Indian
Territory, Missouri, Arkansas, Mississippi, Alabama, Georgia, Florida,
South Carolina, North Carolina, Kentucky, Tennessee, Virginia, West
Virginia, and Maryland, Hartford, C.T.: American Publishing Co., 1875.
Courtesy of Thomas Cooper Library, University of South Carolina.

in the most glaring light some of the atrocities of the present system. The Conservatives alleged, and it was, indeed, clearly proven, that four hundred negroes were imported from Edisto Island at one time, to create a majority in Charleston for the so-called "Republicans." None but Radical supervisors of the elections were appointed, and the right of challenge at every poll-precinct was denied. The law required every person voting to swear that he was a citizen of Charleston, but the imported voters were provided with the printed forms of the oath, from which the clause concerning the place of residence was omitted.

With no power of interference, and no chance to dispute at the polls or in the counting of the votes, this city of 50,000 inhabitants, possessing $30,000,000 worth of taxable property, was delivered over, bound hand and foot, to the tender of the ignorant and the vicious. The party then in power admitted the abnormal condition of affairs. Governor Moses* told an editor in Charleston that

---

*Franklin Moses Jr. (1838–1906), elected Republican governor in 1872 with enormous black support. His father was born in Charleston to a prominent Jewish family, and his mother was Scotch-Irish. A secessionist before the war, afterward he supported

every citizen of South Carolina could vote in that city, if he chose, without hindrance; the Charlestonians could not help themselves. The result of this latter election, in which the negro party was, of course, victorious, was a ferment, culminating in mass-meetings, investigations, and finally in a series of arguments. It was charged and shown that the commissioners for the elections did not designate all the polling-places so that the general public would know where they were, but that they stealthily opened them during the election, and there "rushed through" the illegal voters. It was also affirmed by the supporters of the corrupt State Government that a "residence in the city without limit as to time," in the county, sixty days, and in the State, one year, were qualifications sufficient for a voter under the act of 1873. The board of managers consisted, at the city election in 1873, almost entirely of negroes. Several hundred special deputy sheriffs were appointed to "maintain order" if the Conservatives made any attempt to challenge voters at the polls; and the managers refused to give the reporters of the city press any information concerning the changes made in the polling-places the night before the election. The Republican or Radical ticket was elected, and the protest of the citizens of Charleston having been entered, the "board of commissioners," appointed by the Legislature, then published a formal announcement that the election was "legal and valid," and that the "protest was overruled."

The Conservatives were bitterly grieved at this, as they had made a very firm stand, and it showed them how completely they were at the mercy of their present masters. They were not especially dissatisfied with the choice for Mayor, as the successful candidate, Mr. Cunningham, is an honest man;* but the other municipal officers elected they regarded quite differently. The present police force of the city is about equally divided into black and white, and there are nine colored aldermen in the new board. It is not because of the presence of the negro in these offices of trust and honor that the Charlestonians are angry and grieved, but because he refuses them their proper share in the government. As they are now situated, the intelligence and property of the city are as completely

---

integration of the state university, established new social programs and public funding of old-age pensions, and created a black militia to help protect freedmen from white paramilitary insurgents. He hosted blacks socially, both as governor and a private citizen. Notorious for his extravagant use of money before and after the war, he was indicted in 1874. The court ruled that he could not be prosecuted while he served as governor, but his enemies labelled him the "Robber Governor." Ginsberg, *Moses of South Carolina*, 39–66.

* George Irvin Cunningham (1835–1902) succeeded John A. Wagener, serving two terms (1873–1877). Born in Monroe County, TN, he was to date the last Republican mayor of Charleston.

shut out from political representation as if they were imprisoned within walls of adamant.

Charleston's city tax, in 1872, amounted to two per cent, but in 1873 was somewhat reduced. The combined city, county, and State tax, however, now amounts to three and a-half per cent. The assessments are always fully up to, and usually over, the actual value of property. The property holder, in the first instance, makes his returns. If the county auditor is not satisfied with the estimates, he changes them to suit himself; and the citizen then has the refuge of appeal to a "board of equalization." The Constitution requires that all property be taxed at its value.

The present city debt is nearly $5,000,000, some of which was incurred by subscriptions to railroads before the war. The city, before the war, invested $1,000,000 in the Blue Ridge railroad, and the State about $1,300,000. In 1868 or '69, the State stock, a majority, was sold for $13,000, to a ring. Shortly before this the State had guaranteed $4,000,000 of bonds of the road; these were hypothecated by the company. The ring secured the passage of a law authorizing the State Treasurer to issue $1,800,000 of revenue bond scrip upon the surrender to him of the $4,000,000 guaranteed bonds, said scrip receivable for taxes. Exchange was made, and bonds have been canceled, but the State Supreme Court has decided that the act authorizing the issue of the scrip is unconstitutional and void.* The "licenses" which business and professions are already compelled to submit to are grievous burdens, and the people consider them such an odious form of municipal taxation that when the Legislature passed a law for collecting State licenses also, it was resisted, and finally its repeal was deemed expedient. The astute legislators even imposed a license-tax upon the railroads, which were, of course, already licensed by charter.

Thus cut off, politically, Charleston, with grim patience, awaits a turn in the tide of affairs, and catches a little inspiration from the development of the

---

* The Blue Ridge Railroad, reorganized in 1868, had resumed construction that included tunnels that were partly completed in four states when the "ring" plundered the funds and defrauded the state (and not for the first time). The ring was made up of Reconstruction Republicans in state government including Col. John J. Patterson and Hiram H. Kimpton, a New York financial agent for the state of South Carolina from 1868 to 1873, and the members of the Financial Board—Governor Robert K. Scott, Ex-Governor and Attorney-General Daniel H. Chamberlain, Treasurer Niles G. Parker and Comptroller-General John L. Neagle. Hiram Kimpton, who had negotiated the sale of the bonds, "seemed chosen to bear the brunt of the blame for the crime." He ran off to New York and was considered a fugitive from justice when Gov. Wade Hampton, newly in office, tried to have him extradited from New York, to no avail. Fleming, ed., *Documents Relating to Reconstruction,* nos. 4 and 5, "Public Frauds In South Carolina."

scheme for a new railway route from Chicago to Charleston. This superb air line, when built, will pass by Columbia and Spartanburg, in South Carolina, northward to Asheville, in the North Carolina Mountains—thence through Cumberland Gap into Lexington, in Kentucky, and so onward to Chicago, giving an outlet on the sea 100 miles nearer the North-west than New York now is by any existing line. The towns mentioned above are situated directly on the route originally projected for the connection between the North-west and the Atlantic, and pronounced by all who have surveyed it as one of the most economical and practical ways across the Blue Ridge and the Alleghenies "to be found from the head-waters of the Susquehanna to the southern termination of those ranges."

The extensive marl-beds of the South Carolina lowlands, all comparatively near Charleston, have long been known; but they were first especially noticed by Edmund Ruffin, of Virginia, a noted agriculturist,* who had been very successful in renovating worn-out lands in his own State with marl. He examined the South Carolina marls, and found them much richer in carbonate of lime than those of Virginia, but the carbonate was so combined with and mineralized by silex, oxide of iron, phosphate of lime, and other substances, as to necessitate a chemical change by burning before it could be applied to agricultural purposes.

Among these marl deposits, which abound in the immediate vicinity of Charleston, are found hard nodular bodies of all sizes, varying from that of a pin's head to masses weighing hundreds of pounds. These nodules are now known as phosphate rock, and have been described as "incalculable heaps of animal remains thrown or washed together." Beautiful specimens of ribs, vertebræ, and teeth of land and sea monsters of the early tertiary period are found in profusion at a little distance below the surface, and are readily dug up with pick and shovel. The negroes are said even to dive for them to the river-beds, and to bring up large quantities.

The people have at last awakened to the immense value of these deposits, and a number of establishments devoted to their conversion into phosphate-manures have sprung up since the war. In these manufactories the nodules are baked thoroughly dry, then ground to a powder, which is finally mixed with sulphuric acid and charged with ammonia. The Wando Company, which first undertook the production of these fertilizers, made thirty per cent. profit, and there are now two dozen companies in the State organized for the purposes either of mining or manufacturing these phosphates. One company is organized with a capital of $2,000,000 to mine in all the navigable rivers in the State; and there are several

---

*Edmund Ruffin (1794–1865) had published *Report of the Commencement and Progress of the Agricultural Survey of South Carolina* (1843).

manufacturing corporations which have each a million dollars capital. The Etiwan Company claims to have the largest acid-chamber in the United States; and in the Wando, Etiwan, Pacific, Guano, Atlantic, Stono and Wappoo mills, four or five millions of dollars have been invested since 1868.*

Important as is this industry, there are a variety of others already developed in Charleston which promise great future success. In the manufacture of doors, blinds, sashes, and machinery, and in ship-building, a large capital is invested. The enterprising citizens are even constructing ready-made houses and churches, which can be shipped in sections to new States and territories. A cotton-mill and several tanneries are projected. The "truck farms" vie with those of Norfolk, and are supplying the Northern markets with early vegetables. The city's jobbing trade amounted to about $6,000,000 in 1872, and steadily increases at the rate of twenty-five per cent.

The highways leading out of the city are all richly embowered in loveliest foliage; the oak, the magnolia, the myrtle, the jessamine, vie with each other in tropical splendor. Splendid shell roads have been projected, but are not yet completed. The visitor hardly knows which most to admire—the cultivated bloom and glory of the gardens, the tangled thickets where the luxuriant cane rises thirty and forty feet, the shimmering sheets of water on the marshes, or the long sandy pathways, over which stretch the long arms of moss-hung oaks. A palmetto, standing lonely under the rich glow of the splendid Southern moon, will fill even the prosaic with poetic enthusiasm; a cabin, overgrown with vines and tendrils, and half concealed in a green and odorous thicket, behind which one catches the gleam of the river current, will make one enamored of the sweet silence and restful perfection of the lowland capital's suburbs. The mansion with closed doors, and decaying verandas, from which "Life and thought have gone away," will recall the late revolution's worst phase to him who had almost forgotten it in the city's commercial bustle.

---

* A few years after the war, the commercial potential of phosphates as a fertilizer took off, creating a speculation bubble as land prices rose and owners of abandoned rice fields along regional rivers scrabbled to unload their plantations. From 1867, many mining companies were founded, many with northern investors, and these companies "ravaged the regional landscape and riverbanks" looking for phosphates, taking advantage of freed slaves as an unskilled labor force. Some made fast fortunes to revive those lost in the war; however, phosphate mining ultimately failed as an industry beginning around 1888, when higher quality phosphates were discovered in Florida and Tennessee. State political fights, concerning what of the industry's revenues were due the state, exacerbated its decline. By World War I, mining operations in the region had ceased altogether. Hendrix, *Down & Dirty*, 116–18.

Along the Ashley, the old manorial houses and estates, like Drayton Hall and the Middleton homestead, stand like sorrowful ghosts lamenting the past; on James's Island one may wander among rich cotton plantations, now over-spreading the maze of fortifications which sprang up during the war; there is no more silence and absolute calm, as there is no more of beauty and luxuriance, in Magnolia cemetery, than in the vast parks surrounding these ruined and desolate homes. The monuments in the cemetery are beautiful and tasteful; so are the battered and broken monuments to a dead civilization and a broken-down system which one finds upon the old plantations.

There is a wide belt of forsaken plantations near the Cooper River, along the famous Goose Creek, upon whose banks stands the venerable St. James's Church, built in 1711. Around this ancient building the ambitious forest is fast weaving a network difficult to penetrate; and the very graves are hidden under festoons of wild vines and flowers. Along the harbor there are also deserted and bankrupt towns, like pretty Mount Pleasant, filled with moss-grown and rotting houses, whose owners have fled, unless too poor to get away.

The climate of South Carolina being as mild and genial as that of the most favored portion of southern Europe, it is not strange that the lower classes of Italy and other countries should feel inclined to emigrate to the Palmetto State. But the people have been slow to show a proper intelligence on the subject of immigration. The legislators have taken care to encourage certain Northern classes to come—since they are sure that they will not; and have discouraged foreigners from attempting to settle in the State, since they fear that might lead to a new deal in politics. The Italians who went into the common-wealth some time since were offered $100 per year, and a little meal and bacon weekly; but they haughtily rejected any such terms. The white laborer who enters South Carolina must be offered good wages and given land at cheap rates; and the sooner the natives learn that he is not to be expected to work and live as the negroes do, the better it will be for their interest.

Recently the whites have become thoroughly aroused to the importance of this subject, and there is a great change in the temper with which immigrants are now received. The determination seems to be to make much of them as a sure, if slow, means of working out the political regeneration of the State, and securing its material prosperity. A State Commissioner of Immigration was appointed by the late Taxpayers' Convention, and the counties are appointing local Commissioners. An effort is now making at Charleston to establish a direct steamship line to Liverpool, which, it is hoped, will not only give a stimulus to immigration, but to inward freights as well.

The negro is not especially anxious to see immigration come in. The spirit of race is strong within him. He is desirous of seeing the lands in the commonwealth in the hands of his own people before the rest of the world's poor are invited to partake. He is impressed with the idea that South Carolina should be in some measure a black man's government, and is jealous of white intervention. This is not the sentiment, certainly, of the intelligent and refined colored people, but the mass are ignorant, and think that they are right in taking that stand. The black man lets the African in him run riot for the time being. He even dislikes to see the mulatto progress; and when he criticizes him, it is as he were necessarily an inferior.

So, too, the negro secretly dislikes the white adventurer, or "carpet-bagger," as our Southern friends call him. Black rogue has quickly learned from white rogue all he wishes to know, and now proposes to go alone. He has found, now that he has obtained power, a strange fascination in the use of political machinery for purposes of oppression and spoliation. He thinks too, grimly, in the words of the Carolinian black's savage song:

"De bottom rail's on de top,
An' we's gwine to keep it dar."

RADICAL MEMBERS

OF THE FIRST LEGISLATURE AFTER THE WAR

SOUTH CAROLINA

Dusenberry	Mayes	Demars	Rivers	Miteford	Smith	Swails
McKinlay	Jillson	Brodie	Duncan	White	Pettengill	Perrin
Dickson	Lomax	Hayes	BOOZER	Barton	Hyde	James
Wilder	Jackson	Cain	Smythe	Boston	Lee	Johnston
Hoyt	Thomas	Maxwell	Wright	Shrewsbury	Simonds	Wimbush
Randolph	Webb	Martin	MOSES	Mickey	Chesnut	Hayes
Harris	Bozeman	Cook	Sancho	Henderson	McDaniel	Ferr
	Tomlinson	Miller	Sanders	Howell	Williams	Meade
	Wright *		Nuckles	Hayne	Gardner	Thompson
				Mobley		Rainey
				Hudson		
				Nash		
				Carmand		

* Afterwards associate Justice of the Supreme
Court of the State

Radical members of the first legislature after the war, South Carolina, c. 1876.
Photomontage of members of the first South Carolina legislature following
the Civil War, mounted on card with each member identified.

Sir George Campbell, M.P. (1878)

"The Petrel State"

Sir George Campbell, M.P. "The Petrel State" from *White and Black: The Outcome of a Visit to the United States* (London, Chatto & Windus), 1879.

Sir George Campbell (1824–1892), author, Indian administrator, and Scottish Member of Parliament, was the son of Sir George Campbell from Fifeshire, an assistant surgeon for the East India Company who was knighted in 1833. Young George was educated at Hamilton Academy, once known as one of the finest schools in Scotland. He embarked in 1842 for India, where he served in the North-West Provinces and the Punjab. Returning to England in 1851 on furlough, he studied law at Inner Temple and was appointed in 1854 by his uncle (then lord chief-justice) as an associate of the court of Queen's Bench. Having given evidence before a committee regarding a renewal of the East India Company's charter, he published a useful descriptive handbook, *Modern India* (1852). In the following year, he also published a long pamphlet on his view of needful reforms. In 1862 Campbell was appointed a judge of the High Court, Calcutta, and was head of a commission on the Orissa Famine of 1866–1867, after which he was appointed chief commissioner of the Central Provinces. He served as lieutenant-governor of Bengal from 1871 until his retirement in 1874, when he was elected Liberal M.P. from Scotland (1875–1892).

Known to be uncompromising, Campbell was not altogether successful at either his Indian service or as a politician. His true interest was ethnology, and he wrote on ethnological subjects for the *Quarterly Ethnological Journal* and the *Journal of the Bengal Asiatic Society*. In 1874, he edited *Specimens of the Language of India* and authored *A Handy Book on the Eastern Question* (1876). After *Black and White* (1879), he published *The British Empire* (1887). His *Memoirs of My Indian Career* (1893) was published posthumously.

Campbell was active in the British and Foreign Anti-Slavery Society and committed to the worldwide abolition of slavery. (The organization continues today as Anti-Slavery International.) As he was interested in the welfare of native races, he traveled to America to study the unsettled racial situation. In Washington, he met with President Rutherford Hayes and wrote: "The President takes a very favourable view of the position and prospects of the negro. He thinks the present race of negroes are not equal to white men; but then, according to his views, the qualities of mankind are very much a matter of climate. Whether white or black, he thinks men are inferior in hot climates." From Washington, he traveled into the South, spending most of his time in Virginia, North and South Carolina, and Georgia.

Campbell had heard South Carolina referred to as "the petrel state," as in "stormy petrel" or one who brings discord, a rebel. He arrived in the state capital, Columbia, during the November election of 1878. Reconstruction had ended, but tensions were high as this was the first election held since the governor's race of 1876, when Wade Hampton III (1818–1902) had been elected in a contentious and bloody contest. Hampton represented the state's old Bourbon elites, yet his campaign had been rampant with statewide violence by the "Red Shirts," a paramilitary group that served the Democratic Party by disrupting elections and suppressing the black vote in the state. They had intimidated and attacked Republicans during the 1876 campaign to ensure Hampton's election, and reestablish white supremacy in South Carolina. The violence had tilted the political balance to the Democrats, resulting in the "redemption" of South Carolina after years of Republican rule. Two years had passed, and although Hampton's reelection seemed secure, there was anxiety that the elections on the larger ticket would once more lead to violence. Campbell "justly observes" that the struggle for political power, as well as the question of whether blacks were going to be allowed to vote freely, was the cause of all the trouble.

He wrote:

> I entered the "Petrel" State of South Carolina on the day of the election, and the first station in that State that we came to was full of people dressed in the famous red shirt, which we also saw continually at all the stations as we came along. In this part of the State there does not seem to be a very serious contest; it is only in the lower regions, where the black population is very numerous, that there is any doubt about the result of the elections. The constitution of South Carolina is still that which was imposed upon it after the war. It has not been revised, and is still of the popular character dictated by Northern ideas. All the county and local officers are elected; there is no such system of nomination as prevails in North Carolina. Here the elections for Congress, for the State Assembly,

and for the local offices, all take place together—are all entered in one "ticket." Mr. Wade Hampton, the present Governor, is a moderate Democrat, and his re-election is not opposed on this occasion. Where there is a serious contest is in regard to the members of Congress and State Assembly, and the local officers. Red shirts now seem to be only a party badge. I saw no appearance of actual 'bull-dosing,' but there were many signs of election-day—many people about, a good deal of talking and shouting and galloping about on horseback, and some few symptoms of whisky. There were a good many negroes about, and they did not look terrorized. There is no need to terrorize them just here, as they have no chance—the whites having it all their own way. A few blacks go with the Democrats, and I saw one or two of them wearing the red shirt. On my arrival in Columbia in the evening, things seemed pretty quiet: the election had passed without any serious trouble.

Next morning he found an account of the elections in the newspapers and wrote: "As there are no Republican papers here, one cannot hear that side. The local papers assert that this has been the quietest election ever known. There has been no violence, only some attempts at fraud on the part of the blacks, which have been promptly and properly repressed. I observe, however, that it is admitted that at several places the United States supervisor, who is entitled to be present at each polling place, has protested against the rejection of black votes. At one place near this some young men are said to have done good service by putting a stop to the frauds of the blacks. It is suggested that some black employees who voted wrong must be dismissed. It seems to be assumed that all the elections in this State have certainly gone in favour of the Democrats. That was indeed a foregone conclusion."

After breakfast, he sought out Governor Wade Hampton at the Capitol. He wrote: "He is generally reputed to be a very superior man, and evidently has great influence. Originally a Carolina man, he had also large property in Mississippi, like a good many others of the rich people in this part of the country; but he was quite ruined by the war. Cotton, being the great resource of the Southern States, was captured or burnt by the Federal armies, and he lost 5,000 bales. He now lives, I understand, in a cottage in a humble way. All his conversation gave one the idea of a very moderate man."

He continued:

Mr. Wade Hampton talks very strongly of the misconduct and fraud of the carpet-bag Government which was displaced last year. At one time, he says, 98 out of 124 members of the Assembly were blacks, and there was unlimited fraud and stealing. He gave me the report of the committee appointed to investigate these frauds. The debt of the State, he says, is not so very large—about seven million dollars; he would rather pay than repudiate. Meantime, while the matter is under the consideration of the Legislature, the money for the interest is lodged in the Treasury. Although the county officers are elected, it seems that the justices of the peace are nominated by the Governor, and are now mostly Democrats, but some of the other side are nominated also. Some blacks are put upon juries, but not many. The Governor speaks of the black population in terms similar to what I had heard before. He says the better class of whites certainly want to conserve the negro; the lower whites are less favourable, and will not admit them to social equity; but the bitterness is only political and not carried into labour questions.

Campbell talked with several other men who happened to be about the Capitol and concluded: "They all admit that the ballot at elections is an utter farce, and that there is no pretense at secrecy. A common dodge is to print tickets in imitation of those of the enemy, and to foist them upon illiterate voters of the other side. More frequently the ballot is 'stuffed' by putting in several thin tickets wrapt together. The rule is that if more vote tickets are found in the box than the number of voters the excess number is drawn out by a man blindfolded for the purpose. He can very well distinguish the tickets of his own party; they are generally on a different kind of paper. My informants account, however, for their victory in the elections by saying that they managed to influence many of the blacks. They say the red shirt was merely a political emblem got up in mockery of some phrase about 'bloody shirts' used by an Indiana senator. It never meant anything more serious. The Klu-klux was at one time bad, but not so very bad; they sometimes tarred and feathered, but seldom murdered. In short, South Carolina is altogether not so black as it has been painted, according to their account."

Having taken the temperature of the capital of "The Petrel State," Campbell ventured on to study post-Reconstruction conditions in the lowcountry—particularly those of the region's blacks.

SOURCES

Buckland, Charles Edward. *Bengal Under The Lieutenant-Governors.* Calcutta: S. K. Lahiri & Co., 1901.

Cisco, Walter Brian. *Wade Hampton: Confederate Warrior, Conservative Statesman.* Lincoln: University of Nebraska Press, 2011.

Lee, Sidney. "Sir George Campbell." In *Dictionary of National Biography*. London: Elder and Smith, 1901: Supplement Vol. I.
"Three British Views of America," *The Nation* 29 (Sept.11, 1879): 181–82.

"The Petrel State"

I travelled from Columbia to Charleston through the night in a very comfortable sleeping-car belonging to the local railway. In the glimpses of the night I could only see that we passed through a great deal of pine-forest. At daylight I found that there were many tall pines near the route; but approaching Charleston the country became more open, with fine soil and good cultivation. Strawberries, cabbages, sweet potatoes, and common potatoes seemed to be largely grown. The potatoes are not yet killed by frost. I went to the Charleston Hotel, which was comfortable. After breakfast I walked about the town. The site is flat, and the country not striking, but the vegetation is extremely fine—very much of a semi-tropical character. There are many orange-trees in full bearing and other fruit-trees and shrubs. Many of the houses are extremely good, and very prettily arranged, with gardens about them. The climate here is said to be very good; the hot weather is tempered by the trade winds and sea-breezes. In summer the thermometer rises to about 90°, and there is little hard frost in the winter. The magnolias and evergreen oaks are fine trees, and very abundant. I called on Colonel T—, a gentleman engaged in the cotton business,* who gave me much assistance. He introduced me to the Carolina Club,† and to several gentlemen there, with whom I had a great deal of talk. They say they had hoped the negroes would have turned out good small cultivators and paid rent, and that they, as owners, would have had an easy time; but the negro fails in that respect; he is improvident and careless, lets down the land, and spoils it. But Mr. S—, a gentleman who manages a large rice estate, and lives there, happened to come in. He gives quite a different account; he says that the higher part of the estate is let

---

* Col. William Lee Trenholm (1836–1901), who, like his father, George A. Trenholm, had served as a high-ranking official of the Confederate treasury department during the war, was now an advocate of New South spirit. He and his father had reorganized a cotton brokerage from bankruptcy. However, in 1889 he would give up on Charleston and become president of American Surety Co. in New York. Phillips, *City of the Silent*, 171–72.

† The Carolina Rifle Club was organized in 1869, after local military units were banned. Confederate veterans, not trusting federal troops to maintain order, formed such clubs described as "the military arm of the Democratic Party" from which the Red Shirts had arisen in the Upcountry in the 1876 governor's election. After federal troops withdrew in 1878, the clubs became military units. Later the Carolina Rifles Armory, built in 1889 at 158–160 King Street, housed the club. Stockton, "Do You Know Your Charleston," Dec. 19, 1977.

out to negroes who really cultivate exceedingly well, and raise cotton much better than he could have expected. He charges $30 to each family, and they cultivate as much cotton and corn as they can, he undertaking to take out half the rent in labour, and in practice generally taking out the whole in this shape by employing them at fifty cents a day on the rice-lands, and setting off the wages against the rent. When I put to the other gentlemen the contradiction which this account seemed to imply to their views they said that these were especially good negroes; that they came from the upper country, where they had been mixed with whites and accustomed to labour. It seems that during the war there were large migrations. Many from this part of the country went up with the Northern armies, and many up-country negroes came down with them. One gentleman said he had heard of a large number of negroes from an estate in this neighbourhood who settled up-country, and, he is told, now all own land.* It seems generally agreed that the negroes are very good labourers, and do well when they have white men to look over them and set them an example. The native whites manage them better and get more work out of them than any Northerners or foreigners. When, however, the negroes get together in masses and out of the control and direction of white men they are apt to go back. These gentlemen instanced a case of some blacks on estates within their own knowledge, who were good mechanics before the war, but now are worth very little. There are few blacks among the higher mechanics, but some of them earn very high wages here as stevedores for lading ships. In the cold weather a good many white people have come up to work here, but they do not seem to have been very successful. Some Irish come, but I do not gather that they are here now. Irish women, however, much improved and civilised, one finds everywhere. The housemaid at the hotel here is an Irishwoman, and seems very decent and good. She came originally from Dublin, married an American, who was killed in the war, on the Confederate side, as was also her brother, and now she has settled down into service.

The people I have met today are much interested in rice, which is cultivated in this part of the country. It had gone out very much. Since the war some estates

---

* In 1869 the state legislature established the Land Commission, the only southern state to promote the redistribution of land for freedmen. Innumerable blacks purchased land before the commission failed after two decades, like most Reconstruction experiments, due to inefficiency and corruption. However, a few black families who purchased lots in the 1870s held onto their land and increased their holdings in the 1880s. Twenty families owned over one hundred acres, the most successful on record being the retention of "The Promised Land" community in Greenwood. For more on the subject, see Carol Bleser, *The Promised Land: The History of the South Carolina Land Commission, 1869–1890*, and Elizabeth Bethel, *Promiseland: A Century of Life in a Negro Community*.

have been quite abandoned. For instance, I hear of one estate which was worth 500,000 dollars before the war, and for which after the war 275,000 dollars was offered and refused; it has since wholly broken down and fallen out of cultivation, and was bought the other day for 6,000 dollars by some gentlemen who are trying to resuscitate it. On the other hand, a good many estates, the owners of which were able to hold on and keep up the cultivation, are now doing pretty well. The truth, however, seems to be that rice is only grown in the United States by the aid of an exorbitant protective duty, and it is used in America only—none is exported. The Indian rice beats it in foreign markets. People here say they are no longer for free trade; there is nothing like protection. The jute-bagging used for rice and cotton is highly protected. Here they have only one jute-mill, lately erected,* but they hope to have more. They are trying experiments to grow jute, and jute-seed for the purpose has lately been distributed.

The Sea Islands, on which the long cotton grows, or used to grow, lie along the shore in this neighbourhood and southwards to Savannah. They are not islands out in the ocean, but flat tracts along the shore, more or less separated from the mainland by narrow channels. The soil is very good, but the only culture to which it has been hitherto very specially devoted was the long-staple cotton, the cultivation of which has now greatly declined. These cotton lands form the outermost belt next to the sea; behind them are the rice lands, which usually lie along the rivers and fresh-water estuaries. Behind the rice lands and the pine-belt come the upland cotton lands. All the cotton grown in this part of the world, except the Sea Island, is classed as upland. New Orleans cotton is classed separately, and seems to be a better and stronger staple. There is still more cotton shipped from New Orleans than from Charleston or any other port. The long cotton, or Sea Island, is a different variety of the plant from the common cotton. It requires more careful cultivation, and produces very much less cotton—generally only a third or a fourth of the quantity that is got from a good field of short cotton. It still fetches a very much higher price than the short cotton, but not so high in proportion as it did before, and in consequence comparatively little of it is raised.

In the evening I went a little way out into the country. There seems to be an immense cultivation of strawberries here for the Northern markets. One sees great fields of strawberries. There is a good drive, metalled with oyster-shells and lined

---

* Charleston Bagging Co., which wove fiber bags for cotton, opened in 1878 at The Tower Depot on John Street.

with fine magnolias, called Magnolia Avenue. The beauty and fashion of Charleston were out for the evening, principally driving fast-trotting horses. I am told that there were and still are some French mulattos in Charleston in a much higher position than the ordinary coloured people—like those in a considerable position in New Orleans—but they form an exclusive class by themselves, and are not so well off as they were before the war, in which they lost heavily. Altogether the "genteel" coloured people keep very much to themselves.

Next morning I called on Mr. A—, a gentleman* who was most kind in assisting me. He is interested in the Phosphate Beds, and he showed me a large collection of fine fossils found there, in excellent preservation. I also called on the City Superintendent of Schools, who is at the same time the Episcopalian clergyman.[†] He lived in a poor house, and did not seem a prosperous parson. He is a Carolina man, and does not think much of the blacks; but the city schools are, he says, good. I saw many nice-looking girls and young women going to school, with their books. The Charleston people generally impress me favourably. The place is not what it has been, but on the whole it is wonderfully well maintained, and the citizens make the best of the situation.

Today I made the acquaintance of Mr. W—, a lawyer, who has just been elected to the State Legislature,[‡] and is a very pleasant and well-informed man; and also of one or two other gentlemen. Talking over South Carolina affairs, I gather that the principal people of this State were not so far gone in difficulties before the war as those in Virginia. Many of them had great plantations in Mississippi, to which they transferred large bodies of their surplus slaves; and at one time they made a great deal of money, in consequence of which they took to expensive living, keeping racehorses and other fine things. When cotton fell in price their profits diminished, but they looked for future improvement, and did not mind some debt. After that came the war and great destruction of property, especially of cotton, the stores of which were captured or plundered, while the whole of the slave property was lost by emancipation. Land became a drug in the market, and they had no means of meeting their debts; and so it was that many of them have now become very poor. There seems to be no doubt that

---

*Likely Robert Adger (1814–1891), founder of Coosaw Mining Company and another advocate of the New South.

[†] Rev. Joseph B. Seabrook (1809–1877), superintendent of Charleston public schools from 1874 and pastor of a black congregation at St. Mark's Episcopal Church.

[‡] George Rivers Walker (1847–1882) was the son of Henry Pinckney Walker (1816–1890), British consul for Charleston. He was a partner in Walker & Bacot. Walker represented Charleston County (1878–1880) for Christ Church Parish, and was Democratic chairman. He lived in the village of Mount Pleasant. American Bar Association, *Annual Report*, 162–63.

many ladies who were once well-to-do now fill almost menial offices or take in sewing; and the estates and places which were finely kept have now deteriorated, especially those in the low country, where, since long cotton has gone down in the world, they have not succeeded in finding other suitable staples. The Charleston people say that if only this low country could be restored Charleston must still flourish. The negro labour is very good, and there is great abundance of it; but the negroes like regular pay, and do not care to be kept in arrears or paid by cheques, as is too often the case. A cheque is an order on the employer's employee store. If the negro is in debt it is set off; if not, he is kept waiting for his money, or is obliged to take goods on the truck system.

I went to see Mr. D—, a pure negro and notable character.* He has been in England and in Africa, and has seen the world. He is now a justice of the peace here—Trial Justice, they call it. He was appointed by Wade Hampton. He seems a very characteristic, pleasant, amusing sort of person, and talks well. He was educated in the North. He is in favour of Wade Hampton, who, he says, appoints black men when they really are educated and fit. I hear he quite holds his own as a justice.

I also made the acquaintance of R—, a model Democratic negro and friend of the white man.† His story seemed to me a little too much as if it had been rehearsed. He tells very fluently how he was a slave, and how he was educated by his mistress; and how after emancipation his master and mistress, being reduced to poverty, he supported them both, and eventually buried them both—he lays great stress upon the *burying*. He stuck to the whites in bad times amid the persecution of his own race, and now is a prosperous livery-stable keeper, and a friend of the party in power, while his own race have also become friendly to him.

Mr. W— invited me to go over with him to his house, on the other side of the river, in what is called Christ-Church parish, where I should see blacks in

---

* This was Martin Delany, first mentioned in the Whitelaw Reid account. Delany had remained in South Carolina. He had switched his party loyalty to support Democrat Wade Hampton in the 1876 election for governor, and Hampton's victory was partly the result of black swing votes encouraged by Delany. Hampton rewarded him with an appointment as trial justice, which he held until 1879. He afterward practiced medicine in Charleston.

† Stephney Riley, the owner of a fashionable livery stable at 68 Smith Street that catered mostly to whites, supported the Democratic Party. He was the wealthiest African American in town when in 1885, a prominent white physician, Dr. Amos Northrop Bellinger (1837–1908), witnessed him whipping his horse on Smith Street. Bellinger ordered him to stop and an altercation ensued, during which Bellinger shot and killed Riley. He was found not guilty, infuriating blacks in the region. Williams and Hoffius, *Upheaval in Charleston*, 81–82.

great abundance; and we started together. A parish is a mere popular term for a tract of country; it is not now a real division, civil or ecclesiastical. Since I have come into the land of blacks I notice signs of the abundance of labour. Instead of having to carry one's own bag and take care of one's self, as one has in the North, one is constantly beset by blacks who want to carry one's things and do all sorts of services for one. Crossing over, I talked with a large fruit and vegetable farmer, who raises for the Northern markets. He employs nothing but black labour, and finds it very good indeed; but, again, he has something to say against the blacks, alleging that they are loose and immoral in their ways, and dishonest in small things. Women work as well as men. In this Christ-Church parish the negroes are almost fifty to one. The whole of this part of the country outside of the town is almost entirely a negro country. This is part of the county which Mr. W— is to represent. He seems to be on extremely friendly terms with the people, but frankly admits that he cannot get them to vote for him. In the evening we went out and saw the negro population making their purchases in the village. The people do not seem to be of a high type—rather inferior, I thought, to those I had seen up-country, but very good-natured and cheerful. They seem to have got very much into the ways of white people, and do their shopping much as white people do in other parts of the world. The only difference seems to be that they are black, and perhaps a little dirtier than the average of civilised mankind. The storekeepers are Germans—they seem almost to monopolise that sort of business; the negroes scarcely ever rise to keep stores. Mr. W— talks and shakes hands with the blacks, and they reciprocate and laugh immoderately when he tells them that he has beaten them this election, and means to do so again. Certainly there does not seem to be any of the bitterness which one might have expected, after all one has heard of South Carolina, especially considering the way in which this election has been carried.

Next day I went with Mr. W— a long expedition into the country, which is of the Sea Island character. Much of the land is what is called "old field"; that is, land which was once cultivated, but is now overgrown with wood. I am told that after the war many Northerners came up, expecting to make large fortunes by buying good land cheap in this part of the country, and they began by attempting high farming, with high-class stock and so on; but they almost all failed and went back. The live-oaks and magnolias are really very handsome trees, large, round, and spreading. There is still a good deal of cotton cultivation—almost all long cotton; short cotton does not answer here. It seems that short cotton tends to grow long here, while long cotton grows short upcountry. The negroes cultivate it tolerably well. We saw one considerable planter's farm superintended, as bailiff, by an Englishman from Birmingham. Like most improving farmers in these days, he is trying to introduce better breeds of cattle. We came across a good many small negro farmers. They generally rent land, paying as much as four dollars an acre for it, but this is on account of the vicinity of Charleston. Further away in the country they can get it for two dollars an acre. It is said that the rent is very troublesome to collect, and that this same land is sold at eight to ten dollars an acre. We heard the usual tenant's complaints: that though the rent is so high the proprietors do not keep up the house and fences, &c., as they ought. Many of the blacks, however, have their own houses and little patches of land, renting as much more as is necessary to make up a decent farm; and most of them go out as labourers besides, more or less. I understand that in most parts of the low country the proprietors are willing and anxious to sell plots of land to the negroes, because that fixes them to the soil and secures a supply of labour when it is needed. I feel sure that this is the right policy. Here the negroes are generally well off, when they can get employment and are really paid. The difficulty seems, rather, to be to get employment, than for employers to get hands; but I am told that any man who works well and steadily, and is honest, is sure of employment. There is much complaint about their stealing chickens and such things; otherwise they seem to be a good sort of people. I am again struck by the easy, laughing familiarity between Mr. W—and the blacks, and the free chaff which passes about the election. One disagreeable result, however, of the less independent character of the negroes in these parts, and of the election-eering which has been going on, is, that very many of them seem ready to beg for assistance in one shape or another. On the other hand, they are always ready to give any little assistance and to do odd jobs whenever they are asked to do so, and are perfectly content when a little tobacco is given them in return. They certainly seem a remarkably easily-managed, good-natured set of people. The next day was Sunday; we went out to visit a rural chapel in the woods, and found the congregation in full and tremendous chorus of psalmody; one could hear them half a mile off. The whole thing was very pleasant, I thought. Afterwards we returned to Charleston, and I went to a black church in the city—rather a fine one. The preacher was as black as night—a typical negro—and perhaps a little ridiculous in his manners; but I thought him a stirring and effective preacher. Every now and then during the sermon some of the congregation grunted out devout ejaculations in token of assent or by way of emphasising the preacher's good points. I was greatly disappointed, however, to find that instead of the fine, bold singing which I had heard in the country, there was a choir and a poor, thin imitation of civilised singing.

The following day I went to see Dr. B—, the United States postmaster, a coloured man, and said to be the best specimen of his class in this part of the country;* in fact, according to my informants, the only man appointed by the Republicans who is not hopelessly corrupt. He seemed a dapper, pleasant, well-educated man, and reminded me of some of the more educated East Indians in Calcutta. He is quite a Northerner. He admits that the blacks have not come much to the front in any way, and that in commerce they do not keep stores or attain any considerable position, but he explains it all by saying that the social prejudice against coloured people is so great that they have not a chance. Like many of his class, he favours the idea of Liberia, and the great Black Republic that is to be there. I paid a visit to my namesake Mr. C—, the independent Democrat, who stood for State Senator for this district, but was defeated.† He is a lawyer, and all agree that he is a very superior man. I found him very moderate, and not at all inclined to be vituperative, although the election was bitterly contested. He says that he represented the principle of Conciliation against those who would not yield anything. The election was won by simple cheating; that is, by stuffing the ballot-boxes. At one polling-place not more than a thousand voted, but there were three thousand five hundred papers in the box. There was not much intimidation, but only cheating.

Afterwards I went over to James Island, to see a good long-cotton plantation, still maintained on the high farming system by Mr. H—‡ The cotton-fields seemed really very fine; they are highly manured, and give a large yield to the

---

* Benjamin A. Boseman (1840–1881) was Charleston's first black postmaster. Born free in New York, he graduated from the Medical School of Maine at Bowdoin College in 1864. He had served as an assistant physician at Hilton Head in the war and afterward set up a successful medical practice in Charleston. In 1868, he was one of several blacks in the state elected to Congress for the first time. He became the only politician, black or white, elected to three consecutive terms in the state House of Representatives during Reconstruction. During his term, in addition to his political service, he was appointed physician to the Charleston City Jail in 1869 and served on the Board of Regents of the state Lunatic Asylum. After completing his last term as congressman, he was appointed postmaster by President Ulysses S. Grant in 1873.

† James Butler Campbell (1808–1883) from Oxford, Massachusetts, who first came to Edisto Island in 1826 as a teacher. He studied law and settled in Charleston, marrying Anna Margaret Bennett (1812–1851), the daughter of ex-Gov. Thomas Bennett. A Unionist before the war, Campbell served in the state House of Representatives (1850–1855 and 1862–1866) and was elected to the state Senate in 1877. A businessman, he was director of the Savannah and Charleston Railroad Co., the Edisto and Ashley Canal Co., and other companies. James Butler Campbell Papers, 1814–1897. [1015.00] South Carolina Historical Society.

‡ William Godber Hinson (1838–1919) of Stiles Point Plantation, one of the last planters of long-staple cotton and one of the foremost agronomists of his day. His methods of drainage and fertilizing were nationally renowned, and he was an officer in almost every agricultural organization in the state.

acre. The cost of raising it in this expensive way is, however, so great that it seems doubtful whether it pays very well. Like all who have to do with them, he speaks very well of the blacks as labourers. He is trying experiments in raising jute, but does not seem to know how to grow it. At present he has it only in single rows, from which he hopes to get seed; but it is doubtful whether that will ripen sufficiently. I spent the evening at Colonel T—'s; a very nice house and pleasant party. I had a good deal of talk with several people, among them Capt. D—, an Englishman, who came out as a young man, fought in the war on the Confederate side, and is now editor of the principal newspaper here.*

They say that in this lower country they have always been for conciliation, and have supported Wade Hampton in that policy against Geary [*sic*]† and the violent white party who are in the upper country. They point to the unopposed acceptance of Wade Hampton in the present election as a proof of his success.

As a general result of all that I have been able to learn about the elections in this part of the country, I may say that there does not seem to be the least doubt that they were won by the most wholesale cheating. That is avowed in the most open way. Most people seem to praise the negroes, and to be on very good terms with them; but they all admit that, while the blacks will do almost anything else for them, when it comes to voting they cannot be influenced, and insist on voting

---

* Francis Warrington Dawson (1840–1889), editor of the *News and Courier* and a major operative in the Democratic Party. As he ran one of the South's most powerful papers, he was also a national celebrity. Dawson was later shot to death by his neighbor, Dr. Thomas B. McDow, a story that would make headlines throughout the country in 1889.

† Gen. Martin W. Gary (1831–1881), a Harvard-educated attorney from Edgefield elected to the state Senate in 1876, had played a major role in the campaign to elect Wade Hampton. He was among the most uncompromising and outspoken leaders stressing white supremacy and solidarity, while vigorously opposing any cooperation with Republicans or blacks. His plan for the campaign, frequently known as the "Edgefield plan," "advocated the use of electoral fraud, physical intimidation, and even murder to keep blacks and other Republicans from voting." Gary had organized rifle clubs of white Democrats (the Red Shirts) to put his plan into action. In 1878, Edgefield had reelected Gary to the state Senate, although his ambitions were for higher office. Believing himself chiefly responsible for the Democrat's 1876 victory, he broke with Hampton and other party leaders when he failed to be rewarded with a seat in the US Senate in 1877 and 1879. Therefore, from 1877 he was the Hampton machine's most bitter and vocal opponent, protesting payment of the state debt and tax funding for public schools, championing a usury law, and vehemently opposing Hampton's policy of magnanimity toward blacks. Hampton's supporters, including much of the lowcountry, would thwart Gary's campaign for governor in 1880. See Henry H. Lesesne, "Gray, Martin Witherspoon (1831–1881)." In Walter Edgar, ed., *South Carolina Encyclopedia* (Columbia: University of South Carolina Press), 2006.

with their party. At one place that I visited, where a considerable number of Republican votes were recorded, an old Democratic gentleman jocularly remarked that this had been the only honest poll in the whole district. They say the Republicans made the election law to suit their own purpose of cheating, and had arranged the electoral districts so as to swamp the whites with black votes. Now they are hoist with their own petard, and serve them right. The blacks seem to have accepted their defeat as a foregone conclusion, and therefore it is that they are quite good-natured over it. Perhaps, too, they really have to some degree accepted Wade Hampton and his policy, and are not so anxious to fight as they otherwise might be. Both parties seem to assume as a matter of course that whichever controls the machinery of the elections will win the elections. I am told that Wade Hampton generally appointed two Democrats and one Radical as election commissioners; that the radical was always corrupt and could be bought, and that therefore the Democrats always had it their own way. The Democrats of Charleston have done something to conciliate those blacks who accept the Democratic ticket. In this district seventeen members are sent up to the State Assembly, and of these three are Democratic blacks. The county officers are whites, but there are some blacks in the Charleston municipality. For the State Assembly the Republicans adopted a fusion ticket, including the five best of the Democrats.

Hitherto three Congressional districts in the black part of South Carolina have been represented by black men, and I am told that they were all very fair specimens. The representative of the Charleston district was a well-educated negro, from the North.* The Georgetown district was represented by an extremely polished black gentleman, who was formerly a very popular barber in Charleston,† and is not at all a bad sort of person. The Beaufort district has long

---

* Rev. Richard Harvey Cain (1825–1887), born a free black in West Virginia, was raised in Ohio. He attended Wilberforce University, and divinity school in Hannibal, Missouri. Licensed to preach for the Methodist Episcopal Church, in 1861 he became a pastor in Brooklyn, New York. After the Civil War, Cain moved to Charleston as superintendent of African Methodist Episcopal missions. He became the pastor of the congregations that would become Emanuel ("God with us") AME and Morris Brown AME churches. He became active in politics, first serving as a delegate to the state constitutional convention in 1868. In 1872, after serving in the South Carolina Senate (1868–72), Cain was elected as a Republican Congressman in the US House of Representatives (1873–1875 and 1877–1879).

† Joseph Hayne Rainey (1832–1887), born into slavery in Georgetown, was freed in the 1840s when his father purchased the freedom of his entire family. Of mixed race, he became, like his father, a barber. In 1862, he left with his family for Bermuda, returning to Charleston in 1866. He became involved in politics, joining the executive committee of the state Republican Party. He served in the state Senate for Georgetown County

been represented by General S—, who, while a slave, was employed as a pilot, and in the war distinguished himself by carrying off a Confederate vessel and delivering her to the Federals. He has now great influence among his own race, and is not unpopular among white people. He behaved well towards his former master's family and assisted them.* In spite, however, of this favourable account, there is a general accusation that under the Carpet-bag Government all were corrupt, both black and white. Honesty was a thing unknown.

I observe that in a great number of the elections for county and local offices in these Southern States the opportunity is taken to provide for the veterans of the Confederate army who are not eligible for pensions. I saw several notices of elections of one-legged and one-armed ex-soldiers to county offices. These offices are profitable—if not paid by salaries they have considerable fees.

Looking over the accounts of the elections in other States, of which the papers are full, I observe that Governor Nicholls, of Louisiana, is said to be conciliatory and to have followed the same policy as Wade Hampton; but there the negroes fought more successfully than here; and in some cases the Democrats carried the seats in Congress only by adopting a fusion ticket and giving the blacks a good many county offices. There seems to be more "bulldozing" in Mississippi than anywhere else. That is called "the Mississippi plan." South Carolina seems to be the only State which carried everything solidly Democratic. In all the others there has been more or less success of Republican or independent candidates.

(1868–1870) and was a delegate in 1868 to the state constitutional convention. He afterward served four terms in the US House of Representatives (1870–1879), the first black to serve in Congress, where he established a record of length of service for a black Congressman. After leaving Congress, he was appointed a federal agent of the US Treasury for internal revenue in South Carolina. He held this position for two years, after which he began a career in private commerce and worked in brokerage and banking in Washington, D.C. for five years. He retired in 1886, and died in Georgetown.

* Gen. Robert Smalls, first mentioned in the Peck account, had run for his freedom on the C.S.S *Planter* in 1862. He was afterward assigned by the Union to pilot the *Planter* as a federal naval ship. Commissioned as a second lieutenant in Company B, 33rd Regiment, US Colored Troops, he fought in seventeen battles in the Civil War. Promoted to full captain in 1863, he was named commanding officer of the *Planter*. After the war, Smalls returned to his native Beaufort, and opened a store for freedmen. He purchased his former master's house, and allowed his former mistress, Mrs. Henry (Jane Bond) McKee, who was elderly, to move back home prior to her death. He served in the state House of Representatives (1868–1870) as a Republican and in the state Senate (1870–1875). Tried, convicted, and eventually pardoned for allegedly accepting a bribe, he afterward served five terms in the US Congress (1875–1887). Although he lost his seat from 1880 to 1881, he regained it in 1881, after contesting the results. In 1889 he was appointed US collector of Customs in Beaufort.

I have heard a good deal here about the late exodus to Liberia, which was such a wretched failure. The upper class of blacks do not go themselves, but preach to their countrymen the advantage of going. There seems no doubt that the unhappy people who went found themselves much worse off than if they had stayed at home.* There seems to be a much more promising field for emigration from Mississippi and the States in that part of the country to the back parts of Kansas and the Territories where land is to be got free. The negroes seem to have been less domiciled in Mississippi than they were here, and since emancipation they have been more migratory. They are now entitled to homesteads on the same terms as white men; and if they can manage the means of cultivating virgin lands in the Far West they will do very well.

*From the 1850s Martin Delany was convinced whites would not allow blacks to become leaders in society. In his book, *The Condition, Elevation, Emigration, and Destiny of the Colored People of the United States, Politically Considered* (1852), he argued that blacks had no future in the country and should found a new nation. The plan for emigration to Liberia had grown after 1876 and the overthrow of the Radical Republican government. Among adherents, Congressman Richard H. Cain called for a million men to leave for Africa. In 1877, the Liberian Exodus Joint Stock Steamship Company was formed in Charleston with a fund of $6,000, and blacks began arriving in January 1878. The company purchased a bark called the *Azor,* which arrived in Charleston and on April 21 set sail with 206 emigrants aboard. A reporter for the *News and Courier,* Alfred Brockenbrough Williams (1856–1930) accompanied the emigrants to Monrovia and wrote an account of the voyage, during which management blunders resulted in the deaths of twenty-three emigrants. Contrary to law, no physician was on board, and although one of the organizers, George Curtis, volunteered as physician, he had no medical knowledge. After a voyage of forty-two days, emigrants found themselves impoverished, without supplies, and dependent on charity, as well as victims of exaggerated claims of the land's fertility. Eighteen returned in December 1879, to report that not a single passenger of the *Azor* would stay in Liberia if he had the means to return. The Liberian Exodus Company, unable to pay heavy, unforeseen expenses, collapsed. However, among those who stayed, success did eventually come. By 1880, most had found livelihood. By 1890, the *Azor* passengers were well represented among Liberia's most prominent citizens. Saul Hill, a native of York, South Carolina, although financially secure when he left for Liberia, established a successful seven-hundred-acre coffee farm and sold coffee to a Philadelphia firm. Clement Irons from Charleston built the first steamship constructed in Liberia. C. L. Parsons from Charleston was chief justice of the Liberian Supreme Court. Rev. David Frazier opened a coffee farm with twenty-thousand trees and was elected to the Liberian Senate in 1891. One passenger, Daniel Frank Tolbert, originally from Ninety-Six, propagated one of the largest Americo-Liberian families in Liberia. He was the grandfather of William R. Tolbert Jr., president of Liberia (1971–1980). Williams, *Liberian Exodus*; Tindall, *South Carolina Negroes, 1877–1900*, 166–68; Tindall, "The Liberian Exodus of 1878," 133–45.

I have been looking over some of the legislation of South Carolina. It does not seem very different from that which I have noticed in other States. There is, as usual, a good deal of legislation on small subjects, such as an Act to legitimise a child, and another to make an adopted child an heir. There is a regular poor law, providing for a poor-house and outdoor relief. Nothing is said of able-bodied paupers. The relief seems to be confined to really necessitous cases. The road law gives the option of contributing either labour or money for the making of roads. There is a provision for inspecting and classifying flour and some other things, the same as I noticed at Chicago, and a limit to the rates for grinding flour. There is a 7 per cent usury law; but I understand that in practice it is almost entirely evaded. Few people can get money here at 7 per cent, the credit is so bad. There is a law of limited partnership for sleeping partners, but companies seem to be only incorporated by special Acts, of which there are many. There is not now in South Carolina any law prohibiting the intermarriage of white and black people.*

I have had a very pleasant visit to Charleston, and have received much kindness here. Mr. A——, whom I have already mentioned, and who has throughout given me much assistance, has kindly arranged for me a visit to the country. I am to go to a son-in-law of his,† who has an estate in the rice country.

Travelling in this part of the country is sometimes very difficult, if one has to stop at places on the way, for there are seldom more than two trains, sometimes only one, in the course of the twenty-four hours, and they seem generally to manage to arrive and depart in the very middle of the night. However, by getting up very early I made a start from Charleston. The country through which we ran seemed mostly forest, with occasional cultivation. At Greenpond I was met by Mr. W——, who drove me through the forest to his rice plantation, some miles off. After breakfast we had a long and pleasant ride over his land. He has a very large

* South Carolina legalized interracial marriage for some years during Reconstruction. However, once Democrats took power in the South during "redemption," antimiscegenation laws were reenacted and enforced, just as Jim Crow laws would be enacted to enforce other forms of racial segregation. It would take South Carolina until 1998 to officially amend the state constitution to remove language prohibiting miscegenation.
† Robert Adger's son-in-law, William Dalton Warren (1839–1896) from York. He married Sarah Elizabeth Adger (d.1878). Warren had only just purchased Paul Plantation on the Combahee River (later known as Paul and Dalton Plantation) near Green Pond. He also owned Ashtabula Plantation in Pendleton, where he bred cattle. Warren would leave the state for Colorado in 1882, to engage in mining and agriculture. In 1891, he settled in Charlottesville, Virginia.

extent of fine rice-fields. His farm is nearly a thousand acres, and he has several neighbours who have also large plantations; so altogether there is in this part of the country a rice district of which the cultivation is well maintained. Mr. W— has a very elaborate system of tidal canals for the irrigation of the rice. The salt water is banked out, and the fresh water is regulated by sluices, the land being irrigated when the tides rise to the necessary level. The rice seems large and fine, and the yield is said to be large—sometimes as much as eighty bushels of un-husked rice to the acre; but the expense of the irrigation and other arrangements is considerable. Still they would do well if it were not for the competition of Indian rice which has been invading the American market. The planters keep the rice-lands in their own hands, and, beyond a little fodder for their mules, &c., grow little else. The higher grounds they give over to the negroes, who cultivate corn and vegetables for themselves, and a little cotton. In lieu of rent for the land they give two days' labour in the week, and generally work two days more, at fifty cents a day. In most cases they are put upon task-work. In this part of the country the women seem to work as freely as the men, both in the fields and in the thrashing-mills. The negroes keep a large number of cattle and pigs; but Mr. W— says that is a serious difficulty, as the animals increase too much, and the proprietor is expected to find grazing for them. The fence law is a great subject of dispute in this part of the country. The question is, whether the owner of the land is bound to fence cattle out, or the owner of the cattle to keep them in. Each county decides for itself, but it seems to be a burning question. Mr. W— speaks extremely well of his negroes, and they appear to be on very good terms with him. They have quite a respectful manner, and in this out-of-the-way place the little negro girls curtsey like English Sunday-school children. There has only been one strike in this neighbourhood, but that was a bad one.* The negroes struck for more pay for harvest-work, and very violently drove away others who wished to work. Mr. W— was away, and his manager could get no assistance from the Rad-ical Government; so he was obliged to yield for that time, but he has since come back to the old rates, and all has gone smoothly; there has been no more trouble. During the war the people of this part of the country suffered very much from the destruction of property by raiding parties from the Federal fleet; and after the war, when the Federal people established the Radical rule, their feelings were apt to be hurt by their being arrested by black soldiers, and so on. However, they do not seem to have suffered very severely; and now, if money were only more plen-tiful, and there was a better demand for their produce, they would do very well.

---

* For an account of the labor strike, see Margaret Belser Hollis and Allen H. Stokes, eds., *Twilight on the South Carolina Rice Fields* (Columbia: USC Press, 2012).

Talking of these arrests, I may mention that arrest means very little in the United States. Under their old-fashioned English laws every process, criminal or civil, is commenced by arrest, followed by bail. De Tocqueville instances this as showing how an English law favourable to the rich, who can give bail, has prevailed even under Democratic institutions.

Mr. W— has laid out a good deal of land in lots, which he offers to the negroes for sale. Some of them have bought, but most have not the means. He, like others, speaks of their immorality and want of fidelity to their spouses. They are religious in their way, but have their own peculiar ideas of religion, and do not appreciate some of our theology.

In this lower country, so much peopled by blacks, who can stand the climate, the whites are generally obliged to go away from the plantations, in the hot weather to healthier places. In slave days the white overseers were a bad set, and little educated. They had no accounts, there being no money to pay, and they were mere slave-drivers. Now Mr. W—has two or three educated young men under him, and they take it turn and turn about to stay during the unhealthy season. He has also some property up-country, and he says that the blacks there are more intelligent, speak better English, and often make good farmers. On the other hand, the low country people are more simple and more easily managed; and it is a great advantage that the women work here.

There is plenty of game about here. Mr. W— gave me venison of his own shooting. These Southerners habitually eat sweet potatoes, and hominy made of Indian corn. One sees very little of potatoes proper, called "Irish potatoes."

I enjoyed my visit very much; and the impression left upon my mind is, that the relations between a planter and the negroes upon his property may well be pleasant and satisfactory. A little more money and profit only is needed to make things go along very satisfactorily.

The following day Mr. W— drove me to Kusaw [*sic*],* *en route* for Beaufort. All this is quite a negro country. There never were many whites; and after leaving the rice plantations we find that most of the planters have disappeared since the war and the decadence of long cotton. We saw nothing but scattered negro huts. The negroes seem now never to live in villages; they have left the old slave lines and set up isolated houses on their farms. At the meeting of cross-roads you may find small stores, generally kept by Germans.

At [Coosaw] we went over the Phosphate Company's works. They seem to be very active and energetic. The material (composed of animal fossils) is dredged

---

* Coosaw.

or dived for in the river, and is then cleaned and crushed and prepared for export. All the labour is black. I talked to Mr. C—, the son of the former proprietor of all the land about here, and now a manager of the Phosphate Company.* He speaks very highly indeed of the free negro labour, and I myself saw the negroes working as well as any men in the world can work. Evidently these people are not wanting in physical capacity, and make excellent hired labourers. Mr. C— says he has tried Irishmen, but he found them no better workmen than negroes, and very troublesome, so he got rid of them. The blacks, however, only do the manual labour; they are not what is called "responsible," and not to be trusted with machines or anything of that kind. There are, however, some good black carpenters and blacksmiths. Most of these black labourers have land of their own over on the Islands. After doing their ploughing and sowing they leave the women and children to hoe and weed and come over here. They get a dollar a day, and some of the better men a dollar and a quarter, but they seldom save. After they have made a little money they like to go and spend it. They drink, but not to such a degree as to interfere with their work. They go home and get drunk on Saturday night, go to church on Sunday, and generally are back at their work on Monday. He has had only one small strike. The men stayed away on the Saturday, but came back on the Monday. He carried on his work all through the Radical rule, but has had no trouble on account of political difficulties. He could always get on with the black labourers. All that the negroes require is to get their wages regularly paid in cash. On the day of the election they would not stay at work. They all went off to vote at Greenpond, which was the regular polling-place; but when they got there, fifteen miles off, they were told that there would be no poll.

I was kindly sent on to Beaufort in the Phosphate Company's little steamer, which took me through the river-channels. The appearance of this flat country, in which land and water are a good deal intermixed, reminded me very much of the lower parts of Bengal—the tall pine-trees take the place of the Bengal palms, looking in the distance not unlike them. The Sea Islands are situated very like the "Soonderbun" tracts. Two large islands lie between [Coosaw] and Beaufort, and we threaded through the channels separating them. Before the war these islands were filled with large plantations of Sea Island cotton; and here, too, after the war, Northerners came and spent much money, but were disappointed; so the land is now entirely given up to the negroes.

---

*From 1870, Coosaw Mining Company was mining deposits in the Coosaw River, although innumerable other river mining companies were competing in the region.

African Americans working, Charleston, S.C.: Gossiping at the gate.
c. 1879, stereograph. Library of Congress.

"B." (Eliza Houston Barr) (1880)

"Inside Southern Cabins"

"B." (Eliza Houston Barr), "Inside Southern Cabins. III.—Charleston, South Carolina," *Harper's Weekly* 24, November 27, 1880: 765–66.

"B." wrote the serial "Inside Southern Cabins," which ran in *Harper's Weekly* in November and December of 1880. A travel memoir describing the social conditions, work, religious practices, and customs of ex-slaves, the first two articles featured Georgia blacks, the third featured Alabama, and the fourth featured Charleston. The author signed these articles only with the initial "B."

"B." was Eliza "Lilly" Houston Barr (1853–1933), who published as "Lillie E. Barr" or "Lily Barr." Born in Scotland, her family emigrated in 1856 from England to Texas, where her father, Robert Barr, an accountant, secured a position in the land office under Governor Sam Houston. When her father died of yellow fever, her mother, Amelia Edith Barr (1831–1919), took her three girls to live in New York City, where she became a best-selling novelist, famous in her day. Amelia Barr wrote more than seventy novels, including *Remember the Alamo* (1888).

Over her lifetime, Lilly Barr published magazine articles, poetry, and fiction for juveniles, including *Dot and Dime: Two Characters in Ebony* (1877) about black children living on a Texas plantation. She also served as administrator for her more successful mother, during Amelia Barr's long literary career. However, around 1880 Lilly left for mission work with the American Missionary Society (AMS), a journey that brought her to the southern states. The AMS, originally a Protestant, New York–based abolitionist organization, played a major role during the Reconstruction era promoting education for freedmen. The organization founded schools and colleges for blacks in the South, including Atlanta University and Fisk University, among others. The AMS founded Avery Normal Institute, Charleston's first accredited secondary school for blacks, in 1865. The group also conducted Christian missionary work for freedman throughout the South in the decades following the war.

In Charleston Lilly Barr met pioneer civil rights activist Albion Tourgée (1838–1909), who had recently published *A Fool's Errand* (1879), a best seller focused on Klan violence in the early days of Reconstruction. It was followed by *Bricks Without Straw* (1880), also a best seller. Tourgée advised Barr to go to John's Island, where she would find blacks "far different from the usual," and natural surroundings of great beauty and interest.

On John's Island, Lilly befriended Mr. and Mrs. Thomas Fenn Hunt Peck, who lived at Headquarters Plantation (Fenwick Hall) in the "fine old manor house" and invited her to live with them. Her mother wrote: "Every brick in this house had been brought from England by Lord Fenwick its builder, and its noble entrance hall, leaded library windows, and magnificent cypress paneling were still in beautiful preservation. It received its name from having been headquarters during the war of the Revolution." Before the war, Thomas F. H. Peck had been chief engineer on the ships of his father, Captain Fenn Peck (1806–1873), who distinguished himself during the Civil War by running more blockades of Confederate ports than any other skipper without being caught or losing a ship. During Lilly's tenure on John's Island, Peck was planting Sea Island cotton and mining the Stono River for phosphates. From Headquarters, she ventured out to aid and observe blacks on the island and in Charleston, while writing articles for the *Independent* and *Harper's Weekly*. As her mother revealed, Lilly accompanied Mrs. Peck on trips to Charleston "in the longboat, rowed by six black men," whose leader, Binyard, led them in singing spirituals to the rhythm of the oars.

On her return east, Lilly Barr moved up the Hudson River to Cornwall-on-Hudson, New York, where her mother purchased Cherry Croft, a house on the slopes of Storm King Mountain. In 1895, she married Canadian businessman Edward A. Munro, who disappeared from her life at some point. After her mother's death, she undertook the care of an invalid sister. After the death of her sister, Lilly lived the last years of her life alone on a hilltop overlooking Prescott, Arizona, a beloved eccentric to the locals.

In the following article, Barr describes several the region's blacks and their conditions in 1880.

SOURCES

Barr, Amelia Edith Huddleston. *All the Days of My Life: An Autobiography*. New York: D. Appleton and Co., 1913.
Barr, Lillie E. "Three Months on a Cotton Plantation" *Independent* 33 (30 June 1881): 1–2.
———. "Three Months on a Cotton Plantation" *Independent* 33 (14 July 1881): 4–5.
———. "Negro Sayings and Superstitions." *Independent* 35 (17 September 1883): 1222–23.

"Blockade Runner Who Was Never Captured." *The Bamberg (SC) Herald,* 1891–1972 (April 30, 1914): 6.

Hills, William Henry, and Robert Luce. "Personal Gossip about Authors." *The Writer* 29, 1917: 75–76.

Kownslar, Allan O. *The European Texans.* College Station: Texas A&M University Press, 2004.

"Mrs. Munro of Prescott Dead." *Prescott (AZ) Evening Courier,* Feb. 6, 1933: 1, 8.

"Notes on Authors." *Publisher's Weekly* 32: 815, Sept. 10, 1887: 267–68.

Thompson, Robert Ellis, and Wharton Barker. "Authors and Publishers." *The American: A National Journal* 13–14:324, 1886: 300, 368.

"Inside Southern Cabins"

The Charleston negroes are the aristocracy—so far as I have seen—of their race. They copy the whites, and that very fairly, in courtesy, hospitality, and especially in that air of "we are the cream of humanity" which the white Charlestonian is sure to inform you is the case, if he or she thinks you have failed to make the discovery for yourself.

The division between the rich and poor negroes is far more decided here than in any other place I visited. The colored upper-ten include a great number who have never been slaves; and the majority are of very light color—indeed, all but white. This social division line is, however, a slight one compared with the color line, which among Charleston negroes is of the most intense and prejudiced character. In talking with the wife of a white Northern minister, pastor of a colored church there, she told me that several of her husband's light—or, as they prefer being called, "bright"—members called upon her, and requested that she would not be so familiar with the black members of the congregation. "There is no necessity for you to shake hands with them when you meet them on the street," was the monition given her. In the colored boarding-schools the "bright" girls make indignant protests against occupying the same room with the black girls. This color line I found to exist both in Georgia and Alabama, but in a much less pronounced way. Still, there is undoubtedly among very light colored people a persuasion of their superiority; yet, singularly enough, this feeling is generally blended with an intense dislike to white people. One of the most prominent traits of Negro character here is their readiness to adopt children. It is almost impossible to find a home in which there are not one, two, or more adopted children. Perhaps a neighbor dies, leaving three or four little ones. Some nursing woman instantly claims the baby, "because she can 'tend best to it," and the rest are taken readily by others on equally satisfactory grounds, and I believe they receive just as much love and care from the adopting mother as they did from their own; at any rate, I never saw any difference in the treatment of natural and of adopted children—both were made equally welcome to the ragged bed and the corn-dodger, even in the poorest house. The universality of this custom implies that negro women still regard their interest and right in their children as paramount, the father's being really as small as it was in the days of slavery, for I never once heard of a father objecting to this partition of his family.

They have also another custom that savors strongly of slavery—that of giving children away. A mother, when her eldest daughter marries, will frequently give her as a wedding present a younger brother or sister, and this gift is as complete and real as a sale was twenty years ago. The child given belongs to the daughter, to the sister, or friend, as absolutely as if it was an inanimate object, and henceforward transfers its regard and obedience solely to its new protector, looking entirely to him or her for food, clothing, and education. This ownership of brothers, sisters, nephews, and nieces is one of the most significant remnants of slavery. I saw it in South Carolina, Georgia, and Alabama, and was told that it existed all over the South.

The affection between brothers and sisters is often a singularly tender one, and in Charleston many beautiful instances of it came under my notice; one especially of a young man who worked almost night and day at his trade—shoemaking—in order to give his sister a fine education, he himself spelling out, while at his work-bench, such lessons as with her help he was able to manage.

I doubt if it would be possible to find a colored home in Charleston in which Solomon's little remark about sparing the rod and spoiling the child is not practically illustrated by the most unmerciful use of the strap, or "lash," as they call it, and oftener, I fear, to the spoiling than the saving of the child. This is the more remarkable because many of these mothers must retain a very lively memory of their own floggings; and even the younger ones, born after emancipation, have all listened to the stories of the old uncles and aunties, and sympathetically shared their sufferings.

For here, as in Georgia, every little cabin shelters some gray-headed man or woman "who ain't got no folks to care for them." They have a corner for their chest and comforters, and not only share the coffee, corn-bread, and bacon, but are also, in some way or other, supplied with their beloved tobacco or snuff.

In Charleston there are many beautiful residences owned by colored men, and I shall always remember with pleasure my entertainment by Mr. Hall, a prominent colored cotton merchant, who owns a fine house on Rutledge Street.*

* John W. Hall was a cotton shipper who accumulated real estate and personal property valued at $10,000. Hall was from a rising generation that would soon overshadow the

It is surrounded by a lovely flower garden, and handsomely and appropriately furnished throughout. No dining-room could have been better appointed; the silver, the china, the cooking, were all in the best taste and of the most perfect quality; the servants were dressed in clean white linen suits.

Both Mr. and Mrs. Hall had been slaves, and have educated themselves since they were set free. They talked intelligently and grammatically of the events commented on in the newspapers, and were people whose sympathies stretched out to all suffering wrong or oppression, no matter what their creed or nationality. Still, I noticed that the majority of his books referred to his own race and to slavery. They had no children, but, following the usual custom, had adopted three, and were educating them for useful and honorable lives.

Among the higher class of Charleston Negroes the fashion of wearing mourning for deceased friends is carried to such a ridiculous pitch that I wonder it has not caused its entire disregard among white people. For the death of relatives of the most remote consanguinity, for infants which have scarcely breathed, they assume the deepest trappings of woe; and even babies may frequently be seen dressed in black. That they have never seen these relatives, or that they have been in life on the very worst terms with them, does not alter the conditions. As soon as they are dead, they are deemed worthy of the longest crape veil that can be procured.

Turning from the higher class of Charleston negroes to the laborers, one stands appalled before the mass of poverty, ignorance, and superstition that is apparent on all sides.

From most of the streets in Charleston lanes and alleys branch off, and these lead into courts full of vice and misery—places which almost anyone who had no knowledge of negro character would refuse to enter.

But push open the doors, and in every cabin you will find a welcome. The best chair or soap box will be carefully wiped off for you. Everywhere black babies, dogs, cats, and dirt are so mixed up that it is impossible to say which is the dirtiest. Everywhere you hear the same pitiful story of hard work, miserable pay, high rents, hunger, nakedness, and sickness.

The women, as a rule, are ragged and dirty, and rarely seen without the snuff-stick in their mouths. Their language is coarse and brutal, and the most trifling offenses will elicit terrible threats—not in anger, but just from habit. I have often

---

achievements of the more established free brown elite. According to *Sholes' Directory* (1882), J. W. Hall lived at 41 Rutledge Street and had a butler named Stephen Coleman. The address, 41 Rutledge, was north of Calhoun in that day, at Spring and Rutledge streets. *Sholes' Directory of the City of Charleston*, 246, 329. Powers, *Black Charlestonians*, 167.

been interrupted in the middle of a chapter by, "I'll stomp the life out ob you, you little debbil, ef you don't git that water on," and then in the same breath, "Go on, miss; that's a powerful good chapter." The woman had not the slightest intention of "stomping the life" out of any one; it was only her way of telling her child to put the kettle on.

These very women are probably members of some colored church, and can pray in the most intense language for the conversion of their "dear partners," as they call their husbands, and their "beloved children." Yet I don't remember ever hearing a single word of love or praise given to a child, no matter how well it had done its task; and when I asked a woman why they refused such encourage-ment to their children, she answered, "Lord, chile! You ken't praise niggers; ef you do, they git the big head so bad that heaven ken't hold 'em."

The immorality of this class is a common subject of remark, and I have frequently had it pointed out to me as a complete settlement of the negro ques-tion. "What can possibly be done for such men and women?" is asked. I think the answer is very easy. Give them proper places to live in. As long as parents and children, young men and young women, sometimes even two families, are crowded into one room, the ordinary rules of decency are almost of necessity disregarded. I did not discover any unusual immorality among the higher class of Charleston negroes, and with regard to the laboring class, everywhere and among all races, we see "Evil effects from evil causes spring."

Still, even in these wretched courts, I met with some singularly beautiful characters—men and women who, hungry, suffering, bent with ill-usage and toil, have told me with radiant faces how "de Lord Jesus come and sot right down on dat chair" and talked with them; men and women who, in the beauty and sim-plicity of a wonderful faith, have had visions, and seen the "golden chariots swing low," and Jordan shine like the river of God.

"Yes, ma'am," said one of these women to me, "I am de richest woman in Charleston."

I looked round at the few pennyworths of peanut-candy, the can of milk, and the half-dozen sticks of green wood which composed her whole stock in trade, and then at the bright black face bound round with a white kerchief, and asked, "How is that, Ellen?"

"Well, chile," she answered, her face brightening all over, "I don't know A B C, but I know de Lord Jesus Christ! Let me tell you how, chile. Four years ago I buried my dear partner, and when I came back from de funeral, thar was jist bread 'nough for supper, and no more. Well, 'bout five o'clock next morning I riz up from my bed, and I got down on my bendings [knees] right thar, and I battled with de Lord fur breakfast fur me and de chillen. By-'n'-by comes a boy fur a nickel's worth ob milk. I gib it to him, and then down I knelt ag'in, and I says, 'Thank you, Lord, thank you; but 'tain't 'nough, Lord; send some more, good Lord, send some more, Lord.' Pretty soon a boy come 'long, and he buys twenty cents worth ob wood. Den I goes and wakes up de chillen. 'Come,' says I, 'git up now, chillen; Jesus done sent de money for de breakfast; and I's gwine to git it.' Ebery day since He's gi'en me 'nough; and some days more 'an 'nough. I don't know A B C, miss, but I know de Lord Jesus Christ—and I'm de richest woman in Charleston."

Incidents of simple faith as remarkable as this are abundant in these wretched hovels, and setting aside the religious aspect of the question altogether, I could not but regard with wonder the influence of this intangible comforter. St. Paul has told us what faith was to the early Christians; if he stood among these Charleston negroes today, I think he would give a still broader definition. He would say, "Faith is a faculty of the soul which enables men who have nothing to possess everything."

Hid away in a dark hot little room in one of the inner courts I found a woman utterly destitute, blind, and helpless, yet as calm and content as a child. "The Good Master"—a favorite name for the Lord—she said, "He saw I was so much taken up wid what was a-gwine on by de wayside, and didn't gib 'tention 'nough to what was a-doing in my soul's house, so He sent His angel to draw de curtains ober my eyes."

"De Lord is mighty curious 'bout de way He does wid His chillen," answered another woman.

Religion is, indeed, so much a part of these negroes' lives that it is impossible to speak truthfully of them without giving it an apparent predominance. Yet if there is any place in this world where mountains could be moved by faith, I should say that these are the people who could work the miracle.

Generally the woman is the provider for the total family, and even when the man works, the wife takes in washing or sewing, or goes out to day's work, it being an understood thing that she is to provide clothing, while he undertakes for the rent and food. In most cases, however, the woman takes care of the whole family.

The most picturesque and interesting class of Charleston negroes are, I think, the licensed vendors. Some of them, both men and women, are very handsome, and all of them seemed to be endowed with most amusing eloquence. If the vendor was of a religious turn of mind, he mixed up Scripture and vegetables, fish and fruit, in a style which could hardly fail to attract attention.

I have heard them with an intense solemnity inform the inhabitants of a street that this was their last chance to buy vegetables, the last time they were going through the street that day, and that no more beans or potatoes were to be bought, though perhaps a stout handsome negress, with large gold hoops and bright turban, and a great flat basket on her head, was crying "Beans and potatoes" a block behind him.

Sometimes their local and political hits are very clever, and elicit hearty laughs. Again, their peculiar use of any long, fine-sounding word that they have caught is very amusing. I once heard an old man crying: "Strawberries, superfine straw-berries gwine by; strawberries, supernoctial straw-berries gwine by."

Charleston market, to an epicure, would be a place to loiter in and dream of dinners. Every delicacy that can tempt the eye and the palate is there. The place is sweet and fresh, with a marvellous wealth of flowers, and there is a never-ending free entertainment in the piquant and comical invitations to buy from the negro women, seated, not on the ground, but up among their wares. One thing detracts from the idyllic charm of this really picturesque market—the number of buzzards that abide there, seemingly quite at home, and on the most familiar terms with all the habitués of the place. They are, however, the scavengers of the city, and are protected by law, a fine of five dollars being imposed for injuring them.

There is hardly anything the colored men and women dread so much as going to the hospital. Yet the Roper Hospital, a portion of which is open to them, is a beautiful building, admirably ordered, and scrupulously clean. I visited it very often during a stay of nine weeks, and I believe that the colored patients were kindly and intelligently treated.

But the negro is a born herbalist; his faith is in weeds and roots, and it was really pitiful to see their anguish of disappointment when I refused to smuggle in their beloved plantain leaf. One man suffering with acute rheumatism begged me in the most impassioned manner to get him some rattlesnake oil to rub himself with, assuring me that it would cure him. After some search I succeeded in getting it from some country negroes. It was clear, not unlike olive-oil in appearance, and had a faint indescribable smell. It was extracted, so the negroes told me, by hanging the snake before a slow fire, the oil dropping from between the body and the skin. Whether the oil or his faith in it worked the cure, I know not, but certainly he was immediately relieved by its use. I must not forget to state that the head of the rattlesnake is cut off before it is subjected to the fire process.

The negroes' fear of the poor-house is still greater than his fear of the hospital, and I must say that this terror has a just foundation. There is one comfortably sized building and numerous rows of cabins, but into every room three or four paupers are crowded. Gaunt poverty, decrepit old age, terrible deformities, consumption, dropsy, paralysis, and disease in some of its most loathsome forms hold here a delightful carnival.

From statistics given me by the ward physicians it is evident that consumption and dropsy make great havoc among the colored race since their emancipation— the dropsy, I believe, in most cases the result of insufficient or improper food. The slightest bruise, in nine cases out of ten, if not attended to at once, becomes in negroes an ugly eating ulcer. During my short stay in Charleston I knew six women with ulcers of two to three years' standing.

One of these women I thought I could cure, and I went every day to attend to her. She had a large brindle dog called Prince, that had received a very ugly bite from a neighbor's dog. When I first attended his mistress, he regarded me with the utmost suspicion, and, standing close by me, watched everything I did with a critical eye. After three days' consideration of my ways, he seemed to have satisfied himself that I was no quack, for after I had finished with his mistress, he came and lay down at my feet, licked his own sore, and looked rather authoritatively in my face. After a little hesitation I bathed and dressed his wound, he standing perfectly still during the operation. Every morning, when he saw me coming, he followed me into the house, and waited until I had dressed his wound, and this he repeated until he was quite well, when he never noticed me again. I was disappointed at his want of gratitude, but that is exactly how Prince treated me. I can only suppose that his instinct taught him that in my heart I hated and dreaded dogs, and that therefore, though he was willing to take advantage of my charity, he felt no more kindness to me for it than the patients in a hospital feel for its supporters. And though I did not gain his affection, I gained his confidence, for he never afterward barked at me, and he suffered me to go into his mistress's room without following and watching me.

I saw a class of negroes in Charleston who greatly interested me, but whom I had not time enough to visit, because they live far out of the city, and their speech is so barbarous that it would require some little time to establish an intelligent communication with them. Some of this class work in the rice fields; others, still more picturesque, live on the sand-bars and islands adjacent, and are the fishermen of this locality.

I think, from what I saw of them, that their lives would afford very distinct traits, songs, and traditions; and I hope at some future day to touch it below the surface. I tried to talk to them, and understood enough to feel sure that, as far as their religion is concerned, they need a missionary as much as any tribe in Central Africa.

There is among the Charleston negroes, as elsewhere, a kind of religious aristocracy. The elite of colored society go to St. Mark's Episcopal Church,* the well-to-do middle class to the Centenary Methodist Church.† Here, as in Georgia and Alabama, there exists many congregations of "shouters." I was present at one of their services. The women crowded about the altar, keeping up a constant half-step dance to a really beautiful song, of which I only remember one line:

"Let us walk in the light of God."

The sermon was nearly an hour long, and consisted only of these words, "David, the son of Jesse; shout, brudders, shout!" Evidently this was a mere word of command or encouragement, the real worship consisting in the dance, the singing, and the shouting. I cannot say that as a service it commended itself to my spiritual nature, but in some inscrutable way it really did seem to comfort and satisfy the poor creatures who participated in it.

The Baptists are the strong body among the Southern negroes. The Roman Catholics cannot gain any permanent hold upon them, mainly, I believe, because they dearly love to have a voice in the church services themselves. They have intensely religious natures, but they are actively, not passively, religious; and they like to do their own singing and praying—yes, and their own preaching likewise.

* St. Mark's Church was organized as an independent parish in 1865 by a group of prominent black Episcopalians who were without a place to worship after the white Episcopalian churches were evacuated because of the city's occupation by Union Forces. A permanent church building, constructed at the corner of Warren and Thomas streets, was consecrated in 1878.
† Centenary Methodist Episcopal Church was formed after the Civil War with the withdrawal of black members from Trinity United Methodist Church. In 1866, the congregation purchased its building at 60 Wentworth Street.

Judge Heyward's Mansion, Church Street, where President Washington
was Entertained in 1791. View Of House As It Looked in 1883.
Thomas Heyward, Jr. House, 87 Church Street, Charleston, Charleston
County, S.C. By George Barnard (1819–1902), photographer.
Photocopy of photograph. Library of Congress.

LADY DUFFUS HARDY (1883)

"A Ghost of Dead Days"

Lady Duffus Hardy, "A Ghost of Dead Days" from *Down South* (London: Chapman and Hall), 1883.

Lady Duffus Hardy (née Mary Anne MacDowell) (1824–1891), born in London, was one of the most popular British novelists and travel writers of her day. Her father died five months before she was born and she was educated at home by her mother. In 1850 she became the wife of Sir Thomas Duffus Hardy (1804–1878), archivist and antiquary, who served as deputy keeper (chief executive officer) of the Public Record Office at the Tower of London and at Rolls House. Lady Hardy became one of the most famous London hostesses of her age.

However, before she was thirty years old, under the pseudonym Addlestone Hill, she published her first novel, *Savile House* (1853), followed by her second, *The Artist's Family* (1857). Her first significant novel was *Paul Wynter's Sacrifice* (1869), and her novel, *Daisy Nicholl* (1870) achieved great success in America. She published thirteen additional books, innumerable short stories, and articles for magazines and journals.

In 1880 and 1881, Lady Hardy traveled throughout the United States. In 1882 she returned to visit the chief southern states. Her tours prompted two travel books, *Through Cities and Prairie Lands: Sketches of an American Tour* (1881) and *Down South* (1883). In the South on her second tour, she traveled from Virginia to Charleston with her daughter, Iza Duffus Hardy (1850–1922), a romance novelist and travel writer, who chronicled this same visit in *Between Two Oceans* (1884).

The following account begins as the Lady Hardy travels toward Charleston by train. According to Iza, after passing through miles of swampland and the train neared Charleston little black boys came on board the train selling wildflowers—which she thought a very nice touch.

SOURCES

Black, Helen C. *Notable Women Authors of the Day*. London: Maclaren and Co., 1906.

Hardy, Iza Duffus. *Between Two Oceans, Or, Sketches of American Travel*. London: Hurst and Blackett, 1884.

Lee, Elizabeth, "Mary Anne Hardy." In *Dictionary of National Biography,* 1901 Supplement, ed. Sir Sidney Lee. London: Smith, Elder, & Company, 1901.

"A Ghost of Dead Days"

After much loitering and a keen enjoyment of the wilder beauties of Virginia we start on our way to Charleston, one of the oldest historic cities in America.

Our way lies through wide stretches of uncultivated lands, dotted here and there by negro huts with black babies and pigs tumbling together in the mire. In the course of a few hours we emerge from these uninteresting wilds, and are running through the great swamps which extend for miles along either side of our iron road, and are strictly impassable for either man or beast, though it is said that hundreds of poor human creatures in the old days chafed and fretted and grew discontented with their condition of life, and in their foolish endeavour to escape from it were lost in these wilds. Who knows what cries to God for help and mercy have gone up from the inner gloom of these dismal swamps?

The idea of a swamp had always presented itself to our mind's eye as a vast expanse of shiny, slushy soil, half mud, half water, with here and there a rank undergrowth of bushes and stiff grass, and briers, through which it must be a melancholy task to travel—but it is not so. In travelling through these swampy regions the prospect is neither a dull nor an uninteresting one; whole forests of grand old trees rise up luxuriantly, and in such impenetrable masses that scarce a ray of sunshine comes glinting through.

For hours, nay, for the whole day long we speed through this world of green, now and again the great trees turning their leafy arms into a perfect arch above our heads, as we go thundering on.

Some of our fellow travellers go to sleep, others yawn over a book which they have not energy enough to read, some get out the cards and play poker or écarté, according as the spirit of gambling moves them; we hear murmured complaints, "There is nothing to see," and "What a horribly monotonous journey."

But to us it is not monotonous; there is life and beauty in the ever-changing lights and shadows of the forest, sometimes most Rembrandt-like in their depth and dim obscurity; in the dainty colouring of the leaves, and the many strange formations of these ancient kings of the forest, standing in deep rank and file, sentinels and guardians of the silent land, their green heads lifted to the skies, their gnarled and knotted feet firmly planted on the earth below.

We are lost in contemplation, with our thoughts wandering through the soft luxuriant beauty of this forest land, when we slowly emerge from its density into the open country. The landscape changes, widens—Charleston is in sight! In a few minutes the cling-clanging of the engine bell tells us we are nearing the station—another moment, and we are there.

It is evening now, the lamps are lighted, and but a few scattered groups are making their way homeward through the quiet streets, for they keep early hours in Charleston, and by ten o'clock all decent folk are at home in their beds.

The gloomy grandeur of the "Charleston House"—and it is really a handsome stone building—attracts us not; we stop at the "Pavilion," a pretty homelike hotel with a verandahed front, and balcony filled with evergreens and flowers, on the opposite corner of Meeting Street. Our room has the usual regulation furniture, without any pretensions to luxury—clean, comfortable beds, chilly-looking marble-topped tables, and the inevitable rocking chairs, without which the humblest home would be incomplete. We go to bed and sleep soundly after our twenty-four hours' run.

Within all was bright and pleasant enough, but without the prospect was anything but cheering. Our windows opened upon a dingy courtyard, surrounded on three sides by dilapidated buildings two stories high; the rickety doors hung loosely on their rusty hinges, the windows were broken or patched with paper or old rags, and the Venetian blinds swung outside in a miserably crippled condition—all awry and crooked, every lath splintered or broken, the paint was worn off in rain-stained patches everywhere, and the woodwork was worm-eaten and rotten. The place had altogether a miserable appearance, as though the ghost of the old dead days was haunting and brooding over it in the poverty of the present. It seemed to be deserted too, for as we looked out upon it in the light of the early morning, we heard no sound, nor saw a human creature anywhere.

We learned afterwards that these had been the original slave quarters, and are still occupied by the same inhabitants—the freedmen of today, the slaves of yesterday, in many cases still serving their old masters in the old way. The servants of the hotel, waiters, chambermaids, etc., are all coloured, or rather coal-black; for as we go farther South the mixed breeds are more rarely to be met with; it is only here and there we come across the mulatto or others of mixed blood, which is rather a surprise to us, for we expected the half breeds greatly to outnumber the original race.

In Charleston two thirds of the population are black, and almost without exception in all Southern cities they largely preponderate over the whites, whose superiority they tacitly acknowledge, and work under their direction with amiable contentment. Their inherent respect for the white race is exemplified in many ways, especially in the small matters of everyday life.

The master mechanics, builders, carpenters, black-smiths, etc., are generally white, while the journeymen and labourers are coloured; it is the same with the shopkeepers and small traders, their employee's being of the opposite race.

The great drawback in the labour market throughout the Southern States is the uncertainty of the labour supply. The blacks as a rule are excellent mechanics, but they will not work well unless under strict supervision, and they will only work while necessity demands they should. They have no sense of the responsibility which rests upon their employer, and cannot see that their idle self-indulgence must result in his ruin and ultimately in their own. So soon as they have earned a few dollars they enjoy a spell of idleness till they have eaten them up, and then go to work for more; but this peculiarity is not confined to the dark race. They are a good-natured and simple people; today is all; they apply the scriptural text literally, and "take no thought of to-morrow." Gay, thoughtless, fond of pleasure and every kind of self-indulgence, and having led for generations past a life of dependence on the will and direction of others, they can exercise no discretion of their own. Generations must pass before they can learn the lesson of self-government, and be led to feel that their own prosperity must be the outcome of their co-operation with the prosperity of others. I speak of the general character of the people; of course there are exceptions to this rule, and many of them. Education is doing its work slowly but surely; there are schools everywhere, and consequently the coloured population of today is a great advance on the enslaved race of twenty years ago.

We spend our first day in Charleston in a rambling promenade through the city. It is a bright sunny day, with a cool fresh breeze blowing, not at all the sort of weather we ought to have considering the season; instead of the hot sun blazing and burning in vindication of its Southern character, compelling us to creep along every inch of shade, and melting us even then, it simply looks down upon us with a kind, genial eye, occasionally winking and playing bo-peep with the woolly white clouds which come sailing across the azure sky, and the balmy breath of the wind is sufficiently cool to render our wraps not only comfortable but absolutely necessary.

Before we have gone many steps on our way we come upon a pleasant party of some half dozen negroes, sitting on a fence, each one whittling a stick and chewing tobacco in solemn silence—basking in the sunshine in supreme idleness.

On returning some hours later, we find them inexactly the same place, whittling the same stick and chewing the same quid; they do not seem to have stirred an inch. In odd nooks and corners, entangled in the ragged edges of the city, we come upon similar groups.

The aspect Charleston presents at the first glance to the stranger's eye is impressive in the extreme apart from the historical and romantic interest which clings to the place, it has a character peculiarly its own, and bears slight resemblance to any other city we have seen. It seems to have stood still during the last century, and is strictly conservative in its appearance and in its ways.

Quaintly tangled streets and alleys cling to the main thoroughfares, running up and down, in and out, in a sort of thread-my-grandmother's-needle fashion; making a loop here, tying themselves into knots there, and resolving themselves into a perfect puzzle which the pedestrian has hard matter to piece together with his weary feet.

The houses in these out-of-the-way parts of the town are old-fashioned, odd-looking places, some so crippled in their lower limbs as to need the support of strong oaken beams, or patches of bricks and mortar; some are rickety in their upper stories, and lean affectionately on one side so as to support themselves on the strength of their neighbours. Everything seems pining for a fresh coat of paint; but they do their best to conceal their need of it, covering themselves with creeping plants or tawdry hangings, hiding their discolorations and bruises with gorgeous hued flowers, and clasping their green mantle round them as we may have seen an aristocratic beggar draw his robe across his breast to hide his rags and tatters. Occasionally, in some obscure corner of the city, we come upon a rambling old mansion of quaint, picturesque architecture, once the home of refinement and wealth, where the great ones of the country lived in a state of ease, luxury, and almost feudal splendour. It is occupied now by hosts of coloured folk; swarms of black babies crowd the verandahs or climb and tumble about the steps and passages, while the dilapidated balconies are filled with lines of clothes to dry; the negro smokes his pipe beneath the eaves, and the women folk, with their heads turbanned in gay-coloured handkerchiefs, laugh and chatter from the windows and lounge in the doorways. How long ago is it since the clank of the cavaliers' spurs rang upon the crumbling pavement, and sweet ladies with their pretty patched faces laughed from the verandahs, while merry voices and music and hospitality echoed from the now dingy, time-dishonoured halls, and stately dames in the decorous dress and manners of the old days walked to and fro, adding by their gracious presence to the attraction of the festive scene? But these good old days are over; no imperious dames, in stiff brocades and jewelled slippers, pace the wide corridors, or dance the graceful minuet upon the floor; there is no sound of flute and tabor now, but the many sounding notes of labour, the tramp of busy hives of working men and women, and the plaintive voices of the negroes singing is heard instead of it, and who shall say which makes the better music?

We may catch a glimpse of life as it was in this Charleston of old times from a writer in 1763,* who says:

> The inhabitants of this Carolina province are generally of a good stature and well made, with lively and agreeable countenances. The personal qualities of the ladies are much to their credit and advantage; they are genteel and slender, they have fair complexions—without the aid of art— and regular, refined features, their manners are easy and natural, their eyes sparkling and enchantingly sweet. They are fond of dancing; many sing well, and play upon the harpsichord and guitar with great skill.
>
> In summer riding on horseback or in carriages—which few are without —is greatly practiced. In the autumn, winter, and spring, there is variety and plenty of game for the gun or dogs; and the gentlemen are by no means backward in the chase. During the season, once in two weeks, there is a dancing assembly in Charleston, where there is always a brilliant appearance of lovely and well dressed women: we have likewise a genteel playhouse, where a very tolerable set of actors, called "The American Company of Comedians," exhibit. Concerts of instrumental music are frequently performed by gentlemen. Madeira wine and punch are the common drinks of the inhabitants, but few gentlemen are without claret, port, Lisbon, and other wines of Spanish, French, or Portugal vintages. The ladies are very temperate, and only drink water, which in Charleston is very unwholesome. There are about 1,100 houses in the town, some of wood, some of brick; many of them have a genteel appearance, though generally encumbered with balconies or piazzas, and are all most luxuriously furnished. The apartments are arranged for coolness, which is very necessary.

Charleston, as I have said before, is strictly conservative in its principles, and in many respects is much the same today as it was then. In spite of all its reverses— it still retains many of its old characteristics; its features are the same, though cruelly scarred with the names and sword of war. We pass on our way through Meeting Street, one of the chief thorough-fares of the city; it is a long, straight, not overwide, shady street, with beautiful trees on either side, and has a look of almost cloistered quiet about it.

There are several handsome churches embosomed in bowers of green, and the ruins of an ancient cathedral, which was burned by accident more than twenty

---

* Milligan, "A Description of the Province," 516.

years ago; they point this out as proudly, and cherish it as fondly, as though it were a legitimate ruin, a wreck that old time had left upon their shores.

The long stretch of houses on either side are not of any specially varied or picturesque style of architecture; they are three stories high, and have a rather curious appearance, as they turn their backs upon the streets, or rather stand sideways like pews in a church, their fronts facing seaward, to catch the cool sea breeze which blows down from the battery above. The three-storied piazzas running round every house, the green Venetians wholly or partly closed, not a soul in sight, either from within or without, give an appearance of almost oriental seclusion to the place; one half expects to see some dark, laughing beauty peeping out from among the flowers. The dear old city is full of romance and beauty everywhere, and as we pass through the silent street—silent, yet speaking with an eloquence that surpasses speech—the ghost of the dead days seems marching with muffled feet beside us, and the very stones seem to have a story to tell. We feel as though we have fallen upon an enchanted land, where time is standing still, and the years have grown grey with watching. Here and there we come upon a large empty mansion, one of the grand dwellings of old colonial days, whence the tenants have been driven by adverse circumstances; it stands staring down upon the street with blank, glassy eyes, perhaps with a rent in its side, and its face bruised and battered, its discoloured, painted skin peeling off, and slowly rotting. People have neither time nor money to rehabilitate these ancient mansions; they must needs be deserted by their owners, who have gone to seek their fortunes in the eastern cities, while the old homes are left to decay.

From this pretty shady street we come out upon the Battery, and stand for a moment to look round upon the peaceful scene, and enjoy the balmy breeze which sweeps straight from the near Gulf Stream. This is a delightful promenade and pleasure ground, where the good Charlestonians from time immemorial have come for their evening stroll, or to sit under the leafy shade of the scrub-oaks, gossiping with their neighbours. The Battery grounds front the land-locked bay—a sheet of crystal water about three miles wide—around which, and on the opposite side, lies a perfect garland of softly-swelling green islands, which stretch far away out of our sight. On each side, running like arms from the bay, are the Ashley and Cooper rivers, holding the town in their watery embrace. Around three sides of the Battery there runs an elevated promenade, raised about two feet from the grounds, which are beautifully laid out in pretty, white shell walks, grassy turf, and gorgeous flower beds, while groups of fine old forest trees, that have heard the whispering of many centuries, spread their leafy branches far and wide. Turning their backs upon the town and facing this lovely land-and-water scene, stands a variegated collection of fine old-fashioned houses of quaint architecture. Some are landmarks of the old colonial days; each one differs in form and colour from the other, but all are fanciful structures with elaborate ornamentation; some are circular, some flat fronted, some curving in a fantastic fashion, and seeming to look round the corner on their friends and neighbours, to assure them they are not proud though they have turned their backs upon them; some have wide balconies of stone, some light verandahs with green Venetian blinds or graceful ironwork clinging to their front; but everywhere creeping plants and brilliant flowers are growing.

The view on all sides is most picturesque and lovely, and the fragrant air is a delight to the senses. Here is the real aristocratic part of the city, and here to this day, in spite of the many freaks of fortune, the descendants of the old Huguenot and Cavalier families inhabit the homes of their ancestors, whose familiar names still echo on the ears of the town. With lagging footsteps we take our way homeward through the city, losing ourselves and finding ourselves more than once.

Altogether we come to the conclusion that Charleston is a sober suited, gentlemanly city strongly impregnated with the savour of old days; somewhat worn and grey, but thoroughly dignified and pleasant, full of old-world prejudices and decorum that no flighty tourist would care to outrage.

As we enter our chamber after our long ramble we hear the sounds of merry voices, and the passing of people to and fro in the courtyard; then suddenly amid the shouting and the laughter there rises a choir of voices, a hush falls everywhere—they are singing "The sweet by and by." We approach the window and look out. A group of coal-black negroes are sitting round one table piling up rich ripe strawberries for our dessert; close by is another party shelling peas. It is these groups who are singing. Their plaintive melancholy voices affect us solemnly; but even as the last notes are trembling on their lips they begin to play tricks on one another, turning somersaults in the air, grinning, and chattering.

A closer acquaintance with Charleston, its surroundings, and its people, deepens our first impression. A dignified gravity seems to be set like a seal upon their lives, whence all light frivolous things have been cast out, and replaced by high hopes and noble aspirations, born of a past sorrow. There is a look of preoccupation on their faces, as though their thoughts and desires have outstripped their powers of action, and they are pushing the world's work forward that they may come up with them and realize the state of their holy ambitions. They dress somberly, in dark neutral tints, with a quiet elegance and simplicity. They are as the sober setting to a brilliant picture, where the coloured folks supply the flaunting figures and gaudy colouring—the blacker they are the more gorgeous are their personal adornments.

The many handsome churches and public buildings add largely to the attractions of Charleston, and are, to a certain extent, a reflex of the minds of the people. As the descendants of old families concentrate their energies and their pride on their ancestral home, so the good Charlestonians from generation to generation have devoted theirs to the glorification of their beloved city; and in erecting new buildings, public companies as well as private individuals, instead of building according to their own special taste, have had some regard to that of their neighbours; every stone has been laid thoughtfully one upon the other, not only with regard to its own features, but as a part of a whole, and in perfect harmony with the general aspect of the city. One building never mars the effect of the other; the eye is hurt by no incongruity of architecture, no false colouring, but everywhere is a pleasant blending of symmetrical forms and delicate tints. The effect upon the eye is the same as that of a perfect melody upon the ear—no slurred notes, no flat where a sharp should be, nothing jarring, no false rhythm anywhere.

The first question you are asked on entering a southern city is: "Have you been to the cemetery?"

This is one of the chief places of interest which everybody is anxious to point out; for next to the city of the living they cherish the city of their dead. It is here they come to while away their leisure hours, and bring the fresh flowers of every season to lay above the dust of their departed—for you seldom see an undecorated grave.

The Magnolia Cemetery is about three miles from the city; we pass first through a grand avenue to the German burial-ground,* which is beautifully kept, with shining white walks winding among blooming flower beds and rare shrubberies, shaded by grand old oaks, clothed in their mantles of soft grey moss. Carved upon the headstones the solemn words "Her ruhet in Gott" meet the eye at every turn. Passing through this grave-garden, we soon come to the main entrance to Magnolia Cemetery; within the massive gates a colossal bell is suspended from a lofty scaffolding, which tolls slowly as the funeral approaches; a pretty Gothic chapel, where the services are held, stands to the left. Passing under the archway we come upon a few score of white wooden headstones, which stand like special guardians at the gates of death; beneath these lie the Federal dead. Farther on lies the wide Confederate burial-ground; here, side by side, and rank on rank, by hundreds—nay, by thousands—lie the soldiers of the lost cause sleeping their last sleep, happily unconscious of the ruin that fell on the land

---

*Bethany Cemetery (c.1856), adjacent to Magnolia Cemetery, is owned and maintained by St. Matthew's Lutheran Church.

they loved before yet the grass grew over their graves. Few, very few, have an inscription to mark who rests beneath, but soft green hillocks swell in low waves
on all sides of us; these hide the unknown dead, and over them are daisies and
sweet wild flowers growing. Beyond these again lie the more fortunate, who have
died at home, surrounded by friends and kindred, and fitly mourned in monuments of marble; there are symbolical urns and broken columns, groups of
mourning friends in every possible or impossible attitude of depression; there
is a cherub blowing a trumpet as though striving to wake up the heavenly host
with the news "another recruit is coming." He is blowing so hard he seems to
have blown himself out of his draperies, which are fluttering in the wind behind
him, and weeping angels are drying their eyes with stony pocket-handkerchiefs,
as though bemoaning that all the virtues of all the world lay perishing beneath
them—at least, so says the inscription written there.

Passing through this silent world, we find ourselves in a wide white street
which runs through the Catholic cemetery* from east to west, in the centre
and at the highest point of which stands a gigantic black cross. Cedar and ash
and willow trees are growing in picturesque masses; green shrubberies refresh
the sight, and rich red and cream roses are blooming everywhere. The grave
gardens here are laid out in various shapes and sizes—square, circular, triangular, &c.—like a geometrical puzzle spread over the ground. The simplest grave
has a cross above it, sometimes of wood, of iron, or of stone; the symbol of
Christianity, as though growing out from the hearts of the sleepers, is lifted on
all sides.

The sun is shining, the sweet air blowing, and a look of serene calm and
most perfect peace is smiling everywhere. How the vexed and troubled folk, who
wander here to get away from the busy, noisy world, must long to creep down
under the roses and hide from this world's noisy strife, and lie beside the sleeper
under the sod, with hands crossed, eyes closed, at rest for ever more. Here is a
grave covered with "forget-me-nots," and a cry—a hard, cold cry—written in
stone, craving to be "kept green in men's memories." Tall costly shafts of gran-
ite, wreathed with everlasting flowers, prick the skies, and elaborate architectural designs are erected here and there; one has brass cannon at the gates and
sabres crossed upon the threshold, pointing the way the sleeper took to his death.
After wandering about for some time we sit down to rest under a cedar tree,
luxuriating in the sweet scent and bright colour of the waving flower-beds, quite
alone, as we thought, till a voice rather suggestive of "beer and skittles" came

---

* St. Lawrence Cemetery (c.1854), the third Catholic cemetery established in Charleston.

out of the silence: "Nice weather, marm; things is sort o' springin' up every-wheres, and some on 'em is full blowed, ain't they?"

I look up; the owner of the voice has evidently just sidled round from the other side of the tree. He is an elderly man, with a ragged beard and patched clothing—the forlorn and decaying remnants of military glory; his face has a sodden, dissipated look, and his eyes a weak gin-and-watery appearance, any-thing but pre-possessing. He was not exactly a nice kind of human ghoul to meet in such a solitary spot. I answered with an assenting smile or some kind of commonplace cheap civility, which evidently satisfied him, for he edged a little nearer, adding philosophically—

"Yes, it takes a good deal o' sunshine to set things a startin' out; sometimes I think I'd as lief be lyin' down there in the dark as starvin' up here in the sunshine—leastways the sun don't always shine, not on me. I've been a soldier, marm," he added with a slightly Irish accent, "and done my duty on many a gory field, and—oh! a—ah!"

He groaned a low guttural sort of groan—his feelings were evidently too much for him; he took out a red cotton handkerchief, shook it out for one mo-ment as though unfurling a battle flag, then buried his face in it and boo-hoo'd behind it till his broad shoulders shook with emotion. I felt embarrassed. I was not sure I should not have that six feet of suffering manhood in another moment grovelling at my feet; but he recovered his mental equilibrium, replaced his hand-kerchief, shook his hat well forward on his head, and said somewhat irrelevantly but with a mournful intonation—

"'Tain't no use trying to cross yer fate. I've tried it, and it don't answer; but one thing always puts me in mind of another; n' flowers, n' trees, n' grass, n' sich-like strikes me jist now as oncommon like human natur, for the sun o' char-ity must shine on the human heart, before it will open up and give out the per-fume from its inhuman pockets as it oughter—" There was a momentary and suspicious silence on my part; then my ragged and somewhat poetic philosopher added insinuatingly, "Yer don't happen to hev a stray quarter hanging about yer clo'es anywheres? 'cause a sight of it would do me a deal o good."

This ancient sinner wheedled the quarter out of my "clo'es."

We saunter on, and looking from the eastern point of Magnolia we have a magnificent panorama of the city and the clustering vessels afloat in the har-bour, while stern and grim Fort Sumter looms in the distance; the white sails flutter to and fro, and dainty vessels curtsey to their own shadows reflected on the placid water; not a ripple stirs its surface, and the sun pours down a flood of silver on this sea of glass, lighting up and brightening the prospect all around, the purple pines and low-lying forts on the surrounding islands forming a charming background to the panoramic scene.

Charleston is reported by its inhabitants (and surely they ought to know) to be a perfectly healthy city, free from epidemics of any kind; if you dared to doubt it, all good Charlestonians would have you stoned to death on the spot. It certainly may be true within the limits of the city, but of its surroundings the healthfulness is more than doubtful. It lies low, and is surrounded by marshy lands, which at certain seasons of the year are covered with water—the overflow of the two rivers, which compass it on either side.

On returning through the suburbs from our visit to the cemetery, we come upon a very handsome house in a solitary situation, surrounded by a somewhat neglected garden and wide-spreading meadows. Leading to the entrance is an avenue of fine old English oaks, draped with grey Spanish moss. Although secluded, it has the spires and steeples and other prominent features of Charleston city in full view. It is in a state of perfect preservation, with no signs of dilapidation anywhere—it is simply deserted utterly both by man and beast. The dog kennels are empty, not a bird sings from the boughs, not even the domestic cat crouches upon the tiles or creeps along the weedy garden paths; even the stone lions which guard the entrance look in a damp depressed condition, as though they too would be glad to get away if they only could!

On inquiring the cause of this desertion, I am answered:

"Oh, it belongs to a very fine family—they cleared out some weeks ago. They always leave in March and come back in October."

Presently we are overtaken by waggon loads of men, both black and white— all singing merry rollicking songs, and driving at a rapid pace towards the city. We draw our modest vehicle to one side as they rattle and clatter past us. We then learn that they are the factory phosphate hands, driving back to their homes in the city. Although the phosphate works are only an hour's distance from Charleston they are totally deserted every evening; not a single living creature remains upon the premises, as it is injurious to breathe the poisonous air after the sun has set, for then the noxious vapours rise and fill the air with disease and death. Over the extensive works, where the sound of pickaxe and shovel and whirring wheels and human voices are echoing all the day, a silence falls, and the malarial fiend wanders through its confined space seeking, but seeking in vain, for some human prey to torment and kill with its subtle kiss.

This lurking evil lies only in the one direction of the city; on the other side and extending round the harbour are some delightful summer resorts, Mount Pleasant and Sullivan Island being among the most prominent, both being easily reached by a pleasant river trip. The Ferry Company's boats make the journey in about an hour, and make it many times in the day; but perhaps the loveliest of all Charleston's surroundings is Summerville, which is reached by the South Carolina railway. It is situated in the heart of the pine woods, on a ridge which extends from the Ashley to the Cooper river; the climate is health-giving and invigorating, and in summer, though the days are warm, there is always a deliciously cool breeze in the evening, and there are no mosquitoes to make night horrible to the sleeper; it is serene and peaceful as a corner of the original paradise.

On our way to Fort Sumter we have to pass through the market, which is quite unique of its kind. It is a remarkably fine building in the form of a temple; the front faces Meeting Street, the most picturesque of all Charleston thoroughfares. Passing through a handsome lofty archway with a carved stone front and iron gates—now open, as the marketing operations are in full swing—we find ourselves in a long narrow corridor with groined roof and wide windows and doors on either side, where gawky, ill-looking buzzards are gathered, flapping their wings and feeding upon refuse.

As we walk up this narrow aisle piles of rich luscious fruit rise to the right and the left of us; there are hills of pine-apples, and yellow and red bananas, festoons of purple grapes, and mountains of strawberries, bushels of black and white currants, pumpkins, and that arch impostor, the great green water-melon, all artistically arranged, and forming a perfect mosaic of nature's own colouring —only the rough red face of the honest British gooseberry is nowhere to be seen.

Next comes the vegetable department, where everything green looks crisp and fresh, with the diamond dew-drops still decorating the folded leaves, and everything coloured seems painted in Nature's brightest hues. Dainty young carrots, and tiny turnips, looking like baby snowballs, are nestling among the sedate old cabbages, whose great white hearts seem enlarged almost to bursting; and the oyster and eggplant, unknown in European markets, are hiding among the common but useful rough-coated potato; and the delicate asparagus, with its purple tips and straight white stems, bound up in big bundles, the large and well-proportioned rallying round and covering up the crippled weaklings of their kind. The scarlet runners and fine marrowfat peas seem bursting out of their skins with joy at being gathered at last; from the very moment when they first unfolded their pink and purple buds they have been forced to creep up and cling to those tormenting sticks, twisting and twining and working so hard, night and day, till they were tired of living, and would really have gone soon to seed, and once more hidden themselves in their native earth. Now they are at rest—they don't know they are going to be boiled in an hour. Here and there we come upon a silly-looking turtle lying on its back, its flabby nippers wriggling feebly as though trying to turn over and crawl back to its native element.

Next we arrive at the fish and poultry division. There are golden pats of butter dressed in white frills and ornamented with violets, which, it is said, impart to it a delicious fragrance and flavour; and eggs from all the feathery tribe, white and brown, speckled and light blue. Here plump young chickens, who were unfortunate enough to be born in the early spring, are strung up beside their tough old grandfathers; and prairie hens, and other wild birds from desolate regions, hang with stretched necks and drooping wings above the slabs of white marble, where fish from all waters are spread in tempting array. The shining red mullet, and the fat ugly sheep's-head, and even the humble red horse, lie side by side with the aristocratic salmon; and the poor little baby porker, slaughtered in its infancy, before it had even had time to wear a ring through its nose or grout in the gutter, is lying close by, stiff and stark, with a lemon in its mouth.

Framed, like a picture, by the archway at the opposite end of this long aisle, lie the sparkling waters of the bay, with the swelling green hills beyond, and the little wheezy vessel which is to take us to Fort Sumter bobbing up and down by the pier. The little steamer, with the stars and stripes fluttering from the mast-head, is puffing and blowing and making a great fuss,—plunging head foremost, and shrieking like an angry virago for us to make haste, as she is in a hurry to get away.

With the fresh breeze blowing in our faces, and the sun shining in our eyes, as only a Southern sun can shine, we step on board, and in another moment our brisk little convoy is dancing over the water like a joyous child released from school; it trembles and leaps like a living thing, and we almost fancy that its iron heart must be beating with a feeling of sentient enjoyment like our own.

All kinds and conditions of men are crowded round us—high and low, rich and poor; evidently we are all out for a holiday, and in the most perfect sang-froid fashion, and without the slightest ceremony, everybody talks to everybody else. A lady from the North sits beside me, and shading her complexion from the sun, softly drones into my ear her whole family history, from the birth of her first baby to the vaccination of her last.

With the exception of ourselves they were all Americans on board—men from the East, men from the West; some were for the first time making a tour through their own Southern States, but east and west, north and south, walked up and down the deck, side by side, fraternising in the most friendly fashion, chatting upon passing scenes, or talking quietly one with another, indulging in reminiscences of that long ago, when the links of brotherhood had been for a time broken. Close by was an old man with a stubbly grey beard and a mangy fur cap, that looked like a drowned kitten tied round his head; he had gathered a few hoary-headed comrades round him, and they were talking of old days, fighting their battles over again, setting up their guns, and drawing plans upon the deck. So, as the future narrows and closes round us, we are driven to the past for comfort. Flashes of sentiment and scraps of conversation were floating round us, and the very air seemed impregnated with a subtle something that was new and strange to us. While looking round upon this pleasant peaceful scene, the white sails dipping and coquetting with their own shadow in the water, the soft green hills and the grim old forts beyond, all bathed in peaceful sunshine, it is impossible but the mind will travel back to the day when the air was filled with lurid battle smoke, and the cannon, stationed all around the shore belched forth blazing fires, while a hundred hungry, angry tongues of flame leapt from their iron mouths. Just such a calm as this lay upon the city the day the first gun was fired, though the passions of men were brooding below like a strong and silent tide, which is soon to overflow and flood the nations.

We pass by "Sullivan Island," girdled by its beach of golden sand, with a beadwork of white foam embroidered in living light fringing the shore, and its pretty homes surrounded by lovely gardens and farmsteads, and tall church steeples, gleaming in the sunshine. We have but a distant view of Fort Moultrie, which is a striking feature on the low-lying land, but we have no time to pay it a visit, our hearts and our eyes too are anchored on Fort Sumter, and thither-ward our saucy vessel turns its head, a crazy plank is flung to the shore, and we land at last. Federals and confederates, foreigners and strangers, saunter on together.

There is little of the old fort standing; it is a ruin now—a grim picturesque rugged ruin, almost levelled to a mound of rock and sand; desolation, with its empty socketless eyes, stares from the narrow loopholes, where twenty years ago there flashed the fiery orbs of war. We descended, or rather scrambled, down a flight of broken steps—it seemed we were going into the bowels of the earth—peeped into what looked like dark, narrow graves, where the men used to lie, smothered and half stifled, while they worked their guns, and living through this death in life for four long years, they came out of their darkness to the light of the sun to find their martyrdom had been in vain—their cause was lost. But the gates are closed upon all these things.

President and Mrs. Roosevelt in Charleston.
George Grantham Bain Collection. Library of Congress.

OWEN WISTER (1901 AND 1902)

"Enchanted"

Owen Wister, "Enchanted" from *Roosevelt, the Story of a Friendship*
(New York: Macmillan Company, 1930), 101–4. Reprint rights have been
granted from Walter H. Stokes and Alice Stokes, literary executors, Owen
Wister Estate.

Owen Wister (1860–1938) was born in Philadelphia. However, his great-great-grandfather, Pierce Butler (1744–1822), one of the founding fathers of the country, had been a South Carolina soldier, planter, and statesman who married into the Middleton family of Charleston. Pierce Butler's son, Pierce Mease Butler (1806–1867), married British-born Fanny Kemble, one of the most famous actresses of the nineteenth century. Kemble chronicled her own impressions of Charleston in her antislavery journal, *Journal of a Residence on a Georgian Plantation in 1838–1839* (1863).

Wister's father was a physician and his mother wrote for magazines. An only child, he attended boarding schools in New England and Switzerland before he entered Harvard in 1878, where he was a classmate of Theodore Roosevelt (1858–1919). At Harvard, Wister discovered a talent for musical composition and dramatic writing, and afterward spent a year studying music in Paris. When his father pressured him to pursue a more practical career, in 1883 he took a junior position in a Philadelphia law firm and planned to enter Harvard Law School, but he suffered a breakdown. He was sent out west to recover. Fascinated with Wyoming and the West, he began to write stories and sketches of western life. He made extended trips to the West ten times between 1885 and 1895 to escape "the boredom of law studies" after he entered Harvard Law. In 1895, he published his first volume of short stories, *Red Men and White*, followed by *Lin McLain* (1897) and *The Jimmyjohn Boss and Other Stories* (1900).

In 1898, Wister married a cousin, Mary "Molly" Channing (1870–1898). The couple came to Charleston on their honeymoon and they were "enchanted" with the city. Wister wrote his mother, "Of all the American towns I've ever come into as a stranger, it's incomparably the most charming." In 1901, Molly was asked to serve as the Commissioner from Pennsylvania for the Women's Department at the South Carolina Interstate and West Indian Exposition, and they returned for an extended visit. At the time, Wister was integrating his western short stories with new material for his novel, *The Virginian*. It was also during this stay that his old friend, President Roosevelt, traveled to Charleston on a three-day official visit to the Exposition, which Wister reveals in *Roosevelt, the Story of a Friendship*.

Soon after his Charleston visit, Wister became the official originator of the cowboy genre when he published the enormously popular *The Virginian: A Horseman of the Plains* (1902). He dedicated the book to Roosevelt. *The Virginian* went through forty printings from April 1902 to October 1911. In 1904, there was a stage version performed in New York, and despite lukewarm reviews, *The Virginian* had a four-month run on Broadway and toured successfully throughout the country for a decade. Cecil B. DeMille began his career as a film director by producing the first film version in 1914. Other film versions appeared in 1923, 1929 (starring Gary Cooper as the Virginian), and 1946. The novel later served as the basis for the NBC television series, *The Virginian*, which ran from September 19, 1962, to March 24, 1971. Paperback copies of the book still sell well today. Wister wrote other western stories after *The Virginian*. Then, as he turned his efforts to a novel about high-society manners in a fictional Charleston, he made a third visit to town to serve as tour guide to his friend, Henry James, who was writing his own chapter on Charleston for *The American Scene*. Wister soon published *Lady Baltimore* (1905), which became a best seller.

Following the success of *Lady Baltimore,* Wister remained in Philadelphia and lived as a celebrity man of letters. In 1906, he experienced another breakdown. After his recovery, he gravitated to politics and strongly supported Theodore Roosevelt's third party candidacy for the presidency in 1912. When Wister later ran as a reform candidate for the Philadelphia City Council and lost, he was encouraged by Roosevelt to write a novel set in Philadelphia. He began a novel with a narrator based on Henry James, and the characters on real Philadelphians. By 1913 he had written some 48,000 words when his wife, Molly, died in childbirth, and he was unable to finish the book. In 2001, the novel was published (incomplete) by James A. Butler in *Romney: And Other New Works about Philadelphia by Owen Wister.*

For the rest of his life, Wister remained profoundly involved in the social web of Philadelphia and for four decades was a member of the Philadelphia bar.

In 1930, he published *Roosevelt, the Story of a Friendship*, from which the following Charleston excerpt is taken.

SOURCES

Butler, James A. Introduction. *Romney: And Other New Works about Philadelphia by Owen Wister*. University Park, Pa.: Penn State Press, 2001.

———. "The Remarkable Wisters at Belfield." In *Local History Essays*. Book 2. Reprinted from *La Salle: A Quarterly La Salle University Magazine* (Spring 1994). http://digitalcommons.lasalle.edu/essays/2 .

Cobbs, John L. "Charleston: The Image of Aristocracy in Owen Wister's Lady Baltimore." *South Carolina Review* 9:1 (Fall 1976): 44–51.

Freeman, Castle, Jr. "Brief Life of a Western Mythmaker: 1860–1938." *Harvard Magazine* (July–August 2002): 42.

Hoover, Bob. "There's More to Author Than 'The Virginian.'" *Pittsburg Post-Gazette*, April 7, 2002.

Jalowitz, Alan. "Owen Wister." Accessed Oct. 18, 2015. http://pabook.libraries.psu .edu/palitmap/bios/WisterOwen.html.

Mason, Julian. "Owen Wister: Champion of Old Charleston." *Quarterly Journal of the Library of Congress* 29 (1972): 162–85.

"Mrs. Owen Wister Dies." *New York Times*, Aug. 25, 1913: 5, Col. 4.

"Wister Services Held." *New York Times*, July 25, 1938: 29.

"Enchanted"

We had found ourselves enchanted with Charleston, my wife and I, when we went there directly from our wedding in April, 1898. At that time we had prolonged our stay considerably. We had hoped for a chance to return there ever since, and now the chance came. Charleston was to hold an exhibition, and my wife was appointed to represent Pennsylvania in an official capacity appropriate to her. In the Autumn of 1901, I went to Charleston in search of a house for us and our three young children; and soon after the first of the New Year, we all arrived to spend the Winter and most of the Spring.

The town which had fired on Fort Sumter looked forward with warm enthusiasm to Roosevelt's coming there. It had invited him to come and speak at the Exposition, and he had accepted. Since the Civil War, no President had paid Charleston a visit. That this one was not a Democrat did not count much; he was the youngest President in our history—forty-three when his office began, only forty-four now, and this was interesting; more interesting still to these Southerners was his character. His whole career, his outright and downright ways, his picturesque unmistakableness in speech and in action, all this was greatly to their liking. They set out to do their very best for him. The various stages of his welcome were carefully planned by the Committee in charge of this—dinner at the Charleston Hotel, presentation of a sword to Major Jenkins, of the Rough Riders, by his former Lieutenant-Colonel,* visit to the Exposition and Ladies lunch there, visit to the Summerville, boat excursion to view harbor and Forts Sumter and Moultrie, and so forth: and every one was eager to be gracious and cordial to the heroic Lieutenant-Colonel, now President, and a gentleman in whose veins flowed Southern blood.[†]

Behind the ceremony of the sword, was the stunning praise which Roosevelt had written in his account of the Rough Riders about the courage of Major Jenkins. When it was known that the President had accepted the invitation to visit Charleston and speak at the Exposition, this led the South Carolina legislature to make an appropriation for a sword, which the President would be asked to present to the gallant officer who had served under him in the Spanish War.

---

* During the Spanish American War, Maj. Michah John Jenkins (1857–1912) from Yonges Island had served in Roosevelt's famous volunteer cavalry unit, the Rough Riders, and was promoted to major of the regiment. Roosevelt had famously distinguished himself by leading the Rough Riders on a charge—on foot—up San Juan Hill on the outskirts of Santiago, Cuba. The contingent suffered heavy casualties but those who survived returned to the United States as war heroes. In 1899, Roosevelt had published *The Rough Riders* to great acclaim.

[†] Like Wister, Theodore Roosevelt had southern connections. His mother, Martha Bulloch, was a native of Georgia. He frequently boasted that "half my blood is Southern," and got into trouble politically when he wrote in one of his books that the men of the Confederacy were better fighters than the soldiers of the North. When running for vice president in 1900, Roosevelt said that he was "proud of the courage of the men who wore the gray." However, in April 1906, soon after the publication of *Lady Baltimore*, Roosevelt sent a lengthy letter to Wister on the faults of Southerners in general and Charlestonians in particular. He wrote, in part: "The Southerners have developed traits of a very unhealthy kind. They are not as dishonest as, they do not repudiate their debts as frequently, as their predecessors did . . . but they do not send as valuable men into the national councils as the Northerners. They are not on the whole as efficient, and they exaggerate the common American tendency of using bombastic language; which is not made good by performance. Your particular heroes, the Charleston aristocrats, offer as melancholy an example as I know of people whose whole life for generations has been warped by their own wilful perversity. . . . They drank and dueled and made speeches, but they contributed very, very little toward anything of which we as Americans are now proud. . . . Reconstruction was a mistake as it was actually carried out, and there is very much to reprobate in what was done by Sumner and Seward and their followers. But the blame attaching to them is as nothing compared to the blame attaching to the Southerners for forty years preceding the war, and for the years immediately succeeding it. . . . As for the days of reconstruction, they brought their punishment on themselves, and are, in my judgment, entitled to not one particle of a sympathy." Pringle, "Theodore Roosevelt and the South,", 14–25.

The prevailing and spontaneous cordiality in Charleston had been anything but chilled by an affair that had happened in Washington during the Autumn, and that was still quite fresh in Charleston's memory. Senator Tillman, from South Carolina* had been invited to dine at the White House, and had accepted the invitation. Before the appointed day, Senator Tillman, in the Senate, fell upon his brother senator from South Carolina with both fists, and they had what is sometimes termed a little difference. It made a wide stir.[†] Thereupon a suggestion quietly reached Senator Tillman that he withdraw his acceptance to dine at the White House. He did not take this suggestion. In consequence the White House withdrew its invitation. This made a very wide stir indeed. A distinguished foreigner was involved in this, rather oddly, as shall presently appear. The Tillman incident had highly pleased Charleston. He was from the "up country," rustic, forcible, honest, anything but urbane, hostile by birth to the civilized Charlestonians, and he seldom had lost a chance to let them know it. But there was another aspect of the matter. Directly the President's projected visit to Charleston was known, threatening letters began to arrive. Threats never stopped him from anything that he intended to do, they merely made him intend to do it more—but those who were near him felt anxious. This anxiety was shared, I think, in Charleston, although I cannot recall that anybody there spoke a word of it to me; but the Committee of Arrangements was peculiarly strict in making known its decision that the President was to enter no private house whatever.

He came. He won their hearts by his good easy manner, his ready tongue, his vivacity; won them not politically, be it well understood; that most solid part of the Solid South would never vote for him, or for any Republican; he knew this; but personally he won their hearts—and lost them all in the twinkling of an eye.

---

* Benjamin Tillman (1847–1918) was known as "Pitchfork Ben," not only because of his agricultural advocacy but because he once threatened to impale President Grover Cleveland on a pitchfork. A Democrat from Edgefield, he was governor (1890–1894) and a senator from 1895 until his death. During Reconstruction, he led the Red Shirts during South Carolina's violent 1876 election. On the Senate floor, Tillman regularly ridiculed blacks and boasted of having helped kill them during the 1876 campaign.

† In a Senate speech, Tillman accused Senator John L. McLaurin (1860–1934) of corruption, whereupon McLaurin, an ex-Tillmanite, called him a liar. Tillman rushed across the Senate floor and punched McLaurin in the face. McLaurin reciprocated, giving Tillman a bloody nose. The Senate immediately went into closed session and held both men in contempt. They considered suspension, but Tillman argued that it was unfair to deprive South Carolina of her representation. In the end, both men were censured. Kantrowitz, *Ben Tillman and the Reconstruction of White Supremacy*, 168–69; Simkins, *Pitchfork Ben Tillman*, 257–59.

But not then. That came later. While he was there, he was *persona gratissima* to Charleston. This came to us from every side, and we were rather mixed in and up with a good part of it. In his speech he had one sentence, not of local or occasional application, but as permanent in the truth it expressed as any which lies at the foundation of sane government anywhere:

"You can not create prosperity," were his words (or words to this effect) "by law. Sustained thrift, industry, application, intelligence, are the only things that ever do, or ever will, create prosperity. *But you can very easily destroy prosperity by law.*"

That was an example of the sort of bromide which Roosevelt meant when he told me that he had to use bromides in his business: but he could put old truths home in his own vivid fashion which made whatever he said striking.

Some bad moments of anxiety came to those who knew about the threatening letters, while they waited at the Exposition grounds for the ceremony of presenting the sword, and watched the thick uncontrolled crowd pressing and encroaching:—some bad moments, and then a long breath of relief. Just as it looked as if the Committee had lost its grip on precautions, marines appeared, led by Captain Leonard,* cutting through the confusion, shoving the trespassers back, and order was restored and maintained. At the sight of Captain Leonard's one arm, Roosevelt's extraordinary memory flashed into action. During the troubles in China, Leonard had jumped into a river where a soldier—a brother officer, if I remember—was going under, and saved his life; but somehow got an infected arm, and lost it.† The President spoke a few words to him about that, beginning by hailing him by name; and Captain Leonard was a proud and happy man.

And now, back come Senator Tillman and the White House dinner again, together with the distinguished foreigner: they have as direct a bearing upon the sword, and upon the strict orders that the President was to enter no private house in Charleston.

Benjamin Ryan Tillman's relations with his brother Senator from South Carolina, John L. McLaurin, had been growing worse and worse for some time before the day when what he said caused McLaurin to retort that he was a liar.

---

* Capt. Henry Leonard of the US Marine Corps was in charge of troops guarding Roosevelt over his three-day visit.
† In 1900 at the Battle of Tientsin, the bloodiest battle of the Boxer Rebellion in Northern China, Leonard (who went on to become a successful Washington attorney) had saved his lieutenant, Smedley Darlington Butler. Butler, known as "The Fighting Quaker," became the most decorated Marine in US history. Maj. Gen. Butler was also assisting Roosevelt at the Charleston Exposition, courtesy of the US Marines.

This promptly produced the physical encounter between the Senators. Up in the visitor's gallery was Prince Henry, of Prussia, travelling *incognito,* as it is called in diplomacy, not a guest of the nation, a personal guest at the White House. He had come to represent his brother the Kaiser, whose new yacht, built in the United States, the Kaiser had asked Alice Roosevelt to christen. The dinner to which Tillman had been invited and uninvited was given in honor of Prince Henry, who had witnessed the brief fight in the Senate.

Now if Charleston had been pleased by that rebuke to the upcountry Senator, the up-country was so little pleased that it set out to spoil the plan of the sword. Tillman had a nephew of the same name, and the nephew was lieutenant-governor of South Carolina.* He gave out that there would be no sword and no presentation. Upon this, Mr. Gonzales, the editor of the *Columbia State* and compiler of certain volumes of negro folklore in the "gullah" dialect as admirable as anything of the sort I have met,† started a popular subscription through the columns of his paper, inviting everybody to contribute one cent. In this he was joined by other papers. It was successful. The sword was procured. Hugh S. Thompson, a former Governor of the State, and a former colleague with Roosevelt on the Civil Service Commission,‡ represented the legion of contributors. He presented the sword to Roosevelt, who then presented it with a few words to Major Jenkins, who replied while my mind wandered back to the White House dinner, and I reflected that now every vibration arising from that incident was finished. Long afterwards I discovered my mistake.§

---

* James Hammond Tillman (1869–1911), a newspaper reporter before he was a politician.
† Ambrose E. Gonzales (1857–1926) and his brother, Narciso Gener Gonzales (1858–1903), born on Edisto Island, were founders of *The State* newspaper, which supported a number of progressive causes. They were the sons of a Cuban revolutionary and Confederate officer, Ambrosio Gonzales, and Harriet Rutledge Elliott, a member of the lowcountry planter aristocracy. Ambrose published Gullah sketches in the newspaper and would later publish *The Black Border* (1922) and *With Aesop Along the Black Border* (1924).
‡ Hugh Smith Thompson (1836–1904), from Charleston, was governor from 1882 to 1886. He afterward served as assistant secretary of the Treasury under President Grover Cleveland, and in 1889 was appointed commissioner of the US Civil Service Commission by President Benjamin Harrison. He had retired from public service in 1892 and was comptroller of New York Life Insurance Company.
§ Wister refers to the fact that in 1903, James Hammond Tillman, still lieutenant-governor, shot Narciso Gonzales over a crusade Gonzales waged against him in *The State*, helping ensure Tillman's defeat in the 1902 governor's race. Gonzales died four days later. Tillman was acquitted ostensibly on a shaky self-defense theory. In reality, the jury (considered rigged and highly partisan) believed James Tillman was right in taking justice into his own hands.

At those Exposition grounds, when the procession was forming to march I forget where, a comical incident passed before my eyes. The director of the procession was a Mr. Hemphill, at that time editor of the Charleston *News and Courier.** He seemed very much aware of his responsibility, and read out his directions in a voice of perfect importance. He was telling us all what positions we should take, and he began (I think) with where the President of the United States was to stand. The President misunderstood him, apparently, and took a few obedient steps. "Not there," said Mr. Hemphill, peremptorily; "there." And he pointed.

"I will go wherever I ought," murmured Roosevelt with an inflection of meekness that wholly upset my gravity, and caused some heads to turn in surprise at me.

During these crowded Charleston hours, somewhere, I went back to our old disagreement about "Balaam and Pedro."† I told him that I was drawing near the end of *The Virginian,* working every day at it, sometimes nine hours; that the book was to be published in the Spring. Did he still insist that I ought to suppress those details which had so shocked him nine years ago?

"Speak now," I said, "or forever after hold your peace."

"I shall never change my mind about that," he said. "I beg you won't keep that passage. It will deform the book."

I went to my desk and re-wrote the page, and recorded the fact in my dedication of the novel to him.

Of Charleston at the time when Roosevelt came there early in this twentieth century, the ancient Charleston of fine traditions and fierce prejudices, something still was left. Though its prosperity lay shattered and its wharves and warehouses gaped with silence, more mellow beauty hung over the town, its houses, tiled roofs, gardens, grave yards, streets, and unexpected nooks, than ever I have seen elsewhere, even in New Orleans, where an enchanted fragment of the past also lurks, unpoisoned, unmocked by the present, waiting its curtain down. Amid this visible fragrance of time, enclosed by walls and roses, there dwelt in much quiet, with entire absence of show and aversion to show, a group of ladies. Their dress was a sort of seclusion in itself. Elderly they were; their voices, their manner, their ease and simplicity, which was the reverse of rustic and came from

---

* James Calvin Hemphill (1850–1927), a graduate of Erskine who succeeded Francis Warrington Dawson as editor of the *News and Courier* after Dawson's murder in 1889.

† In January of 1894 Wister published a story about a Wyoming rancher and his horse, "Balaam and Pedro," in *Harper's Monthly.* Roosevelt, as enamored of the West as Wister, claimed he was sickened by the violence in the story. Don D. Walker, "Wister, Roosevelt and James," 358–66.

something within them that many educated generations had seasoned and transmitted, would have prevented their feeling at a loss, no matter in what company they found themselves. As girls they had known the crest of the wave, and next its darkest gulf, they had looked upon the Civil War, lost their men folk down to brothers in their teens during those four years, and were still sitting in the shadow of that, because it was the final eclipse of their sun. They referred to it hardly more than they would have imparted family secrets. Being of the true metal, the uses of adversity had merely tempered them still more. They were very few in number. One of their qualities was to wear their poverty lightly, more naturally than many wear their riches; and in their hospitality to be as spontaneous with their scantiness as they would have been with their plenty. They opened their doors to kindred no matter how remote. They opened their hearts, never hastily, but when they had become sure. They shut firmly out certain things that are more than welcome today, such as publicity in the social columns, and conversations about the stock market and such other matters, which they deemed proper in a men's office, and out of place in the drawing room.

Upon the point of social publicity, I recall that it made its first appearance in the winter of the Exposition, 1902; and that the female editor of that column apologized for the innovation by saying that the time had come for Charleston to follow the lead of the age.* Upon this same point I held a most characteristic

---

* The Exposition was an opportunity for the Charleston newspaper to increase its readership with the city's first society column, "The Social World," by Sallie Rhett Roman (1844–1921). Well-connected in South Carolina society as the daughter of Robert Barnwell Rhett, she was the wife of Col. Alfred Roman of Louisiana. Roman had previously written a social column for a New Orleans newspaper, and from 1891 had been an accomplished editorialist of political pieces, as well as a fiction writer, for the *New Orleans Times-Democrat*. In introducing Charleston readers to the new social column, Roman wrote, "The social life of Charleston is preeminently distinguished, both in tone and manners. Its entertainments are emphasized by richness, simplicity and cordiality—the hall mark of high breeding—which gives them a singular fascination, while thoroughly good taste is the key-stone of US superstructure. To edit the column devoted to the social news of the city on the *Evening Post*, wherein will be recorded events taking place among the elevated class of the community, will, therefore, be a pleasure. It is hardly necessary to call attention to the fact that mode and manners change with epochs—and that what is accepted at one period as an essential, may be discarded at another. The present point of view is the one to be considered. Today, no center of any importance, and no progressive newspaper is without a weekly record of social events, a modern phase of life as obligatory as street cars, asphalted streets, scientific sanitation, well-lit thoroughfares, and the artistic adornment of cities. During the exposition months, when Charleston is crowded with prominent strangers from all parts of the country, when the governors of far distant cites, bankers, capitalists and the social leaders of the greatest cities of the country are being entertained by the people of Charleston; when even the

talk with one of the elderly ladies who, knowing who I was, introduced herself to me at the Women's Exchange, early in my stay.

"I am So-and-so's aunt," she said. "And how do you like our Exposition?"

"Extremely. There's only one thing."

"And what is that?"

"So few of your beautiful portraits by Romney and Gainsborough and Reynolds that I see in your houses seem to have been lent to the picture gallery in the Fine Arts Building."

"I will explain that to you. We in Charleston are very old-fashioned, and we do not care to expose our private ancestors to the public gaze."

When Charleston accepted any stranger within its gates, I doubt if one of its fashions of so doing could be, for the very charm and delicacy of its grace, matched anywhere in the world. My wife and I had arrived there from the north late one night to spend our honeymoon. By breakfast time next morning, a bowl of fresh garden flowers was brought to us with a card and the greetings of a lady we had never yet seen. She, with certain other friends of my family, was aware of our coming beforehand. The bowl was of rare china; and had not my mother given me instructions what to do in case such a welcome met us, I should have been obliged either to reason it out in embarrassed suspense, or else to ask the lady who kept our boarding house for guidance. The proper conduct in a case like this was to acknowledge the compliment at once, and to keep the bowl until the flowers were faded, and then return it with a suitable message. With an ancestress by the name of Mary Middleton buried in the churchyard of St.

president honors the city and exposition with his presence, the social news of the town assumes very important proportion, and certainly deserves special mention." Shortly after, an article was published in the *Oregon Daily Journal* entitled "Charleston is Shocked." It reads: "Charleston society is being inexpressibly shocked nowadays by the publication in the *Evening Post* of the happenings in the gay world of the conservative old Southern city. It is the first time in the history of the place and of its society that such events have found their way into print. Innovation has shocked fashionable Charleston beyond all words. The editor of this new department of the *Post* is Mrs. S. Rhett Roman, herself a Charleston woman of aristocratic lineage and experienced in newspaper work. The members of the exclusive set need to be taught that they belong to the twentieth century, and the *Evening Post* will perform a great service to Charleston and to the South in acting as its schoolmaster." However, given the unwritten law of the St. Cecilia Society that its members were never to be mentioned in the newspaper, no proper Charlestonian would agree to be included in Roman's "society" column. As a result, the column did not last long. Mrs. Roman later lived (and died) in Columbia. *Nebraska State Journal* (Sunday, April 20, 1902), 14; "Charleston is Shocked," *Oregon Daily Journal* (Wednesday, April 30, 1902), 3. For more on Sallie Roman, see Nancy Dixon, *Fortune and Misery: Sallie Rhett Roman of New Orleans: A Biographical Portrait and Selected Fiction, 1891–1920* (Baton Rouge: University of Louisiana Press, 1999.)

Michael's at Charleston, I fell heir to the roses in that bowl and to the open doors of very distant cousins and *their* cousins, as my mother and aunt had done before me.

Those of their generation that were still living revealed the constancy in kinship and friendship which was so deeply marked in old Charleston people. Some of them had relations in Europe. After the Civil War, many Southerners left the United States never to return, and were to be found established in various cities—London, Paris, Florence, Rome. And so it befell that at the age of twelve, in Rome, I made the acquaintance of an exile from old Charleston, so handsome, so stately, so truly a presence, a personage, that thing we no longer produce, a great lady, that I can remember her still.* Her father's story draws an important side of Charleston character as it still persisted, even as late as the visit of Roosevelt. Should you ever find yourself in St. Michael's churchyard, read his long and beautifully worded epitaph. His name was Pettigrew [*sic*], and he was a judge. When South Carolina seceded from the Union, he stood almost alone in his dissent, and although he lived in this wildest storm centre of slavery and secession, he not only never changed his mind, but so greatly was he esteemed and revered for his integrity, that he never lost the regard of his fellow citizens; and when he came to die, they surrounded his memory with the feeling and the admiration which may be read in that epitaph.

He had another daughter; and through a word she once dropped to William Makepeace Thackeray, another trait in Charleston character is drawn. When the author of *Vanity Fair* was presented to her, he somewhat oddly and unwisely remarked that he was delighted to make her acquaintance, for he had heard that she was the fastest woman in South Carolina.

"Oh, you mustn't believe everything you hear," said she. "I heard that you were a gentleman."†

---

* Caroline Petigru Carson (1820–1892), the daughter of James Louis Petigru and sister of Susan Petigru King. A staunch Unionist like her father, at the start of the Civil War she lived in New York and later in Rome, creating a life as an artist. For more on Caroline Carson, see William H. Pease and Jane H. Pease, eds., *The Roman Years of a South Carolina Artist: Caroline Carson's Letters Home, 1872–1892* (Columbia: University of South Carolina Press, 2003).

† Susan Petigru King Bowen (1824–1875), Charleston novelist and society figure infamous for her repartee. In the 1850s, she had exchanged barbs with Thackeray during his lecture tour to Charleston. In 1870, King had married her second husband, Christopher Columbus Bowen (1832–1880), a Rhode Island–born South Carolina Radical Republican with a shady history. Seven years King's junior, he was a forger suspected of murder and allegedly a bigamist. Provocative before the war, Susan Bowen became even more so after the war. For more on Susan King and her second marriage, see William H. Pease

Now that happened quite a number of years before ever I saw Charleston; forty at least, I should think, if not fifty; but had they forgotten it? Not at all. In this proud little place, once so busy and important, now a lost echo of what had once been, it was cherished as a legend; and during my first seven days there I fancy that it was quite seven times repeated to me by ladies and gentlemen who, at the time when Thackeray visited Charleston, were either very young indeed, or else not yet born.

Metamorphosed as to its particulars, but the same in its underlying principle, this passage-at-arms between the great author and the great lady served as a valuable brush stroke in the portrait of the place and its people which I was to attempt several years later, although no such ambition dawned upon me when I first learned it from such a series of informants in 1898, nor even during my second and much longer sojourn in the winter and spring of 1902. In those months it may well be that this portrait, not yet contemplated, was nevertheless taking on not so much shape as color, all unknown to me, as I pegged away at *The Virginian,* or marvelled at Charleston during Roosevelt's vertiginous visit, or wandered and meditated and looked across the dreamy, empty rivers to their dreamy, empty shores and the grey-veiled live-oaks that were all of a piece with the wistful silence.

All of a piece. That is exactly what Charleston had remained, exactly what New York had not. Here was a city, not a village, though much smaller than many villages. Such places as Worcester or Springfield had revealed to me that a village can swell and swell, yet always be a village. Charleston now revealed to me that you can shrink and shrink, yet always remain a city, a centre, a capital in prestige. Full of echoes this little, coherent, self-respecting place was also full of life; retaining its native identity, it's English-thinking, English-feeling, English-believing authenticity; holding on tight to George Washington and the true American tradition, even though loyal to its lost cause. What an oasis in our great American desert of mongrel din and haste. To be behind the times, yet intensely vital; to keep itself whole and never break into a litter of fragments that didn't match and so lose its personality as New York had done.

What a lady had once said to Thackeray was still vivid and ready for telling to a stranger; a stranger with what Charleston held to be the right to walk in was received at once; a stranger with wrong credentials could no more cross its social frontier than a traveller without a passport and proper visas can enter a European country today.

---

and Jane H. Pease, *A Family of Women: The Carolina Petigrus in Peace and War.* (Chapel Hill: University of North Carolina Press, 1999).

The forefathers of Charleston and their families had been painted in London by English masters of the eighteenth century, their sons and grandsons had studied law in the Inner Temple, their daughters had danced in the great world, a Charleston boy had attempted to help Lafayette escape from his Austrian prison,* and the mark of the great world was still set upon this civilization, plain to see. Yet it bore this stamp of the past without losing grip on life; side-tracked as the town had been since 1865, in its deep old roots it possessed the secret of persistence.

In *Lady Baltimore,* my portrait of Charleston, the emphasis is laid upon the passing elders more than upon the coming youth, for the sake of a precious thing that was never to return. Roosevelt quarrelled with it, as will be seen, falling heavily on my praise of the South at the expense of the North. I agreed and made changes. As much as he I was Union, never anything else. Any *idee fixe,* like the Southern view of a State, must perish when it begins to hinder growth.

"After all," said Mrs. St. Julien Ravenel to me (she was one of the elders),† "it is much better for us that the Union won. Had we split off, by now we should be split into several republics."

Roosevelt's three whirling days in Charleston gave him no chance to see and know the place. He brought there his historic knowledge, his Union patriotism, and his general passion for social justice. He took just that away. Friendship with people like Mrs. Ravenel would have tempered his severity. I possess a collection of perfectly good grandmothers; but the one who lies beneath the spire of St. Michael's has a special value for me.

---

* Francis Kinloch Huger (1773–1855) led a failed attempt to rescue Lafayette from captivity in Olmütz in 1794, during the wars surrounding the French Revolution.
† Mrs. St. Julien (Harriott Horry Rutledge) Ravenel (1832–1912), Charleston author.

State Street Shops, C. H. White, c. 1907. Etching on japan paper,
National Gallery of Canada.

CHARLES HENRY WHITE (1907)

"Charleston"

Charles Henry White, "Charleston" from *Harper's Monthly,* Nov. 1907: 852–61.

Charles Henry White (1878–1918), born in Hamilton, Ontario, Canada, studied at the Art Student League in New York City. He worked in illustration and pen drawing before he traveled to Venice, where in 1901 he took up etching with famed American etcher Joseph Pennell and he began to etch plates of Venetian cities. After further study in England with artist James McNeill Whistler, he returned to America, where there was little competition in etching. White arrived in New York just in time to participate in the burgeoning of printmaking as an art form, and he made important contributions to that revival in the United States. He taught the first etching classes of the printmaking program at the Art Students League. (After White's early death, Pennell returned to take over and expand the program.)

In 1902 White produced a set of etchings of the east side of New York that appeared in *Harper's Monthly*, after which he began a long series of "humorous and sprightly" travel sketches of American cities for the magazine. The articles were accompanied by illustrations of his etchings, which "emphasized the old truth that there is beauty to be found in every-day surroundings and in our own land." He soon acquired a reputation for his ability to reproduce the picturesque qualities "of street and alley, of waterfront and factory district." Over the next decade, he published impressions of New York, Pittsburgh, Chicago, Richmond, New Orleans, Boston, Philadelphia, Washington, DC, Salem, Massachusetts, and Charleston. In doing so, he set a standard for quality etchings and created a distinctly American idiom for urban and industrial subjects. His artwork was exhibited in New York galleries and influenced the American etching revival, a movement known for its realistic treatment of subject matter. Meanwhile, White was hired as an illustrator by the Frederick J. Quinby Company in Boston who had decided to illustrate, translate, and publish the writings of

French novelist Charles Paul de Kock (1794–1871). White's work appeared in de Kock's *Adhémar* (1904), published by Quinby, among other novels.

In 1909, White left for France and Italy. Although he lived abroad, he exhibited in Chicago, New York, and Philadelphia. He was one of the three hundred artists whose works were included in the New York Armory Show of 1913. He also translated ten tales of *The Second Odd Number: Thirteen Tales* by Guy de Maupassant for Harper Brothers in 1917. He died on the French Riviera the next year, at age forty. Of his 124 etchings, forty were of European cities and the rest of American cities.

When artist Birge Harrison (1854–1929) saw White's Charleston etchings in *Harper's Monthly* and read his article about the gracious old city, he was inspired to travel south to Charleston. Harrison, the director of the esteemed Art Student Leagues in Woodstock, New York, became a winter resident. He befriended Charleston artist Alice Huger Smith (1876–1958), who became influential in the local art community from this association and in turn influenced Charleston artist Elizabeth O'Neill Verner (1883–1979). Birge Harrison inspired his early art instructor, Alfred Hutty (1877–1954), to summer in Charleston. Primarily an oil and watercolor artist, Hutty did not seriously turn to etching until he took up residence in Charleston in 1919. Shortly after his arrival, he served as the first director of the School of the Carolina Art Association and founded the Charleston Etchers Club. Other artists followed Hutty to town to interpret the region's visual beauty in their art, attracting national attention through their widely distributed illustrations. This was the genesis of an artistic and cultural phenomenon now known as the Charleston Renaissance, when artists united with Charleston poets and writers, preservationists, and civic leaders, to shape the city's revitalization into the 1940s.

In the following article, Charles Henry White depicts the charms of Charleston in 1907.

SOURCES

De Maupassant, Guy. *The Second Odd Number: Thirteen Tales*. New York: Harper Brothers, 1917: see Publisher's Note.

Martin, Denis. *Printmaking in Québec, 1900–1950*. Québec: Musée du Québec, 1990.

Tolerton, H. H. *Illustrated Catalogue of Etchings by American Artists*. Chicago: Roullier's Art Galleries, 1913.

Tovell, Rosemarie L. "Charles Henry White (1878–1918), Canada's Painter-Etcher of American Cities." *Imprint* 22:1 (Spring 1997): 2–10.

———. *A New Class of Art: The Artist's Print in Canadian Art, 1877–1920*. Ottawa, Ontario: National Gallery of Canada, 1996.

Weitenkampf, F. *American Graphic Art*. New York: Henry Holt and Co., 1912.

"Charleston"

A turquoise-blue sky hovering in hazy drowsy indolence over a sea of undulating tile roofs, on either side an uneven aisle of faded stucco facades, running the whole gamut of pinks and grays, and strung along this luminous background innumerable exquisite wrought-iron balconies, festooned by multicolored washing flapping idly in the soft salt air that rings with the clear laughter of children peeping at you through their dainty screen of iron ornament.

Such may be your first impression of one phase of Charleston, but her moods are infinite; and, as you press on, you are thrilled with a sense of the endless variety and superabundance of beauty that lures you in a zigzag course across the city, fearful that something may escape you; here, standing on some deserted wharf listening to the distant singing of negroes, syncopating their movements as they shell oysters in the factory, or retreating into the cool shade of a renaissance arcade to drink in the quiet vista of Tradd Street, its roofs a sea of deep umber tiles, its walls glowing with golden stucco. Reflect this luminous mass of molten gold in a canal, add a few fruit-boats for a foreground, and you have Venice.

Yet within a day's journey from New York, this graceful colonial city of roses, with its dim, half-forgotten gardens, where one might think the old resident had spent his idle hours improvising in stucco and sketching in iron, is only beginning to be discovered by the tourist, and is still shunned by the artist, whose instinctive, aesthetic flunkeyism sends him to Dordrecht or Venice, to grope about for a mildewed motive worked threadbare by generations of painters.

I had come to Charleston with no serious purpose—not to study its history or its legends, as graceful as you will find this beautiful land over, nor its churches and secluded graveyards worthy of Gray's "Elegy." I came merely to etch: to impede the traffic by opening a three-legged stool in odd corners, attracting the negroes, the flies, and those nondescript drifters who congregate to watch you rid yourself of an impression with the aid of a small needle on a copper plate; to lose myself in the intricacies of this Elysium, pausing to jot down in my sketchbook rough notes on the quaint piazzas, superposed and treated with Ionic orders below and Corinthian above; or stopping with a thrill to pull myself up and peep shamelessly over some stucco wall into the privacy of a Charleston garden, its sundial tufted with ivy, and its piazzas a fluttering array of golden trumpet-flowers. Any room taken at random in this Arcadia entrenches an etcher in an inexhaustible wealth of material. I therefore turn to a policeman—

"Just around the co-nah there is a place with Ionic capitals where you will be very comfortable."

One gasps at the policeman's erudition until he remembers that this is a city where a man's childhood may be spent playing hide and seek behind the best of the orders; his courtship discreetly conducted in the lee of a great Corinthian column; in later life elbowing daily the posts of his own classic portico. It is therefore not surprising that even an untutored layman in Charleston is apt to know and appreciate an architectural order when he sees it.

So I locate the house by its mighty row of columns, looking out over the sea, and by a cow—a topographical afterthought of the policeman—grazing on the lawn, doing likewise. There is a distinction to this old mansion* that wins you over immediately, and emphasizes the questionable taste of a few of the modern encroachments along East Battery.

Its bricks are now mellow with age, and the two wrought-iron balconies, each treated with a rondelle, are large enough for one to sit in comfortably, almost overhanging the water, and watch the lingering rays of the sun sift over the most delightful, the most wistful harbor in America. Just as you enter—but I am giving too much away. You may be a Philistine and unworthy to live here.

I shall therefore confine myself to stating that a graceful staircase of black cypress takes a great sweep into a lofty hall above, where, in the gloomy recesses behind heavy portieres, there is a picture-gallery, locked and sealed these many years, presenting pleasant material for speculation when you hear that a Romney —a Charlestonian family heirloom—being sold not so long ago under the stress of need for a small fortune.

On the floor above I paused for breath while the negress stopped to unlock a door. Here at last is a place where a man may practice the art of living. Through the window you look out upon a sunny harbor, dotted at times with distant lumber-schooners, eastward bound under a full head of said, to lose themselves over the horizon smudged with the smoke of outgoing steamers.

If I tire of this vista, one flight of stairs brings me down to Holloway, my companion at late breakfasts, who gave me the freedom of his chambers, consisting of two beautiful Georgian rooms, littered with books and rare prints, an undersized dog, a second-hand piano, a few old portraits, and an exceptionally good mahogany cellarette, about which a small group of stragglers gather at night when a musical member of the coterie seats himself at the piano.

---

* The Capt. James Missroon House (c. 1789) at 40 East Bay was converted in 1905 to a boarding house called the Shamrock Terrace Hotel, under the same management as the Villa Margherita. Damaged in the 1911 hurricane, it was sold by George H. Moffett and renovated in 1925 as the Omar Shrine Temple. It is now headquarters the Historic Charleston Foundation. Smith and Smith, *Dwelling Houses of Charleston*, 91–92.

On these evenings if you pass this way you may have heard a deep bass voice wishing you good-night from beneath the palmettos where a ragged silhouette is barely visible. Apart from his negro origin, revealed in the peculiar "timbre" of his voice, there was little upon which to form a reasonable hypothesis for his nightly vigils, until I hit upon it by accident late one moonlight night as I was homeward bound along the Battery.

A great luminous expanse of water stretched like a sea of silver as far as the eye could follow, into the East, mirroring in its depths the port and starboard lights of a distant fleet of schooners—motionless at their moorings—barely perceptible in the envelopment of the evening. Nothing disturbed the thrilling silence save the distant song of some benighted negro as he rowed for the Cooper River, wailing his spontaneous invocation to the night, and leaving in his wake a thin ripple of silver.

As I rounded the corner, the sonorous cadences of a Chopin ballad told me that the musical member had dropped in at Holloway's, and prompted me to pause and hear the selection out beneath the magnolias. I was tiptoeing about, selecting a suitable trunk to lean against, when my attention was attracted by something beneath Holloway's balcony.

It was the figure of a man whose legs and arms dangled loose and disjointed as if his body were suspended by an invisible cord to the balcony above. As I stole nearer, carefully obliterating myself in the deep shadow of the trees, I recognized in this solitary shuffling figure my negro of the deep bass voice. And the ballad, issuing from the window above, flooded the night with swelling crescendos he swayed from head to foot, flapping his rags as he shuffled his feet in amazing syncopated rhythms, dancing himself out of his hat into a dripping perspiration, till the final chord resounding above brought his big feet down with a delirious whack that sent the echoes hurtling along the weather-beaten walls into the glimmering void above.

I stepped out to say something to him just as a policeman passed, going his rounds. "Keep a-mov-in', niggah," was all the guardian of the peace had to offer, and the colored enigma vanished into the night.

This innate, uncontrollable craving of the negro for rhythm is nowhere better exemplified than in a colored barber's manipulation of an ordinary democratic whisk-broom. You may think that you have been whisked in New York, but the best of our boot-blacks and barber's assistants merely brush your trousers from the knee down, with a few conventional, cold movements, and a perfunctory pass at your collar. Their whisking is at best a calculating, soulless business proposition. But in Charleston all this is changed. To be sure, your negro begins brushing you with a sordid end—the tip—in view: but the moment he begins a

Barber Shop, C. H. White,
c. 1907. Etching on japan
paper, National Gallery
of Canada.

prelude with his whisk on your coat lapels, his work, like that of the artist, becomes the labor of love. He loses sight of its commercial possibilities in its technical resources. In his hands it is manipulated until it becomes a vehicle of expression and takes its place among the instruments of percussion.

If you show even a moderate interest in the skill with which the colored apprentice drums the dust out of your clothing, the proprietor will leave his customer with his face buried beneath a sea of suds, snatch the whisk away from the boy with a "Go 'way, chile," and reveal the possibilities of the implement. Your collar-bone will be approached with a capriccioso movement that will soon shape itself into an allegro non troppo as he reaches your shoulders. In the variegated rhythms that follow in quick succession you unconsciously formulate well-remembered airs. As he reached my ribs, for an instant he was agitato, and I thought I traced Schumann's delightful "I'll ne'er complain"—only for a moment, for he had shifted to elaborate double syncopations. This time the tempo was unmistakable:—"I don' care if yo' nevah come back,"—but doubtless realizing the inappropriateness of the selection, he drifted gracefully into a delirious and exquisite bit of ragtime, drumming as he whistled in a faint pianissimo, "Every li'l bit helps," softly hissing the melody after the manner of a groom when he uses the curry-comb on a horse.

Indeed, as the thing progressed, I became conscious of the fact that I was beginning to feel like a horse, and possibly might look so, to pedestrians as they passed.

Every artifice, every combination in time art of syncopated drumming seemed to have been exhausted as he went flip-flap, pit-a-pat over my person till he reached my abdomen, where he varied things with a tremolo that con amore, and I thought I detected the opening movement of Grieg's "Ich liebe dich"; but in the excitement and nervous exaltation of the moment this may have been a foolish delusion. I soon realized that he still held in reserve the magnificent resources of an unlimited technique when he approached my legs, which are thin and wiry, and made them vibrate to a sustained and furious agitato movement, in which he dropped each third beat, catching himself a resounding slap on his stomach, ostensibly to shake the dust from the whisk, but actually to vary his orchestration with a round, mellow tone. Now he was working his feet against his hands in a sort of rhythmical counterpoint, and the entire force of employees shuffled about, moving their razors in unison.

I felt the climax coming. In the cloud of dust enveloping me I caught a fleeting glimpse of the maestro's shiny pate and heard him wheezing for breath. I steadied myself, while my hat rocked about at a perilous angle as he beat a fortissimo between my shoulder-blades to the timeworn: "First in peace, first in war,

Now I can say I am whisked!"

The Englishman who occupied the chair next to mine was about due for a brushing, so I stopped to light a cigarette and see how I must have looked. But when Rufus* toyed with an exquisite little rhythm on his neck, as a forerunner to better things, the soulless stranger cut him short with: "Oh, I say, my man, caunt y' stop that evahlawsting drumming and brush me off a bit, don't y' know? I've got to catch a train."

Which merely goes to show that in the arts, the higher a man aspires, the smaller he finds the zone of an appreciative public.

*Rufus Emmanuel Felder (ca. 1850–1941) owned the Felder Palace Barbershop, which catered largely to whites. Felder operated on Wentworth Street, then on King Street from 1892. For more on the family see Edmund Drago and Eugene Hunt, Oral History Interview with Felder Hutchinson (July 16, 1985), Avery Normal Institute Oral History Project, Avery Research Center, College of Charleston.

But time flies in old Charles Town, and my return ticket stares me in my face like an impending ban of excommunication. The lovely vistas of faded stucco, the secluded gardens rums wild with roses, each exquisite portico fluttering with exotic flowers, that nod to me on terms of intimacy in my daily rambles, must be renounced.

And as the hour of this renunciation approaches, I found myself returning once more to satiate myself with the unobtrusive beauty of familiar corners. Again I mount the wrought-iron staircase to the old mansion facing the water, which I visited first at the end of a day's work, ascending the sweep of stairs to pull a highly polished brass knob which brought, a moment later, an old ante-bellum negro butler, its a white-duck jacket with pearl buttons, who with great dignity—a dernier-regime manner carefully appropriated from his master—led me into a vast hallway interspaced with Corinthian pilasters, and thence up a stairway past a high Palladian window through which one caught a glimpse of a quiet garden glowing with heavy clusters of ripe oranges relieved against a pink and white mist of azaleas. From the spacious landing above, where in the old days an orchestra played, while below the young people glided through the candle-lit hall, one has access to a great reception-room panelled to the ceiling.

To attempt to catch Charleston's peculiar flavor were as futile as to describe the perfume of a flower. Its charm is insidious, and once under its influence Charleston becomes a habit. Thus many a balcony room is occupied by some ensnared visitor, who thinks he is just passing through as he lingers year after year, unable to renounce the roses, the balconies with their rows of flower-pots glowing with geraniums, the long unfrequented walks by the river at sunset.

Shortly before leaving Charleston, Holloway and I were returning, late one evening, from a section along the river hitherto unexplored by me, when an old residence at the corner well screened by a heavy magnolia caught my attention.

Holloway became reminiscent. "If you had told any of the German musical world of the late seventies that their most noted tenor and exponent of Wagner title roles would be quietly spending his old age watering his peach-trees and training his grape-vines in an old Charleston garden, they would have been incredulous. Yet here he is, merely another instance of those chance visitors we were speaking of who come for a night and are held indefinitely. He may be at home now; if you like, we can cross over."

A few steps across time encroachment of railroad tracks, that have destroyed the character of a once distinguished neighborhood, brought us to the garden. Holloway peeped over the fence and beckoned to me. Half hidden by a rustling

Dismantled Charleston, C. H. White, c. 1907. Etching on japan paper,
National Gallery of Canada.

canopy of foliage an elderly colossus stood absorbed in stringing his vines overhead, after the fashion of an Italian garden. His hair amid beard were silver gray,
yet the fullness of his massive neck and the clean-cut, muscular frame seemed to
speak him an elderly athletic gentleman of distinguished antecedents, magnificently preserved for his three-score years.

He was humming softly to himself as he caught up vines here and there to
arrange them in festoons along his shady piazzas; and, as he approached us, I
recognized the "Evening Star" song from Tannhauser; at first almost inaudible,
but as he continued, the poetry of this fine Charleston evening seemed to carry
him with it till his voice soared in rich sonorous tones that echoed along the
quiet piazzas and awakened a mockingbird in the depths of his magnolia.

Holloway coughed.

In an instant the song ceased. With a hearty roar of laughter the singer took
the steps of his piazza two at a time, and a moment later grasped my hand.

"This was good of you to wander into this wilderness to visit an old man
singing in his garden." He laughed as he led us through a spacious hallway,
whose walls were hung with innumerable oil sketches—some rough notes, others

of exceptional interest—done by him at odd moments during his professional career.

"They are only for myself," he explained apologetically, dismissing them all with a peremptory wave of his arm. "A divertissement for me in my travels."

In the large salon adjoining the piazza there was hardly a spot on the walls where some canvas did not commemorate an important musical event of the late "seventies." The itinerary of the first Wagner-Opera Company to enter Italy, in which he sang the title roles, could be traced distinctly in the dusty paintings rambling in uneven procession above his piano. Even London with her veil of blue mist was represented in a few impressions he had managed to record between rehearsals at the time he sang the role of Rienzi at its premiere.

But among all these paintings I still call to mind an especially fine Bavarian landscape, that stood out clearly among the others, by the delicate tenderness with which he had rendered a mediaeval stronghold with draw-bridge and embattlements towering defiantly above a quiet valley, encircled by distant wooded hills, shimmering in the flame midsummer light that sifted over tower and gables, gilding each pinnacle with burnished gold.

"It is Castle Eisenach," he explained, flipping the dust off its surface with his handkerchief. "Grimm, in his fairy-tales, describes the tower-room accurately. Is it not a curious thing that by playing the role of Tannhauser, and at times Wolfram, for that matter, I was able to buy the castle where, in 1205, Wolfram von Eschenbach wrote Parsifal?"

"You still own it?" I gasped.

"Yes," he replied, simply. "But it is quite a tax on me to keep it up now."

Later, as we sat tilting our chairs on the broad piazza, his son, a young German army officer on leave of absence, appeared, and as the shadows lengthened the old gentleman drifted into reminiscences, revealing with many a racy idiom the comedy lurking behind the scene of the grand-opera tragedy, or chuckling as he recalled the eccentricities of von Bulow,* who, when the ballet-girls supplied him by the Hamburg Opera House were too fat and bulky, would bring this to the notice of the management, at the same time gratifying his Teutonic

---

* Baron Hans von Bülow (1830–1894), German virtuoso pianist, composer and one of the most famous conductors of the nineteenth century, was also one of the earliest European musicians to tour the United States. An early student of Franz Liszt, he was instrumental in the successes of major composers including Richard Wagner and Johannes Brahms. In 1857, he married Liszt's daughter Cosima, who left him for Wagner. Perhaps due to ill health, Bülow was high strung, nervous, and irritable and known for an acerbic tongue he failed to curb, which made him many enemies.

sense of humor by increasing the tempo of the orchestra during rehearsals, and screaming: "Faster! Faster!" until they fell exhausted on the stage.

As I write, I can still see this fine old gentleman* standing in his portico at dusk, a romantic figure among his roses, waving us a hearty "aufwiedersehen."

---

*The opera tenor White describes closely resembles Jean de Reszke (1850–1925), Polish tenor and exponent of Wagnerian opera. In 1874 he made his debut as a baritone in Venice as Jan de Reschi. He took several years off for vocal study, and in 1884 returned to the stage as a tenor. He became the greatest tenor of his generation, admired for his French repertory, Wagner roles, and Italian repertoire, and renowned for his incredible physique. A star at Covent Garden (and a favorite of Queen Victoria's), he made his Metropolitan Opera debut in 1893. His career at the Met lasted only six seasons but was a string of triumphs in Italian, French, and German roles, often opposite his good friend opera diva Nellie Melba. Like the tenor White encounters, de Reszke usually warmed up with "Song to the Evening Star" from Wagner's "Tannhäuser." He voluntarily retired from the stage in 1904 (just as Caruso arrived internationally) and taught voice in Paris beginning in late 1907, so he *could* have been in Charleston. However, although he sang Wagner roles and was said to be the greatest Lohengrin, Tristan, and Siegfried the world had ever seen, this author found no evidence that de Reszke sang the role of Rienzi for the London premiere (in fact, it was English tenor Joseph Maas, who died in 1886), or at all. Nor did I find evidence of his ownership of "Castle Eisenach" in Germany. Wartburg Castle in Eisenach was in possession of the Grand Duchy of Saxe-Weimar-Eisenach until 1922, when a foundation was formed for its maintenance. Jean de Reszke did acquire vast estates in Poland near Warsaw, one that included an ancient castle, and he owned other estate properties with his brother, famous basso Edouard de Reszke (1853–1917). Clara Leiser wrote in *Jean de Reszke and the Great Days of the Opera*: "There have been varied—and sometimes ridiculous—stories about the 'castles' and properties of the de Reszkes in Poland." De Reszke himself may have been the source of inflated stories about his many castles. Additionally, although Jean de Reszke's only son by Comtesse Marie de Mailly-Nesle would have been too young to be "a German officer on leave" at the time of White's visit in 1907, as a boy Jean de Reszke Jr. "enthused over everything that had to do with war, horses, guns, swords, and drums, used to make remarkable sketches of soldiers." He was obsessed with uniforms and wore various ones constantly, play-acting soldiers. (He later joined the French army and died in action in 1918.) Or perhaps it was another young soldier staying with de Reszke (there were rumors). For whatever reason, White was unwilling to reveal the identity of the tenor, and as I found no *certain* evidence that this was, indeed, de Reszke, the tenor in Charleston remains a mystery. Clara Leiser, *Jean de Reszke and the Great Days of the Opera*, 133; "Obituary: Jean de Reszke, Jr." *Musical Times*, 420–21; "Death Of Lieut. De Reszke, *New York Times*, June 23, 1918, 45.

King Street, south, Charleston, S.C., between 1900 and 1915.
Detroit Publishing Co., publisher. Library of Congress.

Edward Hungerford (1912)

"Where Romance And Courtesy Do Not Forget"

Edward Hungerford, "Where Romance And Courtesy Do Not Forget"
from *The Personality of American Cities* (New York: McBride, Nast &
Co., 1913).

Edward Hungerford (1875–1948) was a railroad historian, author, and publicist who wrote books and articles about the railroad. Born in Watertown, New
York, he was sent to Williston Seminary in Easthampton, Massachusetts, where
he was a poor student and spent his childhood watching trains on the Rome,
Watertown and Ogdensburg Railroad. His father wanted him to become an
architect and he enrolled in an architecture program at Syracuse University.
However, he abandoned his studies and went to Western New York, where in
1896 he obtained a job as a reporter with the *Rochester Herald*. After three years
in Rochester, he obtained reporting and editing jobs on various newspapers
including the *New York Evening Sun* and the *New York Herald*. He also wrote
for *Harper's Monthly, Harper's Weekly, The Saturday Evening Post, Redbook,
Trains Magazine,* and *Travel,* among other publications, with the railroad industry eventually becoming his main interest. For seven years Hungerford was
press representative for the Brooklyn Rapid Transit Company. He was also advertising manager for Wells & Company Express, and director of publications
at the University of Rochester.

Hungerford organized highly successful railroad exhibitions. As centennial
director for the Baltimore and Ohio Railroad, in 1927 he created an extravagant
exhibition outside Baltimore, "The Fair of The Iron Horse," which included
displays and a two-hour play, *Pageant of The Iron Horse*. It drew crowds aver-
aging fifty thousand a day. He created five more transportation pageants during
the 1930s including one for the 1939 New York World's Fair, where visitors could
experience the birth and growth of the industry in a three thousand–seat theater.
Using contributions from twenty-seven railroad companies, the show featured
twenty-five locomotives and forty horses. It was a seventeen-acre international
display of electric and diesel engines and cars brought from Canada, England,

and Italy. Hungerford wrote a five-act drama, "Railroads on Parade," with a cast of 250 to embellish his exhibit. The attraction drew 2.6 million visitors during its two-year run.

He wrote too many books to mention, many of them about railroads. One of his popular nonrailroad titles was *With the Doughboy in France* (1920), a journal of his World War I experiences, and one of his best sellers was *Planning a Trip Abroad* (1923). Among his prodigious list of books, he wrote histories of Macy's, the Waldorf Astoria, and Wells Fargo; a biography of Louis Sherry, the Gilded Age restaurateur, caterer, confectioner and hotelier; and innumerable novels.

Hungerford traveled annually more than 75,000 rail miles "just for the fun of it." In the following chapter from his book, *The Personality of American Cities* (1913), he describes coming down the tracks from New York to the city "Where Romance and Courtesy Do Not Forget."

"Where Romance and Courtesy Do Not Forget"

You are not going to write your book and leave out Charleston?" said the Man who Makes Magazines.

We hesitated at acknowledging the truth. In some way or other Charleston had escaped us upon our travels. The Magazine Maker read our answer before we could gain strength to make it.

"Well, you can't afford to miss that town," he said conclusively. "It's great stuff."

"Great stuff?" we ventured.

"If you are looking into the personality of American cities you must include Charleston. She has more personality than any of the other old Colonial towns —save Boston. She's personality personified, old age glorified, charm and sweetness magnified the flavor of the past hangs in every one of her old houses and her narrow streets. You cannot pass by Charleston."

After that we went over to a railroad ticket office in Fifth Avenue and purchased a round-trip ticket to the metropolis of South Carolina. And a week later we were on a southbound train, running like mad across the Jersey meadows. Five days in Charleston! It seemed almost sacrilege. Five miserable days in the town which the Maker of Magazines averred fairly oozed personality. But five days were better than no days at all—

The greater part of one day crossing New Jersey, Pennsylvania, the up stretched head of little Delaware, Maryland finally the Old Dominion and the real South. A day spent behind the glass of the car window the brisk and busy Jersey towns, the Delaware easily crossed; Philadelphia, with her great outspreading of suburbs; Wilmington; a short cut through the basements of Baltimore; the afternoon light dying on the superb dome of the Washington Capitol—after that the Potomac. Then a few evening hours through Virginia, the southern accent growing more pronounced, the very air softer, the negroes more prevalent, the porter of our car continually more deferential, more polite. After that a few hours of oblivion, even in the clattering Pullman which, after the fashion of all these tremendously safe new steel cars, was a bit chilly and a bit noisy.

In the morning a low and unkempt land, the railroad trestling its way over morass and swamp and bayou on long timber structures, and many times threading sluggish yellow southern rivers by larger bridges. Between these a sandy mainland—thick forests of pine with increasing numbers of live-oaks holding soft moss aloft—at last the outskirts of a town. Other folk might gather their luggage together, the vision of a distant place with its white spires, the soft gray fog that tells of the proximity of the open sea blowing in upon them, held us at the window pane. A river showed itself in the distance to the one side of the train, with mast-heads dominating its shores; another, lined with factories stretched upon the other side. After these, the streets of the town, a trolley car stalled impatient to let our train pass—low streets and mean streets of an unmistakable negro quarter, the broad shed of a sizable railroad station showing at the right.

"Charleston, sah," said the porter. Remember now that he had been a haughty creature in New York and Philadelphia, ebon dignity in Baltimore and in Washington. Now he was docility itself, a courtesy hardly to be measured by the mere expectation of gratuity.

The first glimpse of Charleston a rough paved street—our hotel omnibus finding itself with almost dangerous celerity in front of trolley cars. That unimportant way led into another broad highway of the town and seemingly entitled to distinction.

"Meeting Street," said our driver. "And I can tell you that Charleston is right proud of it, sir," he added.

Charleston has good cause to be proud of its main highway, with the lovely old houses along it rising out of blooming gardens, like fine ladies from their ball gowns; at its upper end the big open square and the adjacent Citadel-pouring out its gray-uniformed boys to drill just as their daddies and their grand-daddies drilled there before them—the charms of St. Michael's, and the never-to-be-forgotten Battery at the foot of the street.

We sped down it and drew up at a snow-white hotel which in its immaculate coat might have sprung up yesterday, were it not for the stately row of great pillars, three stories in height, with which it faced the street. They do not build hotels that way nowadays more's the pity. For when the Charleston Hotel was built it entered a distinguished brotherhood the Tremont in Boston, the Astor and the St. Nicholas in New York, Willard's in Washington, the Monongahela at Pittsburgh, and the St. Charles in New Orleans were among its contemporaries. It was worthy to be ranked with the best of these—a hotel at which the great planters of the Carolinas and of Georgia could feel that the best had been created for them within the very heart of their favorite city.

We pushed our way into the heart of the generous office of the hotel, thronged with the folk who had crowded into Charleston—followers of the races, just then holding sway upon the outskirts of the town, tourists from the North, Carolinians who will never lose the habit of going to Charleston as long as Charleston exists. In due time a brisk and bustling hotel clerk—he was an importation, plainly, none of your courteous, ease-taking Southerners—had placed us in a room big enough for the holding of a reception. From the shutters of the room we could look down into Meeting Street—into the charred remnants of a store that had been burned long before and the débris never removed. When we threw up the window sash we could thrust our heads out and see, a little way down the street, the most distinctive and the most revered of all Charleston's landmarks, the belfried spire of St. Michael's. As we leaned from that window the bells of St. Michael's spoke the quarter-hour, just as they have been speaking quarter-hours close upon a century and a half.

We had been given the first taste of the potent charm of a most distinctive southern town.

"The most appealing, the most lovely, the most wistful town in America; whose visible sadness and distinction seem almost to speak audibly, speak in the sound of the quiet waves that ripple round her southern front, speak in the churchbells on Sunday morning and breathe not only in the soft salt air, but in the perfume of every gentle, old-fashioned rose that blooms behind the high garden walls of falling mellow-tinted plaster; King's Port the retrospective, King's Port the belated, who from her pensive porticoes looks over her two rivers to the marshes and the trees beyond, the live-oaks veiled in gray moss, brooding with memories. Were she my city how I should love her. . . . "

So wrote Owen Wister of the city that he came to know so well. You can read Charleston in *Lady Baltimore* each time he speaks of "King's Port" and read correctly. For it was in Charleston he spun his romance of the last stronghold of old manners, old families, old traditions and old affections. In no other city of the land might he have laid such a story. For no other city of the land bears the memory of tragedy so plaintively, so uncomplainingly as the old town that occupies the flat peninsula between the Cooper and the Ashley rivers at the very gateway of South Carolina. Like a scarred man, Charleston will bear the visible traces of her great disaster until the end of her days. And each of them, like the scars of Richmond, makes her but the more potent in her charm.

Up one street and down another—fascinating path-ways, every blessed one of them. Meeting and King and Queen and Legare and Calhoun and Tradd with their high, narrow ended houses rising right from the side walks and stretching, with their generous spirit of hospitality, inward, beside gardens that blossom as only a southern garden can bloom—with jessamine and narcissus and oleander and japonica. Galleries give to these fragrant gardens. Only Charleston, unique among her sisters of the Southland, does not call them galleries. She calls them piazzas, with the accent strong upon the "pi."

The gardens themselves are more than a little English, speaking clearly something of the old-time English spirit of the town, which has its most visible other expression in the stolid Georgian architecture of its older public buildings and churches. And some of the older folk, defying the Charleston convention of four o'clock dinner, will take tea in the softness of the late afternoon. Local tradition still relates how, in other days, a certain distinguished and elderly citizen, possessing neither garden nor gallery with his house, was wont to have a table and chair placed upon the sidewalk and there take his tea of a late afternoon. And the Charleston of that other day walked upon the far side of the street rather than disturb the gentleman!

Nor is all that spirit quite gone in the Charleston of today. The older negroes will touch their hats, if not remove them, when you glance at them. They will step into the gutter when you pass them upon the narrow sidewalks of the narrow streets. They came of a generation that made more than the small distinction of separate schools and separate places in the railroad cars between white and black. But they are rapidly disappearing from the streets of the old city. Those younger negroes who drive the clumsy two wheeled carts in town and out over the rough paved streets have learned no good manners. And when the burly negresses who amble up the sidewalks balancing huge trays of crabs or fresh fruits or baked stuffs smile at you, theirs is the smile of insolence. Fifty years of the Fifteenth Amendment have done their work any older resident of Charleston will tell you that, and thank God for the inborn courtesy that keeps him from profanity with the telling.

But if oncoming years have worked great changes in the manner of the race which continues to be of numerical importance in the seaport city, it will take more than one or two or three or even four generations to work great changes in the manners of the well-born white-skinned folk who have ruled Charleston through the years by wit, diplomacy, the keen force of intellect more than even the force of arms. And, as the city now runs its course, it will take far more years for her to change her outward guise.

For Charleston does not change easily. She continues to be a city of yellow and of white. Other southern towns may claim distinction because of their red-walled brick houses with their white porticos, but the reds of Charleston long since softened, the green moss and the lichens have grown up and over the old walls—exquisite bits of masonry, every one of them and the products of an age when every artisan was an artist and full master of his craft. The distinctive color of the town shades from a creamy yellow to a grayish white. The houses, as we have already said, stand with their ends to the streets, with flanking walls hiding the rich gardens from the sidewalk, save for a few seductive glimpses through the well-wrought grillings of an occasional gateway. Charleston does not parade herself. The closed windows of her houses seem to close jealously against the Present as if they sought to hold within their great rooms the Past and all of the glories that were of it.

Built of brick in most instances, the larger houses and the two most famous churches, as well, were long ago given plaster coatings that they might conform to the yellow-white dominating color of the town. Invariably very high and almost invariably very narrow and bald of cornice, these old houses are roofed with heavy corrugated tiles, once red but now softened by Time into a dozen different tints. If there is another town in the land where roof-tile has been used to such picturesque advantage we have failed to see it. It gives to Charleston an incredibly foreign aspect. If it were not for the Georgian churches and the older public buildings one might see in the plaster walls and the red-tiled roofs a distinct trace of the French or the Italian. Charleston herself is not unlike many towns that sleep in the south of France or the north of Italy. It only takes the hordes of negroes upon her streets to dispel the illusion that one is again treading some corner of the Old World.

Perhaps the best way that the casual visitor to Charleston can appreciate these negroes is in their street calls—if he has not been up too late upon the preceding night. For long before seven o'clock the brigades of itinerant merchants are on their ways through the narrow streets of the old town. From the soft, deep marshlands behind it and the crevices and the turnings of the sea and all its inlets come the finest and the rarest of delicacies, and these food-stuffs find their way quite naturally to the street vendors. Porgies and garden truck, lobsters and shrimp and crab, home-made candies—the list runs to great length.

You turn restlessly in your bed at dawn. Something has stolen that last precious "forty winks" away from you. If you could find that something. . . . Hark!

There it is: Through the crispness of morning air it comes musically to your ears:

"Swimpy waw, waw. . . . Swimpy waw, waw."

And from another direction comes a slowly modulated:

"Waw cwab. WAW Cwab. Waw Cwa-a-a-b."

A sharp staccato breaks in upon both of these.

"She cwaib, she cwaib, she cwaib," it calls, and you know that there is a preference in crabs. Up one street and down another, male vendors, female vendors old and young, but generally old. If any one wishes to sleep in Charleston —well, he simply cannot sleep late in Charleston. To dream of rest while: "Sweet Pete ate her! Sweet Pete ate her!" comes rolling up to your window in tones as dulcet as ever rang within an opera house would be outrageous. It is a merry jangle to open the day, quite as remote from euphony and as thoroughly delightful as the early morning church-bells of Montreal or of Quebec. By breakfast time it is quite gone—unless you wish to include the coal black mammy who chants: "Come chilluns, get yer monkey meat—monkey—meat." And that old relic of ante-bellum days who rides a two-wheel cart in all the narrow lanes and permeates the very air with his melancholy: "Char—coal. Char—coal."

If you inquire as to "monkey meat," your Charlestonian will tell you of the delectable mixture of cocoanut and molasses candy which is to the younger generation of the town as the incomparable Lady Baltimore cake is to the older.

The churches of Charleston are her greatest charm. And of these, boldly asserting its prerogative by rising from the busiest corner of the town, the most famed is St. Michael's. St. Michael's is the lion of Charleston. Since 1764 she has stood there at Broad and Meeting streets and demanded the obeisance of the port—gladly rendered her. She has stood to her corner through sun-shine and through storm—through the glad busy years when Charleston dreamed of power and of surpassing those upstart northern towns—New York and Boston— through the bitterness of two great wars and the dangers of a third and lesser one, through cyclones and the most devastating earthquake that the Atlantic coast has ever known through all these perils this solidly wrought Temple of the Lord has come safely.

She is the real old lady of Charleston, and when she speaks the folk within the town stand at attention. The soft, sweet bells of St. Michael's are the tenderest memory that can come to a resident of the city when he is gone a long way from her streets and her lovely homes. And when the bells of St. Michael's have been stilled it has been a stilled Charleston.

For there have been times when the bells of St. Michael's have not spoken down from their high white belfry. In fact, they have crossed the Atlantic not less than five times. Cast in the middle of the eighteenth century in an English bell-foundry, they had hardly been hung within their belfry before the Revolution broke out—broke out at Charleston just as did the Civil War. Before the British left the city for the last time the commanding officer had claimed the eight bells as his "perquisite" and had shipped them back to England. An indignant American town demanded their return. Even the British commanding officer at New York, Sir Guy Carleton, did not have it within his heart to countenance such sacrilege. The bells had been already sold in England upon a speculation, but the purchaser was compelled to return them. The people of the Colonial town drew them from the wharf to St. Michael's in formal procession—the swinging of them anew was hardly less ceremonial. The first notes they sang were like unto a religious rite. And for seventy years the soft voice of the old lady of Charleston spoke down to her children—at the quarters of the hours.

After seventy years more war—ugly guns that are remembered with a shudder as "Swamp Angels," pouring shells into a proud, rebellious, hungry, unrelenting city, the stout white tower of St. Michael's a fair and shining mark for northern gunners. Charleston suddenly realized the danger to the voice of her pet old lady. There were few able-bodied men in the town—all of them were fighting within the Confederate lines—but they unshipped those precious bells and sent them up-state—to Columbia, the state capitol, far inland and safe from the possibility of sea marauders. They were hidden there but not so well but that Sherman's men in the march to the sea found them and by an act of vandalism which the South today believes far greater than that of an angered British army, completely destroyed them.

When peace came again Charleston—bruised and battered and bleeding Charleston, with the scars that time could never heal—gave first thought to her bells—a mere mass of molten and broken metal. There was a single chance and Charleston took it. That chance won. The English are a conservative nation—to put it lightly. The old bell-foundry still had the molds in which the chime was first cast—a hundred years before. Once again those old casts were wheeled into the foundry and from them came again the bells of St. Michael's, the sweetness of their tones unchanged. The town had re-gained its voice.

If we have dwelt at length upon the bells of St. Michael's it is because they speak so truly the real personality of the town. The church itself is not of less interest. And the churchyard that surrounds it upon two sides is as filled with charm and rare flavor as any churchyard we have ever seen. Under its old stones sleep forever the folk who lived in Charleston in the days of her glories—Pringles and Pinckneys; Moultries; those three famous "R's" of South Carolina—Rutledge and Ravenel and Rhett—the names within that silent place read like the roster of the colonial aristocracy. Above the silent markers, the moldering and crumbling tombs, rises a riot of God's growing things; in the soft southern air a perpetual tribute to the dead—narcissus, oleander, jessamine, the stately Pride of India bush. And on the morning that we first strolled into the shady, quiet place a red bird—the famous Cardinal Crossbeak of the south—sang to us from his perch in a magnolia tree. Twenty-four hours before and we had crossed the Hudson River at New York in a driving and a blizzard-threatening snowstorm.

The greatest charm of St. Michael's does not rest alone within the little paths of her high-walled churchyard. Within the sturdy church, in the serenity of her sanctuary, in the great square box pews where sat so many years the elect of Charleston, of the very Southland you might say; in the high-set pulpit and the unusual desk underneath where sat the old time "clark" to read the responses and the notices; even the stately pew, set aside from all the others, in which General Washington sat on the occasion of a memorable visit to the South Carolina town, is the fullness of her charm. If you are given imagination, you can see the brown and white church filled as in the old days with the planters and their families—generation after generation of them, coming first to the church, being baptized in its dove-crowned font at the door and then, years later, being carried out of that center aisle for the final time. You can see the congregations of half a century ago, faces white and set and determined. You can see one memorable congregation, as it hears the crash of a Federal shell against the heavy tower, and then listen to the gentle rector finishing the implication of the Litany before he dismisses his little flock.

Dear old St. Michael's! The years—the sunny years and the tragic years—set lightly upon her. When war and storm have wrecked her, it has been her children and her children's children who have arisen to help wipe away the scars. In a memorable storm of August, 1885, the great wooden ball at the top of her weather vane, one hundred and eighty-five feet above the street was sent hurtling down to the ground. They will show you the dent it made in the pavement flag. It was quickly replaced. But within a year worse than cyclone was upon St. Michael's—the memorable earthquake which sank the great tower eight inches deeper into the earth. And only last year another of the fearful summer storms that come now and then upon the place wreaked fearful damage upon the old church. Yet St. Michael's has been patiently repaired each time; she still towers above these disasters—as her quaint weather-vane towers above the town, itself.

After St. Michael's, St. Philip's—although St. Philip's is the real mother church of all Charleston. The old town does not pin her faith upon a single lion. The first time we found our way down Meeting Street, we saw a delicate and belfried spire rising above the greenery of the trees in a distant churchyard. The staunch church from which that spire springs was well worth our attention. And so we found our way to St. Philip's. We turned down Broad street from St. Michael's—to commercial Charleston as its namesake street is to New York —then at the little red-brick library, housed in the same place for nearly three-quarters of a century, we turned again. The south portico of St. Philip's, tall-columned, dignified almost beyond expression, confronted us. And a moment later we found ourselves within a churchyard that ranked in interest and importance with that of St. Michael's, itself.

A shambling negro care-taker came toward us. He had been engaged in helping some children get a kitten down from the upper branches of a tree in the old church-yard. With the intuition of his kind, he saw in us, strangers—manifest possibilities. He devoted himself to attention upon us. And he sounded the praises of his own exhibit in no mild key.

"Yessa defines' church in all de South," he said, as he swung the great door of St. Philip's wide open. He seemed to feel, also intuitively, that we had just come from the rival exhibit. And we felt more than a slight suspicion of jealousy within the air.

The negro was right. St. Philip's, Charleston, is more than the finest church in all the South. Perhaps it is not too much to say that it is the most beautiful church in all the land. It thrusts itself out into the street, indeed, makes the highway take a broad double curve in order to pass its front portico. But St. Philip's commits the fearful Charleston sin of being new. The present structure has only been thrusting its nose out into Church Street for a mere eighty years. The old St. Philip's was burned—one of the most fearful of all Charleston tragedies in 1835. "Yessa a big fire dat," said the caretaker. "They gib two slaves dere freedom for helpin' at dat fire."

But history only records the fact that the efforts to put out the fire in St. Philip's were both feeble and futile. It does tell, however, of a negro sailor who, when the old church was threatened by fire on an earlier occasion, climbed to the tower and tore the blazing shingles from it and was afterward presented with his freedom and a fishing-boat and outfit. Does that sound familiar? It was in our Third Reader—some lurid verses but, alas for the accuracy that should be imparted to the growing mind—it was St. Michael's to whom that wide-spread glory was given.* St. Michael's of the heart of the town once again. No wonder that St. Philip's of the side-street grieves in silence.

* In 1796 St. Philip's Church was saved when an enslaved man risked his life to extinguish a fire in the steeple. For his bravery, he was given his freedom and took the name Will Philip Lining. Hungerford mentions that when Mary Anna Phinney Stansbury (1842–1928) published her poem, "How He Saved St. Michael's," she named the wrong church.

In silence, you say. How about the bells of St. Philip's?

If you are from the North it were better that you did not ask that question. The bells of St. Philip's, in their day hardly less famous than those of the sister church, went into cannon for the defense of the South. When the last of the copper gutters had been torn from the barren houses, when the final iron kettle had gone to the gun-foundry, the supreme sacrifice was made. The bells rang merrily on a Sabbath morn and for a final time. The next day they were unshipping them and one of the silvery voices of Charleston was forever hushed.

But St. Philip's has her own distinctions. In the first place, her own graveyard is a roll-call of the Colonial elect. Within it stands the humble tomb of him who was the greatest of all the great men of South Carolina—John C. Calhoun—while nightly from her high-lifted spire there gleams the only light that ever a church-tower sent far out to sea for the guidance of the mariner. The ship-pilots along the North Atlantic very well know when they pass Charleston light-ship, the range between Fort Sumter and St. Philip's spire shows a clear fairway all the distance up to the wharves of Charleston.

There are other great churches of Charleston—some of them very handsome and with a deal of local history clustering about them, but perhaps none of these can approach in interest the Huguenot edifice at the corner of Queen and Church streets. It is a little church, modestly disdaining such a worldly thing as a spire, in a crumbling churchyard whose tombstones have their inscriptions written in French. A few folk find their way to it on Sunday mornings and there they listen attentively to its scholarly blind preacher, for sixty years the leader of his little flock.* But this little chapel is the sole flame of a famous old faith, which still burns, albeit ever so faintly, in the blackness and the shadow of the New World.

That is the real Charleston—the unexpected confronting you at almost every turn of its quiet streets: here across from the shrine of the Huguenots a ruinous building through which white and negro children play together democratically and at will, and which in its day was the Planters' Hotel and a hostelry to be reckoned with;† down another byway a tiny remnant of the city's one-time wall in the form of a powder magazine; over in Meeting Street the attenuated market

---

The poem was extremely popular, well-loved, and reprinted for over a century, regardless of the fact that Stansbury erred in her Charleston churches. Anna Wells Rutledge, "The Second St. Philip's, 112–14; "Will Philip Lining," *Century Magazine*, 728.

* Dr. Charles Stuart Vedder (1826–1917), who was blind, was pastor of the Huguenot Church for forty-eight years before he became pastor emeritus in 1914.

† The "ruinous" old Planter's Hotel (c. 1809) would languish until it was renovated as the Dock Street Theatre with WPA funds in 1936.

with a Greek temple of a hall set upon one end and the place where they sold the slaves* still pointed out to folk from the North; farther down on Meeting Street the hall of the South Carolina Society,† a really exquisite aged building wherein that distinguished old-time organization together with its still older brother, the St. Andrews, still dines on an appointed day each month and whose polished ballroom floor has felt the light dance falls of the St. Cecilias. "The St. Cecilia Society?" you interrupt; "why, I've heard of that."

Of course you have. For the St. Cecilia typifies Charleston—the social life of the place, which is all there is left to it since her monumental tragedy of half a century ago. In Charleston there is no middle ground.

You are either recognized socially—or else you are not. And the St. Cecilia Society is the sharply-drawn dividing point. Established somewhere before the beginning of the Revolution it has dominated Charleston society these many years. Invitations to its three balls each year are eagerly sought by all the feminine folk within the town. And the privilege of being invited to these formal affairs is never to be scorned—more often it is the cause of many heart burnings.

No one thing shows Charleston the more clearly than the fact that on the following morning you may search the columns of the venerable *News and Courier* almost in vain for a notice of the St. Cecilia ball. In any other town an event of such importance would be a task indeed for the society editor and all of her sub-editresses. If there was not a flashlight photograph there would be the description of the frocks—a list of the out-of-town guests at any rate. Charleston society does not concede a single one of these things. And the most the *News and Courier* ever prints is "The ball of the St. Cecilia Society was held last evening at Hibernian Hall," or a two-line notice of similar purport.

Charleston society concedes little or nothing—not even these new-fashioned meal hours of the upstart Northern towns. In Charleston a meal each four hours —breakfast at eight, a light lunch at sharp noon, dinner at four, supper again at eight. These hours were good enough for other days—ergo, they are good enough for these. And from eleven to two and again from five to seven-thirty remain the smart calling hours among the elect of the place. Those great houses do not yield readily to the Present.

---

* No slaves were sold in the Old Market (c.1840–1841), but the legend has prevailed. Slaves were sold on the north side of the Old Exchange Building (then the Custom House). When in 1856 a city ordinance prohibited this practice of public sales, slave auctions took place at several sales rooms, yards, and marts that opened along Chalmers, State, and Queen streets. In 1859, the Old Slave Mart was built at 6 Chalmers Street. It is now a museum.
† South Carolina Society Hall (c.1804).

Charleston society is never democratic—no matter how Charleston politics may run. Its great houses, behind the exclusion of those high and forbidding walls, are tightly closed to such strangers as come without the right marks of identification. From without you may breathe the hints of old mahogany, of fine silver and china, of impeccable linen, of well-trained servants, but your imagination must meet the every test as to the details. Gentility does not flaunt herself. And if the younger girls of Charleston society *do* drive their motor cars pleasant mornings through the crowded shopping district of King Street, that does not mean that Charleston, the Charleston of the barouche and the closed coupé, will ever approve.

On the April day half a century ago that the first gun blazed defiantly from Fort Sumter and opened a page of history that bade fair to alter the very course of things, Prosperity slipped out of Charleston. Gentility, Courage, Romance alone remained. Prosperity with her giant steamships and her long railroad trains never returned. The great docks along the front of the splendid harbor stand unused, the warehouses upon them molder. A brisk Texas town upon a sand-spit—Galveston—boasts that she is the second ocean-port of America, with the hundreds of thousands of Texas acres turned from grazing ranges into cotton-fields, just behind her. New Orleans is the south gate of the Middle West that has come into existence, since Charleston faced her greatest of tragedies. And the docks along her waterfront grow rusty with disuse.

She lives in her yesterdays of triumphs. Tell her that they have built a tower in New York that is fifty-five stories in height, and she will reply that you can still see the house in Church street where President Washington was entertained in royal fashion by her citizens; hint to her of the great canal to the south, and she will ask you if you remember how the blockade runners slipped night after night through the tight chain that the Federal gun-boats drew across the entrance of her harbor for four long years; bespeak into her ears the social glories of the great hotels and the opera of New York, and she will tell you of the gentle French and English blood that went into the making of her first families. Charleston has lost nothing. For what is Prosperity, she may ask you, but a dollar-mark? Romance and Courtesy are without price. Romance and Courtesy still walk in her streets, in the hot and lazy summer days, in the brilliancy of the southern moon beating down upon her graceful guarding spires, in the thunder of the storm and the soft gray blankets of the ocean mantling her houses and her gardens. And Romance and Courtesy do not forget.

Betty Paschal O'Connor, photograph, frontispiece page from
My Beloved South. New York; London: G. P. Putnam's Sons, 1914, c1913.
Courtesy of Thomas Cooper Library, University of South Carolina.

Mrs. T. P. O'Connor
(Betty Paschal O'Connor) (1913)

"Hospitable Charleston"

Mrs. T. P. O'Connor (Betty Paschal O'Connor), "Hospitable Charleston"
from *My Beloved South* (New York; London: G. P. Putnam's Sons), 1913.

Mrs. T. P. (Elizabeth Paschal) O'Connor (ca. 1850–1931), born near Austin, Texas, was descended from Anne Pope, George Washington's grandmother. She was the daughter of Texas Supreme Court judge, George Washington Paschal, and his second wife. Her mother died when she was young and O'Connor was sent to boarding schools, first to a Georgetown convent near Washington, DC, and later to a school in White Plains, New York. She returned to Washington, where she made her debut. She briefly married F. G. Howard of Washington and had a son, Francis Howard (1874–1954). During the Civil War, with the assistance of Ulysses S. Grant, she obtained a position in the United States War Office. By the early 1880s she had moved to New York City, where, to support herself and her son, she worked as a manuscript reader for Harper Brothers.

Paschal traveled to Ireland, where in 1885 she met and married Thomas Power O'Connor (1848–1929), a journalist and Irish nationalist political figure, who for nearly fifty years was a member of parliament in the House of Commons of the United Kingdom and Ireland. The couple lived in London, where Mrs. O'Connor began her career as a journalist. In 1887, she and her husband published the radical journal *The Star*. Her husband also founded *The Sun* and other newspapers. In 1917 he became the first president of the Board of Film Censors, and in 1924 he was made a member of the Privy Council by the first Labour government. Meanwhile, Elizabeth O'Connor wrote and starred in a play, *The Lady from Texas* (1901), which failed. She published a number of books, including *My Beloved South*. The O'Connors socialized in political and literary circles, and among their acquaintants and friends were James Whistler, George Bernard Shaw, Oscar Wilde, Bret Harte, Arthur Conan Doyle, Henry James, and Ellen Terry.

It is interesting to note that Mrs. O'Connor's son, Francis Howard, became a figure of the London art world. A painter, art critic, exhibition organizer, and art director, he was also a collector whose art collection comprised works by Titian, Van Dyck, Tintoretto, Bassano, Reynolds, Hogart, Sargent, Mann, and other old masters and modern paintings. More interesting is the fact that Francis's son (Mrs. O'Connor's grandson) was poet and aesthete Brian Howard (1905–1958), renowned as one of the wittiest men of his generation. Educated at Eton and Oxford, he was close friends with Evelyn Waugh and in the late 1920s and 1930s was a key figure among London's "Bright Young Things," satirized in such novels as Waugh's *Vile Bodies* (1930). Waugh used Brian Howard as inspiration for his character Anthony Blanche in *Brideshead Revisited* (1945), as did Nancy Mitford in the creation of Cedric Hampton in *Love in a Cold Climate* (1949). Howard, considered the most promising of his talented group of English friends, became famously "bad, mad and dangerous to know," and never fulfilled his promise.

In London in 1912, Elizabeth O'Connor was unwell and longing for the South of her childhood, when she decided to write a book on the South and planned a visit to the region to revive her. Conjuring memories, she claimed she kept a palm leaf fan—something once prevalent in the South—as a treasured reminder. She wrote:

> Very likely [my palm leaf fan] is the only one in London. It is kept in a special drawer, and often in the cold, dark, sleepless nights, as the raw, grey dawn penetrates my room, I will get out of bed, take from its place my old palm leaf fan and lay my tired head upon its uneven surface. It seems to give me a moment's comfort when nothing else can, for it speaks of sunshine, of the magnolia, of the banjo, that oldest of musical instruments. My old fan dissipates the London fog, and conjures a picture of my Aunt Polly Hynes and Aunt Lizzie, rocking slowly in their light cane chairs and fanning themselves on the long gallery that ran across the entire length of my old home in Texas. . . . I love just the ordinary palm leaf fan that is bought for a picayune. Its office has often been beyond rubies and pearls, in saving the sick, comforting the dying, and making life bearable on the hottest days to the living. On every gallery when summer comes numbers of these fans appear. In all the churches they are slipped in between the cushion and the pew, and they can even be found in the dear old musty Court Houses throughout the South.

So overladen with sentiment, O'Connor set out on her tour of Charleston, Savannah, New Orleans, Louisville, and Texas, and on to the Mississippi River.

It was in this mood that she, accompanied by her friend, Bee Clark from Maryland, arrived in Charleston, which she describes in *My Beloved South*.

SOURCES

Catholic Church. "Mrs. Elizabeth Paschal O'Connor." *Catholic Historical Review.* Washington, D.C.: Catholic University of America, Vol. 2 (April 1916 to January 1917).

Lancaster, Marie-Jaqueline. *Brian Howard: Portrait of a Failure.* London: Timewell Press, 2005.

"Mrs. T. P. Connor Dies of Pneumonia." *New York Times,* (Sept. 2), 1931.

"O'Connor, Thomas Power." Correspondence of James McNeill Whistler, University of Glasgow Library Special Collections at http://www.whistler.arts.gla.ac.uk/corre spondence/biog/display/?bid=O_Co_TP (accessed December 13, 2015).

Ratchford, Fannie E. "Elizabeth Paschal O'Connor." *Handbook of Texas,* Texas State Historical Association at http://www.tshaonline.org/handbook/online/articles/foc12/ (accessed December 13, 2015).

"Hospitable Charleston"

Fair were our nation's visions, and as grand
As ever floated out of any fancy-land;
Children were we in simple faith,
But god-like children, whom nor death,
Nor threat of danger drove from honour's path
In the land where we were dreaming .—D. B. Lucas

It was said before the War that one letter of introduction to Charleston would give you twenty-five dinners, and twenty-five letters in New York would give you one dinner. Dinners are, alas, more difficult to give in Charleston now, as the present-day negro does not approve of late hours, but the hearts of the people are as hospitable as ever.

We arrived in that beautiful white city on Saturday, and I had no sooner delivered my letters of introduction than cards were left accompanied by invitations (such a pretty, charming attention), to occupy various pews in St. Michael's, a quaint, interesting church. The old-fashioned pews are so high they almost hide the occupants.

For many years St. Michael's was a church by day and a blessed lighthouse by night, sending out from its tall spire rays of warning to ships at sea. The little sweet old-fashioned churchyard is covered with grass and full of flowers. The old tombs certainly bear witness to the healthy climate, for almost everybody seemed to have lived to the ripe age of seventy-five, seventy-eight, eighty or eighty-two years. Probably the most unique monument in all the world is a rude memorial on one of these ancient graves. A young English settler came to Charleston with his wife and his belongings, among them a very solid oak bedstead. When his wife died he had no money for a headstone, but hoping eventually to buy one he put up temporarily the head of the bed. On it is cut in rude letters: "Mary Ann Luyten, wife of Will Luyten. Died September 9th, 1770, in the 27th year of her age." Perhaps he left Charleston before he could provide another headstone; at any rate, this stout oak memorial is as good today as when it was erected in 1770. Its quaintness making it a subject of keen interest to the tourist, it is now protected by a strong wire netting, and there seems to be no reason why it should not last another century.

Charleston had pleasant memories for me, as my Aunt Polly Hynes had made a visit there in her youth, many years before the War, and, as a little girl, I used to hear her speak of the Rhetts, the Pinckneys, the Middletons, the Vander Horsts, the Barnwells, the Pringles, the Ravenels, the Izards, the Draytons, the Allstons and the Chesnuts, at whose house she visited. The great families apparently lived like princes, and even people who were not rich kept fifteen or twenty servants.

My grandfather, Governor Duval, met the Chesnuts in Washington and corresponded afterwards for many years with her husband. The families interchanged visits, for the Chesnuts were as hospitable as my grandfather.* Mrs. Chesnut got all her gowns from Paris and was distinguished for her beautiful head-dresses and her lovely jewels. Aunt Polly, during her visit, was provided with an accomplished lady's maid, who was an excellent hair-dresser and a wonderful clear-starcher.

In those days ladies wore transparent India muslins embroidered and trimmed with lace, and organdies with a blue or purple ground. These dainty gowns required starch made of gum arabic, which was as transparent as jelly, and not every maid understood the art of using it. Aunt Polly embroidered quite as well as any professional needlewoman; her English thread lace was transferred from one dress to another and her India muslins must have been exquisite, so she appreciated a proper *blanchisseuse*.

Whenever dreams were spoken of, Aunt Polly always related the fortunate dream of her friend, Mrs. Robert Shubrick, which had, under extraordinary circumstances, saved the life of her brother who was coming to Charleston by

* William Pope Duval (1784–1854), appointed the first civil governor of the newly acquired Territory of Florida in 1822. Sen. James Chesnut, first mentioned in the Whitelaw Reid account, and his wife, Mary Boykin Chesnut (1823–1886), whose Civil War diary was first published as *A Diary from Dixie* (1905). They lived at Mulberry Plantation in Camden.

boat from Philadelphia. Three times in one night this lady had a recurrent vision of him in a surging sea with a little white flag floating in front of him. So impressed was she with the truth of the warning, that she got her husband to send a pilot boat to cruise in the track of the incoming vessels, and the third day something small and white was seen floating on the waves of the sea, and, coming nearer, a half-starved man was picked up lying on a chicken-coop—the only survivor of a ship which had gone down three days before.

Aunt Polly, who was a famous gardener, had taken back the gardenia with her to Florida and from there she had brought it to Texas. It was named after Doctor Garden* of Charleston, a famous horticulturist, a popular doctor and a Royalist. My mother, who was more proud of her garden than of anything in the world, used to say when she showed the hibiscus, a flower which in the morning was white, in the afternoon rose and in the evening red, and which I always thought in my childhood came from fairyland—"This was sent me from South Carolina by one of the Pinckneys."

The first time I went into the street in Charleston the catalpa, and the sweet bay, and the pink mimosa, all old friends, gave me a fragrant greeting. But the live oaks, draped in moss, were the oldest friends of all. My friend, Bee and I started out intending to take a long walk on Monday morning. The open doors of the library, however, were too tempting and there we stopped.[†] It was organized in 1728 and is truly a delightful place in which to spend an hour or two. It contains some rare and valuable manuscripts and the *Gazette,* Charleston's first newspaper, a tiny little sheet, printed on grey paper with a printer's ink which must have been very rich as it is as thick and black as possible even today. Occasionally, it is cold enough for fires, but the windows and the doors of the library are continually open, the bright yet softened sunlight of the winter streams in, and the air is like champagne, warm enough for comfort and cool enough to be exhilarating, for Charleston has a wide sea frontage. The beautiful East and South Batteries with their splendid houses and avenues of palmettos and magnolias, are suggestive of Nice, but the climate is infinitely superior to that of the South of France, as there is no raw chill with the setting of the sun, but just an agreeable crisp coolness.

---

* Dr. Alexander Garden (1730–1791), Scottish physician, botanist, and zoologist, who arrived in Charleston to practice medicine around 1752. He spent his spare time studying the natural history of the region, sending specimens to botanist Carl Linnaeus in Sweden. During the Revolution he sided with the British. After the war, his property was confiscated, and he had to leave South Carolina.

† The Library Society at 50 Broad Street would soon move to its new location at 164 King Street.

The old houses are stately and beautiful. They combine the best periods of English architecture with the needs of the South. Generally two long balconies, one on the first and one on the second storey, run along the entire side of the house, and there Charleston people live during the summer, which is said to be by no means an unpleasant part of the year, with the bathing and boating by moonlight on the silver sea. The water of Charleston is quite unique, it flows from artesian wells, is very cool and pleasant to drink and highly charged with soda, magnesia, and salt, therefore it is a strong and valuable medicinal water, a splendid aid to the digestion (it was marvellously beneficial to me), and a great skin beautifier. If a little German village possessed the waters of Charleston, half of Europe would be flocking to drink them. A clever doctor from Boston staying in the same house with me, who had suffered for years from indigestion, said the waters of Charleston had completely cured him. He declared that if he was ten years younger he would settle there, open a large sanatorium, which with the combination of the sun, the tonic air, and the curative properties of the waters would enable many a chronic invalid to recover health.

The environs of Charleston are quite delightful. Summerville, a beautiful little place, semi-tropical in verdure, rich in the odour of flowering shrubs, is so extraordinarily profuse in its abundance of wistaria that it looks like a long amethyst picture from a Japanese screen. There is an excellent hotel in the midst of pine and cypress and magnolia trees, and a large tea plantation not far away,* which we drove through. The tea did not interest me so much as the beautiful roses and camellias, but we bought a small package and tried it. In this respect I fear I am de-nationalised, for I infinitely prefer the tea we get in England.

On the other side of Charleston, fifteen or twenty minutes by boat and a little distance by rail, is the Isle of Palms where many of the residents have cottages. It is a charming spot and might with equal appropriateness be called the Isle of Oleanders, for they grow to a fine size and in great luxuriance among the palmetto trees down to the very water's edge. On our return from the Isle of Palms we stopped at Fort Moultrie and saw the tomb of Osceola. The Fort is now a pleasant military post and a fine-looking Irish sergeant showed us over it,

---

* Summerville had become a "curative and restorative" winter resort in the pinelands, as one of the two best places in the world for the treatment and recovery of lung disorders. In 1891, Charlestonian Frederick W. Wagener (1876–1936) opened the Pine Forest Inn on fifty-two acres. The building was razed in the 1960s. Pinehurst Tea Plantation was founded in 1888 by Dr. Charles Shepard (1842–1915), who successfully grew prize-winning tea until his death. Many decades later, some of Shepard's tea plants were salvaged, which eventually led to the founding of Charleston Tea Plantation on Wadmalaw Island, where today the American Classic Tea brand is grown.

and he pointed out with pride Fort Jasper, named in honour of Sergeant Jasper, a gallant non-commissioned officer of the Revolution.* When the British were besieging the fort the flagstaff was shot away and the flag fell, arousing the British to a great cheer, for they thought it meant surrender. Jasper leaped from the wall, seized and tore the flag from the broken staff and, climbing back fastened it to a rod, saying, "Colonel, we must fight under our flag!" and the white crescent rose again. Sergeant McCarthy said it was the only monument of a private soldier in America.

I asked him a good many questions about military service. He had been in the service for years and said it was harder every day to get recruits. America has so many resources and possibilities for the working man that he hesitates to join the army. "Still there are chances even for soldiers," the Sergeant added; "we have a private who owns a restaurant in Charleston."

"How did he manage that?" asked Bee.

"He is a Greek," said the Sergeant. "He enlisted as soon as he came over here and he lent out his first month's pay at a dollar-and-a-quarter interest on the dollar, the money to be returned within the month."

"There is a Greek proverb in the East," I said, "that it takes two Jews to be equal to one Greek."

"Since then," said Sergeant McCarthy, "while never spending a penny himself, he has lent money to the whole regiment."

"And always," I said, "gets back his usurious interest."

"Always," said the Sergeant, "although if the Colonel knew about it he would stop his game. In four years he has made about four thousand dollars, but," he added with a sigh, "only a Greek can do it, not a native-born American nor an Irishman. My pay is good, fifty or so dollars a month. I am a bachelor with no kids to provide for, and yet I go now and then to Calegeiri Clementeanio for a loan."

What a pity that Greek cannot meet Greek only in this world, for evidently he will always get the better of every other nationality.

On my way home it was borne in upon me that I was really in my own leisurely land, for as we were hurrying to the boat the Captain smilingly called out, "We will wait: take your time, take your time, we are not going off without you."

"Now," I said to Bee, "there is the true, considerate, obliging spirit of the South."

---

* Battery Jasper, a coastal gun battery named for Sgt. William Jasper (1750–1779). At its completion in 1898, the battery was transferred to the US Coast Artillery. It was deactivated in 1942.

Charleston socially is one of the most agreeable places in America and one of the most English, though it really has no right to be, for it was not like Virginia, settled by the Cavaliers, but by a mixture of races—English, Scotch, and Irish, Belgian, Swiss, and French Huguenots. But the English curiously enough have left their impress here more clearly than anywhere else in America. The accent is a pretty, softened, musical English, the tastes of the people, the literature, the atmosphere, after all these centuries, are still English.

I went to have a dish of tea with Mrs. St. Julien Ravenel, the author of that delightful book, *Charleston, the Place and the People,* and found that she was intimately conversant with English politics, literature, and present-day affairs. She subscribes to a number of English periodicals, pictorial magazines, and *The Times,* and is as well up in the news of London as any lady living in one of the provincial towns in England. She is a tall, distinguished-looking woman of delicate and fair appearance, not unlike the late Baroness Burdett-Coutts,* for she has the same serious manner and the same cultivated dignity and lovableness. She said she had seen an article lately in one of the Northern magazines which spoke of the want of cultivation in the women who formerly lived on plantations. "There was never a more unfounded assertion than this," she declared, "because women who were brought up on a plantation had little to do except read. They generally had excellent governesses, with access to good libraries and abundance of leisure. There was constant intercourse between England and Charleston. The men of the family were sent to Eton and Oxford to be educated, and their sisters emulated them in learning. Many women knew both Greek and Latin, were well versed in literature and knew French well." This article went on to say that they knew nothing of English literature; yet I remember one friend, who had received her entire education in England, telling me years ago that she had only read four American authors—Poe, Hawthorne's *Marble Faun,* but not his *Yankee Tales,* Washington Irving, and Prescott's *Conquest of Mexico,* "although," she added, "I believe that is mostly fiction."

Mrs. Ravenel herself is certainly one of the most widely read women I have ever met and, indeed, I found all the people of Charleston cultivated and intelligent, with the charming manner inherited from aristocratic ancestors, who already from older countries had great traditions, and pride of family behind them. There is a certain stateliness of deportment still remaining. Quite young people speak to their elders as "Mistress Pinckney," "Mistress Pringle," and so on. Even some of the very old negroes have beautiful manners.

* Angela Georgina Burdett-Coutts (1814–1906) had been one of the wealthiest women in England and a famous philanthropist.

The day I dined with Judge Brawley and his wife (he is one of South Carolina's most distinguished sons, a brave soldier in the Confederate army, who lost one arm in a gallant encounter almost at the beginning of the War),* we drank to the success of our beloved South in fine old Madeira.

On our arrival in Charleston we had been lucky enough to find shelter in the house of Mrs. Dotterer, a handsome, agreeable woman and an excellent housekeeper. Mrs. Chapman, her mother, after the War, started the Woman's Exchange,† a most useful institution with all sorts of interesting objects for sale, authentic antiques, carved looking-glasses, good specimens of genuine Sheffield plate and good copies of old furniture. I bought a wild turkey-tail fan and shall use it in England as a fire-screen. The "Lady Baltimore" cake, the *chef d'oeuvre* of the Exchange, so toothsomely described by Owen Wister, is now known all over the world. The ladies there receive orders from Russia, China, Japan, and I daresay, even from the Balkans. My kind hostesses gave me a little surprise that evening, a "Lady Baltimore" cake all my own. It was exceedingly good, but very rich, being made with layers of delicate white cake filled between with a thick sugared paste of divers sorts of nuts and citron. The top is of richly flavoured icing, and covered with candied flowers.

That night at supper someone told the story of Mrs. Petigru King, one of the idols of my childhood. She had incomparable wit, great charm, and, if not beauty, the reflection of it, for her skin was exquisite, her bright shining nut-brown hair a lovely colour, and her smile was enchanting. Thackeray had heard of her wit, and, to draw out her powers when she asked him the question, "Mr. Thackeray, how do you like America?" his eyes twinkling with mischief, he answered: "Very much, but the Americans, they are vulgar." Whereupon she quickly answered: "That is easily understood, for we are all descendants of the English." He said, laughing, "Forgive my rudeness, it was only to make you unsheathe the dagger of your wit. I am quite satisfied with the result."

There is no function historically more delightful or interesting in America than Charleston's St. Cecilia balls. The society began in 1737 with a concert given on

---

* Judge William H. Brawley (1841–1916), former US congressman, and Marion Emma Porter Brawley (1843–1906) lived at 9 Legare Street, where their "entertainments were among the most elegant ever given in Charleston and the dinner parties of the Brawleys were famous affairs." Breaux, *Autobiography of a Chameleon,* 109.

† Mrs. Henry (Julia Belle Chapman) Dotterer (1863–1935) and her mother, Caroline Connor Chapman (1838–1928), lived at 1 Water Street. The Women's Exchange for Women's Work, founded in 1885 with the intention of helping the "educated poor" become self-sufficient, was managed by a board of fifty women. Social Register Association, *Social Register,* 94; Ayers, *Promise of the New South: Life after Reconstruction,* 77–78.

a Thursday, St. Cecilia's day, and comprised originally a number of earnest musical amateurs who soon became ambitious and paid a large salary to the *chef
d'orchestre,* who in 1773 received five hundred guineas a year. The arts and
graces declined, however, as the years went by, giving place perforce to more
practical interests. Fewer men had time for the study of music, and when President Monroe accompanied by John C. Calhoun, his Secretary of State, visited
Charleston, it was decided that St. Cecilia must give a ball in lieu of a concert.
Since then, except during the War, there has been no interruption of the three
balls given every winter by the St. Cecilia Society. The members are elected by
the society and it is no uncommon thing for the father, grandfather, and great-
grandfather of an applicant to have been members before him. Mrs. Ravenel
says, "If a new resident, or a family recently brought into notice, there will be
inquiry, perhaps hesitation and a good backing will be desirable. When a man
is elected the names of the ladies of his household are at once put upon the list
and remain there forever, changes of fortune affecting them not at all. The members elect the Vice-President, Secretary and Treasurer and Board of Managers;
the managers continue from year to year, vacancies occurring only by death, the
eldest manager becoming President and Vice-President in due order."

The invitations are in themselves quite unique, for every name on them has
figured in history before and during the Revolution, bringing back memories of
the old picturesque life of the plantation gone to come no more. Edward Rutledge, one of the present managers, is a descendant of John Rutledge who wrote
so heroically to Moultrie in 1776: "General Lee wishes you to evacuate the Fort.
You will not do so without an order from me. I will cut off my right hand sooner
than write it.—J. Rutledge."

Joseph W. Barnwell, my escort to supper, a handsome clean-shaven barrister,
with dark humorous eyes is a descendant of "Tuscarora Jack,"* a favourite hero
of my childhood, chiefly I think on account of his name, although he was a
daring, resolute fighter in the wars with the Indians. Another of the family, Robert Woodward Barnwell, a member of the Convention at Montgomery, gave the
casting vote which made Jefferson Davis President of the Confederacy. But every
name—Middleton, Porcher, Vander Horst, Sinkler, Stony, Barker, Ravenel—is
honoured in the history not only of the State of Carolina, but of America, and
these splendid names have been as nearly as possible preserved in the invitations

---

* Joseph Walker Barnwell (1846–1930), an attorney and politician who lived at 48 South
Battery. His ancestor, Col. John Barnwell (d.1724) from Ireland, settled in Charleston in
1701. He was known as "Tuscarora Jack" after commanding an expedition against the
Tuscarora Indians in 1711. He was later a colonel in the war against the Yamasee Indians
(1715).

of the St. Cecilia's Society by the election of sons, grandsons, and great-grandsons throughout the centuries. They are as gallant gentlemen as their great-grandfathers and even in the present-day balls a trace of the old order exists. No sitting out on stair-steps or hiding away in corners is allowed at these historic parties.

A story is told of one of the "Four Hundred," who on her way from Florida to New York received an invitation to a St. Cecilia ball. She sat out one or two of the dances on the staircase outside the ballroom. Such a breach of etiquette was unknown and was certainly not to be allowed, so the President, a man of beautiful manners and charming address, found the lady in a secluded corner and offering his arm said, "I have come, dear Madam, to conduct you to the ballroom. We cannot afford, if only for a brief moment, to lose so brilliant an ornament."

"Oh," she said, "I know I am breaking a rule, but all the world does it in New York and London." The President replied, "New York and London are too large to look after individual guests; here we can see to their welfare, and I fear you will take cold in this draughty hall." The lady laughed, took his arm, and went back to the ballroom.

The men of Charleston subscribe liberally, and the balls are beautifully arranged. The society owns its own napery, silver, glass and table ornaments and, with each table decorated with flowers, the balls have all the refinement of private entertainments. The suppers are served promptly at twelve o'clock, as the dances begin at nine, and are prepared by negro cooks, the ladies of Charleston superintending everything and often cutting sandwiches and preparing some special delicacy with their own hands. The round dances are interspersed with rather stately music when the older people walk round the room, for the St. Cecilias, unlike most balls in America, are by no means given exclusively for young girls. Mammas and even grandmammas are expected to be present and to participate in the evening's enjoyment.

Etiquette requires the president to take down the latest bride to supper, while the vice-president takes the most distinguished stranger. The girls are supposed after each dance to return to their chaperons, and in this way the men are left free to seek in time the partners engaged for the next dance. This is a fashion that might well be introduced at other balls in America. All the invitations of the St. Cecilias are delivered by hand and a stranger must almost belong to the *livre d'or* to receive one. When, however, the guest has arrived she is entertained like a queen; every dance on her programme is filled up, or if she happens not to dance, agreeable partners are provided for conversation, and no one who has attended a St. Cecilia ball is likely to forget its distinctive and hospitable charm.

There was one thing I wanted very much in Charleston that I did not get, a palmetto salad—it is said to be a very great delicacy and is made from the heart of the palmetto tree. It seems a great extravagance to destroy an entire tree for a dish, but on the plantations there are so many trees that one more or less makes very little difference. Those who have eaten of it say there is no flavour so fine and delicate as this round white heart dressed with fresh olive oil, lemon instead of vinegar, and a dash of salt. One of my hostesses, sweet little Mrs. Mitchell,* promised if I would remain a few days longer she would send to her plantation for this luxurious specialty of South Carolina, and make a salad with her own tiny hands. I couldn't wait, but some day I am going back for it.

The morning for our visit to the Magnolia Cemetery was glorious with sunshine, and Bee proposed that we should make a détour and go by the East Battery to take our car. Even grim Fort Moultrie looked cheerful that day; there were several beautiful yachts in the harbour, the avenue of palmettos rustled their leaves in a faint bright breeze, and as I turned to look at the pretty white town, peaceful and prosperous, it seemed amazing that so much of it had survived the five hundred and sixty days of bombardment it had sustained during the Civil War. Certainly no city has suffered in the past more than Charleston, for, after the long siege, when her sons by land and sea kept her "virgin and inviolate to the last," came a severe earthquake. The house we were living in carries a great iron bar across the front in memory of this event. Fate seems indeed to have tried the people in order to prove their courage, which is indomitable.

The cannon along the Battery always detained us for a little; they speak so eloquently of that long bombardment, and each bears a brass tablet telling of the service it had done. A big gun looking directly upon Fort Moultrie had been down in the depths of the sea and this was its honourable record: "This gun, having taken part in the attack on Fort Sumter by an armoured squadron, April 7th, 1863, was recovered from the wreck of the sunken *Keokuk* by an exploit of heroic enterprise, and mounted on Sullivan's Island, where for two years it was used in defense of the city it had once been brought to attack. Removed to this place by the Civil Authority, August, 1889." Some of the guns had seen four years of active service; when the sun shone so brilliantly upon them it turned the black of the iron into a shimmering blue. Fate, with even her hardest knocks, cannot deprive Charleston of its ideal climate, and in another decade all her old prosperity will return to her, for there is no more beautiful spot in America than this

* Belle Witte Mitchell (1874–1965) lived at 8 South Battery. Her husband, Julian Mitchell Jr. (1867–1960), was an attorney, businessman, and state legislator. They owned Point of Pines Plantation on Edisto Island. Social Register Association, *Social Register*, 111.

lovely city by the sea. Even Magnolia Cemetery smiled that day, and the dead seemed in happy peace. The monument to South Carolina's great soldier, General Wade Hampton, stands in the centre of the Confederate dead, whom with such valiant courage he led into heroic action. The most beautiful monuments are not however of stone; they are nature's great live-oaks, with their widely spreading branches, bending tenderly over the hundreds of little headstones, as if to say, "Soldiers, sleep well."

The sun grew so warm that to escape it I sat under one of the trees with the long grey moss softly touching my face like the gentle hand of an old friend. Bee was busy with her Kodak trying to get an impression of one of the ancient oaks carrying seven centuries of mystic gloom, when a lady, dressed in deepest mourning, with a sweet face, old, thin and very white, came and sat beside me. She said, "Good morning; the sun is very warm for this time of the year."

I said, "It is, indeed, but having been out of the South so long I am more than grateful for it."

"Do you," she said, "live abroad?"

"Yes," I said, "I live in London, but now I have no 'dwelling more by sea or shore.'"

"Ah," she said, "then it is better to wander."

"Yes," I said, "perhaps—this is a very beautiful place for rest."

She said, "I try to find it so, for, like Bobbie, the little faithful dog in Edinburgh, who when he lost his master spent his life by the side of his grave, I spend my life here. All my six children sleep over there"—she pointed to a row of graves not far off. "Whenever the sun shines I come here in the morning, and I leave in the evening. I do not always bring flowers, but I talk to them and often I go away comforted, for I feel they have talked to me."

"I, too, have my sorrows, but they are nothing compared to yours."

"I can bear mine," she said, "for I know I shall find my children again. I am a little lonely and I grow weary of waiting, but that is all."

"Good-bye," I said "I shall often think of you."

"I need not give you my address in Charleston," she said, "you will always find me here."

Bee had photographed the noble tree and met me with her camera.

"You look white and fagged, are you tired?" she asked.

"No," I said, "but a broken heart that still lives has been shown to me. The quiet hearts of the dead are at peace; it is the sorrows of the living that are overwhelming."

Old market, Charleston, S.C., between 1900 and 1915.
Detroit Publishing Co., publisher. Library of Congress.

William Dean Howells (1915)

"In Charleston, A Travel Sketch"

William Dean Howells, "In Charleston, A Travel Sketch" from *Harper's Monthly* 131 (October 1915): 747–57.

William Dean Howells (1837–1920), realist novelist, poet, literary critic, and playwright, was born in Martin's Ferry, Ohio. His father was in the newspaper business and by the time Howells was nine years old, he was working the presses. He educated himself through intensive reading and the study of Spanish, French, Latin, and German. By the age of eighteen, he was writing for his family's newspaper, the *Sentinel,* and other Ohio area newspapers, and contributing poems to the *Atlantic Monthly.* Because he did not want to abandon his family during a period of hard times, he declined scholarships to Harvard and became a Columbus correspondent for the *Cincinnati Gazette.* His first editorial job was for the *Ohio State Journal,* a Republican paper in the state capital. While Howells was news editor, the *Journal* became even more partisan once it became apparent that the issue of slavery would cause a major conflict in the country. This venture into partisan politics led to Howells's involvement in Abraham Lincoln's presidential campaign and his authorship of the *Life of Lincoln* (1860). As a reward, in 1861 Lincoln appointed him US consul in Venice, Italy, where he avoided the horrors of the American Civil War.

Meanwhile, Howells had begun his professional writing career in earnest by contributing to the *Atlantic Monthly,* the *Saturday Press,* and the *Cincinnati Dial.* He coauthored his first book, *Poems of Two Friends* (1860) with J. J. Piatt. On Christmas Eve 1862, at the American embassy in Paris, he married Elinor Mead from Vermont, a sister of sculptor Larkin Goldsmith Mead and the architect William Rutherford Mead of the firm McKim, Mead, and White. Upon his return to the United States in 1865, he settled in Boston and became assistant editor of *The Atlantic Monthly* in 1866, and at the same time published two novels based on his experiences in Italy, *Venetian Life* (1866) and *Italian Journeys* (1867). By 1871, Howells had risen to the position of editor of *The Atlantic*

Monthly. Nicknamed "The Dean of American Letters," he became nationally known as editor of the popular journal. During his tenure, he published much of Mark Twain's early work and concentrated on his own writing career.

In 1867 he received a master's degree from Harvard and in 1869 became a university lecturer there. He also endeavored in a period of prolific writing, publishing *Suburban Sketches* (1872), followed by other European novels and producing at least eight books within thirteen years. He was a bestselling novelist in the 1870s. Howells, who rejected artificial sentimentality and romanticism in American fiction, played an important part in the rise of the Realism movement in the United States. He challenged American authors to choose American subjects, to portray them honestly, and to create characters who used Native American speech. In 1881 he resigned from *The Atlantic Monthly* and published another six books between 1881 and 1884. His literary reputation soared with the realist novel *A Modern Instance* (1882). In 1885 he produced his masterwork, *The Rise of Silas Lapham*. Howells spent the rest of his life writing. He wrote over a hundred books in various genres, including novels, poems, literary criticism, plays, memoirs, and travel narratives, as well as essays and sketches in *Harper's Weekly* and other major magazines. In 1886, he became associate editor of *Harper's*.

In 1908 he was elected the first president of the American Academy of Arts and Letters, which instituted the Howells Medal for Fiction in 1915. A resolute critic of racial intolerance, he was a founding member of the National Association for the Advancement of Colored People (NAACP) in 1909. W. E. B. Du Bois praised him with the words: "When a band of earnest men spoke for Negro emancipation, William Dean Howells was among the first to sign the call." Howells became president of the American Anti-Imperialist League and was a strong supporter of women's suffrage in later years. Having come of age in an era of "political corruption, industrial greed, and American imperialism," he remained an outspoken opponent of social injustice; his novels reflect that belief.

His wife died in 1910, and from 1915 to 1918, Howells and his daughter, Mildred, began to winter in St. Augustine, Florida. There he worked on an (unfinished) novel about that city. Perhaps it was merely proximity that led him to Charleston, or his earlier friendship with Constance Fenimore Woolson, who had first wintered in St. Augustine (1873–1879) and published an article on Charleston for *Harper's Monthly* (1875). Woolson's collection of short stories, *Rodman the Keeper: Southern Sketches* (1880), praised by their mutual friend, Henry James, as an apt evocation of "the *voicelessness* of the conquered and reconstructed South," intrigued him. Henry James had published his own account of Charleston in *The American Scene* (1907).

Or Howells may have simply been on assignment when, in the spring of 1915, he and Mildred journeyed to Charleston. They stayed at The Villa Margherita at 4 South Battery, an Italianate villa built in 1892 for Charleston banker Andrew Simonds (1861–1905) and his wife, Daisy Breaux Simonds (1864–1949). After Andrew Simonds's premature death in 1905, Daisy had leased the house to Charlestonian Ina Liese Dawson (1875–1961), who had added an annex and converted the house into a fashionable inn. Daisy Simonds named it after herself: the Villa Margherita—"margherita" being Italian for "daisy." Dawson was a superb hostess with an elegantly trained staff, and the hotel served wealthy northerners on their winter excursions to South Carolina hunting plantations, as well as other seasonal guests. Over its history, many famous guests stayed at the inn. (It was returned to a family residence in 1961).

So from the Villa Margherita in early April 1915, William Dean Howells set about describing Charleston. His subsequent "In Charleston, A Travel Sketch," was accompanied by illustrations executed by Charleston artist Alice Huger Smith. Smith's association with Howells would culminate in her later friendship with his son, architect John Mead Howells (1868–1959), who in 1934 would retire to Charleston, purchase and restore the Col. John Stuart house, and become a key participant in the city's historical revival.

SOURCES

Collister, Peter. *Writing the Self: Henry James and America*. New York: Routledge, 2015.

Goodman, Susan, and Carl Dawson. *William Dean Howells: A Writer's Life*. Berkeley: University of California Press, 2005.

Howells Family Papers. Houghton Library, Harvard University, Boston.

Smith, Alice Ravenel Huger, and Daniel Elliott Huger. *Dwelling Houses of Charleston, South Carolina*. Charleston: History Press, 2007.

"In Charleston, A Travel Sketch"

It was when, through an unseasonable storm of cold rain, we found ourselves housed on the Battery at Charleston that we realized ourselves in a city which was not quite like any other city, and which differenced itself from other cities more and more as our ten days of it passed. They were the first ten days of April, and that they were wet and cold in the beginning instead of bright and warm was a greater grief to the Charlestonians, who almost immediately began making us their friends, than to us we accepted their excuses for the weather quite as if they could have had it otherwise. The fact is that it was the same make of chill that we had been experiencing at St. Augustine during a month past without knowing that it was bad, though people there said it ought to have been indefinitely better. The winter, they said, had been very perverse; but we considered what it must have been in the North and tried not to suffer from it as much as they thought we should.

When the weather cleared at Charleston and the sun came out, the mocking-birds came out with it on the Battery. The flowers seemed never to have been in, but were only waiting to be recognized in the gardens that flanked the houses facing across the space of palmettos and live-oaks and columns and statues and busts, and burly Parrott guns glowering eastward and southward over the sea-walls. The flowers were there to attest the habitual softness of the Charleston winter, but experience of Riviera and Bermuda winters had taught me that flowers are not to be trusted in these matters. Still, I am not saying that the Charleston winter is not mild, and as for the Charleston spring, what I saw and felt of it was divine, especially on the Battery.

It is a city imagined from a civic consciousness quite as intense as that of any of the famed cities of the world, say such as Boston, and it built most of its stateliest dwellings in that place. All the old houses that front upon it are stately; on the South Battery modern houses have intruded themselves in some of the gardened spaces; but on the East Battery the line is yet unbroken. I should not know quite how to justify them in making me think of a line of Venetian palaces, but that was what they did, and the sense of something Venetian in them recurred to me throughout our ten days. Perhaps it was the sea and the sky that conspired to trick my fancy; certainly it was not the spacious gardens beside the spacious houses, nor the make of the houses, though their size, if not their shape, flattered my fond notion. Without being exactly of one pattern, they were of one general type which I found continually repeated throughout the city. A certain rather narrow breadth of stone or brick or wood abuts on the street, and as wide a space of veranda, colonnaded and rising in two or even three stories, looks southward or westward over a more or less ample garden-ground. The street door opens into the house, or perhaps into the veranda, or perhaps you enter by the gate from the garden where the blossoms of our summer paint the April air, and the magnolia shines and darkles over the coarse-turfed lawn. The garden-beds seem more meagerly covered with plants than with us, but there are roses and jasmines in every coign of vantage, and other flowers which my vocabulary fails in the names of, though I think of peach blossoms a month old, but young still, and pear buds freshly blown. Nearly all the gardens are shut in by high brick walls, and it is something fine to pass in or out by the gate of such a garden, with a light iron-work grill overhead and small globes on the high-shouldered brick piers; and it adds I know not just what grace of experience to have one's hostess call up to the colored uncle dusting the second floor of the balcony above, "Wait a moment, Romeo," though in the play I believe it was Juliet on the balcony.

Charleston is a city of some seventy thousand people, black and white, and it covers, I should say, about as much space as Manhattan, rashly judging from what seemed our night-long drive from the railroad station to the hotel on our arrival. Probably, also, the city's extent is an illusion arising from the indefinite repetition of such houses and gardens in every quarter. There are certain distinct business thoroughfares, long, very long, stretching out in shops mostly low; but people who built their dwellings in the old time seem to have built them wherever they liked, unhampered by any dictate of fashion: There is apparently no East Side or West, as in New York; no South End or Back Bay, as in Boston; the court quarter of Charleston was where any of its proud families chose to put their houses. They lived nearly always in houses of that two-story, southward-veranda type, overlooking those spacious gardens. Wherever we walked or drove we counted such houses by scores, by hundreds; if I did not care what I said, I should say there were thousands of such houses. They looked out from their leaves and flowers over streets of modern brick or asphalt, or of primeval sand where the tire buried itself in the dust and the hoof slowed to a walk; or if they varied in this or that stateliness from it, the type, they did not wholly forget or suffer the passing stranger to forget it.

I have the feeling that the streets, whatever make they were of, were better kept than the streets of Northern towns, which have not known the impulse to purge and live cleanly given by Colonel Waring to New York.* Certainly they looked neater than the streets of such a typical New England town as Portsmouth; but how they were kept so I cannot tell; the old tradition of the turkey-buzzard as the scavenger of Charleston dwindled, in my observance, to a solitary bird of the species in the street beside the Old Market. As to other matters of public cleanliness, I should say that the tobacco-chewing habit, so well-nigh extinct in the North, is still rife in the South, if one may judge by the frank provision made for it. In the shuttle-car which carries the traveler into Charleston from the railroad junction when one comes from the South, every seat was equipped with a cuspidor quite a foot across; and a cuspidor was the repulsive convenience obtruded at frequent intervals in the waiting-room of the station when one departed. The cuspidors there were much smaller than those of the shuttle-car; but then they were filthier; and it is with very sensible relief

---

* Much newspaper coverage had been given to Col. George E. Waring Jr., who in 1895 had taken charge of what is now the Department of Sanitation and cleaned up the streets of New York.

that I turn back from them to those far more characteristic streets where I have been asking the reader to accompany me. I rather liked the sandy streets as the more frankly native, and I particularly liked that one which widened to a plaza before the vast old Aiken house, and the kindred houses of like presence which it had, as it were, willed beside it.* Their variance from the prevailing type was decided, but except in this impressive group the type held its own.

The houses of that neighborhood were square rather than oblong, and they wanted the southward verandas, which scarcely happened with any of the other old houses. I have no sense of gardens beside them, but, on the other hand, the space between them had a background of the weather-worn, never-painted hovels which may have been the negroes' quarters in the time of slavery, and may still be the abodes of their poverty. Upon the whole, perhaps because I saw them almost the last of the great old houses, they gave me a strong sense of their surpassing dignity. But when we had left them I reverted with increased content to the typical houses which I think were more naturally evolved from an instinctive obedience to the conditions, climatic, civic, social. The noble mansions on the East Battery are all galleried oblongs, flanked with gardens; though one of the noblest mansions, if not the most noble, in Charleston, the beautiful old Pringle House, fronts the street, a square bulk from a narrow space fenced high with fine iron-work, and with the faltering memory of its lovely old garden lurking sway from the public eye behind it. We looked into this garden from the stairway leading to the drawing-room where we had sat a twilight moment in the presence of the young builder of the house, a blur of vague richness on the panel for which Sir Joshua Reynolds had painted him in his red coat a century and a half ago, and from which he seemed to offer us the hospitality of the mansion, though this had always descended from generation to generation in the female line, and does not even bear the founder's name.†

---

* Howells refers to the Aiken-Rhett House (c. 1820) at 48 Elizabeth Street, once the home of Gov. William Aiken, and Aiken Row, seven identical rental houses Gov. Aiken built after 1830 flanking Wragg Square. Only two of the seven have survived. The Aiken-Rhett house is today a house museum owned and operated by the Historic Charleston Foundation.

† The Miles Brewton House (c.1769) at 27 King Street, also known as the Pringle House, was built by merchant Miles Brewton (1732–1775). It has been owned since by members of the related Brewton-Motte-Alston-Pringle-Manigault families. The house was commandeered as British headquarters after Charleston surrendered to the British in 1780, and a bayonet was thrust through the Joshua Reynolds portrait Howells mentions. At the end of the Civil War in 1865, the house was occupied once more as headquarters for a Union general. Smith and Smith, *Dwelling Houses*, 93–110.

The little moment of that intimation of character, of conditioning, was supreme in its way, as another moment was in that house in the East Battery, where I looked from the veranda and saw Fort Sumter a far-off shadow on the waters. My host pointed it out to me, his fellow-citizen of whatsoever sort, who must wish to visit with my eyes, if by no nearer approach that most venerable monument of our Civil War. But we left each other to our respective thoughts and I leave the reader to imagine mine, for if I did not needlessly obtrude them there I will not here. No other American city has such a monument as that, but it is the only monument in Charleston which commemorates the war for and against our nationality. Her other memorials are of two sorts—one for the insurrectionary Colonies and one for the insurrectionary States. The great Chatham lifts the arms maimed by the British bombardment in enduring demand of English liberties for America; the great Calhoun from the loftiest column of the city proclaims the sovereign right of each member of the Union to nullify the Federal compact.

The pathos of the final defeat of the hopes which his doctrine instilled in his fellow-citizens is most poignant, I think, in that collection of relics and memorials which the Daughters of the Confederacy have gathered into the room over the Old Market House, and which "speak a various language" to the visitor. Whatever his feeling toward the cause which was lost, it has always the appeal of a lost cause, and the battle-shredded banners, the swords sheathed in ultimate defeat, the faded letters-home from the fields of death, the tokens of privation and self-denial steadfastly borne by the women left behind hoping and despairing, they all witness how hard it was to give up that which was taken away. If the North had failed in the war for the Union, it would still have been a great nation, but to the South defeat came with a message of forbidden nationality and all hope of it; and these memorials protested against the doom with a deathless pride which one must reverence at least in the gentlewomanly presence expecting reverence. The collection of Civil War relics in the City Hall, though so intensely Confederate, we found indefinitely less moving, perhaps because there we gave our interest chiefly to the wonderful portrait of Washington by Trumbull.* It is strange that this should not be popularly reproduced as the true portrait, for it shows Washington much more imaginably human and probable than the wooden visage—imperishably expressive of the artificial teeth of the greatest

---

*Artist John Trumbull (1756–1843) was commissioned by the city to paint President George Washington's portrait in 1791, to commemorate Washington's Charleston visit during his Southern Tour. It hangs today in Council Chambers at City Hall.

of Americans, if not men—which the brush of Stuart* has perpetuated. Trumbull portrays him younger, in a vigorous full-length, with deep-set eyes, and a look of energy and life, and the mystery of his exhaustless patience and indomitable will.

If one accused oneself of hypocrisy one could only hope that it was a guiltless hypocrisy whenever one must seem by one's silence to share what must be the prevalent feeling for the lost cause. To this moment I do not know what the prevalent feeling in Charleston is concerning slavery. It was intimated only once, from lips that trembled with old memories in owning and affirming of the negroes, "They were slaves, but they were happy," and then one could dissent only in silence. Happy or most unhappy, their children and grandchildren prevail in Charleston by a good majority of her seventy thousand population; and I must own that their absence would be preferable to their presence in the eye seeking beauty or even gaiety. Their presence is of an almost unbroken gloom, which their complexion relieves by little or no gradation from absolute black to any lighter coloring. This is, of course, morally to be desired; there may be the paler shadings of the mulatto, the quadroon, the octoroon, but I did not notice them, though more than once I took persons for white who would have shown to the trained eye as black as the blackest of that majority now strictly segregated from the genuine whiteness. To the city which so much took my liking their color gave a cast of very loathed, yet pitied, melancholy. If they had gone about in any barbaric brightness of rags, any vivid touch of scarlet or crimson or range, they might even have given some cheer to the street life, but their taste seemed to be for the gloomier dyes. If the garments had holes in them, and lapped in tatters here and there, it was probably not by personal or racial preference; the like happens with the poor everywhere. I have found the destitute in New York as unbeautiful and even as unpicturesque as the segregated in Charleston; poverty is always unlovely; let me be as fair as this to the bygone conditions ending in the poverty one sees in the South. If I speak here of the rude wooden balcony overhanging the pavement of a certain Charleston Street where men, women, and children used to stand and be bidden off at auction by the buyers underneath, it is not to twit the present with the past in a city apparently unconscious of it. But in my impressions of that city my black fellow-creatures persist, a

---

* Artist Gilbert Stuart (1755–1828) painted Washington's portrait in 1796, which Howells compares to a portrait by Trumbull. Known as the Lansdowne portrait, Stuart's iconic oil-on-canvas portrait is on permanent display at the National Portrait Gallery of the Smithsonian. Stuart wrote, "When I painted him, he had just had a set of false teeth inserted, which accounts for the constrained expression so noticeable about the mouth and lower part of the face."

dreary cloud; their freedom was not animated by the smile, much less the light laughter one expects of them; only once did they show any noticeable interest in life, and that was when they stood in a crowd at one side of the street, strictly segregated from the white crowd on the other side, but equally following with it the events of the great fight in Havana between the pugilistic champions of their race and ours,* as the bulletins reported them. I wish they could have pinned their pride and hope to some other champion of their race, like Booker Washington,[†] or their great painter Lewis,[‡] or such a poet (if there is any other such) as Paul Dunbar,[§] but these no doubt were beyond the furthest ken of the crowd listening to the disheartening news of the rounds at Havana.

In the Southern cities their race never looks fitly present, but when one meets them on the country roads, or glimpses them in the forests of pine, they seem to belong. At one place far from town where a herd of wild-looking black women-creatures were plying their axes among the undergrowth of the woods, they seemed to draw the African jungle about them, and revert in it to something native and authentic. But in the hovels of the town and the cabins of the suburbs the Southern negroes are simply a black image of the poverty which infests the world. In Charleston, indeed, this has something of the relief which the meridional sun seems to give poverty everywhere, and I have it on my conscience to instance the black women carrying burdens on their heads as women do in Italy, and a certain quaint mammy who sounded a personal if not racial note of character by peddling vegetables in a baby-carriage, as picturesque exceptions to the monotony otherwise unrelieved. I am also bound to note that the cries of the shrimp-sellers were soft and sweet, and consoled for the gloomy silence which their color otherwise kept; and the little old wrinkled black beldam, who, being hard stared at by the strangers, bobbed a curtsy to them from her threshold, did something to abridge the aloofness of her race from theirs.

Every city has its temperament, and in most things Charleston is like no other city that I know, but there were moments in her long, long streets of rather

* This was April 5, 1915, when at the Oriental Park Racetrack in Havana, Cuba, John Arthur "Jack" Johnson (1878–1946), the first black world heavyweight boxing champion (1908–1915), lost his title to Jess Willard, a white working cowboy from Kansas. At the time, Johnson was the most famous African American in the world. In 1912, he had famously faced public controversy when he was charged with violating the Mann Act, even though there was an obvious lack of evidence and the charge was largely racially biased.
[†] Booker T. Washington (1856–1915), educator and author.
[‡] Edmonia Lewis (1845–1911), sculptor and portraitist, the first African American and American Indian female artist to earn international fame for her work.
[§] Paul Laurence Dunbar (1872–1906), black poet, novelist, and playwright.

small shops which recalled the High streets of English towns. There were even moments when London loomed upon the consciousness, and in breaths of the sea air one was aware of Folkstone. But these were very fleeting illusions, and the place reserved its own strong identity, derived from a history very strenuous in many epochs. I do not know how strenuously the commercial life of the port survives, and I am rather ashamed of having tried so little to know. In the waters widening from the Batteries, South and East, vessels of not a very dominant type lay in the offing or slowly smoked across it. But the walk along the ancient wharves which I went one rather over-warm afternoon did not persuade me of a prospering traffic. The aging warehouses had been visited by many flies which left tumbled walls and tangled pipes and wires in gaps of blackened ruin. The footways were broken, and the coarse grass sprouted between the cobblestones of the wheelways. The freight-cars on many railroad tracks shut me from the piers, and there might have been fleets of commerce lying at them, for all I could see, but I doubt if there were.

Not only those fires had wrought the devastation I saw, but that earthquake which shook Charleston so terribly certain years ago had done its part, though one hears of it mostly for the harm it did to the beautiful houses among those fronting on the East Battery which so flattered my fondness with something vaguely Venetian in their keeping. The great water beyond the Battery could well have been the basin of St. Mark, with a like habit of rising and flooding the shore when the wind and tide conspire. All those beautiful houses had been washed full of the sea so many times that the dwellers in some had abandoned their lowest story to it, and had their domestic and social life above-stairs out of its reach; yet the gardens kept their perennial bloom, and the rose and jasmine garlanded the forsaken galleries of the ground floor, so often the water floor.

You must constantly take account of the galleries and the gardens if you are to sense Charleston aright. The galleries give the city its peculiar grace, and the gardens its noble extent. It is these which spread it wide over the sea-bordered plain where it stands in that proud indifference to Sides or Ends which I have noted, and I am by no means sure that the gardens or the galleries of the East Battery are the finest in the town. There are others in Legare Street and King Street and Meeting Street, not so far from the South Battery as not to be of its neighborhood; yet far from these there are other gardens in I know not what quarters which won my heart as we drove by or trundled by in the trolley-cars abounding in Charleston, as with the purpose of showing it to the stranger. There is a Belt Line most convenient for his curiosity, but I especially liked the little cars on King Street and Meeting Street, which one always found waiting at the Battery corners in a sort of Old Cambridge leisure such as our horse-cars of the eighteen sixties and seventies knew.

If I have hitherto spoken mostly of the fine old houses and the prouder streets, it is not because I look down on lowly dwellings or avert my idle steps from humble avenues. These, if they had any grace of historic decline, like Tradd Street, the home of large and little commerce in the past, took my liking as much as the ample perspectives of Broad Street with its show of handsome public edifices, and I liked passing through alleyways where the small black children glistened at the thresholds of their houses and yards in the proper effulgence of their race. I believe that in the old times the slave children and their young masters played together, but segregation seems to have ended that. The children in the paths of the South Battery were all white, and there was no note of black except in the nurse-maids, who exercised the command with their little charges which everywhere subordinates the children of the rich to the rule of the poor. The sight of one small patrician having clawed out of his mouth the diet of broken shells in which he was indulging from the pathway, while a wild clamor of reproach and menace from the nurse's tongue went up, was an example of this, probably lost upon the boy as soon as his nurse went back to her gossip with the other black nurses. She was kind, if threatening, and those paths of the Battery looked clean enough to eat. The white children played there; not so vigorously as one sees them in Central Park, nor with such a show of ruddy cheeks or sturdy limbs, but with as much of it as could be expected in a semi-tropical climate. The place is charming with its live-oaks and the mocking-birds lyrically nesting in them. I tried to surprise these in some of their orchestral moments when they could be expected to represent the whole line of local songsters, but I was never so fortunate, and I came away from the South with the Northern belief that the mocking-bird does not compare in its "melodious bursts" with our bobolink or oriole, or catbird, and might well be silent in presence of our hermit-thrush. All the more conveniently in the silence of the mocking-bird can you read your novel in that pleasant shade, or, if you are young, live your romance, or, still better, if you are old, look on at others living theirs. In the last event you will not be abashed by those shows of impassioned affection which are so apt to embarrass the beholder in our Northern parks.

The car on Meeting Street (such an acceptable name!) took us by the beautiful old church of St. Michael's, and into a grouping of other churches, with their graveyards so old and so still beside them in the heart of the city. If you are very worthy or very fortunate it will be the Saturday before Easter Sunday when you stray into St. Michael's and find the ladies of the parish trimming the

interior with sprays and flowers, and one of these may show you the more notable among the wall tablets which you have brought the liking for from English
churches. St. Michael's is of a very sisterly likeness to St. Philip's Church in the
architectural charm derived from their mother architecture of the Georgian
churches in the Strand. These two Charleston churches seem to me more beautiful than any of the Strand churches; and St. Philip's is especially fine with the
wide curve of open space before it; and precious for the Chantry bas-relief in
one of its walls. But we went for our own Easter service to the perpendicular
Gothic of the Unitarian church* which keeps the social eminence enjoyed by
that sect in Charleston almost from the time of the break with the elder faith in
Boston. The building was one of those which suffered most in the earthquake,
but the fan-work of the roof has been renewed in its pleasing suggestion of Oxford; and there was I could not say just what keeping in the sermon's appeal to
Tennyson and Emerson for support of the Scriptural texts of immortality which
the Easter service dealt with.

The church has its traditions of a distinguished ministry from the first, and
I was aware of something as authentically local in its spiritual atmosphere as in
that of the ancient Huguenot church which we saw on a week-day by the kindness of the pastor. History was cumulatively present in the names tableted round
the walls from the time of the first emigrations of "the Religion" which the great
Admiral Coligny promoted to the time of the general exile after the Revocation
of the Edict of Nantes. Their names became and remain among the foremost
of the city; but many of the families once Huguenot are now of the Anglican
communion, though there is still a service in French, which perhaps not all the
parishioners of the church understand.

The gardens and the churches embody Charleston to the visitor's recollec-
tion, and then I suppose there remains almost as strongly with him an obscure
sense of her permanence in a tradition which one of the greatest civil wars was
fought to extinguish. For good and all, or for bad and all, South Carolina is
politically in the Union, but in Charleston the sense of her being spiritually still
in the Confederacy, rightly or wrongly, haunts the visitor. How could it be
otherwise, with a people not superhuman? Yet I like to record that on the anniversary of the surrender at Appomattox, which fell on one of our ten days, the
leading journal (I thought it always extremely well written) expressed in frank
and manly terms a sense of Grant's delicate behavior in that affair† which may

---

* The Unitarian Church (c.1854) at 4 Archdale Street.
† On April 9, 1865, Confederate Gen. Robert E. Lee surrendered the Army of Northern
  Virginia to Gen. Ulysses S. Grant at the McLean home in Appomattox, Virginia. Grant
  not only graciously allowed the defeated Lee to choose the place of his surrender, but

well have been prevalent in the community. Still, this could have been without the reconciliation to the result which I should find it difficult to imagine. It is the fatal effect of war, and especially of internecine war, that after the hostilities the hostility abides, and the house once divided against itself cannot stand for generations as it stood before the division.

Society as we saw it a little in Charleston had the informal charm of the vast cousinship which results in a strongly localized community where people of various origins intermarry and meet one another in constant ease and intimacy. It is the charm of all aristocracies, and I suppose Charleston is and always has been an aristocracy; a commercial aristocracy, to be sure; but Venice was a commercial aristocracy. The place has its own laws and usages, and does not trouble itself to conform to those of other aristocracies. In London the best society dines at eight o'clock, and in Madrid at nine, but in Charleston it dines at four, and sups lightly at seven. It makes morning calls as well as afternoon calls, but as the summer approaches the midday heat must invite rather to the airy leisure of the verandas and the cool quiescence of interiors darkened against the fly in the morning and the mosquito at nightfall. We did not stay for any such full effect of the summer, but every day of our stay the mocking-birds increased among the young buds which pushed the old leaves from the spray of the live-oaks (to fall and send up a small, subtle, autumnal scent from the grass beneath); every morning there were more flowers in the garden-beds, more blossoms on the trellises; the wind blew softer than the day before, and something more appreciably temperamental declared itself in the advancing season.

I have always liked places with a compact history, like Florence, for instance, where you do not have to go even so far as the Arno to compass its renown, or like Siena, compacter still in the talc of its civic life; and I found this merit in Charleston, as the reader will understand better if he acquaints himself with the city's past in Mrs. St. Julien Ravenel's very interesting historical study of *The Place and the People*. After Boston, no other American city has had a civic consciousness so intense and so continuous, and in both the very diverse causes and characteristics eventuated in colonial times, at least, in much the same social life. The Puritans and the Proprietors arrived in one city and the other at a like ideal of aristocratic ease and dignity as a proper expression of their quality, and if the Southern city was habitually the gayer, there were extreme moments of the

---

his terms were generous. Lee was not imprisoned, or prosecuted. Officers were allowed to keep their sidearms, and Grant allowed the Confederates to take their horses and mules home to carry out spring planting. He provided Lee with a supply of food rations for his starving army. Further, as Lee left the house and rode away and Grant's men began cheering in celebration, Grant immediately ordered them to stop.

little Northern capital when she relented almost as far. In both the ideal was aristocratic; good society was based (as it still is everywhere) upon the commonalty which consents to social inferiority, and if in Charleston there was the deeper and dismaler underworld of the slave, in Boston slavery was not yet condemned as immoral. In both the leading families ruled, but the Revolution which brought banishment to many of the leading families of Boston confirmed those of Charleston in their primacy.

The very diversity of their origin in Charleston contributes to the picturesqueness of the aspect which its society wears to the strangers. Here for once in the human story the victims of oppression did not suffer for their wrongs even in their pride; the Huguenots who fled from France found not merely refuge in Carolina, but instant worldly honor. Their abounding names are of the first in Charleston; the very names of the streets testify to their equal value in the community proud to welcome them; and the episode of their coming lends unique distinction to annals never poor in distinction. I like to think it was their qualification of the English ideal which has tended to give the Charlestonians their gentle manners. But if I am altogether mistaken in this, I like these manners better than our brusque Northern ways. I like a place where the very ticket-seller makes the question of a Pullman section an affair of social courtesy, and the telegraph-operator stays with my despatch in his hand to invoke my conjectures of the weather. In a world where to-morrow so often galls the kibe of today, it is pleasant to draw breath awhile where the present keeps a leisured pace which seems studied from the past, and mid-April, such as we left in Charleston, promises to stay through the year.

Norman Rockwell, c. 1921.
Underwood & Underwood, photographers. Library of Congress.

NORMAN ROCKWELL (1918)

"The Battle of Charleston 1918"

Norman Rockwell, "The Battle of Charleston 1918" from *Norman Rockwell, My Adventures as an Illustrator* (Garden City, N.Y.: Doubleday), 1960. Reprint permission courtesy of the Norman Rockwell Family Agency.

Norman Rockwell (1894–1978), painter and illustrator, was born in New York City. He attended Chase Art School (The New York School of Art) at the age of fourteen. Two years later, he studied at the National Academy of Design, then at the Art Students League. He painted his first commission before the age of sixteen, and produced his earliest works for *St. Nicholas Magazine*, the Boy Scouts of America publication, *Boys' Life*, and other youth publications. Still in his teens, Rockwell was hired as a staff artist for *Boys' Life* and subsequently served as art editor. When he was twenty-one, his family moved to New Rochelle, New York, where they shared a studio with the cartoonist Clyde Forsythe, who worked for *The Saturday Evening Post*. With Forsythe's help, Rockwell submitted his first successful cover painting, which resulted in forty-seven years with *The Saturday Evening Post* and 321 covers. His success led to covers for the best magazines in his day.

Rockwell was twenty-three years old when he enlisted in the US Navy. His original orders were to take him to a base in Ireland but a German submarine off the East coast detoured his ship to Charleston. Due to his small physique, he never saw active duty. Instead, he served as a morale booster. In August of 1918, he was assigned to draw cartoons and create layouts for *Afloat and Ashore*, the Charleston Navy Yard's official publication. While enlisted as a Painter/Varnisher Third Class, USNRF, Rockwell continued his work for the *The Saturday Evening Post* and other publications. He was not in Charleston long. When the war ended in November of 1918, he was discharged from the Navy.

In 1926, Rockwell resumed work with the Boy Scouts of America and produced fifty-one original illustrations for their annual calendar. The 1930s and 1940s were considered the most fruitful decades of his career. In 1930 he married

Mary Barstow, a schoolteacher, and the couple had three sons. The family moved to Arlington, Vermont, in 1939, and Rockwell's work began to reflect small-town American life. In 1943, inspired by an address President Franklin Roosevelt made to Congress, he painted the *Four Freedoms* paintings, reproduced in four consecutive issues of *The Saturday Evening Post* with essays by contemporary writers. Rockwell's interpretations of *Freedom of Speech, Freedom to Worship, Freedom from Want, and Freedom from Fear* proved to be enormously popular. The works toured the country in an exhibition sponsored by the *Post* and the US Treasury Department and, through the sale of war bonds, raised more than $130 million for the war effort.

In 1953, the Rockwell family moved to Stockbridge, Massachusetts. When his wife died suddenly in 1959, Rockwell took time off, and he and his son, Thomas, produced his autobiography, *My Adventures as an Illustrator.* The *Post* printed excerpts from his book in eight consecutive issues, and it became a best-seller. Among his memories in the book, he reveals his World War I adventures at the Charleston Naval Base.

Rockwell remarried in 1961. His last painting for the *Post* was published in 1963, after which he spent ten years at *Look* magazine depicting his interests in civil rights, poverty, and space exploration. His last commission for the Boy Scouts was completed when Rockwell was eighty-two, concluding a partnership that spanned sixty-four years and generated four hundred and seventy-one Rockwell images for periodicals, guidebooks, calendars, and promotional materials. In 1973 he established a trust to preserve his artistic legacy by placing his works in the custodianship of the Old Corner House Stockbridge Historical Society, now the Norman Rockwell Museum, and had his studio and its contents added to the trust. He received the Presidential Medal of Freedom, America's highest civilian honor, in 1977.

The following excerpt begins in New York, where Rockwell enlisted, and describes his assignment at the Charleston Navy Yard.

SOURCES

"About Norman Rockwell." Norman Rockwell Museum. Accessed Dec. 3, 2015. http://
 www.nrm.org/about-2/about-norman-rockwelll.

"The Battle of Charleston"

When the first draft call of World War I was sent out I was deed exempt. I don't remember why; too many dependents maybe. I didn't object: I wasn't a fire-eater (so far as I know, no Rockwell ever was).

I was pretty well satisfied with myself, knocking out covers and illustrations for *Life,* the *Post, Judge, Leslie's, Country Gentleman,* receiving three or four fan letters a week, making quite a bit of money.

Then one day in June 1917, as I was riding uptown on the subway, six or eight badly wounded merchant seamen boarded the train. I gave one of them my seat—a big, rawboned man on crutches with a bandage over his forehead and one eye. All I could think of as he lowered himself clumsily into the seat was how easily I'd got out of it, of the careless way I rocked on my feet with the motion of the train. By the time I left the train at New Rochelle, I'd made up my mind. I took a taxi to the Pelham Bay Naval Training and Receiving Center.

But the doctors rejected me. I was seventeen pounds underweight for my height and age. I caught a train back to New York. Maybe the doctors at the enlistment center at City Hall would accept me.

The yeoman who weighed me at City Hall had been a student at the Art Students League. "Hello, Norm," he said. "Jump aboard." I got on the scales. "You've overdone the starving artist bit," he said. "You're underweight." I sighed dejectedly. "You really want to get in?" he asked. I told him I did. "Wellll," he said, looking me over, "it won't do any good to weigh you with your clothes on." (I was stripped for the examination.) "Besides, it's against regulations. You *sure* you want to enlist?" "As I hope to paint a good picture," I said, swearing the most terrible oath I knew. "Follow me," he said. "We'll talk to a doctor."

He led me into a dark, drafty little office and explained my problem to a doctor who was sitting with his legs up on a desk, smoking a cigar. "Norm's an artist," he concluded. "If we get him in they'll give him a special assignment, painting the insignia on airplane wings or something. It won't matter if he's underweight." "How much under is he?" asked the doctor, chewing his cigar and looking at me thoughtfully. "Seventeen pounds," said the yeoman. "Won't do," said the doctor. "We can waive ten pounds but not seventeen." The yeoman glanced furtively around. "How about the treatment?" he whispered. "He don't look big enough," said the doctor. "I want to get in," I said, shivering—the chill drafts were running up and down my legs; my feet felt like blocks of ice against the cement floor. "What's the treatment?" "Bananas, doughnuts and water," said the doctor. "You eat seven pounds' worth, we waive the other ten pounds, and you're in." "All right," I said. "It's your stomach," said the doctor, pulling open a large file drawer at the bottom of the desk. "Sit down." The drawer was filled with bananas and doughnuts. I eased onto an icy chair, my teeth chattering. The yeoman drew a pitcher of water at the washbasin in the corner and set it before me on the desk. The doctor heaped bananas and doughnuts around it. "Go to," he said, and I began to eat doughnuts and bananas and drink the water. The doctor scratched a match on the seat of his pants and lit his cigar. The yeoman hummed softly, staring at the ceiling. I ate and drank.

After a while, "Weigh him," said the doctor. I staggered to the scales. "Not yet," said the yeoman. "Five pounds to go." So I ate some more and drank some more. The doctor's cigar went out. The yeoman stopped humming. Both watched me intently. "I'm going to burst," I said, "I'd better quit." But by then the doctor and the yeoman had adopted my enlistment as a personal cause; it wasn't just one sailor more or less anymore; it was their battle against the Kaiser and all his forces of darkness. "Oh no," said the yeoman, "you aren't going to quit now." "Come on," said the doctor, peeling a banana for me. "Four more doughnuts and as many bananas. Wash 'em down with water."

I stuffed. . . and stuffed. . . and stuffed. The yeoman weighed me again. "Hurrah!" he shouted. "We've won." And the doctor and he congratulated each other. I could hardly walk; the seven pounds of doughnuts, bananas, and water sloshing about in my stomach threw me off balance. But I managed to struggle into my clothes—my fingers were so stiff with cold that I couldn't button all the buttons—and totter home.

Not many days later I was called to duty as a "landsman for quartermaster." A grand title, I thought proudly, not realizing that a landsman is defined as "a sailor of little experience rated below an ordinary seaman." I was ordered to report to the Brooklyn Naval Yard where I would embark for the base at Queenstown, Ireland. My duties would be those of a painter and varnisher; I would paint the insignia on airplanes.

We sailed that night, blacked out because of the submarines. I stayed on deck, watching the lights of New York slide away behind us. Suddenly a light sparked from the darkness about two hundred yards ahead of the ship. There was a commotion on the bridge. Somebody yelled, "A submarine!" Then in the faint glare of the light I made out a naval officer standing on what appeared to be the conning tower of a submarine and shining a flashlight on a small American flag. He shouted across to the captain of the ship I was on, ordering him to change course and go down along the coast to Charleston, South Carolina. A German submarine was lurking in the Atlantic just ahead.

The next morning we docked at Charleston. I was issued a uniform, given shots, and detailed with the rest of the new arrivals to pull stumps in a corner of the base where new barracks were to be erected. I set to with a crowbar, pounding it down under a stump, then heaving and wrenching, yanking it out, and jamming it under again until I was wringing wet and panting. I figured if I worked hard they'd make me an admiral and assign me a soft desk job.

But pretty soon the old sailor who was in charge of the work party sauntered over. After he'd watched me for a few minutes he said, "Take it easy. Take it easy. You wanta ruin the navy?" I stopped heaving at my stump and looked around. Everybody was staring at me. "Relax," said the old sailor, "relax. It ain't much fun bein' admiral. Think of the worry. And the paperwork." An enlistee who was standing beside me tittered. I laid down my crowbar and lighted my pipe. But if hard work wouldn't get me anywhere, what would?

It wasn't going to be my martial bearing. I realized that later that night. Flu was raging through the camp like a pack of rabid wolves; men were dying every day. Being short of able-bodied men, the authorities assigned the new arrivals in the camp to guard duty and burial squads. I got a piece of both. At dusk twelve of us were issued guns and marched off behind a wagon laden with rough pine coffins. When we reached the cemetery the coffins were unloaded. Then the bugler bugled taps while the coffins were lowered into the graves, the officer said: "Readyaimfire," and bangety, bang, bang, bang . . . bang, we fired. (That last bang was me; I hardly knew the butt of a rifle from the barrel.)

Guard duty was cold, damp, and frightening, but uneventful. I stood in a mud puddle for four hours, scared silly of snakes, Germans, and my fellow guards, who had a propensity for shooting wildly at anything which made the least sound. As the cold yellow light of morning shimmered in the puddle at my feet I decided that sailoring, or at least the military aspects of it, wasn't for me. But what was I going to do in the navy?

The next day I found out. In the morning we filled out questionnaires on our civilian work experience and training. I put down "illustrator." The chief petty officer, who was looking over the questionnaires, asked if I would do his portrait. I did. That afternoon an ensign saw the portrait and asked if I'd draw him. I did. He showed it to a captain and the captain called me into his office. I entered in my new uniform—bell-bottom trousers, tight blouse, and little white cap; I looked like a toadstool turned upside down. The captain said, "Oh, my God," and assigned me to the camp newspaper, *Afloat and Ashore,* giving me ten days' leave to go to New York and get my art supplies. "Your job's morale," he said. "You'll do more good that way than swabbing decks or stoking boilers." As I left the room he added, "You'd make a helluva sailor anyway."

I disagreed with the captain. I *was* a sailor, an old salt, in fact.

A few nights later, my friend Clyde took me to a dinner for illustrators and artists at the Salmagundi Club in New York. World War I was a poster war. Charles Dana Gibson did posters of beautiful girls dressed as Columbia and calling on America to save the world from the Kaiser; James Montgomery Flagg did his famous poster of Uncle Sam pointing his finger and saying, "I want you."

Posters urged people to buy bonds, conserve coal, nab spies, and save peach pits. If the government wanted something done, not done, or undone they stuck posters up on every blank wall in the country. The dinner at the Salmagundi Club was held to whip up enthusiasm among the illustrators and artists.

When I returned to camp I was installed in a corner room in the Officers' quarters. Two days a week I drew cartoons and made lay-outs for *Afloat and Ashore;* the rest of the time I was allowed to my own work as long as it was in some way related to the navy. I painted a *Post* cover of one sailor showing another a picture of his girl; a *Life* cover of a group of smiling soldiers, sailors, and marines. (Title: "Are we downhearted?" Everywhere you went during the war— in bars, trolleys, meetings—somebody would yell, "Are we downhearted?" and everyone would chorus, "No!") I drew countless portraits of officers and ordinary sailors, not because I was ordered to do so, but because I thought it was a good morale builder. Most of the men sent their portraits home to their wives and sweet-hearts; it seemed to cheer them up considerably, especially if they were about to be shipped overseas. (Promotions were so rapid that I had to paint the officers one rank above their present rank; I expect that cheered them up too.)

I have to admit that doing portraits of officers made my life less complicated. If I wanted a pass to town I'd just ask one of my sitters. He could hardly refuse; I might have elongated his nose or weakened his chin. One portrait I did even saved my life. When I got the flu I went to the hospital. A doctor whose portrait I'd drawn discovered me there. "Get out of here," he said. "The place'll kill you. The germs are as thick as blackstrap molasses. Go back to your hammock and pile blankets on yourself. Sweat it out." I did as he directed and recovered.

But in spite of the fact that I worked hard, it was an easy life. I was getting my room, board, and clothes free and still earning almost as much money as I had as a civilian (an ensign figured that with the free meals, etc., I was making more than an Admiral). I had no military duties and aside from the two days a week at *Afloat and Ashore* could do pretty much as I wished.

I even had an unofficial bodyguard. One day a burly, rough-tough lot named O'Toole asked me to do his portrait. I said sure. When I'd finished he was so pleased that he appointed himself my personal bodyguard. "Any guy tries ta shove ya round, tell *me,*" he'd say. "I'll fix his liver." And he'd pull two brass hammock rings which he sharpened along one edge out of his pocket and, fitting them around his fists like brass knuckles, shadowbox violently with my imaginary enemies.

O'Toole had been a taxi driver in Chicago before the war. Other sailors used to worry about their wives. Not O'Toole. "She kin lick anybody on the block," he'd tell me. "Ain't nobody gonna get aheada her. Nosiree. She'd womp 'em. Did me oncet. I went all blue in the eyes. She's a ten-carat woman. There ain't another like her between Lake Michigan and the stockyards."

I was real proud of O'Toole. He was the he-man who knew how to handle himself. I was the "pale artist plying his sickly trade." He took good care of me. At meals, unless you managed to get a seat at the head of the table where the waiters set the bowls of food, you darn near starved because the bowls were always empty by the time they'd passed six or eight men. When the bugler sounded mess call every sailor on the base would drop what he was doing and rush pell-mell to the mess hall. I'd fling down my brushes and run too. But as I was going out the door O'Toole would lay his hand on my arm. "Slow down," he'd say. "Slow way down there. Ain't no hurry." And we'd walk calmly to the mess hall. When we got there O'Toole would barge and jostle up to the head of the line, dragging me behind him. "What'd I tell ya?" he'd say to me. "No call to rush. No call to sweat up." Nobody ever objected to this highhanded behavior twice. O'Toole flattened them the first time and that was enough.

O'Toole was proud of me too. He'd come into the room where I was working and look at my drawings. "Juuudas Priest," he'd say, "I never knew a guy like you. An artist. Look at that," he'd say to one of the other fellows. "If that ain't Ensign Simmons, it ain't *nothin'*." And Lord help the other fellow if he didn't agree.

It was the considered opinion of O'Toole that I should only do portraits of officers. "It don't get you nothin' drawin' them mugs," O'Toole would say, referring to the ordinary sailors (he was a sharp operator; wangled an easy berth in special services though his only special talent was for crafty undetectable goldbricking). "Leave 'em alone. Say I'm drivin' my hack along Michigan Bulward. A bum waves a bottle of red at me. Do I stop? Not on your sweet head, I don't. I cruises around till I spots a fella with a cane and a shinin' hat on wagglin' his thumb at me. I wouldn't have no hack 'f I picked up bums. Same with you. Officers put ya here. Sailors ain't nothin'."

One day as he was going on like this a sailor stuck his head in the door and asked which one was Norman Rockwell, the artist. Quick as a cobra, O'Toole says, "Me. Whatta ya want?" The sailor asked, "Would you paint my portrait, Mr. Rockwell?" "Sure," says O'Toole. "Come back at four." So the sailor thanked him and left. I asked, "What did you do that for?" "I'll fix him," said O'Toole. "Lemme handle it. You jus' sit over there in the corner and don't say nothin'."

When the sailor returned O'Toole was seated before my easel. "Come in, come in," he says to the sailor in a lofty voice. The sailor came in. O'Toole looked him over in silence for a minute. "Juuudas Priest," he says, "ain't that a fine face. Look at them bones there. Noble, I calls it, noble. It'll be a pleasure to paint that face." Then he led the sailor over to the window and began to pose him, turning him this way and that and muttering to himself, "No, the light ain't right that way. No. No. There. But no. Profile's better." Finally, after having twisted the sailor's head almost off his neck, he sighed and said, "I can't do it justice. But it'll havta do," and he walked over behind the easel upon which he had previously set a huge piece of drawing paper. Then he said to me, "Jack, hand me my brushes," and proceeded to paint, flourishing his brushes and moaning as if in an agony of inspiration.

Every so often O'Toole would ask one of the sailors in the room for his opinion of the picture (he had thoughtfully provided himself with an audience) and the sailor would comment learnedly. "Mr. Rockwell," he'd say to O'Toole in a humble tone, "don't you think the nose is a hair too big? And the eyes a trifle beady?" Then O'Toole would jump up, fling down his brushes, stamp his feet, and swear he couldn't work in such an atmosphere of ignorance. But we'd soothe him, saying it was a masterpiece, caught that aristocratic look about the eyes and all, and after grumbling a bit O'Toole would go back to work.

All this while the poor sailor whose portrait was being painted stood there with his head wrenched over his left shoulder, trembling with anticipation and terribly anxious to see the portrait. If he so much as blinked an eye O'Toole would shout, "It can't be done. If you don't stop wobbling I'll havta ask your pardon and leave." Then the sailor would stiffen, hardly daring to breathe.

Finally O'Toole announced that he was finished. With great fanfare and ceremony he led the sailor over to the portrait. The sailor gasped when he saw it, for it was a hodgepodge of lines and circles in the center of which sat a neat game of ticktacktoe. Wow, was that sailor mad! But you know what O'Toole was, so nothing came of it. O'Toole told him he was a mug and had no business bothering me and sent him packing.

Of course this didn't stop the parade of sailors who wanted their portraits painted. But it provided a diversion, which we sorely needed. We led an easy life but a dull and lonesome one too. Almost every afternoon O'Toole, who got off work at two o'clock (as I said, he was a sharp operator), would come over to my studio and if I wasn't busy we'd take a bus into Charleston. We always wanted to get out of camp, away from the long rows of drab unpainted barracks and the clouds of sand which blew up and down the street, stinging our eyes and leaving a gritty residue in the food, our clothes and hammocks. But when we left the bus at Charleston there was nothing to do. We'd walk around the Plaza or up to the old Slave Market, window-shop, and watch the boats in the harbor. No decent girl would speak to sailors. Bars and grubby dance halls were the only places which would tolerate us.

Finally O'Toole and I, stuffed to the ears with boredom and feeling somewhat guilty about our easy life, decided to transfer from special services to a fighting outfit. One morning we went down to the docks in Charleston to pick a ship. We toured a destroyer, a battleship, and a mine sweeper. None of them appealed to us. Then we came to a navy freighter which had steam up in preparation for departing on a voyage. I said, "We don't want a freighter, O'Toole." "C'mon," he said, "let's look anyway." So we boarded the ship and after a while found ourselves in the huge, gloomy, cavernlike boiler room. In the harsh red glare spouting from the open furnace doors we could see a crew of stokers, stripped to the waist and gleaming with perspiration, shoveling coal. As each shovelful struck the fire, flames would burst out the door and singe the stoker. It was unbelievably hot; the rotten-egg stench of soft coal burning almost choked us. We hadn't been there three minutes before our warlike spirit vanished. We went back to special services, resolved to endure, if not enjoy, our comfortable berths.

The navy wasn't all paradise, though. The food was monotonous: navy beans, navy beans, navy beans, and every Friday night blackberry jam, which no one would eat because we suspected that it was laced with saltpeter to curb weekend wildness. And the regimentation, which galled my independent, artist's soul. Everything in the navy was done on a grand, individual-burying scale. The doctors didn't decide that *you* needed a laxative; they decided that the whole camp needed one. So they'd sneak some into the beans, and all night long there would be long lines of impatient sailors stamping about outside the "head." A hundred and fifty men to do this, a hundred and fifty men to do that; never one man, always a crowd. Everyone muffled under the blanket of blind obedience: a sailor would say, "I think . . ." and the officer would reply, "*You* don't think; *we* do the thinking around here."

Still, it wasn't so bad. Every night we had a movie either at the YMCA (which we didn't like because they wouldn't let you in unless you answered a questionnaire and because there was a small admission charge) or the Knights of Columbus (which we liked because they let anyone in and it was free) or at the camp theater (which was even better because after the movie amateur theatricals were held). Once, I remember, *Poor Little Rich Girl* starring Mary Pickford was shown and as she refused one plate of scrumptious food after another (the poor little rich girl—she didn't want peach melbas or six-inch steaks, she wanted love), the audience got wilder and wilder. "Try her on navy beans," we yelled, "try her on navy beans. That'll fix her precious stomach."

It's amazing the mixture of men you meet in the navy. Some of the fellows hadn't worn shoes before. One man from the backwoods of Kentucky had never used a fork. He ate with his face three inches from the plate, shoveling in the food with his knife. So we all stopped eating and stared at him. Pretty soon he noticed that the table was quiet and looked up. "Waas all th' matter?" he asked. "Oh, nothing," we said, "nothing at all." But after a while he caught on and we saw him begin to experiment with his fork, muttering to himself and cursing and cursing as the beans rolled off it.

The navy was an education to me, too, though in a different way. I'd never lived among men like that. If they were amazed at knowing me ("An artist. My God, *an artist!*"), I was astounded at knowing them. One day I walked into the bathroom and there were two chief petty officers taking showers and swearing at each other at the top of their voices. They were experts and were having a good-natured cussing match. They didn't stop with execrating each other's parents, they dug back to the grandparents and distant cousins. Oh, it was grand to hear. First one would call in question (in a deep, bull-throated voice) the morals of the other's maternal grand-mother, then the other would bellow out a load of imprecations on to his companion's great-uncle's personal habits. Then they'd fall to, thick and fast, on each other's grandfathers. It was magnificent; it was monumental; it was biblical.

I'd never heard such things before. It was a fascination to me. I was glad to get out of the navy (they offered to make me an ensign if I'd take charge of the camp newspaper at the base at Newport News; I refused), yet I was almost sorry to leave all the horseplay and all my friends.

Two months after our tour of the fighting ships, O'Toole and I received a rude jolt. A new commander was appointed to the Charleston naval base. Even O'Toole was perturbed. "I can't figure it," he'd say, shaking his head. "You got to know what kinda officer he is before you can go to get around him. Liable to bump us all off to Russia before we have time to figure him." Then he'd sit about and scratch his head. "Juuuudas Priest," he'd say, "it's the waitin' chews ya."

O'Toole was right. The new commander might transfer all of us from special services to active duty. He might assign all of us to the Russian route. (Duty on the ships which carried supplies to Russia was known to be the worst in the entire navy.)

One afternoon O'Toole and I were in my studio discussing the situation when the door was suddenly flung open, a voice yelled *"A-ten-shun!"* and in walked the new commander in full-dress uniform—white jacket and trousers, gold braid and white gloves—a big, handsome, beefy-looking fellow. His wife—a square, mannish lady smartly dressed—accompanied him.

"Carry on, men, carry on," he said. I went back to work on the portrait I was painting and O'Toole fussed with a pile of old canvases in the corner. The new commander stood behind me, looking at the portrait. After a minute I happened to glance around and saw that he was leaning on my palette table, one of his white-gloved hands squished down in the gobs and smears of oil paint. Oh, Lord, I thought, Siberia, here I come. "Ah, Commander, sir," I said, "your hand, sir. Paint, sir." He lifted his hand and looked at the glove, sticky with paint of many colors. I composed a brave farewell letter to my friends at home. But then he laughed and, stripping off his glove, said, "A souvenir," and handed it to me. He chatted a bit, asking about my work and how I liked the navy, and left the room. O'Toole was of the opinion that the new commander could be "got round," but, he added, the wife was a fish of a different color. She worried him.*

The next day I was transferred to the commander's personal staff and went to live on the U.S.S. *Hartford,* which had been Admiral Farragut's flagship when he sailed into Mobile Bay during the Civil War, saying, "Damn the torpedoes! Go ahead!" and which was now moored in Charleston Harbor as the official headquarters and residence of the commander of the Charleston naval base.

The *Hartford* had been refurbished since Mobile Bay and was a sumptuous palace.† In the center of the ship a grand, red-carpeted staircase swept down to a huge ballroom whose walls were decorated with ornate, hand-carved scrollwork. The staterooms, which were the officers' quarters, were lavishly appointed and hung with all manner of rich velvets and tapestries. Down all the carpeted hallways ran handrails of gleaming brass. The kitchen, stocked with goodies by the merchants of Charleston who hoped to obtain the business of supplying the camp, was staffed by a horde of cooks—meat cooks, pastry cooks, vegetable cooks, salad cooks, sauce cooks, etc. A marine band—scarlet jackets, blue trousers, white belts, and all—was kept always at readiness and marines in full-dress uniforms—dark blue coats, light blue trousers—guarded the gangplanks. O'Toole (I'd got him a job as chauffeur on the commander's staff by drawing a portrait of the ensign in charge of transportation), myself, and a tenor lived in a plush

---

* This was Commanding Officer Mark St. Clair Ellis (1873–1952) and his wife, Rose St. John Mildmay Ellis (1879–1973).

† The U.S.S. *Hartford*, first launched in 1858, had served in prominent campaigns in the Civil War as the flagship of David G. Farragut, most notably in the Battle of Mobile Bay in 1864. It was the receiving ship at Charleston Navy Yard from 1912 to 1938, and although the ship was placed out of commission in 1928, the *Hartford* remained a fixture in Charleston through the Depression. President Franklin Roosevelt, who made many visits to the Charleston Naval Yard while traveling to Warm Springs, Georgia, loved the old ship and planned to have her refurbished with WPA funds. In 1938, the *Hartford* left Charleston for Washington, DC.

stateroom. The tenor and I dined, or rather feasted in barbaric splendor, with the commander and his wife, who very kindly explained how we were to go about using the multitude of forks, spoons, and knives which surrounded our plates. When the commander entertained visiting dignitaries—senators, French or English admirals—the tenor sang and I displayed my work before the assembled guests in the ballroom.

But I soon learned that the real purpose of my being on the *Hartford* was to paint portraits of Captain Mark St. Clair Ellis and his wife. Mrs. Ellis, who was very wealthy and had been the first woman ever to receive a mining degree, had a lot to do with running the camp. Her husband put up a very dignified and military front, but I don't think he had much administrative ability. Every order that he issued was a brief synopsis of some passage from the *Bluejacket's Manual,* which he knew by heart and spoke of in reverential tones. When a situation arose which wasn't covered by the *Manual,* he stretched, squeezed, twisted, or simplified it until it *was* covered by the *Manual.* O'Toole always insisted that Mrs. Ellis was the brains behind the gold braid. All the sailors liked her. If the camp didn't have something—say a movie projector—she'd buy it. We used to cheer her when she passed through camp.

The trait in Captain Ellis' personality which I came in contact with most often was his vanity. I did two portraits of him—one in his uniform and one in civilian clothes. He was very anxious about them. All his ribbons had to be just so. First his eyes didn't have the right sparkle—lively but dignified and stern as befitted the eyes of the commander of the Charleston naval base. Then his chin was too round or his nose too short. He really shouldn't have worried; he *was* a handsome man.

Finally I got everything to his satisfaction and started on the portrait of him in civilian clothes. It was a revelation to me. When he took off his uniform he sank from a mastiff to a spaniel. Still handsome but nowhere near as impressive. He was quite disappointed.

I was just finishing the second portrait when the false armistice burst upon us. O'Toole, the tenor, the marine band, the cooks, and I decamped for Charleston to celebrate. We commandeered a moving van, dumped all the furniture out on the road, and drove into town. There we abandoned the van, hijacked a carriage and, loading five or six girls into it, towed it all over Charleston through the crowds. As we were passing one of the fine hotels an old Southern gentleman with a white goatee and wide-brimmed hat hailed us and insisted on climbing into the carriage among the girls. So we hauled him all over town, stopping at every bar we came to for drinks at his expense. After a while O'Toole became so plastered that he fell under the wheels of the carriage. The third or fourth time this happened he scraped his nose, got mad at the carriage, pulled everyone out of it, and tipped it over. We spent the rest of the night in a combination dance hall and saloon.

The next morning we awoke to find that it had been a false armistice. But everyone knew the real thing wasn't far off and so applied for a discharge. The navy, of course, couldn't allow that. To prevent a stampede, an order was issued that no honorable discharges were to be granted. All leaves were canceled too.

Well, I wanted to get out real bad. I could see there was no use my remaining in the navy; I wasn't doing any good. And I was eager to resume civilian life. So I told Captain Ellis that the only place in the whole country where truly beautiful frames could be bought was Knoedler's in New York. "I can pick out just the right ones," I said, "big, ornate, gold-leafed. It'll make the portraits look marvelous. Knoedler's has the finest frames money can buy or man make." He considered his portraits stunning masterpieces (one tenth because of the painting; nine tenths because of the model), so he sent an aide to look up discharges. The aide reported back that under the existing order prohibiting honorable discharges there were only two ways to get me out of the navy: a dishonorable discharge (that was going too far, even for me) or an inaptitude discharge, which meant that I was unfit for my duties in the navy or, in other words, a moron. "Give him that," said Mrs. Ellis. I agreed. *My God!* said Captain Ellis. "He can't go through life with an inaptitude discharge! What'll his friends say? What'll his wife think of him?" "Don't be silly, Mark," said Mrs. Ellis, and worked at him until he consented to sign my inaptitude discharge.

In the whole Charleston Navy Yard there was only one book, a paperback, describing the procedure to be followed on discharges. Captain Ellis gave it to me so that I could fill out my papers properly. That night when I returned to my stateroom the lights were out and O'Toole and the tenor were asleep. Not wanting to wake them, I laid the book, which was open to the page on inaptitude discharges, face down on the table and undressed in the dark.

The next morning I discovered to my horror that the book was lying face down in flypaper. The only book of its kind in the camp. Ruined. I wouldn't get out of the navy for six months.

After O'Toole had laughed himself sick we set to work to try and unstick the flypaper. We tried everything—steam, hot water, cold water, hair tonic, machine oil, soap, mashed fish scales (that from an old sailor who swore it would rip the skin off a snake's back; maybe it would have, but it didn't work on the flypaper). Finally we succeeded (I've always thought it was sheer wish power that did it), I made out the papers, and on November 12, 1918, one day after the actual armistice, I was discharged as unable to adapt myself to the duties of a "landsman for quartermaster" in the United States Naval Air Reserve. My service record reads:

Discharged with Inaptitude Discharge. Rockwell is an artist and unaccustomed to hard manual labor.

His patriotic impulse caused him to enlist in a rating for which he has no aptitude. Moreover, he is unsuited to Naval routine and hard work.

And below this is the terse comment:

I concur in the above statement.

(signed) Norman Rockwell

The next day I visited Knoedler's in New York and asked them to ship three of their gaudiest frames to Captain Mark St. Clair Ellis at the Charleston naval base. Years later I heard that he had left the navy and was running a swank restaurant outside Paris.

The last vestiges of my stint in the navy soon vanished. I joined the American Legion, but as the meetings were largely taken up with the recounting of gruesome war stories and noble war records, I was left pretty much out in the cold. ("What battles were you in?" "I was in Charleston." "Oh.") After a few meetings and parades I quit. Then one day I ran out of paint rags. That was the end of my uniform.

Photograph of Amy Lowell (1874–1925) at Sevenels,
by Bachrach, Houghton Library, Harvard University.

Amy Lowell (1912–1922)

"And the Garden Was a Fire of Magenta"

Amy Lowell, "'And the Garden Was a Fire of Magenta': Travel Poems" (1912–1922). "Epitaph In A Church-Yard In Charleston, South Carolina," from *A Dome of Many Coloured Glass* (Boston: Houghton Mifflin), 1912: 108–9. The following are from *Poetry, a Magazine of Verse* 21:3 (December 1922): 117–124: "Charleston, South Carolina," "A South Carolina Forest," "The Middleton Place," "Magnolia Gardens," and "The Vow."

Amy Lowell (1874–1925), poet, critic, and lecturer, was from a Boston Brahmin family with a long and distinguished ancestry. Her father, Augustus Lowell, was a businessman, civic leader, and horticulturalist. Her mother, Katherine Lowell, was an accomplished musician and linguist. Her brothers were Abbott Lawrence Lowell, president of Harvard, and astronomer Percival Lowell. Romantic poet James Russell Lowell was a first cousin.

Amy Lowell was educated in private schools and at home by her mother until she was twenty-eight, after which she enjoyed the life of a Boston socialite, and traveled abroad. About 1902, she decided to devote her energies to poetry. It was eight years before her first piece, a sonnet, was published in *The Atlantic Monthly*. Two years later, she published her first volume, *A Dome of Many-Coloured Glass* (1912). On a visit to England in 1913, Lowell met Ezra Pound and discovered his circle, the Imagists, a group of English and American poets who wrote free verse and were devoted to "clarity of expression through the use of precise visual images" in language, a strand of modernism. Pound included one of Lowell's poems in his anthology *Des Imagistes* (1914), and that same year she published a second book, *Sword Blades and Poppy Seed,* her first experimentation with free verse and "polyphonic prose." She was editor of three numbers of *Some Imagist Poets* (1915–1917), a modernist journal that promoted Imagism as an avant-garde movement, and an important force in then-modern poetry. Between 1916 and 1925, numerous volumes of her works saw publication, both poetry and critical works, as well as the two-volume biography, *John Keats* (1925). In 1925, she won the Pulitzer Prize for her collection *What's O'Clock*, and in the years following her death, three volumes of her works were published, including *Ballads for Sale* (1927).

A celebrated poet, Amy Lowell lived at the Lowell family estate, Sevenels, with a houseful of Old English sheepdogs, which she bred. Known as "the wealthiest bachelor woman in Boston," she drove a claret-colored limousine. Portly and eccentric, she was outspoken and a cigar smoker. Her first visit to Charleston was in the spring of 1906, and she found it "entrancing" and "a place for poets indeed." She visited Middleton Place, finding the eighteenth-century gardens "a dream that remained with her always." She visited the Pringle house on King Street and met "the last Miss Pringle," Susan Pringle Frost (1873–1960), and her sister, Mary Pringle Frost (1871–1943), and saw "the jouncing-board on which they had exercised for forty years." In St. Michael's churchyard, she copied the epitaph on the tombstone of George Augustus Clough, who died in 1843 of "strangers' fever," and wrote the sonnet, "Epitaph In A Church-Yard In Charleston, South Carolina."

A frequent lecturer, in 1922 Lowell was invited to Charleston to lecture the Poetry Society of South Carolina. She welcomed a return to the city and to Middleton Place. In fact, she "anticipated a great deal of glamour." However, locals were aghast when Lowell, accustomed to staying up all night and sleeping all day, refused the hospitality of poet Josephine Pinckney at her mansion on King Street and instead checked into the Fort Sumter Hotel. There, she claimed, she could loll on sixteen pillows and "get room service all night long"—and smoke her cigars. (She was reportedly seen smoking a hookah.) When the old city was not at all like Lowell remembered it, she wrote the poem, "Charleston, South Carolina," with the line, "Commerce, are you worth this?" She was disappointed that old families had disappeared and the Pringle house now took in boarders. However, in honor of her prior 1906 visit to the Frost sisters, she wrote "The Vow." Two founders of the Poetry Society, DuBose Heyward (1885–1940) and Hervey Allen (1889–1949), and founding member Josephine Pinckney, took Lowell on a ride through a ghostly forest, and she wrote "A South Carolina Forest." She returned to Middleton, which she found as lovely as before, and wrote "The Middleton Place." Yet in touring Magnolia-on-the-Ashley, recently opened to the public, she found herself disappointed in the color of certain flower blossoms, which she expresses in her poem, "Magnolia Gardens." When on March 30 she arrived at South Carolina Society Hall to lecture the Poetry Society the audience arose at her entrance.

Lowell later feuded with locals via *Poetry* magazine over "Magnolia Gardens," in which she renders certain blossoms "Hateful, /Reeking with sensuality, /Bestial, obscene," colored a shade of "magenta." Charlestonians wrote letters to the magazine challenging her perception of the color of the flowers. In response, Lowell found another poem describing the flowers as magenta, and convinced its author to submit it to *Poetry* with a letter defending her choice of words. She then persuaded *Poetry*'s editor to print the other poet's work. Amy Lowell liked to have the last word. However, she removed some of the contested references before the poem was published again.

The following are the poems inspired by Lowell's two visits to Charleston.

SOURCES

Beardsley, David. "Amy Lowell: Brief Life of an Imagist Poet," *Harvard Magazine* (March 1997).

Damon, S. Foster. *Amy Lowell: A Chronicle.* Boston: Houghton Mifflin, 1935.

"Lowell, Amy" *Encyclopædia Britannica* at http://www.britannica.com/biography /Amy-Lowell (accessed December 2, 2015).

"She is Unconventional: Miss Amy Lowell Tells About Smoking Cigars," *Eugene (OR) Register-Guard* (December 8, 1913): 6.

"And the Garden Was a Fire Of Magenta": Travel Poems"
Epitaph in A Church-Yard In Charleston

GEORGE AUGUSTUS CLOUGH
A NATIVE OF LIVERPOOL,
DIED SUDDENLY OF "STRANGER'S FEVER"
NOV'R 5TH 1843
AGED 22
CHARLESTON, SOUTH CAROLINA

He died of "Stranger's Fever" when his youth
Had scarcely melted into manhood, so
The chiselled legend runs; a brother's woe
Laid bare for epitaph. The savage ruth
Of a sunny, bright, but alien land, uncouth
With cruel caressing dealt a mortal blow,
And by this summer sea where flowers grow
In tropic splendor, witness to the truth
Of ineradicable race he lies.
The law of duty urged that he should roam,
Should sail from fog and chilly airs to skies
Clear with deceitful welcome. He had come
With proud resolve, but still his lonely eyes
Ached with fatigue at never seeing home.

Charleston, South Carolina

Fifteen years is not a long time,
But long enough to build a city over and destroy it;
Long enough to clean a forty-year growth of grass from between cobblestones,
And run street-car lines straight across the heart of romance.
Commerce, are you worth this?
I should like to bring a case to trial:
Prosperity versus Beauty,
Cash registers teetering in a balance against the comfort of the soul.
Then, to-night, I stood looking through a grilled gate
At an old, dark garden.
Live-oak trees dripped branchfuls of leaves over the wall;
Acacias waved dimly beyond the gate, and the smell of their blossoms
Puffed intermittently through the wrought-iron scroll-work.
Challenge and solution—
O loveliness of old, decaying, haunted things!
Little streets untouched, shamefully paved,
Full of mist and fragrance on this rail evening.
"You should come at dawn," said my friend,
"And see the orioles, and thrushes, and mocking-birds
In the garden."
"Yes," I said absent-mindedly,
And remarked the sharp, touch of ivy upon my hand which rested against the
    wall.
But I thought to myself,
There is no dawn here, only sunset,
And an evening rain scented with flowers.

A South Carolina Forest

HUSH, hush, these woods are thick with shapes and voices,
They crowd behind, in front,
Scarcely can one's wheels break through them.
For God's sake, drive quickly!
There are butchered victims behind those trees,
And what you say is moss I know is the dead hair of hanged men.
Drive faster, faster!
The hair will catch in our wheels and clog them;
We are thrown from side to side by the dead bodies in the road.
Do you not smell the reek of them,

And see the jaundiced film that hides the stars?
Stand on the accelerator. I would rather be bumped to a jelly
Than caught by clutching hands I cannot see,
Than be stifled by the press of mouths I cannot feel.
Not in the light glare, you fool, but on either side of it.
Curse these swift, running trees—
Hurl them aside, leap them, crush them down!
Say prayers if you like,
Do anything to drown the screaming silence of this forest,
To hide the spinning shapes that jam the trees.
What mystic adventure is this
In which you have engulfed me?
What no-world have you shot us into?
What Dante dream without a farther edge?
Fright kills, they say, and I believe it.
If you would not have murder on your conscience,
For Heaven's sake, get on!

The Middleton Place, Charleston, S.C.

What would Francis Jammes,* lover of dear, dead elegancies,
Say to this place?
France, stately, formal, stepping in red-heeled shoes
Along a river shore.
France walking a minuet between live oaks waving ghostly fans of Spanish moss.
La Caroline, indeed, my dear Jammes,
With Monsieur Michaux engaged to teach her deportment.
Faint as a whiff of flutes and hautbois,
The great circle of the approach lies beneath the sweeping grasses.
Step lightly down these terraces, they are records of a dream.

Magnolias, pyrus japonicas, azaleas,
Flaunting their scattered blooms with the
		same bravura
That lords and ladies used in the prison of the Conciergerie.

---

*Francis Jammes (1868–1938), French poet and novelist, was best known for his poetry
of the natural world. He praised the simplicity of country life in contrast to the decadent element in French literature of the turn of the century. Jammes had reached the
stature of a patriarch for the young poets of the pre–World War II generation. Lowell
felt he was the greatest living poet.

You were meant to be so gay, so sophisticated, and you are so sad—
Sad as the tomb crouched amid your tangled growth,
Sad as the pale plumes of the Spanish moss
Slowly strangling the live-oak trees.

Sunset wanes along the quiet river,
The afterglow is haunted and nostalgic,
Over the yellow woodland it hangs like
the dying chord of a funeral chant;
And evenly, satirically, the mosses move to its ineffable rhythm,
Like the ostrich fans of palsied dowagers
Telling one another contentedly of the deaths they have lived to see.

Magnolia Gardens, Charleston, S.C.

It was a disappointment,
For I do not like magenta,
And the garden was a fire of magenta
Exploding like a bomb into the light-coloured peace of a Spring afternoon.
Not wistaria dropping through Spanish moss,
Not cherokees sprinkling the tops of trees with moon-shaped stars,
Not the little pricked-out blooms of banksia roses,
Could quench the flare of raw magenta.
Rubens women shaking the fatness of their bodies
In an opulent egotism
Till the curves and colours of flesh
Are nauseous to the sight,
So this magenta.
Hateful,
Reeking with sensuality,
Bestial, obscene—
I remember you as something to be forgotten.
But I cherish the smooth sweep of the colorless river,
And the thin, clear song of the red-winged blackbirds
    In the marsh-grasses on the opposite bank.

The Vow

Tread softly, softly,
Scuffle no dust.

No common thoughts shall thrust
Upon this peaceful decay,
This mold and rust of yesterday.
This is an altar with its incense blown away
By the indifferent wind of a long, sad night;
There are the precincts of the dead who die
Unconquered. Haply
You who haunt this place
May design some gesture of forgiveness
To those of our sundered race
Who come in all humility
Asking an alms of pardon.
Suffer us to feel an ease,
A benefice of love poured down on us from these magnolia-trees.
That, when we leave you, we shall know the bitter wound
Of our long mutual scourging healed at last and sound.

Through an iron gate, fantastically scrolled and garlanded,
Along a path, green with moss, between two rows of high magnolia-trees—
   How lightly the wind drips through the magnolias.
   How slightly the magnolia bend to the wind.

It stands, pushed back into a corner of the piazza—
A jouncing-board, with its paint scaled off,
A jouncing-board which creaks when you sit upon it.
   The wind rattles the stiff leaves of the magnolias:
   So many tinkling banjos drown the weeping of women.

When the Yankees came like a tide of locusts,
When blue uniforms blocked the ends of streets
And foolish, arrogant swords struck through the paintings of a hundred years.
   From gold and ivory coasts come the winds that jingle in the tree-tops;
   But the sigh of the wind in the unshaven grass, from whence is that?

Proud hearts who could not endure desecration,
Who almost loathed the sky because it was blue;
Vengeful spirits, locked in young, arrogant bodies,
You cursed yourselves with a vow:

Never would you set foot again in Charleston streets,
Never leave your piazza till Carolina was rid of Yankees.
  O smooth wind sliding in from the sea,
  It is a matter of no moment to you what flag you are flapping.

Ocean tides, morning and evening, slipping past the sea-islands;
Tides slipping in through the harbor, shaking the palmetto posts,
Slipping out through the harbor;
Pendulum tides, counting themselves upon the sea-islands.
So they jounced, for health's sake,
To be well and able to rejoice when once again the city was free,
And the lost cause won, and the stars and bars afloat over Sumter.
The days which had roared to them called more softly,
The days whispered, the days were silent,
they moved as imperceptibly as mist.

And the proud hearts went with the days, into the dusk of age, the darkness
    of death.
Slowly they were borne away through a Charleston they scarcely remembered.
The jouncing-board was pushed into a corner,
Only the magnolia-trees tossed a petal to it, now and again, if there happened
    to be a strong wind when the blooms were dropping.

Hush, go gently,
Do not move a pebble with your foot.
This is a moment of pause,
A moment to recollect the futility of cause.
A moment to bow the head
And greet the unconcerned dead,
Denying nothing of their indifference,
And then go hence
And forget them again,
Since lives are lived with living men.

View down street to St. Philip's Church, Charleston, South Carolina,
between 1920 and 1926. Arnold Genthe, (1869–1942), photographer.
Library of Congress.

Ludwig Lewisohn (1922)

"A Lingering Fragrance"

Ludwig Lewisohn, "A Lingering Fragrance" from "South Carolina: A
Lingering Fragrance," *The Nation* 115: 2975 (July 12, 1922): 36–38.

Ludwig Lewisohn (1883–1955), novelist, academic, translator, and Zionist
leader, was born in Berlin to an upper-middle-class Jewish family. His father's
financial failures brought the Lewisohns in 1890 to rural St. Matthews, South
Carolina, then in 1892 to Charleston, where the family fared poorly and Lewisohn experienced growing up "as Jewish among a waspish aristocracy." Though
his mother was the daughter of a rabbi, his father, Jacques, was a follower of
the *Aufklaerung* and believed that one religion is equal to every other. He cared
little for religious rites and observances of Judaism, therefore the family was
isolated from both Jews and Gentiles. Ludwig was an active Methodist in his
youth—an attempt, he wrote, to "become as Gentile as his neighbors." An excellent student and valedictorian of his high school class, he entered the College
of Charleston at age fifteen and obtained a bachelor's and master's degree in
only four years. Yet he remained an outsider. He would later describe an "element of pathos" in the proud, insular aristocracy of his Charleston youth,
"which accentuated so often beauty and repose" as analog to the sadness of his
own alienation.

In 1903, Lewisohn published a fifty-thousand-word history of South Carolina literature, which ran in installments in the *News and Courier* as "Books We
Have Made." The same year he left for New York and Columbia University,
where he completed another master's degree but abandoned his dissertation
after an advisor warned his "Jewish birth" would exclude him from attaining an
English faculty appointment. Instead he went to work as an editor for Doubleday Page & Co. "writing literary reviews and serialized potboilers" nights, until
labor activism cost him his job. In 1905 he became a freelance magazine writer,
returned to Charleston, and married (the first of three marriages). When this
domestic situation faltered, he returned to New York and published his first novel,
The Broken Snare (1908), with the blessing of author Theodore Dreiser. Set in

Charleston, it is the story of a young woman's attempts to find herself by running off with a man. The book received good reviews in New York but was rejected by the Charleston *News and Courier* as a "disgusting" and "devilish" work. The paper's editor was horrified "to see the most intimate relationship between a man and a woman portrayed in a manner 'reeking with the sweat of the vulgarest human passions,' and 'particularly by a Charlestonian.'" Those vulgarities included marital unhappiness, elopement, and an accidental abortion: strong stuff for that day. Ultimately the book did not sell, but this was the first of a number of subsequent novels by Lewisohn.

In 1910 he was instructor in German at the University of Wisconsin, and from 1911 he was professor of German language and literature at Ohio State University, until his German nationality and antiwar activism cost him this job. Yet Lewisohn had published several critical works and his reputation as a critic and scholar was well-known, therefore he was offered positions on several journals before he became an editor of *The Nation*. Promoted to associate editor in 1920, he remained there until 1924.

Meanwhile, in 1914 the College of Charleston awarded him the honorary degree doctor of literature. After the death of his mother that same year, he newly committed to his Jewish heritage and increasingly supported Judaism and the Zionist cause. In 1920 Lewisohn began lecturing on both Jewish and general interest topics. After he left *The Nation* in 1924 he wrote and lectured extensively until 1943, when he became editor of *The New Palestine*. In 1948, he became one of the thirteen original faculty members at Brandeis University, holding the position as professor of comparative literature until his death.

Lewisohn authored innumerable articles and thirty-one books of criticism, history, fiction, biography, and Jewish affairs. Some of his better-known works include his memoir, *Upstream: An American Chronicle* (1922), in which he wrote of his love-hate relationship with Charleston (which he renamed Queenshaven). *Mid-Channel* (1929), his second autobiographical book, was a treatment of the problems of Jews in America. *Haven* (1940) was the third and last volume of his autobiography. Of the fifteen novels he published, the third, *The Case of Mr. Crump* (1926), brought him international acclaim. He afterward published *Island Within* (1928), his best-known novel, followed by *Expression in America* (1932) and *Renegade* (1942), among others.

Lewisohn authored several works on Judaica and Zionism and translated several German works including Franz Werfel's *The Song of Bernadette*. He was a member of the Jewish Academy of Arts and Sciences and an honorary secretary of the Zionist Organization of America. In his last decades, he was an outspoken opponent of Nazi Germany, a leading promoter of Jewish resettlement in Palestine, a forthright critic of American Jewish assimilation, and one of the earliest voices advocating Jewish renewal in America. For four decades, he was a force in American journalism, literature, Zionism, and education.

When, in 1922, Lewisohn published "South Carolina: A Lingering Fragrance" in *The Nation,* neither Charleston nor the Upcountry was pleased. In 1977, South Carolinian Louis B. Wright (1899–1984), a scholar, librarian, and director of the Folger Shakespeare Library published *South Carolina: A Bicentennial History.* In his introduction (which he titled "A Lingering Fragrance") Wright claimed he had waited more than fifty years to respond to Lewisohn's "repugnant" article in *The Nation.* He wrote: "It was supercilious, arrogant, and derogatory—so irritating that for more than half a century I remembered it with distaste. Lewisohn's descriptions of both Charleston and the Up Country were libels." He continued, "If for Ludwig Lewisohn South Carolina had the lingering fragrance of a vanished civilization, for me it was the opposite. I was not the only one irritated. August Kohn, correspondent at the time for the Charleston *News and Courier,* told me with an appropriate gesture of holding his nose, 'There is a fragrance about Lewisohn—the fragrance of a rotten egg.'" Wright, a native of Greenwood, took particular umbrage at Lewisohn's tendency "to damn the whole Upcountry as a land of ignorant barbarians—rednecks and hoodlums—whose very religion, a strict Protestantism, was a stench in the nostrils of cultivated man." Wright wrote, "The author of this diatribe, while purporting to praise the ancient cultivation of Charlestonians, contrived also to insult their descendants." And: "We do not relish an expatriate ingrate, just because he made some little literary success in New York, looking down his nose and calling us names."

In his 1922 essay for *The Nation,* Lewisohn looks back to the city that he both loved and hated. He ponders Charleston's cultivated past and questions the city's diminished place in the state given the progress of the Upcountry during the New South era.

SOURCES

"Biographical Sketch." Ludwig Lewisohn Manuscript Collection [166]. American Jewish Archives. Cincinnati, Ohio. Accessed Nov. 30, 2015. http://collections.american jewisharchives.org/ms/ms0166/ms0166.html.

Chyet, Stanley F. "Ludwig Lewisohn in Charleston (1892–1903)," *American Jewish Historical Quarterly* 54:3 (March, 1965): 296–322.

Klingenstein, Susanne. *Jews in the American Academy, 1900–1940: The Dynamics of Intellectual Assimilation.* Syracuse University Press, 1998.

Melnick, Ralph. *Life and Work of Ludwig Lewisohn: A Touch of Wildness.* Wayne State University Press, 1998.

Melnick, Ralph, *Life and Work of Ludwig Lewisohn: This Dark and Desperate Age.*
    Wayne State University Press, 1998.
Proctor, Samuel, Louis Schmier, and Malcolm H. Stern, eds. *Jews of the South: Se-
    lected Essays from the Southern Jewish Historical Society.* Mercer University Press,
    1984.
Wright, Louis B. *South Carolina: A Bicentennial History (States and the Nation).*
    W. W. Norton & Company, 1977.

"A Lingering Fragrance"

A tiny tongue of land extending from Broad Street in Charleston to the beautiful bay formed by the confluence of the Ashley and the Cooper rivers is all of
South Carolina that has counted in the past; the memories that cling to the little
peninsula are all that count today. More than thirty years have passed since Ben
Tillman led the revolt of the agrarians, the "poor white trash," the "wool-hats"
of the "upper country" against the old Charlestonian aristocracy. He won. The
time-spirit was with him. The new men control the State; they control the State
University; they will not send their sons to the College of Charleston; they have
industrialized the "upper country" and made it hum with spindles and prosperity and their particular brand of righteousness. Spartanburg is both a more
progressive and a more moral city than Charleston. It even indulges in cultural
gestures and is visited by a symphony orchestra once a year. It is the headquarters of the cotton-mill men and of the Methodists; it is the seat of Wofford College where they cultivate Christian prosperity and the tradition of the sainted
Bishop Duncan:* "In my time I used to read Shakespeare and Scott and all those
writers. But nowadays I read nothing but the Bible because I know it is the word
of my God. . . ."

   The new men brought neither freedom nor enlightenment. They oppress
and bedevil the Negro without the old gentry's vivid and human even if strictly
feudal sympathy with his character and needs; they sentimentalize in political
speeches and commencement orations about the Old South. Of its genuine qualities, as these were represented in old Charleston, they know nothing. It was,
indeed, in mute deference to them that the president of the College of Charleston ceased, long before the days of prohibition, to serve wine at his receptions
and permitted engineering courses to be added to the undergraduate curriculum. In this atmosphere the sons of the Charleston gentry who, until a few years
ago, studied Greek as a matter of course, have sunk into that appalling and intolerant ignorance and meanness of spirit that mark the cultural vacuum known

---

*Bishop William Wallace Duncan (1839–1908), who spent much of his life serving both
  Wofford College and the Methodist Church.

as the New South. They no longer study in Europe or found periodicals or issue shy volumes of verse or cultivate a perfectly genuine though somewhat pseudo-Roman and oratorical spirit of service to the State and nation. They are letting their civilization perish without resistance.

They are, of course, vastly outnumbered and energy died out of the stock long before they were born. They are mere descendants and cling to the husks. In the early years of the present century one of the last of the Pinckneys wrote a "Life of Calhoun"* in which he defended the doctrine of nullification as fundamentally necessary to the structure of American government. Then he went mad. At the reunions of Confederate Veterans the contemporaries of this gentleman spoke with tears of the glories of the Old South. They did not mean the spirit of true civilization which, somehow, old Charleston had possessed; they meant the "peculiar institution of slavery" and the oligarchical rule of the planters of the sea-board counties. Yet at that very time faint remnants of the old Charleston spirit could be observed. The Master in Equity, a *novus homo,* but long accepted through association and marriage into, let us say, the South Carolina Society and the St. Cecilia Society, desired to publish in a volume the poems he had written in the course of a lifetime beautifully though rather ineffectually dedicated to literature and learning. A group of his friends—colleagues of the Charleston bar—made up a purse for him and the book was duly brought out by a New York firm noted for its sharp business practice and its long association with American literature. That was a last flicker of the life of old Charleston. I seem to be detailing gossip. But these anecdotes are significant and they are, at least, authentic. They should be corrected in the impression they convey by others. The old Charleston group had its darker side. William Gilmore Simms was treated shabbily,[†] though I am willing to believe that he was a man of rude manners and unprintable speech; Henry Timrod, the best of their poets,[‡] was treated abominably. He was, in the first place, the son of a German tradesman and poor and a tutor in planters' families. More sinister in its meaning is the bit

---

* Gustavus M. Pinckney (1872–1912) wrote *Life of John C. Calhoun* (1903).

† William Gilmore Simms (1806–1870), whose novels achieved great prominence. He edited several newspapers and important southern journals. Simms lived at Woodlands Plantation near Bamberg. He was born in Charleston but was never accepted by Charlestonians. There were exceptions. Poet Paul Hamilton Hayne (1830–1886) wrote that he was one of a "band of brilliant youths who used to meet for literary suppers at [Simms] beautiful home; and here it was that the love for old Elizabethan lore, and the study of the classics of the English tongue . . . found one of its best stimulants."

‡ Henry Timrod (1828–1867), whose first collection, *Poems,* was published in 1859, was an important southern poet of the nineteenth century. Following his death, *Poems of Henry Timrod* (1872) was published by his friend, Paul Hamilton Hayne.

of gossip which floated down the years that he or the young woman to whom he was betrothed had "a touch of the tar-brush." This thing—interesting and picturesque if true of the poet himself—was whispered to me in a kind of murderous secrecy as a sufficient excuse for whatever need, misery, humiliation poor Timrod was permitted to endure. The old Charlestonians, in brief, loved letters and learning and romance. They were often capable of a fine and gallant and even intellectual gesture; they bore themselves not without distinction. Under that cultivation and distinction, as under the cultivation and distinction of the eighteenth-century type everywhere, lurked cruelty, violent intolerances, stealthy and relentless lusts.

It is hard to realize that today. Quiet has stolen into the old houses of the lower city; scarcely a breath seems to ruffle the wistaria vines in spring! In such a spring Mr. Owen Wister visited shady drawing-rooms—and talked to exquisite old ladies and wrote "Lady Baltimore." Henry James communed with such frail figures during his last stay in this country. He saw a long disused harp, a lovely colonial cabinet, autograph letters of Hayne, and was told that Mr. Thackeray, when he lectured here, took tea in this very room. And it caressed his ear when old ladies with delicate shadows amid their porcelain-like wrinkles sounded the vowels of English as he knew, from the rhymes, Pope must have sounded them, but as he never expected to hear them upon mortal lips. These "values" pleased him amid the violent and raw distractions of the American scene. They are soothing. I, too, have lingered among them and savored them. But they do not tell the complete story of the civilization from which they derived.

That tight and peculiar Charleston culture was created by settlers partly of English, partly of French descent. Names, put down almost at random, will help to convey its quality and atmosphere. Among the English names are Wragg, Middleton, Pinckney, Gadsden, Drayton, Hayne, Trescott, Bull; among the French are Manigault, Gaillard, Huger, Simon, Legare, Porcher, de Saussure, Jervey (Gervais). The Ravenels were probably Marranos; the French settlers were Huguenots and though many of them, under the political and cultural domination of Britain, went to augment the Anglican parishes of St. Michael and St. Philip, enough clung to their ancestral faith to make the only Huguenot church in America a quaint and agreeable projects Charleston landmark to this day. There were dissenters from other countries, like the Dutch Mazycks; there was, from a very early period on, a small colony of Sephardic Jews—Lopez, De Leon, Moise, Ottolengui. All the names I have mentioned exist in Charleston today. Of the immediate youngsters I cannot speak. The bearers of these able names who are now approaching middle age all, or nearly all, preserved within them something of the spirit of their ancestral civilization.

They were not Puritans in the fierce, vulgar, persecuting and self-persecuting sense. Their theological and moralistic assents were social gestures; they had, themselves, large mental reservations and though in their own persons they considered it rather bad form to parade those reservations, they were not intolerant of the type of conscience that held silence to be hypocritical. They were snobs to the marrow, but a few of them, at least, were capable of contemplating that fact consciously and a little sorrowfully. A Charleston gentleman, almost of the ancient regime, was heard to say to a friend of his: "I don't blame you at all for leaving a city where your social standing will never be quite what you deserve. It is a pity; Charleston needs you. But I should do the same in your place." Yes, they were snobs and facile assenters who made the free life more difficult. But they had a real respect for the arts, for the things of the mind, for the critical spirit they could never quite share. They were and are, when every deduction has been made, among the most civilized of Americans. They had, in addition, grace, ease, personal charm. When I think of the people who are pressing them hard—the horse-dealer from central Georgia, some hustler from the Middle West—I am inclined to lend them an almost legendary worth. I must, at all events, set down this fact: the present descendants of most of the old Charleston families are poor. The men are still members of the learned professions, as their fathers were. They still consider them learned professions—even the law. The handsome new houses in elegant Charleston are the houses of new people. Many a beautiful or almost and time-mellowed mansion on Legare Street is in a state of gradual decay.

The history of the old Charleston group is, of course, like the history of other such urban and patrician groups in other parts of the world. It can be matched in Mantua and in Lubeck. The pathos of its downfall lies in the fact that it has gone down not before the authentic spirit of the modern world, but before the mean barbarism of sharp business men and Ku Klux Klanners. Its enemies and conquerors would consider the personalities it produced at its best moments—Hugh Swinton Legare, Paul Hamilton Hayne, William Henry Trescott [*sic*]*—very much as a Tulsa or Winesburg hundred percenter would consider, if he could consider them at all, Nietzsche or Verlaine or Bertrand Russell.

* William Henry Trescot (1822–1898), Charleston attorney and author of numerous American history books, had served as assistant secretary of state under President Buchanan and had been an important intermediary during the early part of the Fort Sumter crisis. He went on to a brilliant career as a diplomatist. He authored *Foreign Policy of the United States* (1849); *Diplomacy of the Revolution* (1852); *An American View of the Eastern Question* (1854); *Diplomatic History of the Administrations of Washington and Adams* (1857); besides various memoirs, addresses, and pamphlets.

For what Legare and [Trescott] had was the critical and distinguishing mind, the culture of the intellect. Legare, a diplomat, a scholar, a brilliant and romantic personality, a writer like the Edinburgh reviewers of the early days, hastened home from Brussels to protest against secession; [Trescott], a statesman who cultivated quietly a gift for extraordinarily limpid and expressive prose wrote, soon after the Civil War, reflections that blended human warmth with philosophical detachment.

These men and Robert Hayne and Calhoun were, however, less intimately characteristic of the Charleston culture that projects feebly into the present than the minors—the shy spiritual and literary adventurers found in almost every family. In the very early days they were bolder, like Washington Allston, the poet and painter and friend of Coleridge.* Later their efforts were more tentative and hushed like the verses of the Simon [sic] brothers,† or the really admirable poems of the almost legendary James Mathew Legare,‡ or the Crashaw-like outpourings of Caroline Poyas.§ Often they sought anonymity and printed verse and prose in the Charleston periodicals which succeeded each other from before the Revolution to the founding of the *The Nineteenth Century Magazine* in 1870. And when one considers that the contents of these magazines were all written in Charleston and that Charleston, which has fewer than seventy-thousand inhabitants today, was a very small town indeed, one gains a high notion of the pervasiveness of the literary culture and spiritual aliveness that existed in the city between the Revolution and the Civil War. Much of this writing was, of course, feeble and jejune. There is scarcely an original note. The Byronic lyric succeeds the couplet and the didacticism of the late eighteenth century; the emergence of Keats can be noted almost to a day; later that of Tennyson. But behind this imitative expression there was an extraordinary number of cultivated, impassioned, vivid personalities. Everybody wrote—men of public affairs like William

* Washington Allston (1779–1843), poet and artist born at Brookgreen Plantation near Georgetown into the Alston/Allston family of planters. He graduated from Harvard, studied art at the Royal Academy in London, and traveled in Europe before he pioneered America's Romantic movement of landscape painting. He befriended Samuel Taylor Coleridge in Italy. His poetry was published in *The Sylphs of the Seasons* (1813) and posthumously in *Lectures on Art and Poems* (1850).
† The Simmons brothers, poet William Hayne Simmons (1784–1870) and author James Wright Simmons (1790–1858), born in Charleston.
‡ James Matthews Legare (1823–1859), who contributed mainly to magazines, published a single volume, *Orta-Undis and Other Poems* (1848).
§ Catharine Gendron Poyas (1813–1882) published *Huguenot Daughters, and Other Poems* (1849) and *Year of Grief, and Other Poems* (1869).

Crafts;* merchants like Isaac Harby.† One Manigault published anonymous novels,‡ another was a really able scientist who brought home a great collection of natural history that is still to be seen.§ Still others expressed themselves through exotic adventure like Joel R. Poinsett, who found in Mexico the decorative flower that bears his name. I am deliberately jumbling periods. The spirit of the civilization of old Charleston was, while it lasted, one. From Alexander Garden—discoverer of the Gardenia—before the Revolution to Dr. Dixon Bruns of the Civil War period and to Professor Yates Snowden today,** one of the marks of the gentleman and the eminent citizen has been to turn out an elegant or a stirring copy of verses at will. But the last or almost the last has been written. Only the descendants of the Sephardic Jews have shown a queer kind of vitality and have produced in the last generation and in this two writers of the shabbily popular variety—Rodriguez Ottolengui,†† and Octavus Roy Cohen.‡‡

---

* William Crafts (1787–1826), lawyer, member of the legislature, and editor of the *Charleston Courier*, published *Sullivan's Island, The Raciad, and Other Poems* (1820) and *A Selection in Prose and Poetry, from the Miscellaneous Writings of the Late William Crafts* (1828).

† Isaac Harby (1788–1828), schoolmaster, editor, essayist, playwright, and political writer. For more on Harby, see Gary Phillip Zola, *Isaac Harby of Charleston, 1788–1828: Jewish Reformer and Intellectual* (Tuscaloosa: University of Alabama Press, 1994.)

‡ Gabriel Manigault (1809–1888), lawyer and planter, published the anonymous novel, *Ellen Woodville* (1844), and the three-volume *Saint Cecilia: A Modern Tale From Real Life* (1871–1872). He is believed to have authored *The Actress in High Life* (1860), which was initially credited to author Susan Petigru King as a ruse. Manigault also published nonfiction works, including *The United States Unmasked* (1879).

§ Although Charles Manigault (1795–1874) was a noted collector of art and scientific objects, Lewisohn likely refers to his son, Gabriel Edward Manigault (1833–1899), who obtained a medical degree and studied in Europe but never practiced medicine. He was a planter who devoted much of his life to natural history pursuits. He was curator of the Museum of Natural History at the College, and curator at the Charleston Museum.

** Dr. John Dickson Bruns (1836–1883), a surgeon and poet from Charleston. Yates Snowden (1858–1933), professor of history at South Carolina College, published poetry as well as books and articles on state history.

†† Rodrigues Ottolengui (1861–1937), a dentist born in Charleston, moved to New York and was editor for thirty-five years of *Items of Interest: A Monthly Magazine of Dental Art, Science, and Literature*, while he published detective fiction, four novels, and a short story collection.

‡‡ Octavus Roy Cohen (1891–1959) worked for numerous newspapers before he became popular for his stories about blacks published in *The Saturday Evening Post*. Admitted to the South Carolina bar, he practiced law in Charleston for two years. From 1917 until his death he published fifty-six books, including humorous and detective novels, plays, and collections of short stories, and composed successful Broadway plays and radio, film, and television scripts.

From Charleston "neck" to the Piedmont region there may well come the indignant question: Is Charleston gossip an adequate account of the great, proud State of South Carolina? It is. Or shall one record the labor condition in the cotton mills or the antics of former Governor Blease* or expatiate on the lynching statistics?—I once travelled with Blease from Charleston to Cincinnati. He was going to a national meeting of the Elks. He was, with a touch of consciousness, almost of staginess, the typical leader of the democracy of the New South —ostentatiously large wool hat, dark rather fierce eyes, heavy black mustache, gaudy insignia on a heavy watch-chain, a man who radiated or wanted to radiate a constant ferocity against the irreligious, the impure, "Nigger-lovers," aristocrats, "pap-suckers," Yankees, intellectuals, a son of the soil and of the mob with a chip on his shoulder. His conversation had a steady note of the belligerent and the self-righteous. A noisy, astute yet hectic obscurantist. He might have been from Georgia or Mississippi. He despised Charleston with a touch of inverted envy. A South Carolinian quite merged in a larger and lower unity and without any relation to the specific character of the State. Finally shall one make much of the fact that though, whether through the influence of race or climate, the demands of the senses are rather exorbitant in South Carolina, the State has the amusing distinction of being the only commonwealth in the civilized world to tolerate no provision for divorce on its statute books?† In Charleston, least, there has never been a lynching and her citizens have, at need, disregarded their Draconian lawgivers. Also, they and their ancestors have created a beautiful thing—the city that clings to the bay. Linger in these streets and lanes and gardens and enter a few shadowy interiors beyond the deep verandas that turn to the South. A race lived here that loved dignity without ostentation, books and wine and human distinction. Its sins, which were many, fade into the past. They were always less vulgar and ugly than those who have come after.

---

* Coleman Livingston Blease (1868–1942), Democratic state legislator, governor (1911–1915), and later US Senator, played on the prejudices of poor whites to gain their votes. He was pro-lynching, anti–black education, and against "lying newspapers." As senator, he would advocate penalties for interracial couples attempting to get married and criticize First Lady Lou Hoover for inviting a black guest to tea at the White House.
† In South Carolina, divorce was abolished from 1879 to 1948.

O'Donnel House, 21 King Street, Charleston, Charleston County, S.C.
Historic American Buildings Survey, creator. Library of Congress.

SCHUYLER LIVINGSTON PARSONS (1928)

"Mr. Parsons' Mansion"

Schuyler Livingston Parsons, "Mr. Parsons' Mansion" from *Untold Friendships* (Boston: Houghton Mifflin), 1955. Reprint permission granted from Stephanie Wharton Holbrook, Schuyler Parsons Estate.

Schuyler Livingston Parsons (1892–1967) was from one of New York's oldest families. His father ran the family business, Parsons & Petit, a wholesale chemical import firm that supplied gunpowder and explosives. Parsons grew up on a forty-acre family estate, Whileaway, in Islip, New York, and in New York City, where he attended private school before he was sent to St. Marks in Southborough, Massachusetts. After attending Harvard and law school, he served in the ambulance corps in World War I. In 1919 he married Betty Bierne Pierson (1900–1982), a twenty-year-old from another old New York family who would become better known as Betty Parsons, New York art dealer, collector, and early promoter of Abstract Expressionism. Schuyler Parsons was ten years her senior. When "he proved to be as captivated by men as she was by women" (and, according to her, his drinking and gambling got to be too much), the couple divorced amicably in Paris on the grounds of incompatibility.

Parsons worked for his father's chemical company for a time, although he traveled seasonally between New York, Long Island, Newport, Aiken, and Palm Beach. His close friends included Charlie Chaplin, Gertrude Lawrence, Elsa Maxwell, Elsie de Wolfe, and the Duke and Duchess of Windsor. It was at his estate, Pleasure Island, in Islip that George Gershwin began composing *Rhapsody in Blue*, writing the first notes in Parson's guest book.

In 1928, Parsons' doctor recommended that he convalesce in Charleston, where he first rented the Pinckney mansion at 21 King Street, and afterward purchased 18 Lamboll Street. He was in town during the stock market crash of 1929. A collector in the past, Parsons began to sell antiques in both Charleston and Aiken in the years he frequented South Carolina. Most of all, he mingled with the socialites of his day. Parsons did not remain in Charleston long but was soon on his way.

By the 1950s, Parson's favorite havens for the rich, Newport and Palm Beach, had fallen off. "Frankly, I can't remember when I had a white tie on last," he said. His financial situation had become dire and most of his famous friends were dead, when in 1955 he published *Untold Friendships*. He lived another twelve years after the publication of his memoir. Retired to a small house in Palm Beach, he spent his last days "awash in the memories of untold friendships."

The following excerpt begins in New York City, where, after an accident, Parsons is advised to recover in Charleston.

SOURCES

Bruno, Lisa Doll. "From Chaplin to Lindbergh, Pleasure Island in Islip Boasts 90 Years of Celebrity History." *Newsweek* (Oct. 16, 2013).

Burghardt, Laura. "The Movement of Architectural Elements within Charleston, South Carolina." Thesis, Clemson University, May 2009.

Frost, Susan Pringle. "Miss Frost Tells History of Her Restoration Work," *Charleston News and Courier,* Feb. 24, 1941.

Malcolm, Tom. *William Barclay Parsons: A Renaissance Man of Old New York*. New York: Parsons Brinckerhoff, 2010.

Samuel, Lawrence R. *Rich: The Rise and Fall of American Wealth Culture*. New York: Amacon-American Management Association, 2009.

Stein, Judith E., and Helène Aylon. "The Parsons Effect." *Art in America* (Nov. 1, 2013). http://www.artinamericamagazine.com/news-features/magazine/betty-parsons/.

Weeks, Lyman Horace, *Prominent Families of New York*. New York: Historical Company, 1898.

"Mr. Parsons' Mansion"

In the autumn of 1928 I started making cross-country business trips which by now I enjoyed, since I had friends everywhere. In New York that winter I gave a dance and several dinners for my niece who was coming out. Somehow I sensed that I should cut down, but stocks were going up every day, I was back in the market, and to provide ready cash I put a large mortgage on the Seventy-second Street house, which had doubled in value since I bought it and for which I received fabulous offers all the time. So I just fell in with the spirit of the times, disregarded my better judgment, and gave ever bigger and better parties.

Christmas came and went. By now I was drinking far too much and one evening got into a dreadful row with my sister Helena when she told me I was in no condition to take my niece to Birdie Vanderbilt's Christmas party. It was the only fight I ever had with her and it hurt us both deeply. Shortly afterwards, while on a business trip to Cleveland, I heard of a lovely house at Newport which could be bought cheaply, and I decided to go to see it, but by stopping over a day to visit Niagara Falls, I missed the opportunity and returned to New York tired and discouraged. The next night I went to a wild party which lasted until morning. I was to report for jury duty that day and after breakfast, before setting out, had to see the cook because I was giving a large formal dinner that night. I started for the kitchen door which was down a dark hail with the cellar door next to it. In a daze from lack of sleep and the drinking of the night before, I opened the wrong door. I had not been told that the cellar stairs had been removed and the new ones not yet put in. As I stepped through the door, I hurtled into space, somehow hit a standard which broke my fall, but landed right on my head on the cement floor of the cellar.

I had suffered a double fracture of the skull, but although I could hardly see or hear, I never lost consciousness. For days I hung between life and death, bleeding from the eyes, my head swathed in bandages. A troupe of consultants were called in, and with their help, the skill, personality and philosophy of Dr. Fred Tilney* pulled me through.

After six weeks it was decided that I must go to a warmer climate. Dr. Robert Wilson† in Charleston was a friend and colleague of Tilney's so it was decided I should go there. Again the caravan was on the move with the devoted Whartons,‡ a nucleus of white servants, two trained nurses, two dogs, trunks, a surgical bed, and two cars sent ahead. At Charleston I rented the old Pinckney house on King Street a very comfortable large house which was promptly termed by the chauffeur "Mr. Parsons' Mansion." As there was an elevator I could have the room on the top floor which overlooked the rooftops and had a wonderful view of the harbor. We inherited the Pinckney cook, Victoria, as great a character as she was a cook. She could not write except to sign her name which she did with a flourish, "Victoria R." The R. we found out was for Rutledge, a family her parents had served as slaves. My two nurses were Canadians and used to wear their blue veils in the street, a great novelty to Charleston, and when I was well enough to get into a wheel chair, we would have a platoon of little blacks following us down the street. My head hurt terribly at times and no one could touch it without my going into a paroxysm of pain and fear. Most of the time I had on a black silk hood so I could not use my eyes, but later a patch was adequate.

Behind the garden at King Street was a lovely yard which ran at right angles and was the back of the property at 18 Lamboll Street. The house was a typical

---

* Frederick Tilney (1876–1938), noted brain specialist and professor of neurology at Columbia University.
† Robert Wilson Jr. (1867–1946), Charleston physician and dean of the Medical College.
‡ Richard Thomas Wharton (1876–1933) and Helena Parsons Wharton (1878–1936), Parson's brother-in-law and sister.

Charleston one, gable end to the street with porches on the first and second floors the full length of the house. It was just what we wanted and we bought it, for by then I knew it would be years before I could work again. The kindness of people was very touching and there was no Mason and Dixon Line visible. Besides our Southern friends we had plenty of Northern ones who came from Aiken over the slippery roads of those days. However, I saw very few people because I could not always manage to say what I wished and had a horror that people would think I had lost my mind.

It was about this time I felt I had to have some outside help to give me the courage to overcome the pain and paralysis. Mrs. Thomas Hastings, one of the truest friends and greatest wits of my acquaintance, came from Aiken* laden with Christian Science books, but I could not take in their philosophy, nor could I concentrate long enough to understand their meaning. So I evolved a system of prayer and listening which has stood me in good stead since. I began to worry about my finances, but I still had enough collateral on which to borrow a considerable sum—enough to see me through at least two years.

In the spring I went up to New York to see the doctor, who said I was greatly improved but must have a specially trained neurological nurse. Miss Tyler soon became one of the family, being with me day and night for three years, by which time she had me back in the land of the living. That summer I spent the life of an invalid at Newport, loafing about the beach and our garden and taking rides in the speed boat.

Before leaving for Charleston in the fall, the New York doctors told me I would have to have one eye out, but luckily I insisted on further examinations which showed that I had made an amazing recovery and it was agreed that I could get away with a patch over one eye, do certain exercises and be checked up on regularly. I wore the patch for just seven years, but the eye was saved and according to the doctors, this was a miracle. Before going south I resigned from my chemical firm, closing an era of my life

The fall of 1929! I was alone when I got the news of the panic in Charleston, but it did not upset me greatly since the rent from the New York house took care of my mortgage. I had plenty of cash left from my loan, and I owned a big block

---

*Helen Ripley Benedict Hastings (1865–1936), equestrian and sportswoman, daughter of Elias Cornelius Benedict, New York City banker. She was married to Thomas Hastings, Beaux-Arts architect and a partner at Carrère & Hastings, which designed the New York Public Library, as well as famous homes and public buildings around the world. It was said to be a marriage of convenience as both were gay. In 1928, Hastings designed the couple a winter residence called Horsehaven at the winter colony of Aiken. Mosette Broderick, *Triumvirate*, 368.

of stock in our family real estate company, which I considered as sound as the Rock of Gibraltar. Few of my friends in Charleston were badly hit since few had enough money to speculate, so I lived in a fool's paradise for a few months.

Again I had, I think, created a lovely house, and according to the guest book it was not long before the procession of visitors started, keeping up in a steady stream throughout the winter and into late May. Dick Wharton retired in January and he and my sister arrived shortly after. Several of our friends came to look for plantations, for the North was then discovering South Carolina. People who had saved what they could from the crash wanted a place where they could live outside the gloom of New York and others used us as a convenient stopping-off place en route to Palm Beach. It was very exciting. Every day almost, a telegram and a new guest.

Late that spring Charleston was celebrating an anniversary with all sorts of high jinx, and the mayor asked me if I knew someone who could review the parade and make the main address. I at once thought of that lovable character Nick Longworth, then Speaker of the House.* He accepted and planned to spend a few days beforehand with Laura Curtis at Aiken.† I was to have a large and important lunch for him at two, and a police escort was waiting at North Charleston at eleven-fifteen to usher the party into the city, but there was no sign of them. The telephone wires began to burn. They had left Aiken on time; a scouting party went out, all to no avail. The Committee was furious, I was mortified, and it was a most downhearted gathering that assembled for two o'clock dinner. But just as we were to go in, we heard the welcome sound of sirens and there they were. It took Nick only a few seconds and his charm to prevent a second civil war. I found out later that he had decided he could not take the heat of reviewing a parade, having been up very late the night before in Aiken, so he had ordered the chauffeur to drive into a grove of welcoming live oaks and the entire party took a refreshing nap. However, he made a rousing speech in the afternoon and even those who had objected to a Northerner as the main speaker relented completely. What a man!

In odd moments that winter I studied much of Charleston's history and became imbued with the legends and characters of the place. I still could not get around enough to do much sightseeing, but took many drives to the plantations,

* Nicholas Longworth III (1869–1931), speaker of the House of Representatives (1925–1931) and husband of Alice Roosevelt Longworth, the daughter of Teddy Roosevelt.
† Laura Merriam Curtis (1850–1943), the socialite wife of prominent lawyer James Freeman Curtis, former assistant secretary of the US Treasury and first counsel of the Federal Reserve Bank. She was Nick Longworth's mistress. In 1931 Longworth died at Laura Curtis's house in Aiken. Amanda Smith, *Newspaper Titan*, 328–29.

seeing many of them before they were sold to Northerners as shooting properties. The captain had brought the *Efoyad* down and we had lots of picnics and trips up the various rivers and along the inland waterways, where Dick and I found a derelict plantation with a grove of really big camellia trees which we bought and transplanted to our yard in town. One of our friends was an expert landscape gardener and planted a beautiful herbaceous border which gave us a riot of color all winter long. We conformed to most Charleston customs save two. First, we furnished our downstairs porch and used it even on mild winter days, an unheard-of practice since the Charlestonians considered their porches too hot in summer and too cold in winter. The only furniture on most of them was the ubiquitous "joggling board." Many Charleston proposals have been made on these joggling boards! Our second revolutionary action was to pay our colored servants to stay until after the evening meal. We still had Remy and Ida who lived in a charming Colonial cottage in the yard and in addition there was a raft of hangers-on who came and went in rapid succession.

The house when I bought it had a very plain entrance door which I replaced with a beautiful one I had found in Newport and which was said to have come from Charleston originally. Few people realize that Newport was started as a summer resort in the eighteen-thirties by the rich Charleston planters, the Middletons, the Rutledges and the Draytons.

Fall River in those days was the headquarters of the fertilizer market. The planter's family would embark on the company schooner in early June, completely equipped even to cow, horses and carriages. After unloading the family and their possessions in Newport, the schooner would go on to Fall River for a load of nitrates. In the fall, it would bring up the cotton crop and after the planter had disposed of this, would stop at Newport for the family's return to Charleston. "Stone Villa" in Newport, once the home of Gordon Bennett and now owned by Bill Whitehouse, was built by a Charlestonian.* There is another interesting sidelight on the Charleston invasion of Newport. The planters naturally brought slave help and body servants, and as these grew old, they were manumitted there and pensioned by their owners, becoming the forerunners of the highly respectable Negro colony now in Newport, so many of whom have Charleston surnames. When I first brought up my Charleston servants I was

* The Middleton family were the original owners of Stone Villa (c. 1833). Once the home of James Gordon Bennett, founder, editor, and publisher of the *New York Herald*, the last owner was William F. Fitzhugh Whitehouse from New York. Two years after his death in 1955, Stone Villa was acquired by developers and demolished for a shopping center.

astounded at their many callers, who, I found out, were the descendants of common ancestors who had come from Charleston three generations before.

Charleston in my early days there was a lovely place to live. The tempo of life was slow, the cooking superb, and the people charming. The houses may have needed painting on the outside but the interiors had great dignity, even though many fine pieces of furniture had been sold to Northern buyers. To my eye, used to the polish and gleam of English mahogany, these pieces seemed very dull and I soon found out why. A legend told of a visit by Stanford White* at the turn of the century who said that the best furniture preservative was a mixture of oil and pumice! As I have said before, the main form of entertainment was a cocktail party or an evening of cards, with the hostess herself serving the cold supper left in the icebox. Once when I was asked to midday Sunday dinner at a fine house on Legare Street, just as I reached the gate an old lady I knew was passing and as I bowed, she spoke up. "Are you going in there for Sunday dinner?" "Yes," I said. The old lady shook her head. "I don't understand those people having an outsider to Sunday dinner, and a damned Yankee to boot. You certainly have arrived." There was so much that was foreign to us in those days. The street cries of the peddlers hawking their wares were so colorful it was a pleasure to be awakened by them. Many had songs which had come down for generations, the most familiar being, "He crab, she crab." She crabs were a greatly prized delicacy on account of the roe. Another I loved was: "Here come yo' paper boy.

Why esk for more?"

The man who cried "Drum-fish roe never got far, as this." In the late spring, this was the greatest of all delicacies to the Carolinian. I loved the shrimp, and the Charleston shrimp pies for which I give the recipe for those interested:

2 cupfuls of cooked rice
½ lb. of cooked and peeled shrimp
1 ½ cups of canned tomatoes or about 4 fresh ones
1 small chopped onion

---

*Stanford White (1853–1906), architect and partner in the firm of McKim, Mead & White, who was murdered by millionaire Harry Kendall Thaw. White's mother, Alexina Black Mease (1830–1921), was from a Charleston family. From his post–wedding trip in the South with his wife, Bessie, in 1886, White wrote his mother from a train between Charleston and Savannah, "Here we are—happy as two Long Island clams at high water. We were both wild about Charleston. It is a most lovely old city, with the swellest old houses I have ever seen on this side of the water. The Battery is almost as pretty as ours must have been." Charles C. Baldwin, *Stanford White*, 31, 172.

½ lb. of butter or bacon drippings
1 teaspoon of Worcestershire sauce
Salt and pepper to taste

Melt the butter or drippings and mix all the ingredients together. Put in a Pyrex dish, sprinkle buttered bread crumbs over the top, and bake in a hot oven about thirty minutes.

I could never tell one black from another and made some awful mistakes. Once Laszlo Széchenyi* came to stay with me for a week while he was Hungarian Minister in Washington and of all my guests was most liked by the Charlestonians, who outdid themselves in entertaining him. On the station platform as he was leaving he said, "I could never live here, for I couldn't tell my servants from those of my neighbors. Take that butler of yours, William. He would see me out of your house and when I got to a party, there was his duplicate with a different coat on, and again at the next house." I explained that William was not just my butler but the best hired man you could get in Charleston. Afterwards he was "mine," and from me went to Elizabeth Arden Graham,† with whom he remained until he died last year. Laszlo wore a patch and when we were together, he would have me wear mine on the other eye.

The Charleston Negro was filled with unique superstitions and under the veneer of civilization was still the African native. Many in the country still spoke Gullah or sang the Gullah spirituals. We had a very cunning little maid who brought up my sister's breakfast one day looking quite sick. The poor girl said she had an awful pain but would be all right soon, for she had just taken a large glass of vinegar and bicarbonate of soda! She then rushed from the room, there was a resounding explosion and she literally blew up and died then and there on the stair landing. I screamed for a young house boy we had, called Isaiah, and the first thing he did was to bend her legs under her body and take her in his arms. He said, "Get a car quick," which I did, and he held her that way until he put her on her own bed, when he let her legs stretch out. Then there was a convulsive movement and it looked to her family as if she had died in her own bed. Isaiah told me afterwards that if she had died in our Yankee house, there would be a curse on us forever and no Negro would work for us again.

* Count László Széchenyi de Sárvár-felsővidék (1879–1938), Austro-Hungarian military officer, diplomat and venture capitalist, married to heiress Gladys Vanderbilt.
† Elizabeth Arden, born Florence Nightingale Graham (1878–1966), founder of the cosmetics empire. From 1938 to 1954, she owned a fifteen-room winter residence at Summerville.

I often went to plantations to hear the spirituals sung an eerie form of entertainment in the moonlight, with Spanish moss hanging like wraiths from the live oaks and the African rhythms intoned in Gullah. The revival meetings were interesting, especially those of the sect known as Holy Jumpers. Once at one of these gatherings a young boy got so carried away he frothed at the mouth and threw a fit in the aisle. His grandmother was in front of me and cried in delight, "My gran he got religion." No one touched the poor boy but he soon recovered. Others got their conversion in a far different way. When they were carried to a pitch by the singing and the stomping, the men would find partners and continue their wild dancing in the bushes.

Once we went to a wedding in a little country church where we were seated up in front since the groom came from a friend's plantation. To our horror, when the bride appeared she was what is known as "heavy with child," but dressed in bridal veil and satin. It was all pleasantly condoned because dates showed that bride and groom had both "got religion" at a revival meeting. Motoring through the countryside you would often see a door or the shutters of one room painted sky blue. I was told that this was to let the angels in, for there was a sinner or an invalid in that house. I had a very highly educated cook at one time who was a master at her trade. One of my guests, a prominent New Yorker, had obtained from her the recipes of a certain luncheon that was exceptionally good. One evening many months later I was quietly reading when I heard the most awful wailing and sputtering in Gullah. Elizabeth ran into my room waving a paper in a frightening manner. My guest had unwittingly given the recipes as her own to Cholly Knickerbocker,[*] and here they were in print! It was some time before I could quiet Elizabeth or get her to speak in English again.

The Holy Jumpers' greatest claim to fame was to get so carried away that they could jump over the altar table—no small feat, as there was little room for a take-off and the altar was five feet high and at least two feet wide.

The Gullah spirituals have been preserved in Charleston by the splendid work of the Society for the Preservation of Spirituals, which long antedates the tape recorder. When I was there, its leading spirit was Miss Caroline Rutledge[†] and its membership included only descendants of owners of the large plantations. The funds necessary for its work were raised by concerts given in the tourist season, at which the ladies were dressed in crinolines, usually authentic and always historically correct, and the men wore stocks, frilled shirts, fobs and

[*] Cholly Knickerbocker, a pseudonym used by a series of society columnists writing for New York newspapers.

[†] Caroline Rutledge (1876–1952) was the sister of poet and author Archibald Rutledge (1883–1973) of Hampton Plantation in McClellanville.

pointed shoes. They would be grouped on a stage set with a well-head in a grove
of live oaks with hanging moss and a planting of azaleas. It was both fascinating
and humorous when Miss Caroline, regal and stately, would step out of her role
and suddenly strut a cake-walk. One evening I gave a dinner before such a gathering and a visiting Englishwoman, Marion Cran in her book, *Gardens in America,* wrote it up as follows:

> The night before I left [Charleston] I dined with Mr. Schuyler Parsons
> and spent an evening I can never forget. He is a man of taste with a very
> charming house in Charleston and by the time I arrived there I was so
> battered by the beauty of everything, by the sense of history and the
> rich, forceful personality of this land of America of which I had been
> deplorably ignorant all my life, that nothing surprised me any more.
>
> So when I found among the guests several men in frilled shirts, black
> stocks and fobs and all the rest of an ancient garb, I took them for
> granted as part of the astonishing town in which Time had vanished,
> and one moved in another age.
>
> It appeared, however, that we were going on to a concert where this
> dress was worn by the male voices; and later on I heard them sing with
> the rest of the Charleston Society for the Preservation of Spirituals.

My best friends in Charleston were the Felix Chisolms,[*] who had a large
house in the harbor, the Norwood Hasties,[†] and Ben Kittredge, Jr. The Hasties
owned "Magnolia Gardens" and Ben's parents, "Dean Hall" on the grounds of
which the Cypress Gardens were afterwards developed.[‡] These two now familiar
tourist meccas became my second homes. "Magnolia" had been a fine country
estate for generations and the park was planted informally with azaleas and
magnolias along paths that wove through live oaks and streams. To me the blaze
of color here at the height of bloom is the eighth wonder of the world. I have
seen it in sun and rain, at dawn, twilight and moonlight and I have never tired
of wandering through the paths. "Dean Hall" on the other hand was a shooting
preserve. After Mr. Kittredge decided he was a little old for shooting, he began
to develop a cypress swamp with planting to give it color. Until that time we
used to picnic on the banks where they had an outdoor cooking stove and simple
benches and tables. At the end of the meal the colored people would come up

[*] Felix Chisolm (1888–1951) and Elizabeth Simonds Chisolm (1895–1974).
[†] Norwood Hastie (1877–1951) and Sara Calhoun Simons (1892–1981).
[‡] Ben Kittredge Sr. (1859–1951) purchased Dean Hall Plantation in Moncks Corner in
   1909. The property was transformed into Cypress Gardens, which opened it to the public in 1932.

from the cabins and sing for us. Each year there was a bit more planting, and almost without one's realizing it a sensationally beautiful spot was created. No words can convey the sense of unreality as one is poled through a grove of towering cypress trees floating on still water; clear but almost black, with vistas of the banks ablaze with azaleas and daffodils. Another beauty spot, difficult to get permission to see and quite a long day's trip from Charleston, was the nesting place of the white egret. On reaching the Santee Gun Club* one got into "bateaus" that looked like dugouts, in which one was poled in silence through a cypress swamp for an hour. Suddenly quite without warning one arrived at a semicircle of brilliant green trees set widely apart. Against this brilliant green flew hundreds or thousands of lovely, graceful, blindingly white birds. The only person who has ever captured the romance, poetry and beauty of this scene in water color is Miss Alice Huger Smith, a truly great artist. I had the pleasure also of knowing Josephine Pinckney, whose "Mansion" originally inspired me to settle in Charleston. She was the leading spirit of the Poetry Society in those days and was trying out her hand in experimental writing. She has since through her novels given outsiders a vivid picture of the glamour of this romantic city,[†] so steeped in the tradition of the past.

Membership in the St. Cecilia Society was proof that you were of the elite. The St. Cecilia claimed to be the first social organization or club in the country. It started as a musical society, but by 1930 no longer had its own club rooms and existed solely for the purpose of giving two balls a year. The parties were not what could be called fun, but were most traditionally carried out. There was a bride of the year and a debutante of the year. Without my knowledge, I was put up for membership. There was a complicated system of voting, with the last and deciding round in the hands of the governing board, with one blackball enough to keep you out. No divorced person had ever been admitted, but my backers thought they had enough influence to see me through. Their argument was simple logic: in 1930 there were no divorce laws in South Carolina, so no divorce could be recognized. As long as I had not remarried, I had broken no law of the state. When my name came to the final vote there was one blackball. Everyone knew who had cast it; he had refused to waver from the unwritten law which excluded divorced people. Word has it that my main backer got up and said, "If George V or Jesus Christ came up for membership you would blackball them

---

*The Santee Club (c.1898), a private hunting preserve on the Santee River near Georgetown.

[†] Josephine Pinckney published the novels *Hilton Head* (1941); *Three O'Clock Dinner* (1945); *Great Mischief* (1948); *My Son and Foe* (1952); and *Splendid in Ashes* (1958).

because they are not related to the Rutledges." I was sorry not to get the chance to taste one of the sensational St. Cecilia suppers.

By the following winter Charleston was undergoing a great change, with many of my old friends coming down to buy town houses or plantations nearby. Among these new arrivals were the Gerry Chadwicks,* the Ray Shonnards,† Paul Mills,‡ the Robert Goelets,§ Ector Munn,** Mrs. Hartford,†† George Widener,‡‡ Harry Bingham,§§ the Hutton brothers*** and many more. Mrs. Washington Roebling restored the old Gibbs Mansion superbly,††† and Walter Salmon bought a lovely old house where he and his wife, Betty,‡‡‡ made a great addition to the life of the city. That winter I visited Aiken for the first time. I went up with Camilla Beach, who many years before had had a tragic experience there; she was

---

* Elbridge Gerry Chadwick, who managed Vincent Astor's properties, and his wife, Dorothy, purchased Woodville Plantation on the South Santee River in McClellanville. The property is now part of the lands of Wedge Plantation owned by the University of South Carolina.

† Horatio S. Shonnard, New York stockbroker, and his wife, Sophia, purchased Harrietta Plantation near McClellanville.

‡ Stockbroker Paul D. Mills and his wife, Lalla, from Philadelphia purchased Windsor Plantation on the Black River near Georgetown in 1929.

§ Robert Walton Goelet, heir to a New York real estate fortune including the Ritz-Carlton Hotel, and his wife, Anne Marie Guestier, purchased Wedgefield in Georgetown.

** Ector Orr Munn (1891–1993) and his wife, heiress Fernanda Wanamaker Orr (d. 1958) frequented the region in stopovers to and from Palm Beach and Aiken.

†† Henrietta Hartford (1881–1948), Beaufort native and widow of A&P grocery heir Edward Hartford, purchased Lexington Plantation on the Wando River and built a mansion in 1931. She renamed the property Wando Plantation.

‡‡ George D. Widener, a Philadelphia horse-breeder and sportsman, and his wife, Jessie Sloane Dodge, purchased several plantations near Pocataligo, which they combined into Mackay Point Plantation, where in 1930 they constructed a hunting lodge.

§§ Harry Payne Bingham (1887–1955), financier and philanthropist, purchased Cotton Hall Plantation in Yemassee in 1930 and built a twenty-six-room house.

*** Edward Hutton, Wall Street financier, began purchasing South Carolina plantations in 1917 and subsequently owned about 10,000 acres. He wintered at Laurel Springs Plantation on the Combahee River in Colleton County with his wife, General Foods heiress Marjorie Merriweather Post. His brother and partner, Franklyn Hutton, owned several plantations, including Oakhurst in Colleton County, where he built a winter residence. The father of Woolworth heiress Barbara Hutton, she inherited the property at her father's death in 1940.

††† Cornelia Witsell Farrow Roebling (1869–1942), originally from Walterboro, purchased the William Gibbes House at 64 South Battery in 1928. She was the widow of Washington Roebling, a civil engineer known for his work on the Brooklyn Bridge, which was designed by his father, John A. Roebling.

‡‡‡ Walter J. Salmon, New York City real estate investor and developer, bought 14 Legare Street in 1930. Widowed twice, he was married to his third wife, Elizabeth Davy.

attacked by someone in the dark who cut her throat from ear to ear with a razor. There was, of course, a tremendous stir and many friends of Mrs. Beach, including my father, put up a large reward for the capture of the criminal. A money-mad sheriff arrested Mr. Beach for attempted murder, and although he was of course exonerated, the affair remained a mystery and left a very bad taste in everyone's mouth.* Camilla had never been back to Aiken since that time.

I was able to walk again by now, and spent a lot of time in the antique shops of Charleston and in trying to sell antiques for their proud but impoverished owners. I am often asked whether I found it hard, as a Northerner, to live in Charleston. The answer is "Yes and no." The city was in those days almost incredibly shut off from the rest of the country—the through trains did not even stop there until about 1930—and the inhabitants, many of whom had grown up during the rich years "before the war," found it very hard to be reduced to poverty. They resented having to sell their heirlooms, and although they depended on these sales, they never showed any gratitude if you helped them to make them. As long as the Whartons were there, and I could blow off steam to them in the evenings, I was very happy, but Helena had suffered a very serious heart attack in Newport that summer, and could not come south until January, and when I had to keep my worries to myself, they started to fester and I began to wonder whether it was not time I moved on.

It was a warm spring and Miss Tyler and I moved into a small shack at Folly Beach, with the Atlantic at our back door. Mrs. Kittredge had a cottage next door, and her son Ben the one adjoining. Mrs. Kittredge was one of the Marshall sisters,† three of whom had married respectively, George Canfield of New York; his son, George, Jr., by a previous marriage with a Miss Kittredge; and the brother of the first Mrs. Canfield, Benjamin Kittredge! Just to keep things going, of Mr. Canfield Sr.'s children by this second marriage, a son and daughter married a brother and sister, and another son married their first cousin. Try to figure out those relationships if you have an idle moment!

We had a lazy month at the seaside, relieved by a visit from Carola Kip, a charming girl who later married Ben, but at that moment he was so engrossed

---

* Camilla Moss Havemeyer Beach (1869–1934), resident of the winter colony in Aiken, was brutally attacked in 1912, and claimed it was a black man who attacked her in the yard of her Aiken house. Eleven months later, her second husband, millionaire Frederick Ogden "Beauty" Beach was charged with "murderous assault" in the case. After a dramatic trial, he eventually won an acquittal and the couple apparently remained together until his death in 1918. Gene Coughlin, "Camilla Moss' Two Tragedies," 30.

† Elizabeth Marshall Kittredge (1873–1959), Charleston native and wife of Benjamin R. Kittredge Sr.

with a book he was writing* that I had to substitute for him in entertaining Carola, which I found no strain. The Kittredges used to have vegetables and flowers sent down from "Dean Hall," and I shall never forget the buckets of gardenias that came from their gardenia hedge.

I felt much better after a month of this gentle regime, and when the ocean water became hot and the bugs very bad, I woke up one morning and told Tyler to pack up, that I had decided to go north and start an antique business.

---

* Benjamin Kittredge Jr. (1900–1981) and Carola de Peyster "Kip" Kittredge (1904–1975). He published the novel *Crowded Solitude* in 1930.

Church at crossroads on sealevel highway, south of Charleston, South Carolina, c. 1936. U.S. Farm Security Administration. Carl Maydans, photographer. Library of Congress.

M. A. De Wolfe Howe (1930)

"The Song of Charleston"

M. A. De Wolfe Howe, "The Song of Charleston," *Atlantic Monthly* 146 (July 1930): 108–11.

Mark Antony De Wolfe Howe (1864–1960), biographer, editor and historian, was born in Bristol, Rhode Island, the son of Episcopal Bishop Mark Antony De Wolfe Howe. In 1886, he graduated from Lehigh University and completed a master's at Harvard. He married into the eminent Quincy family of Boston, which included congressmen, lawyers, governors, and mayors, when he wed Fanny Huntington Quincy, essayist and writer. She was a descendent of Josiah Quincy, author of a 1773 account of Charleston.

Mark De Wolfe Howe became "the Bostonian of Bostonians," historian of Boston clubs and societies, and biographer of its literary figures including Dr. Oliver Wendell Holmes (for which he won the Pulitzer Prize). He was an editor for *The Atlantic Monthly*, then served as vice president of The Atlantic Monthly Company. At the same time, he held editorial positions on a number of magazines, edited innumerable letters and biographies, and published additional books, including *The Memory of Lincoln* (1889), *Boston: The Place and the People* (1903), *Home Letters of General Sherman* (1909), *Life and Letters of George Bancroft* (1908), *Boston Common: Scenes from Four Centuries* (1910), *Letters of Charles Eliot Norton* (1913), *The Boston Symphony Orchestra* (1914), *The Harvard Volunteers in Europe* (1916), *The Atlantic Monthly and Its Makers* (1919), and many more.

His son, Mark De Wolfe Howe (1906–1967), became a Harvard law professor, historian, biographer, and civil rights leader. In the 1970s the younger Howe's daughter, Fanny Howe (b.1940), poet and author, rebuked her patrician Boston heritage and married black activist Carl Senna. She remains a civil rights activist today. Howe and Senna are parents of the novelist Danzy Senna, who writes about growing up biracial in the 1970s and '80s in her novel *Caucasia* (1998).

In the following article, Howe describes a concert of the Society for the Preservation of Spirituals in "Old Charleston" in 1930.

SOURCES

"Mark De Wolfe Howe Dies; Lawyer, Historian Was 60." *Harvard Crimson* (Mar. 1, 1967).

"The Song of Charleston"

It is a fortunate thing that the spendthrift "collectors" who scour the land for spoils cannot completely sack every place they visit. In all conscience there are objects enough, purchasable and portable, for them to carry home. Some things, by the grace of heaven, cannot be borne away—old houses, old gardens, old essences and flavors. These things can be transplanted only in picture and in memory. Not even in picture, only in memory, can the musical note and rhythm of a town, city, or region—the song that goes on singing itself in your heart—be appropriated by the wayfarer. For every place has its rhythm—indeed, its song. These are of two sorts—the insistent, plainly audible, and the still small voice, speaking for what lies hidden within. In the vast orchestra of city sounds—with many latter-day, local variants upon "great London's central roar"—one instrument after another may dominate the melody and rhythm. The note of smaller places may be less constant, less certain to be recognized. Yet, outward and inward, the two voices of every place bear their part in ranking the *genius loci*—and for all the weight of what you see wherever you go, it is probably what you hear that swells most palpably the homeward-bound luggage of the spirit.

Such are the thoughts that spring to one's mind on a visit to the city which, by the American measure of antiquity, must be called the ancient city of Charleston, South Carolina. There—with good luck in point of time and opportunity—one may hear a note, a definite song, so purely indigenous, so utterly characteristic, that it seems to spring as inevitably from Charleston soil as the porticoed, seaward-looking houses that could be found nowhere else. The positive distinction of line and tone speaks for a civilization, a highly-organized society, that has no American duplicate in scale and effect. Not the dwelling houses alone, but its public buildings, churches, and halls, connote a dignity and leisure that could have sprung only from an order of existence in which a powerful local oligarchy concerned itself with matters of grace and beauty.

It is not here and now a question whether the basis of privilege on which such an order erected itself was valid or the opposite. There it was, and the tangible fruits of it, surviving the repeated assaults of wars, earthquake, fire, and hurricane, stand proud and beautiful today, undefeated if a little wistful, in testimony of the lasting uses to which a society of planters could turn its untold resources of labor. And it is precisely in the songs of the Negro toilers of the great South Carolina low-country plantations, that descendants of their owners are preserving today an admirable spirit of blended gratitude and *noblesse oblige*, the veritable song of Charleston.

Thus the South Carolina counterpart of the "Society for the Preservation of New England Antiquities"—to whose ministrations aging spinsters have been heard to wish themselves eligible—is the Charleston "Society for the Preservation of Spirituals." There is no boasting, but a simple acceptance of the fact that the community lacks funds for any general restoration and preservation of its physical monuments. There is nevertheless a spiritual monument—a monument literally to the spirit—of Charleston in the past which was in actual danger of disintegration until, some eight years ago, a small company of Charlestonians, bearing for the most part the historic names by which the streets and the best houses of the city are known, undertook for their own pleasure to meet and sing together the songs which they had learned as children from the black servants on the plantations that were their homes or places of frequent visitation. These formal gatherings planted a seed of rapid growth. Friends heard the singing and enjoyed it so much that they bespoke a wider hearing for it. A local charity needed help and the loosely organized society sang for its benefit.

As the organization took form, that form rendered it unique among choruses. For one thing, no singer with a trained voice was eligible for membership: what Negro singer of spirituals has had a trained voice? For another, it is essential that the membership should themselves be plantation-bred, or at least plantation "broken"—for plantation life in its essence, be it said, long survived the Civil War. "You either lived on a plantation"—it has been written of this qualification —"or you didn't, and you can't use political influence, money, or good looks, or any other handy asset to turn that trick for you, if you didn't begin earlier in life than this to be eligible for membership." An alien to the childhood influence of spirituals, with a voice trained by the best singing master in the world—a candidate with either or both of these handicaps—is automatically blackballed. You must go to Charleston for a genuinely exclusive club.

Did the society, thus organized, content itself with singing and resinging the spirituals for which its members could draw upon their own earliest memories? By no such process could they have accumulated their present repertory, including about a hundred and twenty songs. Their plan, on the contrary, has been to visit plantations and churches where the older Negroes are still singing their religious melodies, to learn the airs direct, by as many repetitions as need be, from these singers, and, lest the words—in the strange Gullah dialect of the South

Carolina low-country—should evade remembrance, to make written notes of them on the spot. It has always been through such first-hand study—in the Santee country, on Beaufort, Edisto, and James Islands, and at other places in the region tributary to Charleston—that the songs have been gathered. If the spirituals familiar to theatregoers through *Porgy** have seemed to "ring true," the facts that Mr. and Mrs. DuBose Heyward have been active members of the Charleston Society for the Preservation of Spirituals and that songs rescued by that organization have thus found their way to the stage on both sides of the Atlantic may well have something to do with it.

For the first few years of its existence the Society restricted its concerts to Charleston. Then, on demand from Savannah, Columbia, South Carolina, and other cities and towns within relatively easy reach, it appeared before audiences peculiarly qualified to appreciate its distinctive Southern flavor. Only within the past year has it journeyed far afield—to Boston, New York, Philadelphia, and the neighborhood of Wilmington, Delaware. So definitely amateur an organization, made up of ladies and gentlemen whose occupations are at the farthest possible remove from those of a traveling troupe, cannot be made a subject of common exploitation Indeed, one hesitates to expatiate upon its merits even in so utterly unsought a piece of writing as this. Yet after one has experienced, all unprepared, the memorable sensation of hearing the Society give one of its concerts in its own town of Charleston, it was almost churlish to keep that experience to one's self. After all, the tickets are on public sale.

The town was packed with tourists, for the Middleton Place and the Magnolia Gardens—acclaimed by the temperate John Galsworthy 'the most beautiful spot in the world'[†]—were nearing their climax of beauty. The evening in an overcrowded hotel looked a little formidable. But not far away was the local Academy of Music[‡]—such a theatre, though somewhat enlarged, as that in which Napoleon III first saw the Mariette of Guitry's play.[§]

---

* *Porgy: A Play in Four Acts* (1927), adapted by DuBose and Dorothy Heyward from the novel, had premiered on Broadway. It ran a total of fifty-five weeks in New York, and the original cast toured the United States twice and performed for eleven consecutive weeks in London. The play was the basis of the libretto, which DuBose wrote later for the opera, *Porgy and Bess (1935)*.

† John Galsworthy (1867–1933) wrote about Magnolia Gardens in his short story, "The Hedonist," in *The Century Magazine* 102:3 (July, 1921), 321–25.

‡ The Academy of Music stood at the corner of King and Market streets. The building was razed in the 1930s, and the Riviera Theater, built on the site, opened in 1939.

§ Sacha Guitry (1885–1957), French stage actor and playwright whose "Mariette ou Comment on écrit l'histoire," a musical comedy, opened in the Théâtre Édouard VII in

But the chorus on which the curtain rises is no such questionable company as that which the professional theatre so often assembles. Instead one sees some forty ladies and gentlemen who might, without any violent demand upon the imagination, have come together in the fifties of the last century out of the stately houses encompassed in a circle drawn from the theatre to include the Battery and the shores of the Ashley and Cooper rivers. The women's simple dresses of blue and pink are of that earlier time; the men identify themselves completely with it merely by substituting stocks and the semblance of a ruffled shirt front for the more rigid adjuncts of contemporary evening clothes. The president of the Society tells the audience something of its purpose—to preserve a treasured heritage, to employ any tangible gains from so doing for the benefit of old and needy Negroes, and ultimately to publish a book of distinctive Gullah melodies and words, with pictures and historical text provided entirely by Charleston painters, etchers, and writers,* the proceeds from this enterprise to be devoted to help members of the race from which the preserved spirituals are derived. Each song is then introduced, with a word, in accent subtly local, about its origin. And then the chorus sings.

There are sophisticates who have grown a little weary of the singing of spirituals—and no wonder. The colored singers of them on concert stages are too often beguiled into self-consciousness and a certain overdressing of the simple melodies. The white concert singers of the same songs are often, and inevitably, subject to another self-consciousness—that of the imitator, and their voices are of course lacking something of which the origin is distantly African. With the Charleston chorus there is nothing of imitation. It is rather a matter of rendering of a white interpretation of a folk tradition common, though from different angles of practice and enjoyment, to black and white. The simple stage setting of the Southern outdoors, with enough of pendulant Spanish moss in the foreground to localize the scene beyond mistake, the seated group represent with equal certainty the gallantly surviving Charleston of old, the absence of all the stage consciousness usually revealed in bowing soloist or conductor—for conductor there is none, and soloist is soon merged in chorus—attune the spectator, surrounded by an audience quite homogeneous with the chorus itself, to the full effect of the singing. How is this effect, of so remarkable an intensity, produced?

Paris in 1928 and toured in the United States. It tells of Napoleon III meeting a young *soubrette* who becomes his mistress.
* *The Carolina Low-Country* was published in 1931.

A single singer, man or woman, unprompted by a leader or by any setting of the key, launches the melody, in which the others soon join, rising one by one and sitting again in their places without sign of premeditation or direction, swaying their bodies and clapping their hands in those motions strangely defined as "shouting," speeding the tempo, increasing the volume of the song, till that which began as a gentle, deliberate solo ends in an ecstasy of rhythm, rapid movement, and choral mass in which singers and hearers seem joined in that unity of stage and house which is the ultimate test of the power of song and action.

All this, one is well aware, is what an enthusiastic, not yet disillusioned, listener to spirituals might say of them at their best anywhere. Perhaps; but here, one is disposed to insist, there is something different. Here, I for one believe, is that special note which makes the singing of the Preservation Society so indisputably the song of Charleston. You have been told in the afternoon that it took a hundred slaves ten years to bestow upon the gardens of Middleton Place their noble and gracious form; and even the mythical half-year of seven maids with seven mops shrinks in comparison to a minute of time. The measure of things in Charleston seems rather a matter of centuries than of years—centuries of association, in which the interdependence of two races has played no negligible part. Whatever the origin and significance of the religious songs of the low-country Negroes, it is immensely significant that truly representative members of the dominant race are now singing those songs in a spirit of sympathy, reverence, and devotion which are themselves survivals from a less cynical age. How otherwise can true folk song, an indigenous form of art capable of its highest values only by the practice of rigorously art-concealing methods, be adequately preserved? Can the same process be applied in other places, to other species of song, to other forms of folk expression in art than music? The song of Charleston leads one to hope that such things may be, that native American art may flower in many gardens yet untilled.

Meanwhile let Charleston, like Bethlehem, become a place of musical pilgrimage. A festival of spirituals at the time when the gardens are in their glory would not appreciably increase the strain upon the already overtaxed provision for local bed and board. The lovers of flowers and of music are often identical. Old gardens, old houses., old music, all fruits of the same vanishing civilization, are better blended than isolated. And let not the chorus be tempted to stray too often from its own native habitat. Bethlehem with its Bach, Dayton and North-field with their roaming choirs—however beautifully the singers from these places may sing, Bach is an alien in Pennsylvania; the composers of sacred music, from Palestrina to Sullivan, have nothing in particular to do with Ohio and Minnesota.

But Charleston and the low-country spirituals are close of kin: place and music inalienably fit and supplement each other. It would be against nature for such a chorus to be permitted unbrokenly to immure itself at home—and the world beyond Charleston would be the loser if it did. But at home is where one may best hear it, in the Second-Empire-like Academy of Music, with the whole song of Charleston, to which the cadences of the spirituals contribute a moving and determining part, throbbing itself quietly along in one's heart.

Emily Clark Balch by Arthur Davis, artist. Oil on canvas.
Albert and Shirley Small Special Collections Library,
University of Virginia, Charlottesville, Virginia.

EMILY CLARK (1930)

"Supper at the Goose Creek Club"

Emily Clark, "Supper at the Goose Creek Club" from "DuBose Heyward,"
Virginia Quarterly Review 6:4 (Autumn 1930).

Emily Tapscott Clark (ca.1890–1953) was born in Raleigh, North Carolina to
an Episcopal minister. Her mother died in 1894, and two years later her father
moved the family from Fredericksburg, Virginia, to Richmond, where he became
rector of St. James's Episcopal Church. In 1909, Emily graduated from Virginia
Randolph Ellett School for Girls in Richmond. After passing the Bryn Mawr
College entrance exam, she decided not to attend college. She instead wrote
book reviews for the *Richmond Evening-Journal* until the newspaper's book
page was discontinued in 1920, when she and three other contributors founded
The Reviewer, an experimental literary magazine. As volunteer editor for a new
journal, the first few years she supported herself as a staff writer for the *Richmond News Leader*.

    The Reviewer debuted in Richmond in February of 1921 with Clark as editor and contributor and Virginian Hunter Stagg, who reviewed books and acted
as literary editor. Although the journal only ran until 1925, its thirty-five issues
helped spark the Southern Literary Renaissance. It was significant in that not
much else of literary consequence was being published in the South—a fact
publicized by editor and critic H. L Mencken in his essay "The Sahara of the
Bozart," which first appeared in 1917 in the *New York Evening Mail* and was
reprinted in his book, *Prejudices, Second Series* (1920). In the essay, Mencken
described the South as "almost as sterile, artistically, intellectually, culturally,
as the Sahara Desert," and the condition of the modern South especially lamentable because the antebellum South, particularly Virginia, had been the seat of
American civilization. Mencken felt the time was nigh for cultural renewal. *The
Reviewer* was a response, as was the subsequent literary revival, during which
southern authors sought to rid southern literature of the sentiment of the Old
South and began experimenting in the larger liberation of the 1920s.

Emily Clark herself straddled two worlds. A descendant of one of Virginia's "first families" and a member of the Daughters of the American Revolution, she was also a flapper during the Roaring Twenties. Due to a lack of early editorial policy at *The Reviewer*, Clark published both northern and southern writers, women as well as men, experienced writers and fledging ones. Her personal charisma and social connections landed submissions from such well-known writers as Ellen Glasgow, Allen Tate, Sinclair Lewis, Gertrude Stein—and DuBose Heyward. With Mencken's assistance, she also helped such new writers as South Carolinian Julia Peterkin (1880–1961), the first southern novelist to win a Pulitzer Prize for *Scarlet Sister Mary* (1928) in 1929. Clark's editorial policy was: "We are here to discover something—that is our sole excuse for being here at all."

Despite its success, the magazine by 1924 needed funds. Philadelphia millionaire Edwin Swift Balch helped alleviate the problem when he contributed to finances. In the autumn of 1924, after Emily Clark married Balch, a widower, and Hunter Stagg retired, *The Reviewer,* with about 1,200 subscribers and a progressive reputation, was moved to the more liberal Chapel Hill, North Carolina, with playwright Paul Green as editor.

Emily Clark moved to Philadelphia. After Edwin Balch died in 1927, with encouragement from Mencken, she "caused some uproar in Richmond society" with the publication of *Stuffed Peacocks,* thirteen character sketches with a "biting" introduction about the city. She later published an account of *The Reviewer* and its prominent contributors in *Innocence Abroad* (1931). She remained a patron of the arts and her writings appeared in several magazines, including *The Virginia Quarterly Review*. She died in Philadelphia, leaving two-thirds of her estate and some of her letters and manuscripts to the University of Virginia. *The Virginia Quarterly Review* used Clark's bequest to establish the Emily Clark Balch Prize for short stories and poetry, an annual award that continues today.

In the following article written in 1930, Clark recalls a supper she had with DuBose Heyward at the Goose Creek Club in January of 1925—the year Heyward published the novel *Porgy*—and goes on to reveal their literary relationship over the 1920s. Over that decade, Heyward helped found the Poetry Society and collaborated on a book of poems with Hervey Allen, *Carolina Chansons* (1922), followed by his book of verse, *Skylines and Horizons* (1924). After *Porgy*, he published works including *Angel* (1926), *The Half Pint Flask* (1929), and *Mamba's Daughters* (1929). He and his wife, Dorothy, adapted *Porgy: A Play in Four Acts* for the stage in 1927.

Heyward would go on to write the play *Brass Ankle* (1931) and publish the novels *Peter Ashley* (1932) and *Star-Spangled Virgin* (1939) as well as the children's book *The Country Bunny and the Little Gold Shoes* (1939). None of his subsequent works brought the fame of *Porgy*. In the next years, he would famously work with George and Ira Gershwin to produce the opera *Porgy and Bess* (1935).

SOURCES

Langford, Gerald, ed. *Ingénue among the Lions: The Letters of Emily Clark to Joseph Hergesheimer.* Austin: University of Texas Press, 1965.
Smith, L. E. "Emily Tapscott Clark (ca. 1890–1953)." In *Encyclopedia Virginia.* June 14, 2014. http://www.EncyclopediaVirginia.org/Clark_Emily_Tapscott_ca_1890–1953.

"Supper at the Goose Creek Club"

The Reviewer and the Poetry Society of South Carolina were responsible for a succession of letters between DuBose Heyward and me before we met. I had, however, long heard of DuBose, not only a dawning poet, but as a part of the Charleston that every properly brought-up Virginian knows, quite outside the Poetry Society. I had already seen him, through the eyes of friends, under the Lady Banksia roses on Josephine Pinckney's porch in King Street, laying, with Josephine and Hervey Allen and Laura Bragg[*] and Beatrice Ravenel[†] and John Bennett,[‡] the foundations of a Poetry Society later to become unique among Southern poetry societies. But I did not see him with my own eyes until several years later, on a January evening at the Goose Creek Club near Charleston,[§] an evening black enough to serve as a setting for *The Half Pint Flask* should that story ever follow "Porgy" to Broadway. Lady Banksia roses were now a memory and a hope, and the night was as wet and chill as only a far Southern night can be to a visitor who twenty-four hours earlier has left the North in search of sunshine. The group of young men and women, later organized to preserve the spirituals, were not then organized, but quite spontaneously, at their own parties, sang them simply for their own entertainment. That night, at supper at the Goose Creek Club, we were lucky. Several Negroes employed about the place

---

[*] Laura Bragg (1881–1978), New Jersey–born director of the Charleston Museum from 1920 until 1931.
[†] Beatrice St. Julien Ravenel (1904–1990), Charleston poet.
[‡] John Bennett (1865–1956), an Ohio-born author and illustrator, lived in Charleston and was a cofounder of the Poetry Society.
[§] "The Goose Creek Club for Preserving Game" was located on The Oaks Plantation (c. 1680), originally a Middleton family plantation. In 1892, Edwin Parsons (1864–1921), a native of Savannah who inherited a railroad fortune, built a house on the estate as a winter residence. He chartered the Goose Creek Club. By the time of Clark's visit, his widow, Mary Battle Parsons, owned the property.

were later asked to come in and sing, and with their own tropic voices they put all the rest of us to shame. For spirituals are songs of passion, no less because the object of their passion is not to be carnally attained. When white folk sing them, however beautifully, these songs, of necessity, are ever so slightly travestied, since passion is lacking. When the sophisticated Negroes of Manhattan sing them, it is not much better. The simple souls of the unmixed black South, more than any people since the age of chivalry, regard themselves quite honestly as God's children, to whom He will be indulgent so long as they acknowledge the direct relationship—God's children lost in Egypt, it is true, but sturdily confident that He will lead them by the right way, triumphantly, into the land of Canaan; without bleak and dreary moral responsibilities of their own, merely the single obligation of an unshakable faith in His loving-kindness. Across a firelit cabin, with the voice of the black South in my ears, I first saw DuBose, who was smiling the tired, luminous smile that is his most characteristic expression. He looked as if the introductory verses to *Porgy*, those verses which sufficiently state his position towards the Negroes he knows and loves best, were at that moment in his head. And perhaps they were, for it was the winter he was writing *Porgy*.

Porgy, Maria, and Bess,
Robbins, and Peter, and Crown;
Life was a three-stringed harp
Brought from the woods to town.
Marvelous tunes you rang
From passion, and death, and birth,
You who had laughed and wept
On the warm, brown lap of the earth.

Now in your untried hands
An instrument, terrible, new
Is thrust by a master who frowns,
Demanding strange songs of you.
God of the White and Black,
Grant us great hearts on the way
That we may understand
Until you have learned to play.

A little later in the evening he spoke to me of "Porgy," in which he was then absorbed, and this was my first intimation that DuBose, like so many poets of

our day—Mr. Cabell, Elinor Wylie, Robert Nathan,[*] and others—had saga-
ciously regarded his poetry as a training school for prose. He told me too of the
real Porgy, the Charleston beggar of whose name and personality and goat cart
the principal character of the book was born, who is now buried on one of the
sea-islands. And I met Dorothy, who had lately become Dorothy Heyward, as a
result of their meeting at the MacDowell Colony in Peterboro. I noticed, too,
the odd resemblance between the future authors of a spectacularly successful
play, a resemblance which caused Charleston to say they seemed more like twin
brother and sister than like husband and wife. A resemblance which to me,
through their apparent fragility and the not-to-be-ignored appeal of the four
very large, very luminous, very brown eyes which together they own, always
suggests Hansel and Gretel lost in a wood, perhaps of their own making. When
DuBose spoke of "Porgy," I was not surprised. He had written a number of
poems when he first began to write for *The Reviewer.* Some of the verses we
published appeared later in *Skylines and Horizons,* the first and only book of
verse of which he was sole author, for *Carolina Chansons* was written in collab-
oration with Hervey Allen. Both of these books appeared during the life of our
magazine. I like to remember that DuBose's first prose appeared in *The Reviewer.* Its title was "And Once Again—the Negro." This is why the announcement of *Porgy* did not surprise me. I was, however, doubtful of its future, for
Green Thursday had appeared without wide acclamation the preceding autumn,
and *Black April,* Julia Peterkin's first success, did not appear until more than
two years after this winter of 1925.[†] As we drove back into Charleston that night
through a live-oak wood mournful with grey moss draped in damp festoons,
then more black than grey, with none of the smoked-pearliness which in sunshine or moonlight bewitches a Carolina forest, I remembered DuBose's first
public meditations upon Negroes, and my correspondence with him, leading
gradually to that article in *The Reviewer* of October 1923. Since the Poetry
Society of South Carolina was born in Charleston in 1921, almost simultane-
ously with *The Reviewer* in Richmond, my first letter from DuBose, its first
secretary, in 1921, was exclusively concerned with the aims of this society: "The
Poetry Society of South Carolina," it informed me, a bit grandiloquently, "is
actively engaged in fostering literary activity throughout the South. This is not
being done from a provincial or sectional spirit, but because, as Miss Harriet

[*] James Branch Cabell (1879–1958), Elinor Morton Wylie (1885–1928), and Robert Grun-
tal Nathan (1894–1985).
[†] Peterkin was first known for her sympathetic portrayals of black folk life in *Green
Thursday* (1924) and *Black April* (1927).

Monroe* has so well put it: 'no one can deny that the world's most precious masterpieces . . . sprang out of local loyalties, and attained to universality because the locale, grandly handled, becomes as wide as the earth.' We are therefore enclosing you a complimentary copy of the all Southern number of *Poetry* in the hope that you will feel warranted in commenting upon it in your columns. As part of the literary activity of America, a new and vital one, we believe that all sections of the country will be interested. May we call your attention to the editorial contained in the enclosed magazine, which will explain more fully what the Southern Poetical Renaissance is? While it is not the general custom among reviews to comment on current issues of magazines, so much has recently been said in certain quarters about the dearth of aesthetic activity in the South that we feel the other and brighter side of the matter should be presented. Then, too, this issue is in reality the first anthology of contemporary Southern poetry, and may mark a new aspect in American letters."

The next year he wrote, after my retaliative demands for *The Reviewer:* "I read your letter at our last meeting, and gave *The Reviewer* a good shove, but as we have just concluded a subscription campaign for the *Poetry* magazines, I am afraid that the immediate results in the way of subscriptions will be discouraging." (They were!) "We are going to do all we can for you in the future, and will give you a good send off in our Year Book. I have been wanting to send something of mine to *The Reviewer* for some time, but have been unable to give a moment to my own work. However, I am enclosing a sonnet from the negro group of "Carolina Chansons," which, as you know, will be published in the fall by Hervey Allen and myself. If you care for this sonnet, please accept it with my blessings, but if it does not appeal to you, do not hesitate to fire it back, and be assured in advance that I will understand, and will try you again with something else later." Unlike many undesired and now forgotten poets on our list, DuBose was unfailingly good-humoured, and sympathetic with our erratic business methods. When, three months later, I notified him that his first contribution was accepted, with an apology for the unconscionable delay, he wrote from the Mac-Dowell Colony: "I understand too well the difficulties of running an organization without the proper facilities to have the least feeling about the delay in acknowledging my poem. I am glad that you now have it, and that you like it. I do not write rapidly, and my output is small, but, if you want my things, I shall send you something now and then. Next fall I shall make an effort to interest

---

*Harriett Monroe (1860–1936), founding publisher and longtime editor of *Poetry* magazine. Heyward and Hervey Allen had edited a southern issue of *Poetry* in 1922.

some people in *The Reviewer,* and when we get our year book up this October, I will give all the space I can afford to a boost for you. You certainly deserve all of the backing we can give you. Allen and I would like nothing better than to stop over and meet all of you, but we are so desperately anxious to get the last minute of our working time here, that we usually bolt for home without a second to spend on the way." Months later: "I am sending you two poems which express extremely different moods. I hope you will like either or both of these well enough to use in *The Reviewer.* I am wondering whether you received your copy of our *Carolina Chansons.* . . . I want you to see what we are doing in our part of the South." And, when I had, very naturally, accepted them: "I was very glad to hear from you, and to know that you liked my poems well enough to accept them for *The Reviewer.* You have maintained such a splendid standard that I appreciate the distinction of appearing in your magazine. I can quite understand how you are submerged with all of the work that you are doing; here in the South, we all have the same problem, and must do our creative work only in spare moments. . . . If I can do anything at any time for *The Reviewer* please call upon me."

In August 1923, three months after this note, I received DuBose's first bit of prose, "And Once Again—The Negro." To Gerald Johnson* belongs part of the credit for this debut in prose, for DuBose wrote: "I read 'The Congo, Mr. Mencken' [published by Gerald Johnson in *The Reviewer* of July 1923] with an awful joy." He continued: "Encouraged by the suicidal, but ecstatic, spirit that has entered into our fellow rebel, Gerald Johnson, I enclose, for your consideration, an observation or two upon the Negro, but I am only a poet, not an essayist. Perhaps this is a piece of bad prose art. At any rate, please do not hesitate to fire it back if you do not want it." And it is a cause for eternal thanksgiving on the part of *The Reviewer* that we did not "fire it back." It must also be noted that DuBose in this letter for the first time, contrary to the ancient Southern custom, capitalizes the word "Negro." This obscure little herald of "Porgy" filled just four pages with the completely successful social and sociological arrangements prevailing among the Charleston Negroes. These arrangements included a system of divorce, companionate marriage, disposal of the children, and a Lucy Stone League,† all known to their originators by less depressing names. Since the

---

* Gerald White Johnson (1890–1980), journalist and author, and the first professor of journalism at the University of North Carolina.

† The Lucy Stone League, founded in 1921, was one of the first feminist groups to arise from the suffrage movement, the first to fight for women to legally retain their maiden name after marriage. The group took its name from Lucy Stone (1818–1893), the first woman in the country to carry her maiden name through life, despite her marriage in 1855.

article has never been printed outside of *The Reviewer,* I repeat here the last three paragraphs. They follow an account of an essay on Negro enlightenment lately read by DuBose in a magazine which took itself seriously:

> During the past summer, I met, in an advanced art circle, a young couple. The wife insisted upon retaining the 'Miss' and her maiden name. They were really quite devil-may-care, and advanced about it, and submitted to the embarrassment of explaining themselves to hotel clerks, and others who made bold to inquire, for the good of the cause. My washerwoman announced the other day that she had married. To my inquiry as to her present name, she replied: "My Lord, do listen to the gentleman! Yer sure don't think I goin' ter be responsible for any nigger's name. No, sir! And he ain't goin' ter get my name neither. I is a good washerwoman, an' I got my reputation to live up to. He can go along with his shoe-carpentering if he wants to, but it is me as brings home the chicken on Saturday night. Me take his name? No suh! Not me!"
>
> And so I listen to their stories, and let them go, but for them I experience a profound sadness. Are they an aeon behind, or an aeon ahead of us? Who knows? But one thing is certain: the reformer will have them in the fullness of time. They will surely be cleaned, married, conventionalized. They will be taken from the fields, and given to machines, their instinctive feeling for the way that leads to happiness, saved as it is from selfishness, by humour and genuine kindness of heart, will be supplanted by a stifling moral straitjacket. They will languish, but they will submit, because they will be trained into habit of thought that makes blind submission a virtue.
>
> And my stevedore, there out of the window. I look at him again. I cannot see him as a joke. Most certainly I cannot contort him into a menace. I can only be profoundly sorry for him, for there he sits in the sunshine unconsciously awaiting his supreme tragedy. He is about to be saved.

In May 1924 his last contribution to *The Reviewer* arrived, "Song at Parting," soon to appear in *Skylines and Horizons.* A tide of literary visitors had just receded from Richmond towards New York. Joseph Hergesheimer,* alone,

---

* Joseph Hergesheimer (1880–1954), novelist of decadent life among the very wealthy. In a 1922 poll of critics in *Literary Digest,* he was voted the "most important American writer" working at the time. From the peak of acclaim, his reputation fell to obscurity by the time of his death.

had proceeded southward to Charleston. DuBose, who met him there for the
first time, wrote me: "I enjoyed Hergesheimer immensely. He says that he is
coming back another year. I hope so. People like him are splendid for Charlestonians. Elinor Wylie would be wholesome also. She is a remarkable person.
Dorothy and I spent an entire summer with her at MacDowell Colony. She was
doing 'Jennifer' that year,* and would read each week's work to us on Sunday.
She is just about the most brilliant woman that I know. That sounds trite, but I
do mean the word in its usual sense. I mean a sustained hard brightness that
glitters and dazzles. . . . I have set myself the task of earning in eight months
sufficient to support life for twelve, so that I might write for four. When my off
time comes I can only dig into a hole somewhere and get my year's output done
in four months. It shuts out all human intercourse—that is the hell of it."

It was the next winter, after *The Reviewer*'s Chapel Hill migration, that
I met my correspondent, for the first time, in the loveliest of American cities,
against a background closer to the setting of his first novel than to his own ancestral setting; the background, I think, of his next novel. DuBose Heyward is
genealogically a part of that innermost core of Southern society which includes
only portions of Maryland, Virginia, and Charleston, excluding even what is
known to Charlestonians as "up-country" South Carolina. With this imposing
tradition DuBose possesses the inestimable asset, as he himself recognizes with
glee, of a boyhood so beset with poverty as to necessitate a job in a hardware-
store at the age of fourteen. At eleven, in the best Henty and Alger manner,†
he was delivering afternoon papers out of school-hours. A few months ago we
spoke of Thomas Wolfe, one of DuBose's deep affections, who, belonging to a
widely different South,‡ possesses more than one academic degree. DuBose said:
"He will be remembered when all the rest of us are utterly dead." And when
someone said that *Look Homeward, Angel,* had been enormously influenced by
its author's Hellenic passion, he replied very simply: "I know nothing about
that, because I have never studied Greek." DuBose is the eldest son of the eldest
son in direct line from Judge Thomas Heyward, the South Carolina Signer, and,
according to his Charleston clan, should now live in the home of that ancestor,
one of the most perfect eighteenth-century houses in Charleston. He has, to
their disapproval since the success of *Porgy,* insisted on remaining in the house
he built for himself in the North Carolina mountains—now occupied by himself

---

* Wylie's first novel, *Jennifer Lorn* (1923).
† George Alfred Henty (1832–1902) and Horatio Alger (1832–1899) wrote popular books
　for boys.
‡ Thomas Wolfe (1900–1938), major novelist from Asheville, N.C.

and Dorothy and the newest member of the family, Jenifer DuBose Heyward
—instead of buying back the home of his ancestors and returning to it like the
third son in the fairy-tale. A lack of prosperity is shared by most of DuBose's
breed in the South, and his own immediate and peculiarly exigent situation was
the result of a minor Civil War tragedy. His grandfather DuBose and two old
maiden ladies jointly inherited a large slave family, dividing it among themselves. Mr. DuBose later bought the two ladies' shares for himself. He died
leaving a large debt for slaves, freed by the Civil War,—which closely followed
his death. Both houses on the several thousand acres left to DuBose's mother
had been burned, but the debt for vanished slaves endured and had to be met.
After three years in a hardware-store an attack of infantile paralysis kept Du-
Bose completely helpless for three more years. Then, at twenty, he was able to
take odd jobs around the waterfront, mainly clerical work in the warehouses,
where he made friends with the Negro stevedores and collected material for
Porgy. At twenty-two he became, incredibly, an insurance salesman, and in ten
years, as he grew gradually stronger, built up—inexplicably enough—a fairly
good business. But, alas, his business success caused him, in his words, to become "the world's most devoted society man," and a severe break-down of a
year's duration followed it. That decade, which included almost nightly balls,
and membership in all the clubs, is recorded in *Mamba's Daughters,* lately translated into French.

His first poems sprang from his year of illness. They were published in *Poetry,* the *Atlantic Monthly, Contemporary Verse,* and *The Reviewer.* The Poetry
Society, whose home is in South Carolina Hall, older and more beautiful than
Hibernian Hall, the home of the St. Cecilia, helped create an audience for both
DuBose and Hervey Allen. After 1921 he arranged to use three months of the
year for himself in either the North Carolina mountains or Peterboro. In June
1924 Dorothy, whom he had married in 1923, suggested that he give up his job
and write "Porgy." Tragedy faced them if the book failed, for every bridge had
been burned behind them. Dorothy was eager to take the desperate chance, and,
as everyone knows, *Porgy* did not fail. Dorothy then suggested and helped to
make the dramatization of *Porgy* for the Theatre Guild. The rest of DuBose's
story needs no telling, since it has proceeded as it began, in the approved Henty
and Alger fashion. One of its latest chapters was set at a party of mine in New
York, in a more or less cosmopolitan group. Rebecca West,* who met him then
for the first time, was later to meet him in London, where writers descending in

---

* Rebecca West, pseudonym of Cicily Isabel Andrews, née Fairfield (1892–1983), British
journalist, novelist, and critic.

age from Max Beerbohm* to the author of *Serena Blandish*† were gathered for him. On the New York evening when Raimund von Hofmannsthal, son of Hugo von Hofmannsthal,‡ learned that he was talking to the author of *Porgy*, he could not contain his excitement. "My father," he exclaimed, "will be so very pleased when I tell him that I have seen you." And Miss West was equally satisfactory. At slightly exotic parties DuBose is likely to remind me, perhaps half-seriously, not to forget my "Virginia raising." And I on these occasions invariably reply that my ambition includes manners unmistakably of Virginia, and clothes and parties unmistakably of New York. With this he is forced to be content.

His present preoccupation is with the period in the South immediately preceding the War Between the States, and he is now submerged in a study of that period in relation to a future novel, which should give him an opportunity to reach the high-water mark of *Porgy*. I, at least, believe it to be more definitely within his own range than the North Carolina mountain people of *Angel*. My opinion, however, is perhaps unimportant, since within or without the author's range, I do not like to read about mountain people. His next play, probably an early production, is concerned, in his own words, "with that unhappy borderline that exists between the Negro and poor-white classes in the South."

Two years ago an argument of immense entertainment to me raged through several days in the literary columns of the New York *World*. A man wrote to complain that the hypothesis of *Mamba's Daughters* was in no respect valid. Lissa would not, he stated, have succeeded had she really been the product of sacrifices made by her mother and grandmother. "Heyward himself," he said, "is a self-made man. He would not be what he is today if he had been made by his family." He had heard the dramatic tale of the newsboy on the streets of Charleston. Immediately an indignant Charlestonian wrote to protest that DuBose was surely not a self-made man. Selling newspapers, protested the second writer, had nothing whatever to do with the matter. DuBose could never have learned, according to this writer, the things he plainly knew had he been self-made. I was, as I said, entertained. This nice definition of "self-made" is comprehensible only to the Southern mind. In the North, it is true, a newsboy risen to fame would very certainly be self-made, since only a boy badly in need of

---

*Henry Maximilian "Max" Beerbohm (1872–1910), essayist, caricaturist, and drama critic, one of the great figures of London.

† The novel *Serena Blandish* (1924) appeared under the pseudonym "By a Lady of Quality" until the author was proven to be Enid Bagnold (1889–1981), who later would achieve fame with the novel *National Velvet* (1935).

‡ Raimund von Hofmannsthal (1906–1974), son of Hugo von Hofmannsthal (1874–1929), Austrian prodigy, novelist, librettist, poet, essayist, and dramatist.

making sells papers there. In a small section of the South it has been different. Therefore the second writer, in a frantic effort to explain himself, choked helplessly with rage in the public prints. And I do not know if the delicate adjustment upon which he insisted was ever made in the New York mind. The subject of this diverting argument remains quite hopelessly a Southern gentleman. In justice to him I must explain that I mean this in a strictly social, quite unliterary sense. I mean, too, that he is literally gentle, in every connotation of that word. Frances Newman* did him less than justice when, in one of her rare enthusiasms for an American novel, she announced in *Books,* without exactly defining herself, that among her many reasons for liking *Porgy* was its "Southern gentleman's viewpoint." *Porgy* is assuredly no gentleman's job. It grew out of long, hot hours of labour on the waterfront with Porgy's kind, hours in which the labourer learned the hearts and minds of black people, within those always rigidly fixed limits where, alone, white people can ever learn the hearts and minds of black people. From this hardly-come-by knowledge he made his beautiful novel. It is, however, completely true that only a gentleman would have been unafraid of all that *Porgy's* presentation implied. For fear and suspicion of the African race, rather than affection and sympathy, are a part of the middle- and lower-class temper of the white South.

Socially, however, his Southern gentlemanly condition is hopeless to a degree which makes him an enigma to some of his newer friends. At a tea for him at Alan Rinehart's,[†] which I left early to catch a train, I protested against his descending with me through numberless floors of a tall apartment building to secure a taxicab in the street outside. He was plainly very tired, and: "In New York," I explained, "men don't leave parties given in their honour to go down into a cold street to call taxis for women who take unnecessary trains when taxis are so easily picked up." Edna Ferber,[‡] standing near, lifted her hands in a gesture of despair: "He is incurably a Southern gentleman," she said, "and he doesn't know it's not done."

---

*Frances Newman (1883–1928), Atlanta novelist, translator, critic, book reviewer, and librarian.
[†] Alan Rinehart (1900–1982), writer and later a film producer and playwright, was the son of mystery writer Mary Roberts Rinehart. His brothers ran Farrar & Rinehart, book publishers.
[‡] Edna Ferber (1885–1968), author of the Pulitzer Prize–winning novel *So Big* (1924) and the novel *Show Boat* (1926), which was adapted into a celebrated Broadway musical in 1927.

Legareville, South Carolina, c. 1850 by Portia Trenholm, active 1844. Oil on canvas.
Courtesy of Abby Aldrich Rockefeller Folk Art Museum, Colonial Williamsburg, Virginia.

HOLGER CAHILL (1935)

"Scouting for Folk Art"

Holger Cahill "Scouting for Folk Art" from The Rockefeller report (frames 829–832). "Holger Cahill Papers," February 21–March 1, 1935. Series Two: Correspondence Files [Reel 5285]. Courtesy of the Archives of American Art, Smithsonian Institution.

Holger Cahill (1887–1960), curator, writer on art, and arts administrator, was born Sveinn Kristjan Bjarnarson. He either emigrated from Iceland with his parents to the United States in the late 1880s or was born shortly after his parents arrived in St. Paul, Minnesota. In 1904, his father deserted the family, forcing Sveinn to be separated from his mother and sister to work on a farm in North Dakota. He ran away and wandered from job to job until settling in an orphanage in western Canada, where he attended school and became a voracious reader. As a young man, he worked at many different jobs and attended night school. While working on a freighter he visited Hong Kong, beginning a lifelong interest in the Orient. He pursued jobs that promised mobility, first at the Northern Pacific Railway in 1907 and later with Great Lakes boats, and eventually journeyed east, arriving in New York in 1913—the same year that the American art world was capsized by watershed events like New York's Armory Show, or the International Exhibition of Modern Art, the first large exhibition of modern art in America. Sveinn became a newspaper reporter and journalist before he attended the New School and New York University, and changed his name to Edgar Holger Cahill. He began to write articles and monographs on American art in 1918 and wrote publicity for the Society of Independent Artists, through which he made many friends in the arts and assimilated into avant-garde artistic and political circles.

Cahill soon assumed a leading role in this reappraisal of folk art and the large-scale revision of American culture taking place across the arts in the early years of the twentieth century. He was among a group of young and pivotal American modernists who had begun to equate the straightforwardness, abstracted forms, and color of early folk art with the new modernist art they had studied in Europe and were pioneering in America. In the early 1920s he was influenced by the institutional support for folk art that he observed during a summer abroad. As he traveled through Sweden, Norway, and Germany, he was inspired by museums like Stockholm's Nordiska Museet, which housed an impressive Swedish folk art collection. In 1921, he was hired by John Cotton Dana, the director of the Newark Museum, as a publicist. Until 1931, he worked under Dana, who had progressive ideas about the classes of objects that deserved space in American museums. From him, Cahill received his basic experience in museum work, organizing the first large exhibitions of folk art. He soon made another influential summer trip, this time to Ogunquit, Maine, where he became interested in the Maine handicraft that local artists were collecting. Edith Halpert, proprietress of the newly founded Downtown Gallery in New York, which sold only contemporary American art, first interested Cahill in Ogunquit. She soon became his partner in both business and the larger project of revisionism that included the folk art movement. They founded the American Folk Art Gallery on the second floor of the Downtown Gallery, which opened in 1931.

Meanwhile, Cahill's first novel, *Profane Earth,* was published in 1927, followed by monographs on artists Pop Hart (1928) and Max Weber (1930). He also published miscellaneous short stories and a biography of Frederick Townsend Ward. (1930).

He launched his own first series of folk art exhibitions—two at the Newark Museum followed by one at the Museum of Modern Art (MoMA). From 1932 he was the director of exhibitions for the recently founded MoMA. His 1932 MoMA show drew almost exclusively from the collection of Abby Aldrich Rockefeller (1874–1948), the wife of John D. Rockefeller, son of the founder of Standard Oil. Abby Rockefeller was an omnivorous collector who served on the board of MoMA and bought thousands of dollars' worth of folk art from the American Folk Art Gallery.

By 1935 Mrs. Rockefeller's collection had outgrown her Manhattan home and she made plans to loan pieces to the Ludwell-Paradise House, the first building completed as part of her husband's restoration of Colonial Williamsburg. She soon employed Cahill as her "folk art tracker." She not only tasked him with selecting, packing, and installing 250 objects from her collection at the Ludwell-Paradise House, while he was "down there" she sent him to "round out what was essentially a New England collection" with any unknown treasures that he might find south of Williamsburg. By 1935 objects in northern and mid-Atlantic antique shops were picked over, yet the South was "uncharted territory." So in February and March of 1935, Cahill traveled south from Williamsburg through Virginia, North Carolina, South Carolina, Florida, and Georgia, and later through Kentucky, Tennessee, and Alabama and as far south as Louisiana. He reported that in Charleston he "made a real haul." He devoted the second half of his Rockefeller report, from which this account is taken, to the four days he spent scouting in South Carolina in the depth of the Depression. However, he later said, "In general the South does not have the wealth of material that you have in the North. The great big centers of handicraft were states like Massachusetts, Maine, Connecticut, Rhode Island and Pennsylvania, and of course New York."

Cahill "didn't buy enough in the South ever to send it by truck" but he did write Mrs. Rockefeller about more than two dozen works of art, many of which are in the Colonial Williamsburg collection today. The 424 objects collected by Abby Rockefeller between 1929 and 1942 are the core of the collection of the Abby Aldrich Rockefeller Folk Art Museum, founded at Williamsburg in 1957. Ironically, her husband, John D. Rockefeller, Jr., involved in the historical restoration of Colonial Williamsburg from 1927, demolished several historic structures for gas stations in Charleston in the 1920s. Standard Oil was also involved in the demolition of Belvidere Plantation (c. 1800), near Magnolia Cemetery, which became part of the Charleston Country Club in 1901. In 1925, Belvidere was razed to make way for a Standard Oil Company refinery and plant (but several architectural elements were salvaged and moved to other locations in Charleston).

Later in 1935, Cahill was appointed national director of the Federal Art Project of the Works Progress Administration, where he remained until its end in 1943. An authority on both American modernism and folk art as well as an advocate of modern industrial design, he endorsed and oversaw the long compilation of *The Index of American Design* (1950), nearly eighteen thousand watercolors depicting traditional American arts and crafts made before about 1890. In 1938, he organized the countrywide exhibition "American Art Today" for the New York World's Fair. The same year he married Dorothy Canning Miller (1904–2003), the first professionally trained curator hired at MoMA. The Cahills collaborated on influential exhibitions that helped to put American art, especially American modernist art, on the map. (Dorothy Miller would become one of the most influential people in American modern art for more than half of the 20th century.) Following the end of the Federal Art Project, Cahill wrote two novels, *Look South to the Polar Star* (1947) and *The Shadow of My Hand* (1956).

In South Carolina, March 2 through 6 of 1935, Cahill wrote of Charleston to Mrs. Rockefeller, "At first glance the city bears evidences of craftsmanship. There is a lot of fine carving on houses. Superficially, the town reminds one of Boston. A glance in a telephone directory shows that it is full of antique shops.

I made a real haul here, but since it is a long story and this report is already too long, I will postpone it to the next letter." Cahill made several acquisitions, including the painting *Legareville, South Carolina* (c.1850) by Portia Trenholm. From Charleston he traveled on to Columbia, where he procured the notable South Carolina painting *The Old Plantation* (ca. 1785–1795).

   The following account of Cahill scouting for folk art in South Carolina is excerpted from an eight-page report Cahill wrote to Abby Aldrich Rockefeller, chronicling his southern journey between February 21 and March 5, 1935.

SOURCES

Cahill, Holger. "Reminiscences of Holger Cahill." Interview by Joan Pring. Transcript, 1957. Holger Cahill Papers. Biographical Material and Personal Papers [Reel 5285]. Archives of American Art, Smithsonian Institution.

Holger Cahill papers, 1910–1993, bulk 1910–1960. Archives of American Art, Smithsonian Institution.

Jentleson, Katherine. "'Not as Rewarding as the North:' Holger Cahill's Southern Folk Art Expedition." *Archives of American Art Journal* (2014). http://www.aaa.si.edu/essay/katherine-jentleson.

Stillinger, Elizabeth. *A Kind of Archeology: Collecting Folk Art in America, 1876–1976.* Amherst: University of Massachusetts Press, 2011.

"Scouting for Folk Art"

Charleston. Charleston is like Boston. It is filled with antique shops. The street of antiques in Boston is Charles Street, in Charleston it is King Street. I found about fifteen shops listed in the classified section of the telephone directories and spent my first morning in Charleston combing these. I found mostly junk, but in the shop of an auctioneer named Burgess I saw two very good children's portraits. He said they were members of the Ball family of Charleston, and that they had come into his possession through a suit over a storage bill. He wanted a hundred dollars for the pair. I asked him if he could not make a better price since the portraits needed cleaning badly. He said he'd take ninety dollars if I'd tend to the crating and shipping. While we were discussing the pictures a very brisk well-dressed woman who was in the shop came over to the dealer and reminded him in a rather peevish voice that he had promised the pictures to her. I thought my safety lay in silence, so I said nothing and wandered off to look at some other things in the shop. The dealer said he had held the pictures for more than three months. She said that was all right. He seemed to feel that it was too long. Well, she said, if you'll only hold them for a few days longer I want to bring in DuBose Heyward (the author of *Porgy* and the great contemporary literary celebrity of Charleston), and Haskell Coffin (a thoroughly bad but prominent academic portrait painter, now in Charleston painting the leading people)* to look at them.

I began to feel a little nervous but still said nothing. After the conversation between the dealer and the lady had come to an end I said that I thought the price of ninety dollars high because it would cost more than ten dollars to have the pictures crated and shipped. Oh no, said the dealer, Sellers the Moving Man will crate them for five dollars and he's a thoroughly reliable man. I can guarantee that he will do it for that. That's fine said I, then I'll take them and before the brisk lady could say a word I had given the dealer ninety dollars in American Express checks and got his receipt. The lady then came over and talked with me, giving me a lecture on art and telling me how the portraits should be cleaned. She said water in which onions had been boiled was very good. Her methods of restoring pictures were very unusual. I thought there was something of Voodoo in them.

The antique shops yielded little more than that the first day. One of the dealers told me of a woman named Mrs. Volk [*sic*]† who had weather vanes, but when I found her it turned out that she did not. A dealer named Mrs. Fromberg‡ told me she had a weather vane at home. I went to see it but it turned out to be a modern brass mantel ornament.

On the second day, having exhausted the antique shops on King Street, I tried the ones in the outlying sections and hired a taxi man at $1.50 an hour to take me around. He turned out to be a great find, since he had been for some years before the driver of a rubberneck bus and knew Charleston thoroughly. On the second day I found a watercolor of a parrot and a quaint small velvet in the Hawkstone shop. The woman said the watercolor had come from Louisville,

---

* William Haskell Coffin (1878–1941), born in Charleston, studied at the Corcoran School of Art in Washington, D.C., the Art Students League in New York, and in Paris. A painter and commercial illustrator, he specialized in images of women. He was well-known in Charleston for his society portraits of locals. Over the course of his career, Coffin painted more than thirty covers for the *Saturday Evening Post*, covers for *McCall's*, *Pictorial Review, Redbook, Leslie's Illustrated,* and *The American*, and war posters for the US government. His popular "Coffin girl" was found on note cards, sheet music, calendars, decorative boxes, and fashion catalogs. He was also portrait painter of the famous Ziegfeld show girls. His brother, Frank Trenholm Coffyn (1878–1960) was a pioneer aviator and a member of the original Wright Brothers Flying Team.
† Marguerite Sinkler Valk (1894–1979), Charleston interior designer and preservationist who had a shop on Water Street in the 1930s.
‡ Rose Marcus Fromberg (1888–1978), wife of Joseph Fromberg (1890–1961), a special federal prosecutor and police court judge. They lived at 43 Bull Street. After the death of her husband, she returned to her hometown of Savannah and operated Rose Fromberg Antiques. Tinsley E. Yarbrough, *A Passion for Justice,*104–5.

Kentucky. Also I found a needlepoint picture with a palmetto tree (the emblem of South Carolina), and a textile showing Washington and Franklin, etc. I am not very knowing about textiles but I thought this was a rare one and that it might fit in your Washington collection. It seemed to me that it was one of the "toiles de Jouy" which were printed in France beginning about 1760. These were usually printed from engraved copper plates. I feel quite certain this is an example of "toiles de Jouy," after I had a chance to look at it and it is certainly an example of color printing in the 18th century, though textile, of course. Another thing I found was a pair of Charleston doorstops, a bear and a sleeping child. These are characteristic Charleston pieces, so I was informed. In looking over Sonn's book on early American iron* in a Charleston dealers shop, I came across a picture of your cut-out peasant weather vane in the book. I recognized it at once, and since Sonn says he saw it at Zimmerman's in Monterey, Pa., it is undoubtedly the same one.

My taxi driver told me he would look around for more antique and second hand places and he would come get me in the morning. The third day yielded nothing, though we combed the strangest looking places, down to a curious second hand store in the "brass ankle" section. The store was labelled "Noah's Ark—We Fix and Sell every thing Cheap—Closed Saturday until Dark." We went there in the evening since this was Saturday.

On Sunday, I visited the Charleston Museum and the Gibbes Art Gallery. The Gibbes is the art museum. They had a very interesting exhibition of miniatures, a lot of pictures by Theus, the Charleston painter,† three pastels by Henrietta Johnson‡ and quite a lot of quaint old pictures. I talked with the director, a young man named Whitelaw,§ and heard something of the woes of the

---

* Albert H. Sonn (1867–1936) published *Early American Wrought Iron* (1928) in three volumes, which includes early Charleston ironwork.
† Jeremiah Theus (1716–1774), Swiss-born painter primarily of portraits, was active in Charleston, where he was almost without competition for most of his career.
‡ Henrietta Johnston (ca. 1674–1729) remains the first known female artist working in the English colonies and the first known pastel artist in the South. A portraitist of about forty extant works, she came to Charleston around 1708, when her husband, Anglican clergyman Gideon Johnston, was appointed as commissary of the Church of England.
§ Robert Newton Spry Whitelaw (1905–1974), a nationally known maker of miniature dioramas for museums and other institutions, became curator of art at the Charleston Museum in the late 1920s, and director of the Carolina Art Association from 1931 to 1953. He was responsible for managing the Gibbes Art Gallery. Whitelaw developed a collections policy that focused on the work of local artists. However, in 1936 and again in 1938 he would collaborate with Solomon Guggenheim, businessman, art collector, and philanthropist, to bring the first nonobjective art exhibition in America to the Gibbes.

museum director in the South. He said that the only traveling exhibitions that were worth anything were the shows gotten up by the museum of modern art, but his museum was too poor to take advantage of them. The Charleston Museum is a mixture of everything under the sun, from natural history to local history and art. They had two interesting embroidered pictures of the Revolutionary or post-Revolutionary period, a painting of a plantation (the plantation owners before the Civil War had itinerant painters make pictures of their plantation buildings), and an extremely quaint and primitive piece of South Carolina pottery, the portrait of a seated man, about eighteen inches high. I had seen heads in South Carolina pottery before, but never a figure, and they assured me down there that it is a rare piece.

On Sunday morning, before the museums opened I walked about the churchyards. The Old Huguenot Church, and St. Philip's and St. Michael's, and looked for carved tombstones. There were a few interesting ones at the Huguenot Church and at St. Michael's, but St. Philip's is a regular art gallery. In St. Michael's, there is one very peculiar grave marker, a part of a bed, probably a footboard. The grave is marked, "In memory of Mary Luyten, wife of Will Luyten d. Sep. 9th 1770 in the 29th year of her age." This, I believe, is one of the tourist shrines of Charleston, and has been commented on by Believe-it-or-not: Ripley.

In St. Philip's there are many varieties of carved tombstones. The 19th Century ones have willow trees, sheep, etc., while the 18th century ones ran to skulls with wings, cherubs with wings, and portraits. The most interesting carvings were in slate, a very difficult stone to carve. On the graves of Mary Dart (d. 1752) and Mary Owen (d. 1749), there were portrait busts carved in slate. On the grave of Mrs. Ann Scott (d. 1740) there were three cherubs carved in high relief with a floral decoration. There were cherubs with wings on the graves of Mrs. Sarah Creighton (1775), Loyd (1755), and several other graves marked 1744, 1747, 1770. Death's heads, crossbones, hourglasses, coats of arms are frequent on the early 18th century tombstones. There were very interesting portraits carved on the graves of Thomas Ellis (1763), George Hesket (1747), Holmes (1758), and another Holmes (1763). From about 1820 on there are several stones carved with a hand holding a drooping flower, or more frequently simply a drooping flower; 1831, willow trees and urns; 1846, a warship on stylized waves; 1829, 1842, a child kneeling in prayer, carved in high relief: 1850 a mourning lady beside an

---

Guggenheim, who bought a house on the Battery in 1929 and frequented Charleston in the 1930s and early 1940s, would afterward found New York City's Solomon R. Guggenheim Museum, which opened in 1959. Robert N. S. Whitelaw papers, 1892–1973. [263.00]. South Carolina Historical Society.

urn, carved in high relief. A good photographer like Charles Sheeler* could make a fine book out of these carvings in St. Philip's.

Also, on Sunday, I went looking for weathervanes, since Charleston dealers do not seem to know very much about them. On a house at the Fort Sumter Hotel, at the corner of King St., near the Battery, I saw an eagle weathervane on top of a prosperous looking residence. On a business house on King Street, near the corner of Queen, there is another eagle weathervane. On Monday I found two more weathervanes on [a] house owned by a Dr. Rhame, a prosperous Charleston physician.† One of these I was able to get.

On Monday, my taxi driver took me to two women, Mrs. Fuller and Mrs. Schwering [sic],‡ who are scouts for the antique dealers of Charleston. They took me to see a great many people who had paintings, most of which were rather poor. One portrait was rather interesting, a portrait of James Habersham, first governor of the State of Georgia. He holds a large spray of cotton blossoms in his hand. The woman who owns it thinks it is worth $2500.00, but I am afraid she will never realize more than a tenth of that sum. I would date it about 1835. Mrs. Fuller took me to see a man named Hay, who had a still life painted by Major John Cogdell. I was interested at once for on Sunday I had seen two miniatures of Cogdell at the Gibbes Art Gallery, one by Charles Frazer [sic]§ and one by Samuel Smith, Jr.** The miniature by Smith of Cogdell is the only know miniature by that artist, so they told me at the Gibbes, and for this reason the

* Charles Sheeler (1883–1965), a painter, commercial photographer, and collector who helped create an interest in American folk and decorative arts in the 1920s and 1930s. He had been documenting "primitive" objects for more than a decade as the photographer for early collectors of African art. Sheeler is now recognized as one of the founders of American modernism, and one of the master photographers of the twentieth century.
† Dr. Joseph Sumter Rhame (1885–1956), physician, surgeon, and professor of surgery at the Medical University, lived at 59 East Bay.
‡ Mary O'Hagan Schwerin (1886–1963), whose family owned Colonial Antique Shop. Mrs. Fuller was identified by Cahill as her sister. Their father, William James O'Hagan, first opened W. J. O'Hagan & Son, colonial antiques, in 1880 on Queen Street. Mrs. Schwerin also corresponded with Henry Francis du Pont, who from 1927 collected architectural objects from antique dealers, period rooms from demolitions of historic structures, and elements from houses still standing for his Winterthur Museum.
§ Charles Fraser (1782–1860), Charleston artist in the first half of the nineteenth century. An 1857 exhibition of his art included 313 miniatures, 139 landscapes, and other of his works. John Cogdell (1778–1847), lawyer, businessman, artist, and sculptor, had been a close friend of Fraser. The Fraser miniature of Cogdell remains in the Gibbes Museum collection.
** The miniature of John S. Cogdell (ca. 1800) by Samuel Smith Jr. (1776–1812) remains in the Gibbes collection.

name of Cogdell was known to me. Hay got the picture from the Cogdell family. The dates of John S. Cogdell are 1778–1847. He was president of the Bank of South Carolina, 1832–1847, and an officer of the Customs House in Charleston. He is also listed as both painter and sculptor. The miniature of him by Smith at the Gibbes is dated 1802. He is buried at St. Philip's. I copied the inscription on his gravestone. It reads as follows:

> To the memory of John S. Cogdell, a native of South Carolina
> Who was born on the 19th of September, 1778, And died on the 25th day of February, 1847.
>
> In all his relations He was a man to be cherished and loved. He united the kindest Affections with the deepest Sensibility, the purest Virtue with the strictest Honor; He sustained with the great urbanity and the most spotless integrity, Many public offices with Trust and Distinction; and he illustrated and graced them. By an enlightened mind, a cultivated Taste, and a devotion to the fine Arts, at once his Ornament and his Reward. He crowned all his high and endearing qualities by the Humility and Faith of the Christian, and fell asleep in the assurance of awaking in everlasting Life thro' the merits of the Redeemer.

I got the still life by Cogdell, and then was taken by Mrs. Fuller to see a Mrs. Y. F. Legare, an old lady of eighty-five, who lives at a Church Home. She is a member of the famous Legare family of Charleston, of whom Hugh Swinton Legare, one of the most brilliant Charleston writers, minister to Belgium and Secretary of State before the Civil War, was also a member. Mrs. Legare (the name is pronounced Legree, like that of Simon Legree in *Uncle Tom's Cabin*) had three portraits, none of them very good, though one was fairly good, and a very quaint painting of Legareville on St. John's island, near Charleston, which was a great summer place for the local planters before the Civil War. Today, so they say, there is nothing there but a collection of ruinous shacks. I got the landscape from Mrs. Legare because it seemed to me that it was typical of the paintings which the planters used to commission itinerant painters to do, though Mrs. Legare told me that it had not been done by an itinerant but by a Charleston young woman nearly a hundred years ago. She said the woman's name was Miss Portia Trenholm.* Trenholm is also a distinguished Charleston family name.

---

* Portia Ash Burden Trenholm (1813–1892), an amateur artist whose few extant paintings include landscapes. She was the daughter of Kinsey and Mary Legare Burden, and the wife of Charles Louis Trenholm (1808–1865).

Mrs. Fuller then took me to see Dr. Rhame's wife.* Mrs. Rhame said she would sell a weathervane of a fish which she had taken down from a house she owned. I got the fish for $15 plus the scout's commission of 20 percent, $18 in all. She also had a rooster weathervane which seemed badly rusted. She would have sold it, but seemed to want much more for it, so I did not press the matter. I spent the rest of the day going from place to place with Mrs. Fuller but there were no more things worth buying. So I took my departure to Columbia, S.C., taking with me the name of another antique scout, Mr. John O'Hagan,[†] whose address Mrs. Fuller had gave me. Columbia had yielded nothing on my first trip there, but I had hopes that this time I might find something. On the way I stopped at Orangeburg, about halfway between Charleston and Columbia, but found nothing there.

In Columbia I visited the Confederate trophy room in the State Capitol. There are in it a number of quaint things, the best of which are two sign-painter pictures of Confederate troops drilling on Sullivan's Island, which is in Charleston Harbor. I took another look around the antique shops, visited Gittman, the famous book dealer[‡] then went to look up my antique scout. He took me to see a woman named Mrs. Lyles, who doesn't advertise as an antique dealer.[§] She had a house full of furniture and some interesting pictures, the finest of which, by far, was a plantation water color, which she said she had got between Charleston and Orangeburg from an old plantation.[**] She first said she wanted

---

* Willie Brown Rhame (1882–1968), active in the United Daughters of the Confederacy and the Society for the Preservation of Old Buildings.

† John O'Hagan, the brother of Mrs. Fuller and Mrs. Schwerin. Previously involved in antiques, he had gone into the insurance business in Columbia but agreed to scout for Cahill.

‡ James Thornton Gittman (1872–1951) opened Gittman's Book Shop in Columbia prior to World War I. It remained in business until 1967.

§ Mary Earle Lyles (1878–1960), who by at least 1940 was taking in lodgers at her home at 1401 Blanding Street in Columbia.

** Cahill purchased the painting, *The Old Plantation* from Mrs. Lyles. It is one of the only extant depictions of slave life from the eighteen century. He recalled, "I practically fainted when I saw that picture." And: "The style of the picture is based on European-derived tradition, but the Negro types in it are very exact replicas of the Carolina Gullah. [An expert said] they could be recognized as descendants of the Hausa and Yoruba peoples. The banjo in the picture he called an African molo, and the drum of Yoruba origin, called a gudugudu. The dance itself was considered part of a slave wedding." The painting has been attributed to artist John Rose (1752/1753–1802), a plantation owner originally from Beaufort. It now hangs in the Abby Aldrich Rockefeller Folk Art Museum in Williamsburg. For more on the painting and its provenance, see Susan P. Shames, *The Old Plantation: The Artist Revealed* (Colonial Williamsburg), 2010.

The Old Plantation (Slaves Dancing on a South Carolina Plantation),
ca. 1785–1795. Watercolor on paper, attributed to John Rose,
Beaufort County, South Carolina. Courtesy of
Abby Aldrich Rockefeller Folk Art Museum.

fifty dollars for it. I made up my mind to buy it, no matter what she asked, but
said nothing more about it until I had looked over her stock. Then I mentioned
it again. She said, well, I'm sure some tourist will give me fifty dollars for it. I
looked skeptical, the antique scout said he thought it was high, so she came down
to twenty dollars! I bought it.

27 State St. & misc., Charleston, Charleston County, South Carolina, c. 1937.
Frances Benjamin Johnston (1864–1952), photographer. Library of Congress.

EDWARD TWIG (RICHARD COLEMAN) (1940)

"Charleston: The Great Myth"

Edward Twig (Richard Coleman), "Charleston: The Great Myth," *The Forum* 103:1 (January 1940): 1–7.

Richard Coleman (Edward Twig) (1907–1984), who lived in Charleston after 1932, was born in Washington, D.C., where he was educated in Catholic schools through college. He was the author of *Don't You Weep, Don't You Moan* (1935), a controversial novel about Charleston blacks that took its title from "Mary Don't You Weep," a spiritual about delivery from oppression that dates before the Civil War and was recorded as early as 1915 by the Fisk Jubilee Singers. A 1959 recording by The Swan Silvertones, a gospel group, would later make it a familiar anthem for the civil rights movement—quite a stretch from Coleman's novel, which is highly racial, particularly by today's standards. Coleman also published several short stories, including "A Fight for Sister Joe," a Catholic story first published in *Story* in 1937 and reproduced in *They Are People: Modern Short Stories of Nuns, Monks and Priests* (1947). After it appeared in *Story*, the story was purchased by film director Leo McCarey and adapted into sequences of the film *The Bells of St. Mary's* (1946), starring Bing Crosby and Ingrid Bergman. Another of his short stories, "Infamous Mansion" (1947), takes place in Charleston, where a newcomer accidentally wanders into a mansion that turns out to be a whorehouse which has serviced Charleston for seven generations. The establishment, once "one of the most famous brothels in the world," has fallen "from *poularde toulousaine* to collard greens and butts meat." The story has Oscar Wilde wandering into the whorehouse (and fleeing pronto) during his famous 1882 visit to Charleston.

Coleman was a member of the Poetry Society. He later gave lectures on creative writing in Charleston. Among his students in the 1960s was Alexandra Ripley (1934–2004), author of the historical novels *Charleston* (1981) and *On Leaving Charleston* (1984), and *Scarlett: The Sequel to Margaret Mitchell's* Gone with the Wind (1991). A devote Catholic, Coleman befriended author Flannery

O'Connor and published *Flannery O'Connor: A Scrutiny of Two Forms of Her Many-Leveled Art* (1966).

However, when "Charleston: The Great Myth" was published in *The Forum* in 1940, Charlestonians were aghast. The "resulting vituperations" included a storm of letters to the editor sent to the Charleston newspaper in protest, repudiating Coleman for mocking the city, and particularly its preservationists.

In his 1940 article, "Edward Twig" exposes the "myth" of Charleston gentility.

SOURCES

"'Bells of St. Mary's' Adapted in Part, From Story by Charlestonian." *Bulletin of the Catholic Laymen's Association of Georgia* (March 30, 1946): 20.

Bradbury, John M. *Renaissance in the South: A Critical History of the Literature, 1920–1960.* Chapel Hill: University of North Carolina Press, 1963.

Coleman, Richard. "The Infamous Mansion." In *Story: The Fiction of the Forties,* edited by Whit Burnett and Hallie Burnett. New York: E. P. Dutton, 1949.

McDannell, Colleen, *Catholics in the Movies.* New York: Oxford University Press, 2008.

McFee, William, "Picture of a Race," *New York Sun*, March 9, 1935.

Waddell, Gene. Papers. South Carolina Historical Society, Charleston.

Whitelaw, Robert N. S. (director). Correspondence. Civic Services Committee Papers [Folder 17: Frederick P. Keppel from Robert N.S. Whitelaw (Dec. 29, 1939)]. Margaretta Childs Archives, Historic Charleston Foundation, Charleston.

"Charleston: The Great Myth"

Charleston had its day—a brilliant, magnificent day. All that is left of that day are a few mansions, complete with Adams doorways and walled gardens and the memories of another age; quite a bit of history; many records and anecdotes; and a legendary Charleston that exists only in the minds of the self-deluded. There is no such place as the utterly beautiful, charming, gracious old city that the romantics, the wishful thinkers, the fabulists say there is. Remote from that great day of hers is the real Charleston—poor, uncourtly, apathetic, and having as little to do with her own brilliant past as she has with the American present.

Time does not stand still—not even in Charleston, South Carolina, where that claim is forever being made. What time has done to Charleston is devastating, ruthless.

She is like an old woman who has lived too long, disfigured with age, forever dying, yet always still alive. Actually, hers is a kind of life beyond the grave. Charleston at night is an eerie place.

The glorious past of Charleston could not possibly exist in the present city. No place could be less suitable for the grand manner, the elegant ease, the aesthetic and delicate grace of that fabulous town. No place could be less likely to breed either mettlesome or languorous ultrafashionable aristocrats. Culture would be impossible in this stagnation.

Look at this place "where Time stands still," "where the Past lives on in the Present, unchanged and unchanging," "where the fine art of living is the great heritage of her people," "where culture blooms as brilliantly as do the azaleas."

We see that Charleston is first and foremost a poor man's town. Time has robbed her, and Charleston never fights back at time. So the mark of the place is the mark of poverty and neglect—not the genteel poverty of the romances but down-at-the-heels poverty.

We see that Charleston now does not belong to "aristocrats," broken-down or otherwise, but to "nobodies." Theirs is the main street of the city, along with all the rest of the town with the exception of a few hallowed spots. This main street is a lane, narrow as a string, sadly uneager and unstimulating, and a constant reminder that "there is always a Depression in Charleston."

This is a small town "main drag" (one wonders what that other Charleston would think of it), revealing the condition and the tastes of those who buy.

There are too many second-hand stores, too many holes in the wall for "eats" and sundry trash, too many beer hangouts, too many pawnshops.

Here and there on the long street is a bright store that is an oasis in a desert of bleakness.

One remembers that on this street once stood the first department store in America, to which the great ladies of the old South came, often traveling many hundreds of miles, to buy treasures in lace and the like which were imported from far corners of the world.

The rich in Charleston today are generally the damyankees who have come because of these legends and have stayed to try to make some of them real.

Waging an eleventh-hour fight against the time that "stands still," these outsiders have saved some great old houses and many a plantation manor and have converted desquamating old slave quarters in narrow streets into the little pastel gems that are bright enough to be done in full color in ecstatic periodicals. With a few exceptions, the houses that make Charleston look a little as she is meant to look entire, according to the fables, are the restored places of these outsiders who so desperately want the mythical Charleston to exist.

Not Homes—Just Houses

Clustering around these restored mansions and slave quarters that find themselves in so many soft-lighted photographs, water-color sketches, and etchings are the houses that belong to most Charlestonians. And sorrier houses it is hard to imagine. They are that somber paintless hue or a dirty brown or white. Their porches sag precariously. The fact that the porches are often called "galleries" doesn't keep them from being ugly appendages that have atrophied.

Most of the houses are the one-room-wide, single houses of the Low Country, with their sides to the street and their fronts facing the blank backs of the equally gaunt and ugly houses next door. Plants hang from green-painted lard tins, chamber pots, and bona fide flower pots that line the miles of banister railings. And yards are often rock-hard black earth that shines when it rains and smells when the sun draws the dampness out.

Charlestonians often speak disdainfully of the "row" houses of less blessed sections of this country. Yet their identical narrow houses stand side by side in almost every street in Charleston, and are distinguishable only by the color (or lack of it) of their paint, the angle of the porches, the list of the fences, and the individual droop of the houses themselves.

Inside many of these single houses that are the real symbol of Charleston today are monstrous pieces of furniture from the 'seventies and 'eighties, big, black, and forbidding things with mottled marble tops and festoons of rusty chains. The beds are specters in the high, shadowy rooms; and the ancient gas fixtures, converted reluctantly to electricity, hang down like fungoid growths that give off a glow. Many of these Charleston houses are bedecked with the worst wooden lace to be found anywhere in the world, rococo architecture on a binge.

In these houses, in the furniture that haunts them, is the answer to Charleston's well-kept secret. The past *does* live on in the present, but it is not the brilliant past "before" but the bitter and ugly past "after the war that destroyed the old Charleston forever and gave the new an eternal alibi.

The past that stands in every street is the past of 1870. Almost everything in the city today is an actual part of that time or a direct descendant of it.

There's a little of colonial Charleston left, a little more antebellum Charleston left, but it is preposterous to claim that these things are Charleston itself. The Charlestonians who have held on to their mansions and the Charlestonians who never had mansions are like the town. They stem from the "after"; they cannot cross that great gulf. They are separated from their own ancestors by the metamorphosis of the Civil War. They cannot feel or be as their ancestors felt or were. The fantastic thing that was Charleston before the war collapsed completely. Nothing was left alive; nothing grew again among the ruins. Charleston gave herself up completely to inertia and decay.

So many houses are utterly forlorn. Time will make them more so. God knows what will happen to them in the years to come and what will become of Charleston. These houses are filled with a musty smell, are riddled with termites, and actually belong to the giant cockroaches which race across the kitchens, fly about the rooms, and take their ease and fill in the quiet of the gloomy clothes closets.

Not Antique—Just Old

Look at the people who live in these houses. What kind of people are they? Charlestonians are said to have a great heritage, but they are the disinherited of the land. Born into a city that has nothing before it but the grave, they are offered no opportunities and blessed with no ambition. Those few who find a rare urge to succeed, to climb, marking them as different from their fellows, flee the crumbling old tree trunk as soon as they can.

As we see the people on their porches and on the street, we realize again that Charleston is a poor man's town. Charleston's clothes are called "conservative." They're not conservative—they're just old. They look like the contents of a long unopened trunk. They have a little more style and verve than the clothes of the Amish.

Charlestonians are unashamed of their old clothes, their drooping houses, and their empty pocketbooks. Shame is beyond them, just as real pride is. They're content with almost nothing, resigned to the fact that they'll never have more.

Without the tourists, Charlestonians take money out of one pocket and put it in another. They live on each other, and the supply of money is thin.

So the tourists are welcomed but not wanted. The root-deep prejudice against the North is poorly concealed. But the need of Northern money cannot be hidden and is sometimes extremely humiliating to those who really love Charleston.

For instance, there is the new slum-clearance project. Charleston wants all the projects she can get, but this time the old jail stood in the way.

Charleston's jail is (was, now) a medieval structure, complete with everything but a moat and a drawbridge. The wall was a great high thing, and the turret towers were very picturesque. Charleston had kept this jail because she could afford no other (the prime reason for most of the city's clinging to the old). It was a tourist come-on, even if it was such a terrible place that the government never permitted federal prisoners to be kept in it, even overnight.

On the horns of a dilemma, Charlestonians fought for the jail, then for the wall, or they battled for the project. Mr. Strauss [*sic*], the New Deal's representative,* is quoted as having said that the government couldn't worry itself over

---

*Nathan Straus (1848–1931), administrator of the US Housing Authority, was instrumental in the slum-clearance and low-cost housing projects in Charleston. The Old Jail (c.1802) at 21 Magazine Street stood adjacent to an African American neighborhood cited for demolition in the late 1930s. Real estate agent, Susan Pringle Frost, instrumental

old things that stood in the way of better, new things. Many Charlestonians agreed. But the newspaper printed letters of the outraged people who held out for the landmark. These letters played on the theme that, if Charleston didn't keep herself as quaintly attractive as she could, she would lose her life's blood— the tourist money. Few were the genuine lovers of Charleston's past and her relics who begged that this ancient landmark be kept for its own sake. One lady who loves Charleston and is the Society for the Preservation of Old Dwellings has waged a continuous and valiant fight for beautiful or desolate ruins. Time will defeat her, too.

Most Charlestonians have a sort of resentful love of their old city. They wouldn't do much for it but they resent the claim that there is anything the matter with it. They'd tear the whole city down, however, for a project big enough.

These people are the product of the place. They are part of its pretense. They even claim that they don't exist in order to say that Charleston is what she always was. They believe what they say and want everyone else to believe them. They repeat all the myths over and over again, though the realities before them are devastating to such airy nonsense. Many of them are as complacently ignorant as anyone can possibly be and are smug about things that are nonexistent.

Much of Charleston's stagnation is the result of this overpowering self-hypnotism and conceit. Since Charleston is utterly satisfied with herself and believes her ugliness to be beauty, her inertia to be culture, her pretense to be truth, she never lifts a hand to improve herself. Since her people are cultured by inheritance, no books need be read, no art relished.

Not Climate—Just Laziness

A woman in Charleston recently said, in all seriousness, "I never move unless I have to." She is less than forty but she never stirs from her chair unless she has to. This is what time has transformed the "elegant languor" into—lethargy, sloth.

The "fine art of living that is the great heritage of these people" is made up of having a Negro servant for two or three dollars a week; going to bed after a heavy, hot dinner in the middle of the day; playing a bit of bridge, bingo, or poker; and going to the movies. Some fish a little; some hunt a little. Every day is like the next, and even most of the months of the year are the same, because of the mild climate. There is never any festive air on holidays—there is just the

---

in founding the Society for the Preservation of Old Dwellings in 1920, worked to save historic buildings in the city. Thanks to the city's preservationists, the Old Jail survived.

usual blankness and emptiness. Time doesn't stand still in Charleston—it just ticks itself away vacuously. Life goes untasted.

The Charlestonian, with very few exceptions, has a Negro servant of some kind. He may pay the servant as little as fifteen cents a day or as much as five dollars a week. He goes on the assumption that all black females were born cleaners or cooks. This is one of the greatest delusions in Charleston. They break more than they clean and they burn more than they cook. But they keep one from moving unless one has to. And that is the fine art of living—as who should know better than these brilliant descendants of the godlike people of early Charleston?

The habit of going to bed after a hot dinner, upon sizzling, sticky sheets, is certainly unhygienic and is certainly not the sweet siesta of the myths. If life is "unhurried" in Charleston, it is probably owing to metabolic causes—along with the fact that there is nothing to hurry for, nothing apparently to accomplish, nothing to gain.

Incidentally, the legendary mint julep is as little known and as little enjoyed as lobster thermidor. This symbol of "gracious living" is virtually nonexistent. Whisky flows in Charleston but not with mint on the tide.

Endless novels and other works have dwelt on the enervating climate of this ancient American city. It's the heat of her days, so they say, that has made her people less alert, less "efficient," and, in the glamourous jargon of the place, more languorous.

The following are average daily *maximum* summer temperatures:

Charleston	86.5 degrees
Des Moines, Ia	83.5 degrees
Dodge City, Kan	83.4 degrees
Indianapolis, Ind	83.4 degrees
Parkersburg, W.Va	84.0 degrees
St. Louis, Mo	85.8 degrees
Wilmington, NC	83.6 degrees

The average maximum summer temperature of all these less supine places is 85.50 degrees.

That takes care of the maximum temperature. The mean summer average for Charleston is nothing to get so hot about. It is 80 degrees.

The mean humidity of Charleston is 79, which does not make for sultriness. And Charleston is breeze-swept and often utterly delightful, when people are being prostrated in less fortunate cities far north. The leaves of the trees are always aflutter, whereas they are as still as stone in too many towns above Mason and Dixon's line.

The Southern Heat Myth is the tenuous foundation for more nonsense than any other fiction-producing device in America.

According to Vance, in *The Human Geography of the South,* the theory that the Southern sun has made the Southerner take on the characteristics of the Mediterranean European is neat but incapable of demonstration. There is simply no proof whatsoever that the climate is a factor in molding racial temperament and disposition.

Robert De C. Ward, in *The Climates of United States,* says: "The South does not comprise a sharply defined climatic province . . . The slowly graduated effect on solar heat is everywhere modified by wide plains left open to cold winds from Canada and warm moist winds from the Gulf."

It is a little-known fact that neither heat prostration nor sunstroke is nearly so common in the South as in the North, even in Southern slum areas. White women are seen working the heat of the day in the fields of South Carolina and Georgia. And it is a matter of record that summer in Northern and Eastern cities is more intolerable than in the South.

Vance says that the superstition that Southern climate has dangerous effects causes man to do less work than can be done in other sections must pass. "It belongs with Frederick Mayratt's view that the climate America has caused deterioration in original physique of the English settlers."

It is an undeniable fact that a man can do far more work, in much greater comfort, in Charleston than he can in New York or other outlandish places. The heat is never excessive: the winter is balmy and snowless. Sixty-five per cent of the year are sunshiny days, according to fifty-year-long records.

An "outsider" does not find the urge to work or to exert himself growing less when he lives in Charleston than when he lives anyplace else. In fact Charleston has so much good weather that there is endless opportunity—given the desire—for countless activities out of the ordinary.

No—the man who finds the answer to the Charlestonian's disinclination to bestir himself will have to forget the worn-out heat alibi and seek a more prosaic explanation.

Not High Spirits—Just Crime

When one studies Charleston's modern attitude toward crime, one cannot help but wonder if the heat is also to be called on to account for this more serious form of *laissez-faire.* To be languid toward murder is carrying the whole thing too far.

Charleston is near enough the top of the list of homicide rates for American cities to achieve another distinction for herself. And yet murder is treated as lightly as though it were an indiscretion. Only one man has gone to the chair in three years, out of the dozens who took the lives of others, and of course that one made the fatal mistake of killing a police officer. The only man to receive life imprisonment in this same period was the other Negro who had a part in that officer's death.

Within the present decade, Charleston's homicide rate has been twice that of Chicago and four times that of New York. And it steadily maintains the appalling level, year in and year out, of twice to three times the national homicide rate.

In 1939, up to November, there had been twenty-two killings, in only two of which had any defendant been brought to trial. Charleston's population (1930 census) is 62,265.

Four years imprisonment seems adequate here for confessed manslaughter, and twelve years is too long a time to shut up a murderer. Men who have killed deliberately and brutally are turned back into the fold again.

Of course most of this murder is black and is therefore unimportant. So are the slashings and cuttings that are dropped before they ever come to trial. They are everyday occurrences. These crimes are stark and violent. They would reveal more horror than a whole circulating library of murder fiction. Weapons are generally ice picks (which are outnumbering the open-blade razor), jagged broken bottles, flaming hurled lamps, and other remarkable and terrible instruments of death.

In Charleston it is commonplace for a man to lose his life over a woman, a jest, a string of catfish, or a dime.

Stealing goes on in the Riviera-like climate with great abandon. Bicycles alone provide a ten-thousand-dollar-a-year racket.

There is no room here to describe the extraordinary absolutions given fine white gentlemen who do away with thousands and thousands of dollars of other people's money. Even robbing the mails is respectable.

All this lack of concern about crime must surely be part of the "cultural tradition." Charleston is too busy doing nothing gracefully to bother about such things. Moral indignation is as prevalent as snow blindness.

But there is indignation of another sort. It may safely be said that no place on earth is capable of such concerted and violent imagination as Charleston. The town grows apoplectic with indignation when criticized in any way. The old city is allergic to criticism, no matter how honest or indisputable. It is regrettable but manifestly true that Charleston hates criticism far more than crime.

Not Government—Just The Circus

Charlestonians are also aroused from the fine art of inertia when there is an election. Then it takes the Sumter Guards and the fire hoses to calm them down again. Charlestonians bring more zest to their politics than they do to anything else.

The only time there is a quickening in the air is when an election is about to take place. Men live on politics then, and women are caught up in their enthusiasm. An election means a battle, open or hidden. And these people love it. They wouldn't have their politics cleaned up for anything in the world. That would rob them of their one great pleasure. An honest election would be a joyless thing.

So Charleston laughs and boasts about her crooked politics, her slick politicians, her famous battles at the polls. Politics is king in Charleston.

Local political medicine men always put on a good show. They know what is expected of them. The whole thing is as traditional as Punch and Judy, and the last act of the drama is always the frenzied and outraged demand for a recount.

An index of the intelligence and the temperament of too many Charlestonians is the abysmal stuff they applaud at the hustings. It is remarkable that occasionally a good man is elected to some position of trust or prominence. What a man can swallow politically is a fair test of his so-called ideals and standards. A Charlestonian of those other days or of the mythical Charleston would gag on such political claptrap as befouls the balmy air of the city in these times.

No platform or plan is ever put before the voters, but a long-drawn-out dog fight is waged, in which each candidate tries to outdo the rest in crude and extremely stupid backwoods invective. Cultured people would not listen to such stuff and certainly not so avidly and with such apparent pleasure. People of mettle and great standards would chase the inept brayers of these asininities from Charleston's rostrums.

In South Carolina there is performed a unique campaign circus. All candidates for the various political jobs must tour the State together and hold joint meetings at which all must put on their act. This makes for political cataclysms that leave the entertainers limp and the voters hoarse and feverish.

Charleston squirms with expectancy before the local meetings and turns out en masse, armed with fierce prejudices and fervent affiliations. Nothing matters so much as an election, and may the best showman win.

Senator Cotton Ed Smith recently made the marshes of the Ashley River resound with the cries of White Supremacy* and made his opponents seem about

---

*Sen. Ellison "Cotton Ed" Smith (1864–1944), a Democratic US senator (1909–1944) from Lynchburg known for his fierce racist and segregationist views.

as big as so many hominy grits. As long as Cotton Ed travels with the circus, the less gifted and less sincere might as well save their entrance fee. Charleston voted for him two to one, and was stirred by the old political faith he preaches with a rebel yell. If only all showmen were as good as Cotton Ed, Charleston's future and South Carolina's would frighten those of us who really love the city and the State.

Buzzard Town

Incidentally, Charleston is often said by people from the upper part of the State (who love Charleston less than they should) that the old city isn't even in South Carolina. Charleston to them is an alien domain, and currently some of these folk, who care no more for old names and colonial airs than they do for tobacco blight or trouble at the textile mills, are saying that they would like a buffer state between them and Charleston.

These people, who seldom have an ancestor to their name, used to call Charleston "Buzzard Town," because until quite recently the city dump stretched right out in the city, and the buzzards were as much a part of the "old world charm" as the narrow streets, tiled roofs, and feathery iron grillwork.

In spite of the antagonism of Up Country and Low Country, Charleston *is* in South Carolina, and her people are more like those of less pretentious sections than either realize. Ten houses don't make Charleston, nor do twenty people. And all the rest of Charleston has a common denominator with the rest of South Carolina.

Charleston suffers more from South Carolina's unique outlawing of divorce than the rest of the State, because Charleston is a seaport town and is casual about many things which set the camp-meeting section in a ferment. Charleston lawyers long for divorce even more than many a pair of ill-matched mates, but nothing can be done about it. Alimony, at least, isn't among the financial worries of Charlestonians.

It's poorness that shapes these people's lives, makes the pattern of their existence, is both the cause and effect of what they are—poorness, plus a loss of perspective, plus the belief that all things Charlestonian are good and great just because one says they are.

Obviously, this place and its people have no bond or relationship with the old Charleston or with the legendary Charleston. At the beginning of this century, Henry James said that Charleston had an "insidious charm," that she played "a subtle trick on the visitor, but only for one day and night." After that the "feeling of tenderness for the place is gone and the truth all too plain."

The truth is plainer than ever, now. The illusion is fading fast, and the make-believe is all too obvious. Part of the "subtle trick" Charleston plays are her seductive words: Low Country, Mistress So-and-So, Do As You Choose Alley, Strawberry Lane, and countless other charming names that are, after all, just words. Just words, too, are "blue blood," "aristocrat," "illustrious family," and all the rest. Those are dead words, belonging to dead people. Even many Charlestonians themselves are sick of *that* pretense.

The Charleston answer to criticism is often a pointing out of the things that are far from right with many a Northern and Western city or town. What Charlestonians forget is that those places have foisted no fabulous pretense on the rest of us. They are not exhibitionists and narcissists. They do not seduce us with words.

It is a fact which I for one sadly regret, but if you go looking for the Charleston that is so lovely, so glamourous in her age, in her way of living, you will look in vain. There is no such place. Charleston is a myth.

Nature's Mirror, Magnolia-on-the-Ashley, Charleston, S.C.
Library of Congress

MAY SARTON (1941)

"Charleston Plantations"

May Sarton, "Charleston Plantations" from *The Atlantic Monthly* (April 1941): 487. Reprinted by permission of Russell & Volkening as agents for the May Sarton Estate.

May Sarton (1912–1995), poet, novelist, and memoirist, was born in Belgium. She was the daughter of George Sarton, noted chemist and historian of science, and Mabel Elwes Sarton, an English artist and designer. The Sartons arrived in the United States in 1916 fleeing Belgium and the advancing Germans. They settled in Cambridge, Massachusetts, where May's father joined the faculty of Harvard. May attended the "progressive" Shady Hill School in Cambridge before she spent a year at the Institut Belge de Culture Francaise near Brussels. She graduated from Cambridge High and Latin in 1929. By the age of seventeen, Sarton had published her first poems in *Poetry* magazine. She turned down an acceptance to Vassar College to serve as an apprentice for the Civic Repertory Theater, headed by actress Eva LaGallienne. Afterward she founded her own theater company, which failed in the Depression. She felt that this failure helped steer her toward a literary career.

Her first volume of poetry, *Encounter in April* (1937), and first novel, *The Single Hound* (1938), were just the beginning of Sarton's works, which resulted in over fifty books of poetry, fiction, journals and memoirs, essays, children's books, a play, and screenplays. She is best known for her personal journals, including *Journal of a Solitude* (1973), which became a key text in academic women's studies and influenced generations of feminists. In her journals, Sarton sometimes examined her relationships with women. *Mrs. Stevens Hears The Mermaids Singing* (1965), considered her "coming out novel," attracted feminists and gay scholars. In 1974 the book was reissued and brought her renewed recognition, and the 1980s were years of great acclaim, with standing-room only crowds at poetry readings and an increased readership. However, during her lifetime Sarton rued the fact that for most of her writing life, the major critics and the literary establishment had ignored or dismissed her work. Today more than forty of Sarton's books are still in print, and *Journal of a Solitude* has not gone out of print since it was first published in 1973.

Sarton, having published only a first book of poetry, was largely an unknown when, between 1939 and 1940, she undertook a round of poetry readings on a lecture tour of colleges throughout the United States to promote poetry as "the spiritual force of the nation". Tooling the country alone in her new Mercury convertible, she was paid twenty-five dollars for an appearance. In Charleston in the winter of 1940, she wrote in a letter, "I want to live in Charleston—one of the great feminine cities—Venice, Paris. It is so elegant and casual and warm and aristocratic and one could live there so *easily*! It is really lovely, full of light, cool sea air, Utrillo streets, secret gardens, high balconies, and everywhere the darkies laughing and making a warm current under the life of the city. New Orleans is a small very crowded claustrophobic 'Left Bank' but Charleston is just itself."

In her journal, she more fully wrote: "Charleston is a wonderful romantic city, a woman like Venice or Paris, a city that seems to gather up in itself some nostalgia in everyman for a hidden secret part of himself. It is a compound of nostalgias—of the West Indies, the soft voices of the darkies and their laughing birdlike screams, and their bright dresses (a certain pink and a certain blue-green, and purple), mysterious courts and gardens just glimpsed behind iron grilles and high houses with balconies and curved flights of stairs leading to the doors. Some of the houses are painted pink and have *pignons*. They look Dutch. Some of the streets are bare, sad and formal like an Utrillo. Some are elegant, patrician, and almost English. Charleston reminds one of many pasts and of other places and yet is entirely and always itself (as a beautiful woman evokes legends, Helen, Deirdre—and yet is unique and irreplaceable). And when you approach the city it's like entering a legend, for you enter by jungle-swamps, "the low country with long gray mosses hanging from the trees and vivid evil green Virginia creeper and grapevines—something primeval and very soft—."

Sarton published a single poem, "Charleston Plantations," in which she expresses the deeper complexities of the region.

SOURCES

Peters, Margot. *May Sarton: A Biography*. New York: Alfred A. Knopf, 1997.
Sarton, May. *Among the Usual Days: A Portrait*. W. W. Norton & Company, 1993.
Sarton, May, and Susan Sherman. *Sammlung*. New York: W. W. Norton & Company, 1997.

"Charleston Plantations"

You cannot see them from the road: go far and deep,
Down the long avenues where mosses cover up the leaves,
Across the empty terraced lawns neglected and asleep,
To the still place where no dog barks and no dove grieves,
And a black mirror gives you back your face too white
In pools dyed jet by cypress roots: go deep and far,
Deep into time, far into crumbling spaces and half-light
To where they stand, our Egypt and our Nineveh.
Deep in a deathly stillness stand the planters' houses.

The garlands and the little foxes' faces carved
Upon the mantels look on empty walls and water-stains
And the stairs tremble though so elegantly curved
(Outside are waiting the bright creeping vines),
And as your foot falls in the silences, you guess
Decay has been arrested for a moment in the wall,
But the gray plumes upon the trees in deathly loveliness
Will stir when you have passed, and somewhere a stone fall.
Deep in a deathly stillness stand the planters' houses.

There is no rice now and the world that sprang from it
Like an azalea, brilliant from the swamps, has crumbled.
A single century, it is embalmed as Egypt.
A single century, and all that elegance was humbled—
While we who fired that world and watched it burn
Come every spring to whisper near the tomb,
To stare, a little shaken, where the mosses mourn
And the azaleas and magnolias have not ceased to bloom.
Deep in a deathly stillness stand the planters' houses.
© May Sarton Estate

Glenway Wescott, c. 1950s.
Courtesy of Jerry Rosco, Glenway Wescott Estate

Glenway Wescott (1942 and 1946)

"With Maugham at Yemassee"

Glenway Wescott, "With Maugham at Yemassee" from *Continual Lessons: The Journals of Glenway Wescott 1937–1955,* eds. Robert Phelps and Jerry Rosco (New York: Farrar Straus & Giroux), 1991. Reprint permission has been granted by Wescott's literary executor, Jerry Rosco.

Glenway Wescott (1901–1987), poet, novelist, and essayist, was born in Kewaskum, Wisconsin. He experienced conflict with his father, which led to his living with various relatives and wandering as a youth. After dropping out of the University of Chicago, he lived in New Mexico and published his first book of poems, *The Bitterns* (1920). He then went to Germany, where he wrote much of his first novel, *The Apple of the Eye* (1924), and afterward moved to France. As one of the last of the major expatriate American writers living in France in the 1920s and 1930s, Wescott mixed with Gertrude Stein and other famous members of the expatriate community. Openly gay, his relationship with Monroe Wheeler (1899–1988), whom he met at the University of Chicago in 1919, lasted until Wescott's death. Wheeler had a long and active career with the Museum of Modern Art.

Wescott achieved literary acclaim at the age of twenty-six with the publication of his second novel, *The Grandmothers,* the saga of a pioneer family transplanted from New York State to Wisconsin in 1846. It was the winner of the prestigious Harper Prize for 1927, and became a best-seller. He next published *Good-Bye, Wisconsin* (1928), a collection of stories. Despite that literary farewell, he returned to his native state in *The Babe's Bed* (1930), which revealed his ambivalent attitude toward Wisconsin and his native country. Wescott lived in France for eight years, returning to New York in 1934.

In 1940 he published *The Pilgrim Hawk.* Some critics considered it his best work. His last novel, *Apartment in Athens* (1945), was the story of an Athenian family during the German occupation. As a friend of Katherine Anne Porter, Somerset Maugham, and Thornton Wilder, Wescott wrote about them in *Images of Truth: Remembrances and Criticism* (1962). He published another book of poems, essays and reviews, and stories. He was said to be one of the finest stylists of his generation. After his death, two volumes of his journals were published, *Continual Lessons* (1991) and *A Heaven of Words: Last Journals* (2013), as was *A Visit to Priapus and Other Stories* (2013).

Somerset Maugham (1874–1965), British playwright, novelist and short story writer, was one of the most popular and commercially successful authors of the twentieth century. He qualified as a doctor in 1897 but published his first novel, *Liza of Lambeth,* the same year. His play *Lady Frederick* (1907) was his first theatrical success, and his largely autobiographical novel *Of Human Bondage* (1915) became a best seller. It was followed by other highly praised works *The Moon and Sixpence* (1919), *Cakes and Ale* (1930), and *The Razor's Edge* (1945). He wrote more than thirty plays. When the First World War broke out, Maugham served in France as a volunteer member of the British Red Cross's Literary Ambulance Drivers, a group of some twenty-four well-known writers, including Americans John Dos Passos, E. E. Cummings, and Ernest Hemingway. During this time, he met Frederick Gerald Haxton, a young San Franciscan, who became his companion and lover until Haxton's death in 1944. Regardless, Maugham had a child, Liza, by his mistress, Syrie Wellcome, whose husband sued for divorce over the affair. They married in 1917. Syrie Maugham became a noted interior decorator in the 1920s. She divorced Maugham in 1929, finding his relationship and travels with Haxton difficult.

From 1916 Maugham had been recruited into the British Secret Intelligence Service, for which he worked in Switzerland and Russia before the October Revolution of 1917. During and after the war, he travelled in India and Southeast Asia, experiences reflected in his later short stories and novels. In 1926 he bought the Villa La Mauresque at Cap Ferrat on the French Riviera. By 1940 the collapse of France and its occupation by the German Third Reich forced Maugham to leave. He became a refugee, albeit one of the wealthiest and most famous writers in the English-speaking world. After the attack on Pearl Harbor in 1941, there was no need for Maugham's British intelligence work (although there was talk that he had an assignment while he was in the United States). Cut off from his Villa and seeking a place to work on his novel *The Razor's Edge,* he was rescued by his American publisher, Nelson Doubleday (1889–1949) of Long Island, who from 1934 owned Bonny Hall Plantation near Yemassee, South Carolina as a winter retreat. Doubleday and his family wintered in the mansion house while on his acreage some miles away, he built a three bedroom, three bath clapboard cottage, known as Parker's Ferry, for Maugham. Doubleday built two addition cottages, one a writer's studio and the other for three black tenant servants the publisher provided Maugham, a cook (Nora), a maid (Mary), and a gardener

(Sunday), whose nephew (Religious) did odd jobs. Situated on the Combahee River between Charleston and Beaufort, Maugham spent the next four years at Parker's Ferry but for trips and summers on Martha's Vineyard. He wrote, "I face a great marsh, 1000 acres of it, and on the side I have the river Combahee; and behind a great row of magnificent pines. It is a lovely spot, but it is far from everywhere." Haxton, soon bored with the isolation, left for a job with the Office of Strategic Services in Washington. He died in Washington while Maugham was living at Parker's Ferry.

In 1942 Glenway Wescott spent three weeks with Maugham at Yemassee. Twenty-five years younger than Maugham, he was one of Maugham's closest American friends but a world apart in how they lived as gay men. As Wescott pointed out, Maugham, who carefully avoided homosexual themes and gay characters in his works, was from a British generation that lived in mortal terror of the Oscar Wilde trial, which had taken place when Maugham was twenty-one years old. Wescott later recalled his first visit to Yemassee, writing, "Willie was a born teacher. I went down there for three weeks and he taught me everything he knew about writing. We were there all alone, and we'd walk along the swamps and amid the snakes, and then we'd go on to dinner. The whole of the Doubleday staff was there, and Nelson would do anything for him. His wife (Ellen Doubleday) adored Willie. He was their great money maker."

At Parker's Ferry Maugham worked on *The Razor's Edge* (1944), which would prove a great success, particularly to a seventy-year-old author. Ellen Doubleday recorded his routine: "An early morning cup of Nescafé, made by himself, breakfast at eight in his own room where he remained reading 'serious books' until 10 A.M., at which time he went to his writing room and was not seen again until exactly five minutes to one, when gimlets were served, followed by luncheon. Then a nap, the mail, a ride or a walk, and tea. At five he would appear at our house, ready for a game of bridge or gin rummy. At six, we had a drink and when the dinner gong sounded at seven, he usually went home for dinner. To bed around ten, when he usually put himself to sleep with thrillers. There were occasional social, literary, and shopping jaunts to Charleston where he was much admired and sought after. Sometimes, not often, we went to a neighboring plantation. One such evening our host's opening gambit was 'Well, sir, have you found any pretty girls in green hats to write about in the Low Country?' Mr. M. winked at me deliberately, put on his monocle, and told his host he was too busy working to have an opportunity of meeting pretty girls." He taught the cook, Nora, how to prepare onion soup and *truite au bleu* and *duck à l'orang* and almond *soufflé*, making it a point of good housekeeping that the servants eat as well as he did, thereby expanding their horizons.

Maugham spent his seventieth birthday at Yemassee and wrote, "My own birthday passed without ceremony. I worked as usual in the morning and went for a walk in the solitary woods behind my house. I have never been able to discover what it is that gives these woods their mysterious attractiveness. They are like no woods I have ever known. Their silence seems more intense than any other silence. The live oaks with their massive foliage are festooned with the grey of the Spanish moss as if with a ragged shroud, the gum trees at this season are bare of leaf and the clustered berries of the wild China tree are dried and yellow; here and there tall pines, their rich green flaming, tower over the lower trees. There is a strangeness about the bedraggled, abandoned woods, and though you walk alone you do not feel alone, for you have a feeling that unseen beings, neither human nor inhuman, flutter about you. A shadowy something seems to slink from behind a tree trunk and watch you silently as you pass. There is a sense of suspense as though all about you there were a lying in wait for something to come."

Wescott returned to visit Maugham for two weeks in January 1946. Monroe arrived, and remained a few days. Wescott visited again for two weeks in February 1946, during which he made a trip to Charleston for a radio broadcast to publicize his novel, *Apartment in Athens*.

The following account of Wescott's visits to Yemassee were excerpted from his journal, *Continual Lessons*.

SOURCES

Doubleday, Ellen. "Mr. Maugham in America." In *W. Somerset Maugham: An Appreciation with Biographical Sketches and a Bibliography*. Garden City, N.Y.: Doubleday & Co., 1965: 9–10.

Maugham, Somerset. *Partial View*. London: Heinemann, 1954.

McDowell, Edwin. "Glenway Wescott, 85, Novelist and Essayist." *New York Times*, Feb. 24, 1987.

Meyers, Jeffrey. *Somerset Maugham: A Life*. New York: Alfred A. Knopf, 2004.

"Maugham, Somerset (1874–1965)." Biography. National Portrait Gallery, London.

Phelps, Robert, and Jerry Rosco, eds. *Glenway Wescott Personally: A Biography*. Madison: University of Wisconsin Press, 2010.

"With Maugham at Yemassee"

1942

February, 1942—Parker's Ferry, Yemassee, South Carolina

Last night in the train a soldier, a farmboy from Bangor, asked me to play rummy, not gin rummy and not for money, but to keep him awake until we reached Richmond because he wanted to mail a last postcard to his wife. They had spent every night together for the last ten months, he informed me. At every important station he stepped out and found someone on the platform willing to mail another postcard to her, so that she could follow his trip. A very common boy with a big behind and bandy legs, pasty-faced but with a sweet smile.

South Carolina's subtle prettiness as usual: the soft stripes of dawn in the pines; glimmering water on the poor ground; leek-shaped tree trunks standing in the water.

William [Maugham] is in lovely temper. Evidently he has really suffered from loneliness this winter, and just now, in N.Y., he found some calamity and quarrel. So he is glad of my company, I gather.

This is Monroe's birthday, which is for me a great holiday, holy day. For, as I understand my story, had he not been born, and joined his heart and strength to mine, I had been born only once, and to little purpose.

Tonight, we've been warned, all our camellias will be frosted. Nelson Sr. and Nelson Jr. picked 879 blossoms this afternoon, and brought us a lot on trays, looking like an eighteenth-century rustic wedding.

Upon our ride yesterday, half remembering a shortcut through an adjoining estate, we took advice of four black children whom we found cracking nuts on a log, and it was bad advice and we got lost. It was lightly wooded upland, burned here and there, with more moss than foliage; and the various tracks we followed petered out in thicket. Then we heard the ringing sound of an ax, and sought that out. It was an immense youth, of a certain beauty, very black, cutting firewood; and he had a little red bullock and a poor old car with which to bring his load back. He began to talk as soon as we came in sight, and, when we asked him the way, began an eager, almost frantic harangue. He had a resoundingly loud voice, he stammered and never paused, sing-song, as a child might recite verses by rote, with the same great gesture of general direction at the end of each stanza. Not one word was comprehensible; doubtless it was that African language called Gullah, but it was also, I thought, insanity. He bared his beautifully white teeth in a rapturous smile, and his eyes were shining, and his ax was as bright as silver. It was a little like listening to a turkey gobbler; I could scarcely keep a straight face, and yet a little fear also crossed my mind, and William's too (he told me afterward). As he would not cease his harangue we interrupted him with our thanks, and turned our horses and rode away; and then he shouted after us his only comprehensible word: "Goodbye!"

Today after tea we took our longest ride, all the way to Clay Hall.* It is the only house in the vicinity that I should be attracted to live not the genuine

---

* Clay Hall, a 2,200-acre plantation in Yemassee then owned by Percy Kierstede Hudson, a member of the New York Stock Exchange.

colonial but of the mere twenties; a wide stone pavilion with large windows, very low on the ground under the shawled live oaks. Its situation is the best, too: very near the sea as the crow flies, only the river is backed up all around it, coiled like a serpent in a nest of banks and islets. When one has been riding some miles through the swamp, where everything is a little broken or rotten, posting through mud and water, ducking one's head down under the loose branches, unable to see where one is headed—and then comes out there on the causeway, in the wonderful flatness and openness, pale blue and silver and grass-gold, it is like being ten years old. I like the swamps, too, but the only sense they make is in yielding to the melancholy.

It is the chilly glassy twilight. William is still out somewhere playing bridge with publishers and such. I walked by myself all by my lonesome on the levee; the river seeming to have no life except a great quivering dimple here and there, shining with reflected dead grasses. I met one bird, minute and green. This kind of place keeps putting me in mind of bad fevers; because of the shapes of so many things that are unseen, because in the vast quiet even the flutter of the timidest bird seems startling, loud and peremptory.

At lunch while good cumbersome black Mary passed the shad roe, then the cucumber salad, I could see by William's face that he had something confidential to tell.

"Last night in a dream—you may scarcely believe it, but it is true—I dreamed that I went down on Shelley.* I remember saying to myself that I mustn't try to bugger him; he wouldn't have liked that."

It gave me just a little tremor to hear this, wondering what lay in his subconsciousness, what object of his appetite the great inappropriate name masked. Not indeed likening myself to Shelley; only finding myself less unlike him than anyone else here on the Combahee.

It is notable that in fact, though frequently complimenting me upon my youthfulness, etc., he has never felt, at least never let me feel, the least strain in this way. His discretion never fails; his good manners never fail except in anger.

Cold, but still shining bright. The white crane swoops *adagio* over the dark blue canals and the tawny reeds. Every morning while I breakfast I read a canto of the *Purgatorio* aloud to myself, in Italian; that is, my notion of Italian: my morning prayers!

---

* Percy Bysshe Shelley (1792–1822).

From a letter to Barbara Wescott:

March 9

Just this morning, Tuesday, our maid heard a rumor across the rice marsh that Mrs. Doubleday's butler at the big house had heard upon the telephone that Mr. Maugham's brother had had a baby. Which rumor Mr. Maugham relayed to my fireside where, with my breakfast, as it happened.

As for Yemassee, S.C., I have never been in so solitary a place. Even the colored people live miles away. Nothing is in sight. The landscape around us is beautiful, a kind of nullity; blessed be nothing, but beautiful and especially immense. Before my window lies one immense fallow rice marsh; it looks like a white, headless wheat field inlaid with large dark sapphires, a thousand acres without a tree. Yesterday afternoon we went for a walk around it, for miles upon a sinuous narrow hummock made by slave labor. Not knowing how far it was, we kept on until we reached Bonny Hall (Doubleday's), eight miles in all. Mr. Doubleday was not pleased, for there was a great slapping wind and it might have been bad for his famous author's heart. But greatness led the way, and I could not tell him that he was too old for it, nor could I pretend that I felt feeble. Our hands and ankles are all injured by the cat briar. Mrs. Doubleday asked us if we had met the old alligator. Happily, we had not.

March 13

I had to spend the better part of two days drafting a broadcast about books for the soldiers and sailors. William was shocked; he couldn't see how it could have taken me more than half an hour. And yet, when I confess that I have not the ordinary talent of writers, everyone says it is a false morbid manner of speaking.

Yesterday we went riding for two hours, a long swampy way on a bank amid a kind of sacred grove of thin gray trees growing in water; then over a plain the name of which is Big State, with savage Negro dwellings scattered on it, solemn Negroes and awful small red cattle.

After dinner we went up to Bonny Hall to hear singing. This was a great barony (hence, as a matter of etymology, bonny); Sherman burned the old mansion, but the live oaks were not harmed. They are gigantic and in perfect health, with their peculiar, rather horizontal boughs, almost as thick halfway out as where they come from the trunk, so that one wonders why the weight has not dismembered them; an open kind of tree, visible all the way through even in full foliage, as pale as olive, veiled with the silvery moss. There is a semicircular grove at the back of the house, with large hedges and extravagant camellias in

between. We sat out there on a terrace, and the vast cloudy branches, crowned
here and there with some stars, made a background for the singers. It was illu-
minated by a fire on a tall cement block, as if it were a pagan altar; it was almost
too flaming, so that it suggested a very serious sacrifice. There was fire enough
for it to be human sacrifice.

It was a choir of four baritones, two basses, and two altos, led by one named
Isaiah. Very soft and sensitive together, well-rehearsed, I should think; with almost that refined musicality which was the fashion in Vienna and bad for Bach,
I used to think. I have never heard more of velvety voices; somehow virginal;
perhaps they have never sung as loud as they could. One of the altos was the
finest, an androgynous note, verging upon countertenor; and she was also the
cleverest musically, in a melancholy play with the rhythm, and certain harmonies
not in our mode at all.

They began with "Good evening, Mr. Doubleday, how do you do. Good evening, Mrs. Doubleday. Good evening, all the guest-es, how do you do." Then for
an hour and a half, spirituals and local variants upon Moody and Sankey hymns:
"A home beyond the city, Where the sun don' go down" and "Nobody knows
the trouble I've seen, Nobody knows but Mr. Doubleday," and "The devil is a
man You cain't under-stan." Now and then they began "How dry I am," no less
piously and sorrowfully than the rest. Whereupon the houseman, one named
Ephraim, brought a trayful of gin and grape juice. It amused me that, even with
the tumblers in their hands, they went right on with the sorrow of the song to
the last verse, for art's sake.

The Negroes here have a quiet and melancholy which is a surprise to me;
none of the good spirits and bird chatter and jolly fidgets which we know in the
North. I have no idea whether that is voodoo, or malaria, or their memory of
injustices.

March 14
This is a fine place to work, except that the days are too short. William gets
all his work done in the morning, and after lunch, he has his nap before I can say
knife. And so far, I have been too sleepy to work at night; the lovely weather for
one thing, I suppose. I arrived in an exhaustion, and no fooling. A poor blown
shadow of myself. As my body reminds me of a kind of reddened canned mush-
room, I have wanted to take sunbaths, but I have renounced them conscientiously.

March 17
Now it is turning to summer heat fast, interspersed with rough sweet rains.
There is fantastic fragrance of tea olive and daphne (which is like lemon peel and

honey) around the houses. Before dinner last night we got the black Isaiah to take us upon the canals in a paddleboat. The perfectly still water is all spotted with last year's lily pads, in a fine variety of rotten colors. Now and then a flock of ducks would whir up ahead of us, splashing the water white; and there were coot and bitterns and one solemnly flying great heron, Herodias. Isaiah says the alligators are still in their winter sleep. We sat close, side by side, in the prow of the narrow damp old craft, with only the faint sound of the paddling behind us, as in a gondola, sliding as if there were a magnet drawing us along. I have been reading A. Huxley's biography of Father Joseph, *L'Eminence grise:** a kind of mysticism beautifully written and rather thrilling but, I think, untrue and even deleterious. So as we slid amid the pale reeds we discussed that.

Later we had a gala meal of terrapin at the big house, more interesting than appetizing, to my taste; and then we played tandem gin rummy, four on each side. The long Doubleday *séjours* here are not really in the way of pleasure-residence but rather a part of his publishing technique. The sub-publishers and their little wives keep coming and going; a full house of them all the time. They are a bit deadly though not dislikable. Mrs. Doubleday is sweet.

Parker's Ferry
March 18

My sitting room adjoins William's bedroom, and after breakfast I can hear him in a strong voice saying some prayer or reciting something; but as he is a shy man and in a way forbidding, I doubtless shall never discover what it is.

1946

Parker's Ferry, Yemassee, South Carolina
January 13

It is astonishing how Monroe has bewitched William [Maugham]. He couldn't be fonder of me, but he knows what I am going to say—and his force of mind is such that I am inclined to say just that, nothing new—he has heard my stories. Whereas Monroe has fascinated him. He mentions him every other minute: he is keeping a plum pudding for the night he will arrive, there is a new version of gin rummy which he will like better than the old, etc.

There is a certain tyranny about all this. He never forgets for an instant that this is the culmination and windup of his American life, and we are to play our great parts to the end. I am very melancholy and pleasantly false, playing my

---

*Aldous Huxley's *Grey Eminence* (1941) a biography of François Leclerc du Tremblay (1577–1638), French advisor to Cardinal de Richelieu.

part. Extremely sensible of the fact that I came out of sense of duty, pseudo-filial.

January 15

For a windup of Wm.'s career Doubleday wants to publish a great omnibus containing *The Painted Veil*, *Christmas Holiday*, *The Summing Up*, two plays, a lot of stories, and the El Greco study.* And now Wm. has asked me to write the prefatory essay, and I have accepted. A tough assignment and fun.

The dreary cold water has ceased to douche down upon us, but instead we have a wind and finger-stiffening, scrotum-squeezing cold. What a fraud, these climatey parts of the world! There is no fireplace in my study, so I stay in the sitting room, sweet with pitch pine, with Gerald Kelly R.A.'s bad portrait of William† in his youth and beauty in a velvet smoking jacket gaping at me.

January 16

This is Alan's thirty-sixth birthday.‡ Wm. was grief-stricken at the loss of his looks; nevertheless all is settled for his companioning and secretaryship from now on to the end: the Villa Mauresque in May, to order the burned garden re-planted, the bombed windowpanes replaced, the pillaged cellar restocked, etc.; then England for the summer, India in the autumn.

Alan is such a funny creature: a lovely cockney cameo face filled out now so that it is more than a bit woodchucky. Kindness personified; very capable; dapper through and through; antique-loving.

There is something nightmarish for me in the repetition of my coming back here; my terrible memory brings back every word, every torn dead shrub, every tethered pig or cow, every whiff of marsh fragrance, and every mouthful of rich food from the other years. For William there is no repetition because his only reality is out there at his desk: the four or five books he has written the while.

January 17

One of the odd things about being here is that I am drinking too much. I want my usual cocktail before dinner, but then every night William brings out one of his bottles of wine, in the selection of which he has taken a good deal of

---

* *The Maugham Reader*, published in 1950. Wescott's essay reappeared as "Somerset Maugham and Posterity" in his *Images of Truth* (1962).

† Maugham's friend, artist Gerald Kelly, painted him as many as sixty times.

‡ Alan Searle, who Maugham had known since 1928, had become his new secretary-companion and would remain so until Maugham's death.

trouble, and bullies us into drinking every drop of it; and it is too much. It is partly not wanting to waste anything and partly an old-fashioned merrie-old-England anti-puritanical principle; and so far I haven't rebelled. But the result is that, while he and Alan play cards after dinner, I sit dozing by the fire with a newspaper or trashy book like some old colonel. I am not even competent to write my letters; and then I go to bed and fail to sleep or sleep badly.

The very cold night cleared away the clouds, and by evening the sunshine had warmed us up a little; so we went for a long walk. There was an incomparable sunset, and as it happened we saw it through the Negroes' cemetery, the voodoo cemetery, which is a grove of the oldest, most twisted, moss-wound oaks: lumpy molten gold, and a stream of pale bright green running away to the south, and a bank of pale bright purple which finally caught fire, Then suddenly it died away, leaving smoke, soot, silt.

Then the full moon rose, just between the swamp and the marsh, and I went down on the levee alone to watch it. The tide was rushing out with a noise, and it shook the golden reflection as if it were a flag whipping in a wind. All around me there were water birds ill at ease, and I heard what William says may have been turtles, growling or barking.

January 19

Alan asked the cook Nora if she enjoyed reading. Oh, yessir, she answered, but I only like exciting books, so I only read detective stories and the Bible. William was charmed by this; it is so close to his own habit and principle.

Alan is a strange man, sweet cockney, so comical to my ear, and indeed to look at—but with wonderful awful tales of his many years work of penology, and (I think) as right as rain for William.

I made rarebit last night—good enough, except that the cheese wasn't ripe. William says that after his seventy-fifth birthday he is going to eat and drink everything he likes, as much as he pleases! and take Nembutal every night. So to speak, to hell with it!

Gossip: When Edward James* was a little boy he happened to arouse the amorousness of Sir William Harcourt, the statesman. He complained to his mother, and she made a hue and cry, and in consequence Sir William committed suicide. (By drowning in the bathtub, if I remember rightly.) Therefore I think we should not be astonished at any of Edward's little-boy naughtinesses now.

---

*Edward James (1907–1984), rich and eccentric British poet known for his patronage of Surrealism.

Parker's Ferry
Yemassee, South Carolina
February 5

Another day—a sunbath upon the fragrant rye grass; the proofs of Wm.'s little historical novel,* which has all sorts of merit but (I'm afraid)—no glory; a walk across the spongy heath, burned over, so that it is like lost charcoal rubbed into gold; a dinner party at Bonny Hall, characterized by amiability, not by wit.

February 9

Our weather is fine, but not dependable and not absolutely warm. It beams, it warbles in every bush, drawing me outdoors; and then breathes icy down the back of my neck. I certainly have been overeating and perhaps have put on a few pounds; but I am not brown. We don't live right; elderly. We mix our nature with so many reminiscences of cities, and our human nature with shoptalk of literature and (in my case) bad conscience about literature. Anyway I have been absurd all week—Byronic, Manfredish, in a vain gloom with a senseless secret —though amiably reasoning and yarning like any Somerset Maugham character the while.

Poor William: his malaria got him down. Perhaps, too, as he is correcting the proofs of *Then and Now,* he finds it dull, with dwindled power. One aspect of his having Alan is not a success from his point of view—spoiled! You'd think he was fifty-two instead of seventy-two. He lost his temper today, getting after Sunday, the chauffeur, like an old red colonel.

February 10

I must begin to plan my return home, when and upon what pretext. I haven't been clever about it with William and I am weak about it, in the oddest way. He is so touching, as he never has been before. I really am his son, part of his family; all the more so now that Alan has come, the companion of the rest of his life.

At sunset, there was a great fire on our marsh, frightening at first—Wm. and I resolved to sleep with our arms around our manuscripts. Half a mile of tall flames, torn up by the wind; fading down, then arising again. I went down alone between the canals, close to it; but when I could hear it panting, its perhaps morbid fascination turned to ordinary fear, which brought me home. It has put itself out now.

---

* *Then and Now* (1946).

106 Tradd St., Col. John Stuart House, Charleston,
Charleston County, South Carolina, c. 1936 or 1937.
Frances Benjamin Johnston, photographer. Library of Congress.

VASHTI MAXWELL GRAYSON (1945)

"Charleston"

Vashti Maxwell Grayson, "Charleston" from *Phylon* 6:1 (1st Qtr., 1945): 64–69.

Vashti Maxwell Grayson (1904–1958), born in Baltimore, was a member of Baltimore's African-American elite. She was the daughter of Professor Joshua E. Maxwell, a teacher in Baltimore schools. She grew up in Morgan Park on the grounds of historically black Morgan State College, where faculty and other residents, including W. E. B. Du Bois, Eubie Blake, and Cab Calloway, lived in architect-designed bungalows, cottages, and international style modern ranch houses. Grayson received a B.A. from Brown University and an M.A. from Columbia University, and was an honor student at both. She completed postgraduate work in Spanish at the University of Puerto Rico, and in Madrid. She taught romance languages at Morgan State in Baltimore and Spanish in Washington schools, and in 1922, was a founder and charter member of the graduate Baltimore Alumnae Chapter of Delta Sigma Theta. She was working on her doctorate in foreign languages when in 1937 she married Dr. William Henry Grayson Jr. (1906–1976), from a leading black Charleston family.

W. H. Grayson was a 1924 graduate of Charleston's Avery Institute, which after its founding in 1865 had become a prestigious school for the African American community that trained blacks for professional careers and leadership roles until its closing in 1954. He afterward received a B.A. from Fisk University, an M.A. from the University of Michigan and Teachers College at Columbia University, and his Ph.D. from Teachers College, Columbia University. At the time of their marriage, he was principal of Simonton School, the first public school for blacks in Charleston (demolished in 1970). Dr. Grayson became the highly respected principal of Burke Industrial School (J. E. Burke High School) from 1939 to 1945. A skillful administrator, he laid the groundwork for a generation of institutional development for blacks by raising the standard of education at Burke, strengthening the industrial and trade curriculum. He also fought for a more academic curriculum, adding liberal arts and college preparation to the course load to prepare black students for a higher education than vocational training, and prepared students for community involvement. He appointed well-educated black teachers, many of them Avery graduates. On leaving Burke, Grayson was superintendent of Charleston's black elementary schools. He also worked for the American Missionary Society, founders of Avery Institute, in race relations. The Graysons lived at 89 Columbus Street, his family home.

Vashti Grayson published a few poems in *Phylon*, a quarterly journal of race and culture associated with Clark Atlanta University, founded in 1940 by W. E. B. Du Bois. The couple later lived in Nashville, where Vashti was on the research staff of the Social Science Institute at Fisk University, and afterward in New York, where W. H. Grayson was a professor at Brooklyn College and New York University. For the last two years of her life, Vashti Grayson was confined to hospitals in New York and Bethesda with skin cancer, from which she died at the age of 54.

Published in 1945, her poem "Charleston" reveals the city from her perspective.

SOURCES

Baker, R. Scott. *Paradoxes of Desegregation: African American Struggles for Educational Equity in Charleston, South Carolina, 1926–1972*. University of South Carolina Press, 2006.

Drago, Edmund L. *Charleston's Avery Center*, edited by W. Marvin Dulaney. Charleston, S.C.: History Press, 2006.

"If You Ask Me: 'God must have a special plan for Vashti M. Grayson.' A lovely flower gone . . . " *Baltimore Afro-American*, Jan. 17, 1959: 16.

"Miss Vashti Maxwell Resigns Feb. First. Accepts Appointment in Spanish at Randal Junior High in Washington." *Afro-American*, Jan. 17, 1925: 8.

"Miss Vashti Maxwell Wed to South Carolina Principal." *Afro-American*, Aug. 21, 1937: 7.

"Mrs. Vashti Grayson Professor's Wife Dies." *Afro-American*, Jan. 3, 1959: 5.

"Mrs. Vashti Maxwell Grayson Is Buried Beside Her Father." *Afro-American*, Jan. 10, 1959: 18.

"Charleston"
Charleston

Do you know Charleston?
nestling neither in, nor out,
but just on the edge of South Carolina?

In 1937,
she was a charming, ancient lady,
sitting primly erect and proud

in her slightly dusty, antique Chippendale,
behind blinded, curtained and portiered windows
in the long crowded back parlor
of her crumbling, unpainted mansion;
romantic, with its damp underground passages
and secret twisting stairways,
its panelled Cypress walls and beams
firmly secured with hand-wrought pegs;
distinctive, with its Spanish blue marble steps;
carved iron balconies; recessed intricate gates
and solid doors deceptively leading to pillared porches;
a graceful, narrow house
stretching lazily over the low marshy shore
where the sky-blue Cooper and swamp-edged Ashley
slip into the uneasy sea.

"Charleston, by the sea" . . .
An antiquated lady with fading blue eyes
and wrinkled, sun-burned skin;
with magnolias, jasmine and japonica;
with azealeas, oleanders and crape myrtle
tumbling luxuriously from her dry, wispy hair.
She sat in her billowy, yellowing dress
magnificently splashed with scarlet poinsettias,
shedding in all her fading glory
a warmth of rich beautiful memories.

Dozing quietly; nodding gently;
she lived her life in moldy dreams;
dreams of Secession and War;
dreams of bitterness between Up-Country and Low-Country;
of desolate abandoned plantation;
of lost rice and indigo cultures;
of the prosperity of the seventies, eighties and nineties;
of flourishing phosphate factories and lumber mills;
of the coming of the Yanks to reclaim the empty land;
of the restoring of gardens and filling of mud-flats;
of busy wharves filled with disgorging ships, and
heavy laden freighters patiently waiting their turns

at the humming docks.
Ah! Those were the good old days!

In 1938,
the old lady often woke from her dreaming and napping,
and with tottering reluctant steps walked
to the windows facing her groups,—and saw
warehouses rotting; docks silent;
business stagnant; and her people poor and hungry.

Returning sadly to her dark parlor, she met
her sons and daughters showing staring strangers
around her house of precious relics and memories.
"They come to see, Mother," her daughters explained.
"And to pay," her sons added.
The old lady shrugged her shoulders, drew her skirts
around her bony body and her chair closer to the fire;
wove her dreams of a bright aristocratic past
and cast them upon the embers and dying flames.

When the strangers had gone to their hotels,
and her children gathered around her for the evening meal,
the old woman asked: "Where are my grands?"
Her sons and daughters looked at each other
in consternation, and then answered:
"They became dissatisfied with us and
our old-fashioned ways and traditions."
"They went to Georgia, to Alabama, to Tennessee."
"They went to New York, to Pennsylvania, to Washington."
"They never came back from college."
"We should never have sent them North."
Again the old lady shrugged and murmured
in her soft, slurring, slightly nasal voice:
"Perhaps it is better they're gone. You,
my sons and daughters, will cherish the old.
The grands would have changed us too much."

Then, munching her grits and boiled shrimps,
she asked for "Mauma" and her children

in the houses in the backyard; in the choked courts;
in the decaying dwellings and the slanting shacks.
Her children cleared their throats and
breathed deeply before they said:
"Mauma's old and weak. She's fast dying.
Her children are with us still, but
they're not like Mauma."
"They don't like to wash and iron."
"They don't like to nurse and cook."
"They'd rather work for the Government."
The old lady clucked her tongue against her teeth,
and shook her head mumbling:
"Watch them and remember the Reconstruction."

Suddenly, in anger, the sea threw a torment
over and around the old lady.
White and black alike cowered in the folds of her skirts.
And the old lady remembered the cyclone of eighty-five.
She remembered the cyclone of eighty-six.
She forgot the Reconstruction and hatred,
and her white and black children joined hands
to restore her buildings and her history.

Once more, the old lady sat nursing
her memories and her traditions.
Her sons and daughters went as usual
to Broad Street and to the government offices.
Their cousins took up the trades.
Mauma's country kin came to town and
sold their wares in their picturesque bandannas
while her children left for the "North,"
or worked in factories or at trades.
All was well in the old lady's house and grounds.

In 1941,
the monster War reared himself to unheard of
magnitude, and brandished his bloody sword,
as he stood straddling the whole of America,
with one gory boot in the waters of the Atlantic,

and the other in the waters of the Pacific.
The old lady's children frantically explained to her
the threatening danger of attack from the sea,
by airplane and submarine.

Scoffingly, the old lady bade them organize
the women in groups to feed, house and clothe
large crowds of civilians who might lose their homes, and
large troops of soldiers who would come to guard
the water-front and the port.
One of the daughters asked in a frightened voice:
"What shall we do about mauma's children?"
"Organize them, too," the old lady counselled, and
added, "Get the ones with education and leisure."
"But, Mother, they want to be called 'Mistress',"
her daughter demurred.
"Well, call them Mistress over the telephone, and
don't call them anything before your friends."
So, it was settled, and her daughters dashed around
in cultured panic,
taking courses, donning uniforms and indulging
their hysterical imaginations.
They prepared for blitzkrieg, fire and famine.

Mauma sat in the kitchen, quiet and smiling;
her daughters served, as much as the old lady's daughters
would allow, but their imaginations
went no further than slavery; lynching; segregation;
prejudice and daily humiliation.
They had a patriotic duty to perform.
They could bear any disaster that came.

Gradually, America and her Allies mustered
their greatest strength and painfully pushed
the threat of attack and invasion back from
Charleston's marshy shores.
The old lady and her daughters relaxed.
The little old lady went back to her dreaming

of the War Between the States,
of the turbulent Reconstruction;
but she was weaker than before, and older.
She slept more hours now than she was awake.
When she showed interest in the things around her,
It was with Mauma's children she was concerned.
She was told:
"Her nephews from the North, who are soldiers
stationed here give us a little trouble."
"They are resentful of our ways here.
They resist our traditions and laws, and
mutter something about
dying here for their own principles, rather than
dying abroad for international principles.
Mauma's older sons are still digging ditches, and
carrying heavy loads, but
they're joining unions and
they're quoting the Constitution;
they're even questioning the Primaries.
And Mauma's daughters have all left the kitchen.
They're building ships, airplanes and guns.
They're wearing slacks, flowers in their hair,
good clothes; and they flourish twenty-dollar bills
in the markets and our best stores."

The old lady sadly murmured:
"Watch them and remember the Reconstruction."

Her children sought to cheer her up with the War News.
"Mother, we are winning the war on both oceans."
"Your grandsons are marching to Berlin."
"Your grandsons are booming Tokyo."
The old lady sniffed petulantly:
"Twaddle, don't tell me about the war.
We always win the war.
Tell me of the city and state elections;
tell me of Mauma's children;
Those are the important things in our lives.

You must remember to keep the votes in your hands;
to keep Mauma's children in their places, and
to keep Washington out of my house and grounds."

In 1944,
her daughters and sons tenderly lifted her
from her straight-backed chair and laid her
in her great Colonial bed.
They tightly closed the blinds, and the drapes
and the heavy oaken doors
to shut out the sight of the throngs of
Up-country whites and Negroes who came
from the plantations and farms
to work in the Navy Yard and War Industries,
who over-ran the venerable house
and trampled down the flowers as
they parked their trailers on the lawn.
Her children sealed the windows
to bar out the sounds of tearing down old buildings
and raising modern structures;
to shut out the voices of a few of the old lady's own sons
who shouted and pled with their brothers
to let go of the Past;
to forget the Reconstruction;
to save the family from decay;
to clean up politics; improve schools;
rebuild shipping; reclaim the harbor;
establish industries for Peace;
to become a part of the United States.
The old lady heard the tumult of change;
She heard the rumbling of stifled tension;
she heard the disturbing talk of her children, but
she was safe and warm in her bed of delusion.
And there she still lies; in the last days of her life.
She intends to hold on to breath as long as she can.
Struggle will only shorten her last sweet hours.
Covering her small ears with her alabaster hands,
she feasts her dim eyes on the old splendor of her room,
which is just as it was in her prime.

She knows it will remain so as long as she can hold
on to breathing.
Her children will preserve the sentiment which is
her very breath.
They will restrain the surging movement of progress
at her very door,
so that the old lady may die with beauty and with dignity,
in her long narrow house
nestling like a shining shell
in the watery palms of two rivers
that flow into the uneasy sea.

Louis De Saussure House, 1 East Battery, Charleston, Charleston County, SC, April, 1940. Historic American Buildings Survey. Library of Congress. C. O. Greene, photographer.

Simone de Beauvoir (1947)

"These Aristocratic Paradises"

Simone de Beauvoir, "These Aristocratic Paradises" from *America Day By Day (L'Amerique au jour le jour)*, trans. Patrick Dudley (London: G. Duckworth), 1952, c. 1948.

Simone de Beauvoir (1908–1986), French existentialist philosopher and writer, was born Simone Lucie-Ernestine-Marie-Bertrand de Beauvoir in Paris, France, the eldest daughter in a "bourgeois family." Raised strictly Catholic, she became an atheist as an adolescent and resolved to dedicate her life to the study of existence. When she was twenty-one, she attended the Sorbonne, where she studied philosophy and graduated in 1929. That same year, she met famed French philosopher Jean-Paul Sartre (1905–1980) forming a life-long relationship that would shape the rest of her life. The two were best friends, lovers, and partners who influenced each other's work and philosophy but never married, due to de Beauvoir's insistence that their relationship should not be defined by institutional norms. After graduating from the Sorbonne, de Beauvoir taught in various French schools before returning to teach at the Sorbonne, where from 1931 to 1943 she developed the basis for her philosophical thought. In 1943, she published her first fictional book, *L'Invitée (She Came to Stay)*, followed by her first philosophical essay "Pyrrhus et Cinéas" in 1944. In 1945, she and Sartre founded and edited *Le Temps Modernes,* a monthly review of philosophical thought and trends.

In January of 1947, de Beauvoir landed at New York on her first trip to America. Although she was known in this country as an intellectual and philosopher, she was lesser known than she would become. She was embraced by "the Condé Nast set in a swirl of cocktail parties in New York" before she set off on a four-month lecture tour from coast to coast, which took her to Vassar, Oberlin, Lynchburg College, Smith, Wellesley, and Yale, among other schools. She visited Washington, D.C., Philadelphia, New York State, Boston, Cleveland, Chicago, Los Angeles, San Francisco, Death Valley, Las Vegas, the Grand Canyon, Virginia, New Orleans, Jacksonville, Charleston, Savannah, and various cities in

New Mexico and Texas. She traveled by car, train, and Greyhound bus, immersing herself in the nation's culture, customs, people, and landscape. She records gambling in a Reno casino, smoking her first marijuana at the Plaza Hotel, and learning firsthand about the underworld of morphine addicts and thieves in Chicago with author Nelson Algren as her guide. De Beauvoir was interested in everything American, including Algren, with whom she had an affair.

On her return to France, she reconstructed the diary of her trip and published it for French readers as *L'Amerique au jour le jour* (1948). The book was first translated by Patrick Dudley (pseudonym) and published in England in 1952, which is the edition from which the below excerpt is taken. In 1999, the University of California Press published a new edition, translated by Carol Cosman.

A first-rate travel writer, de Beauvoir was not always complimentary of Americans. Her description of Charleston in the spring of 1947 is a blip in the larger context of her diary, yet she immediately noticed the inherent racial tensions. From the road, she wrote Sartre: "Yesterday we saw Charleston, a very pretty old English town, and some marvelous and romantic gardens full of flowers, lakes, little bridges and great trees veiled in grey—gardens dating from 1700 in the middle of big plantations, the ultimate luxury in that delicious, horrible civilization. You can still see the slave market at Charleston on your way back from the gardens. Towards Richmond in the northern part of Virginia, the atmosphere is not so stifling. But I shall never forget the black towns of Jacksonville, Savannah, Charleston, etc.—and the hatred and fear of the whites, which you can feel at every moment." These simmering racial tensions would soon erupt.

De Beauvoir gained notoriety with *Le Deuxième Sexe* (*The Second Sex*), published in 1949. The 972-page book, in which she analyzes the reasons why women's role in society was characterized as inferior to men, was greatly controversial. Some critics branded the book pornography and the Vatican placed it on the *Index Librorum Prohibitorum* (Index of Prohibited Books). Published in America in 1953, the English edition was only a shadow of the original, as it was translated by a zoologist with limited skills in French. In 2009, an unedited English volume was published, bolstering de Beauvoir's reputation as a feminist. Her work ultimately has contributed to her reputation as a pioneer "for progress and freedom of all women all over the world."

Over her lifetime, de Beauvoir pushed an exhaustive number of works including novels, essays, biographies, autobiography, and monographs on philosophy, politics, and social issues. Of her novels, *Les Mandarins* (1954), in which she urges the educated population to participate in political activism, is the best known and won her the Prix Goncourt prize. De Beauvoir's own interest in politics, sparked after World War II, led her to criticize capitalism and defend communism. In her later career, she wrote about aging. Her 1981 work, *La Cérémonie des Adieux* (*Adieux: A Farewell to Sartre*), recalls the last years of her partner's life. She died in Paris, six years after Sartre. They share a grave.

As the following short excerpt shows, by 1947 tourism was well underway in Charleston. In future decades, tourism would progressively provide Charleston an economic future. Ironically, this prosperity would drive Charlestonians—no longer able to afford the rising property values—from the peninsula their ancestors founded, cherished, and preserved.

SOURCES

De Beauvoir, *America Day by Day* (Dudley edition), 1952.
De Beauvoir, Simone. *America Day By Day,* trans. by Carol Cosman. Berkeley: University of California Press, 2000.
De Beauvoir, Simone. *Letters to Sartre.* New York: Arcade Publishing, 1993.
"De Beauvoir, Simone (1908–1986)." The Internet Encyclopedia of Philosophy. Accessed Jan. 17, 2016. http://www.iep.utm.edu/.

"These Aristocratic Paradises"

I had been told, "You must see Charleston and its gardens." This morning we asked a taxi-driver to take us some twenty miles out of town to the great plantations which date from the eighteenth century. Today these aristocratic paradises are exploited commercially; you have to pay two dollars to pass through the gate, and white arrows point out the way to the visitor. The gardens were deserted in the sunshine and the fresh morning air. Young colored women, dressed in wide hats and bright cotton frocks, swept up the dead in the autumnal springtime; in the farthest paths colored gardeners were clipping hedges. We remained alone.

How many gardens there are in the world! The gardens of the Alhambra, the flowerbeds at Kew, the terraces of Florence, the scented groves of Cintra— but these are the most enchanting. The riot of azaleas and camellias is as violent as the storms of New Orleans. The tiny wooden bridges, with romantic curves, connect mysterious pools; furtive paths curl amidst flowering shrubs; and beyond the water, lawns and flowers is the extravagant triumph of the Spanish moss, hanging from silent trees. This is a strange parasite, symbolizing in its splendor and abjectness the contradictions of a magnificent and sordid land. In the groves that line the Mississippi it hangs from the trees, gray, dirty and rumpled, like spiders' webs in attics; but in these gardens it becomes delicate and precious like those spiders' webs covered with pearls of dew that catch the rainbow. It decorates the green vaulting of the avenues with vaporous stalactites, and its magic changes the roads into haunted caverns. It is the color of smoke, the color of amber and twilight, the impalpable color of fairy robes, and it recalls the gauze veils, scarves, and flounces of those fortunate young girls who gazed at their reflections in these pools; the moss is fragile, useless, subtle and disturbing as pearls, as the living blue of turquoises. A puff of wind will turn it to dust, and then it looks like the fleecy balls of dust you find under furniture; it is only rubbish. It brings to the tree-tops the dampness of the marshes in which it strikes root. It loses its magic when touched; it is only a bit of vegetable matter, without shape, without smell and almost without color, like cellulose.

Here luxury attains to beauty. To sit on one of these benches, to look, to breathe, is a joy so complete that you understand why these curves and lights, this harmonious affirmation of the human through the riches of nature, might have seemed a supreme value for some people. Men struggled desperately here to preserve a civilization, whose exquisite refinement was embodied in these gardens which had a central place. Looking at these lakes and lawns, I understood them. But it was not just by chance that, on returning to Charleston, the first trace of the past we came upon was the slave market. It is preserved more or less as it appears in the illustrations of *Uncle Tom's Cabin*. In one wing shopkeepers had set up stands between the stakes—Coca-Cola, bananas, ice cream. The other part was deserted. It is a long, rectangular hall, ready to receive human cattle. To create private paradises as extravagant as the Alhambra, it took the immense wealth of the planters and the hell of slavery; the delicate petals of the azaleas and the camellias were tinged with blood.

Much of old Charleston remains, despite the storms which carried away houses built near the sea; and there is still in evidence the middle-class, commercial life of the English ports which the immigrants from overseas led here in the first century of the city's history. The little houses have creamy colors—pink, red, white and yellow—and look like children's toys; they have tiny doors and windows, and the walls are shiny. Antique dealers, inns, old theaters and little shops have kept their signs, and we found ourselves walking through a country town of the eighteenth-century. Beside the sea, a few cannon and cannon-balls recall a battle fought, and one can visit innumerable houses linked with Washington, who spent a few nights in Charleston. The record of his visit is still piously preserved.

We ate in an old English inn, where they served delicious Southern food, then we took the bus again. We went North, and the country began to dry up. There were no more forests, Spanish moss or bayous—only huge fields with dark furrows, where the promised cotton harvest was still invisible. From time to time a dark wooden shack stood out from the barren earth against red clouds of sunset.

Bibliography

MANUSCRIPT COLLECTIONS

South Carolina Historical Society, Charleston, SC

James Butler Campbell Papers, 1814–1897. [1015.00].

Robert N.S. Whitelaw papers, 1892–1973. [263.00].

Washington, D.C.

Archives of American Art, Smithsonian. Holger Cahill Papers, February 21–March 1, 1935. Series Two: Correspondence Files [Reel 5285] from The Rockefeller Report (frames 829–832).

University of North Carolina, Southern Historical Collection, Chapel Hill

Journal of Meta Morris Grimball, South Carolina, December 7 1860–February 7 1866, December 19, 1861.

REPRINTED SOURCES

Andrews, Sidney. *The South Since the War: As Shown by Fourteen Weeks of Travel and Observation in Georgia and the Carolinas.* Boston: Ticknor and Fields, 1866.

"B." (Eliza Houston Barr). "Inside Southern Cabins. III.—Charleston, South Carolina." *Harper's Weekly* 24 (November 27, 1880): 765–66.

Bunce, Oliver Bell. "Charleston and Its Suburbs." *Appletons' Journal* 6 (July 15, 1871): 57–73.

Campbell, Sir George, M. P. *White and Black: The Outcome of a Visit to the United States.* London: Chatto & Windus, 1879.

Clark, Emily. "DuBose Heyward," *Virginia Quarterly Review* 6:4 (Autumn 1930).

De Beauvoir, Simone. *America Day By Day (L'Amerique au jour le jour),* translated by Patrick Dudley. London: G. Duckworth, 1952, c. 1948.

Grayson, Vashti Maxwell. "Charleston" *Phylon* (1940–1956) 6:1 (1st Qtr., 1945): 64–69.

Hardy, Lady Duffus. *Down South.* London: Chapman and Hall, 1883.

Howe, M. A. De Wolfe. "The Song of Charleston." *Atlantic Monthly* 146 (July 1930): 108–11.

Howells, William Dean. "In Charleston, A Travel Sketch." *Harper's Monthly* 131 (Oct. 1915): 747–57.

Hungerford, Edward. *The Personality of American Cities.* New York: McBride, Nast & Co., 1913.

King, Edward. *The Great South; A Record of Journeys in Louisiana, Texas, the Indian Territory, Missouri, Arkansas, Mississippi, Alabama, Georgia, Florida, South*

Carolina, North Carolina, Kentucky, Tennessee, Virginia, West Virginia, and Mary-land. Hartford, CT: American Publishing Co., 1875.

Lewisohn, Ludwig. "South Carolina: A Lingering Fragrance." *The Nation* 115: 2975 (July 12, 1922): 36–38.

Lowell, Amy. "Epitaph in a Church-Yard In Charleston, South Carolina." In *A Dome of Many Coloured Glass*. Boston: Houghton Mifflin, 1912.

———. "Charleston, South Carolina," "A South Carolina Forest," "The Middleton Place," "Magnolia Gardens," and "The Vow." *Poetry, a Magazine of Verse* 21:3 (December 1922): 117–24.

O'Connor, Mrs. T. P. (Betty Paschal O'Connor). *My Beloved South*. New York; London: G. P. Putnam's Sons, 1913.

Parsons, Schuyler Livingston. *Untold Friendships*. Boston: Houghton Mifflin, 1955.

Peck, W. F. G. "Four Years Under Fire." *Harper's New Monthly* 31:183 (August, 1865): 358–66.

Reid, Whitelaw. *After the War: A Southern Tour, May 1, 1865, to May 1, 1866*. London: Sampson Low, Son, & Marston, 1866.

Rockwell, Norman. *Norman Rockwell, My Adventures as an Illustrator*. Garden City, N.Y.: Doubleday, 1960.

Sarton, May. "Charleston Plantations." *The Atlantic Monthly* (Apr. 1941): 487.

Twig, Edward (Richard Coleman). "Charleston: The Great Myth." *The Forum* 103:1 (Jan. 1940): 1–7.

Wescott, Glenway. *Continual Lessons: The Journals of Glenway Wescott, 1937–1955*. Edited by Robert Phelps and Jerry Rosco. New York: Farrar Straus & Giroux, 1991.

White, Charles Henry. "Charleston." *Harper's Monthly* (Nov. 1907): 852–61.

Wister, Owen. *Roosevelt, the Story of a Friendship*. New York: Macmillan Company, 1930.

SOURCES

Anonymous. *Short Sketch of Charleston, S.C.: How It Fared in Two Wars and An Earthquake*. New York: Atlantic Coast Line, 1886.

American Bar Association, *Annual Report of the American Bar Association: Including Proceedings of the Annual Meeting*, Vol. 5, 1883.

"Annual Report of the New York National Freedman's Relief Association," *The American Freedman* 2:6 (June 1866). New York: American Freedmen's and Union Commission.

Applegate, Debby. *The Most Famous Man in America: The Biography of Henry Ward Beecher*. New York: Doubleday, 2006.

Ayers, Edward L. *Promise of the New South: Life after Reconstruction*. New York: Oxford University Press, 1992.

Baldwin, Charles C. *Stanford White*. New York: Dodd Mead Co., 1931.

Bethel, Elizabeth Rauh. *Promiseland: A Century of Life in a Negro Community*. Columbia: University of South Carolina Press, 1997.

Bleser, Carol. *The Promised Land: The History of the South Carolina Land Commission, 1869–1890*. Columbia: University of South Carolina Press, 1969.

Bowers, Claude G. *The Tragic Era: The Revolution after Lincoln.* Boston: Houghton Mifflin Company, 1929.

Breaux, Daisy (Cornelia Donovan O'Donovan Calhoun). *Autobiography of a Chameleon.* Washington, D.C.: Potomac Press, 1930.

Broderick, Mosette. *Triumvirate: McKim, Mead & White: Art, Architecture, Scandal, and Class in America's Gilded Age.* New York: Alfred A. Knopf, 2010.

"Calhoun's Remains," *New York Times,* Nov. 22, 1884: 3.

Coughlin, Gene. "Camilla Moss' Two Tragedies." *Milwaukee Sentinel,* July 9, 1950: 30.

"Death of Lieut. De Reszke; Last of the Family of the Famous Singer, Known to So Many Here," *New York Times,* June 23, 1918: 45.

Drago, Edmund L., and Eugene C. Hunt. Oral History Interview with Felder Hutchinson (July 16, 1985). Avery Normal Institute Oral History Project. Avery Research Center. College of Charleston.

Epps, Garrett. "The Undiscovered Country: Northern Views of the Defeated South and the Political Background of the Fourteenth Amendment." *Temple Political & Civil Rights Law Review* 13:2 (Spring 2004): 411–28.

Fleming, Walter. *Documentary History of Reconstruction: Political, Military, Social, Religious, Educational & Industrial, 1865 to the Present Time,* Vol. 1. Cleveland, O.H.: A. H. Clark Co., 1906.

———. ed. *Documents Relating to Reconstruction.* Morgantown: West Virginia University, 1904: nos. 4 & 5: "Public Frauds in South Carolina."

Freedman's Society, *Freedmen's Record: Organ of the New England Freedmen's Aid Society,* Vol. 1. Boston, Massachusetts: Freedman's Society, 1865.

Ginsberg, Benjamin. *Moses of South Carolina: A Jewish Scalawag during Radical Reconstruction.* Baltimore: Johns Hopkins University Press, 2010.

Grimball, Meta Morris. The Journal of Meta Morris Grimball (unpublished transcript), in *First Person Narratives of the American South 1860–1920* (Chapel Hill: University of North Carolina), at http://memory.loc.gov/ammem/award97/ncuhtml/fpnashome.html.

Hendrix, M. Patrick. *Down & Dirty: Archaeology of the South Carolina Lowcountry.* Charleston: History Press, 2006.

Hollis, Margaret Belser, and Allen H. Stokes, eds. *Twilight on the South Carolina Rice Fields.* Columbia: University of South Carolina Press, 2012.

Jenkins, Wilbert L. *Seizing the New Day: African Americans in Post–Civil War Charleston.* Bloomington: Indiana University Press, 1998.

Kantrowitz, Stephen. *Ben Tillman and the Reconstruction of White Supremacy.* Chapel Hill: University of North Carolina Press, 2000.

Leiser, Clara. *Jean de Reszke and the Great Days of the Opera.* New York: Minton Blalch Co., 1934.

Lesesne, Henry H. "Gray, Martin Witherspoon (1831–1881)." In *The South Carolina Encyclopedia,* edited by Walter Edgar. Columbia: University of South Carolina Press, 2006.

McIntyre, Rebecca C. "Promoting the Gothic South." *Southern Cultures* 11:2 (Summer 2005): 33–61.

McKivigan, John R. *Forgotten Firebrand: James Redpath and the Making of Nineteenth-Century America*. Ithaca, NY: Cornell University Press, 2008.

Meyers, Amrita Chakrabarti. *Forging Freedom: Black Women and the Pursuit of Liberty in Antebellum Charleston*. Chapel Hill: University of North Carolina Press, 2014.

Milligan, John, Dr. "A Description of the Province of South Carolina." In *Historical Collections of South Carolina*, edited by B. R. Carroll, Vol. 2. New York: Harper Brothers, 1836.

Nepveux, Ethel S. *George Alfred Trenholm: And the Company that Went to War 1861–1865*. Anderson, SC: Electric City, 1994.

"Obituary: Jean de Reszke, Jr." *Musical Times* 59. London: Novello, 1918: 420–21.

"Our Charleston Correspondence." *New York Times* (May 22, 1865).

Pease, William H., and Jane H. Pease, eds. *A Family of Women: The Carolina Petigrus in Peace and War*. Chapel Hill: University of North Carolina Press, 1999.

———. *The Roman Years of a South Carolina Artist: Caroline Carson's Letters Home, 1872–1892*. Columbia: University of South Carolina Press, 2003.

Phillips, Ted Ashton, Jr. *City of the Silent*. Columbia: University of South Carolina Press, 2010.

Pinckney, Josephine. "Bulwarks against Change." In *Culture in the South,* edited by W. T. Couch. Chapel Hill: University of North Carolina Press, 1934: 40–51.

Powers, Bernard. *Black Charlestonians: A Social History, 1822–1885*. Fayetteville, AR: University of Arkansas Press, 1994.

Pressley, John G. "Extracts from the Diary of Lieutenant-Colonel John G. Pressley, of the Twenty-Fifth South Carolina Volunteers." *Southern Historical Society Papers,* Vol. 14. Richmond, Virginia: William Jones, 1886: 35–62.

Pringle, Henry F. "Theodore Roosevelt and the South." *Virginia Quarterly Review* 9:1 (January 1933): 14–25.

Racine, Philip N. *Gentlemen Merchants: A Charleston Family's Odyssey, 1828–1870*. Knoxville, TN: University of Tennessee Press, 2008.

Rutledge, Anna Wells. "The Second St. Philip's, 1710–1835." *Journal of Architectural Historians* 18:3 (October 1959): 112–14.

Sholes, A. E. *Sholes' Directory of the City of Charleston*. Charleston: A. E. Sholes, 1882.

Schweninger, Loren. *Black Property Owners in the South, 1790–1915*. Champaign, IL: University of Illinois Press, 1997.

Simkins, Francis Butler. *Pitchfork Ben Tillman: South Carolinian*. Baton Rouge: Louisiana State University Press, 1944.

Simons, Harriett P., and Albert Simons. "The William Burrows House of Charleston." *South Carolina Historical and Genealogical Magazine* 70 (1969): 155–76.

Social Register Association, *Social Register, Richmond, North Carolina, Charleston, Savannah, Augusta, Atlanta* 36:18 (New York: Social Register Assoc.), 1922.

South Carolina Institute. *Premium List of the South Carolina Institute: Incorporated in 1850, for the Promotion and Encouragement of the Arts, Agriculture, Ingenuity, Mechanics, Manufactures, and a General Development of Industry*. Charleston: Walker, Evans & Cogswell, 1870.

Smith, Alice Huger, and D. E. Huger Smith. *Dwelling Houses of Charleston*. Charleston: History Press, 2007.

Smith, Amanda. *Newspaper Titan: The Infamous Life and Monumental Times of Cissy Patterson*. New York: Alfred A. Knopf, 2011.

Stockton, Robert. "Do You Know Your Charleston." *Charleston News & Courier* (Dec. 19, 1977).

Stoney, Samuel G. "Robert N. Gourdin to Robert Anderson, 1861." *South Carolina Historical Magazine* 60:1 (Jan., 1959): 10–14.

Tindall, George Brown. *South Carolina Negroes, 1877–1900*. Columbia: University of South Carolina Press, 1952.

———. "The Liberian Exodus of 1878." *South Carolina Historical Magazine* 53:2 (July 1952): 133–45.

"To The Public," *United States Congressional Serial Set* (Washington, D.C.: US Government Printing Office), 1861, Vol. 1093: 473–75.

Trowbridge, John T. *A Picture of the Desolated States and the Work of Restoration, 1865–1868*. Hartford, CT: L. Stebbins, 1868.

Walker, Don D. "Wister, Roosevelt and James: A Note on the Western." *American Quarterly* 12: 3 (Autumn 1960): 358–66.

Wellford, Drury. "G. T. Beauregard (1818–1893)." In *Encyclopedia Virginia*, edited by Brendan Wolfe. Virginia Foundation for the Humanities.

"Will Philip Lining." *Century Illustrated Monthly Magazine* 44:66 (May 1903): 728.

Williams, Alfred Brockenbrough. *Liberian Exodus. An Account of Voyage of the First Emigrants in the Bark "Azor," and Their Reception at Monrovia, with a Description of Liberia-Its Customs and Civilization, Romances and Prospects*. Charleston: News and Courier Press Books, 1878.

Williams, Susan Millar, and Stephen G. Hoffius. *Upheaval in Charleston: Earthquake and Murder on the Eve of Jim Crow*. Athens, G.A.: University of Georgia Press, 2012.

Woolson, Constance Fenimore. "Up the Ashley and the Cooper." *Harper's New Monthly Magazine* 52:307 (December 1875): 1–24.

Yarbrough, Tinsley E. *A Passion for Justice: J. Waties Waring and Civil Rights*. Oxford University Press, 2001.

Zola, Gary Phillip. *Isaac Harby of Charleston, 1788–1828: Jewish Reformer and Intellectual*. Tuscaloosa: University of Alabama Press, 1994.

Index

Abby Aldrich Rockefeller Folk Art
  Museum (Colonial Williamsburg,
  Va.), ix, xxi, *ill*. 284, 286, 288, 294n5,
  ill. 295
abolition and abolitionists: the American
  Missionary Society (AMS), 111; James
  Beecher as, 40n2; British and Foreign
  Anti-Slavery Society, 89; British pio-
  neer of, 42n2; northern abolitionists,
  37; Ohio and the Underground
  Railroad, 1. *See also* antislavery
Academy of Music, 266, 266n3, 269
Adger, Robert, 96n1, 105n2
African Americans: children and
  orphans of, 78, 78n3, 114, 115;
  Civil War regiments of, 18n1, 40n2,
  78n3, 103n1; conditions of, xv–xvi,
  xxi–xxii, *ill*. 122, 125–26; as Democrats, 91, 97, 102; and the Freedman's
  Bank failure, xxii; and Liberia, 42n2,
  104, 104n1; and lynching, xxii, 244,
  244n1, 334 ; and the "Martyrs of the
  Race Course, 34, 34n1; meeting at
  Zion Church (1865), 39–43; migrations of, xxii, 79, 94, 104; and
  miscegenation laws, xv; 105, 105n1;
  mission work among, xv–xvi, 111;
  as picturesque, xv, 117, 119, 201;
  political disenfranchisement of, xxii;
  poverty of, xxii, 115, 118–19, 198,
  200–201; and the Promised Land,
  94n1; represented by black men
  (1878), 102; and spirituals, 112, 130,
  254–55, 267, 267n1, 273–74, 321–22;
  and the Society for the Preservation
  of Spirituals, xx, 255–56, 264–69;
  slum clearance and public housing,

xxii, 301, 301n1; syncopation by,
  155, 157–59; upper tenth of, 113;
  and voting, 40n1, 80–82; 100, 101–3,
  108; wedding of, 255. *See also* African
  Americans, religion and faith of;
  Gullah; Jim Crow laws
African Americans, and education:
  Burke Industrial School, 329–30;
  postwar state of, 26–27; Charleston
  schools and teachers of, 96; colleges
  founded for, 111; public schools
  (black and white) in 1865, 27. *See
  also* Avery Normal Institute; William
  Henry Grayson
African Americans, employment and
  labor: attitudes toward, 94, 98, 126;
  employees of shopkeepers and small
  trades, 126; as farmers, 41, 99, 106,
  107; fishermen, 119; journeymen,
  126; as unskilled labor, 26–27, 41, 84,
  84n1, 85, 97, 98, 99, 100–101, 108,
  115; and the labor strike, 106, 106n1;
  at Magnolia Gardens, 69–70; prejudice against, 100; work in the fields
  as tenant farmers and sharecroppers,
  xxii, 94, 99, 119; as servants, xii, xvi,
  xx, 35, 114n1, 115, 125, 160, 177,
  182, 189, 203, 249, 252–53, 254, 255,
  256–57, 265, 302, 303, 316–17, 321,
  326, 333; as stevedores, 94, 278, 280.
  See also street vendors
African Americans, religion and faith:
  99, 116–17, *ill*. 262; African Methodist Episcopal Church, 102n1; Baptists
  and Roman Catholics among, 120;
  Centenary Methodist Church, 120,
  120n2; peculiar ideas of, 107; revival

Chadwick, Dorothy (Mrs. Elbridge
Gerry), 258, 258n1
Chadwick, Elbridge Gerry, 258, 258n1
Chamberlain, Daniel H., 82n1
Chaplin, Charlie, 247
Charleston, aristocrats (white gentry),
130; dominance of, 169–70; families
of, 172–73, 182, 240, 252; hierarchy
of, xiii; intermarriage among, 205;
ladies of, 55, 146–48; and northerners, xiii, xiv, xvi, 61, 195, 251–52;
paradises of, xxii– xxiii, 341; poverty
and pride of, xv–xvi, xix, 33, 33n1,
36–37, 97, 128–29, 147, 198, 235, 259,
279, 299, 308; resorts for, 29, 64, 134,
252, *ill.* 284, 293. *See also* St. Cecilia
Society; Society for the Preservation
of Old Dwellings; Society for the
Preservation of Spirituals
Charleston, dance, xx
Charleston, S.C.: *ill.* 58, *ill.* 62; in the
aftermath of defeat, 25–45, 49–56;
and the Charleston Renaissance, xvii,
154; and civil rights, xxiii; in the Civil
War, 2–21; Col John Stuart House in,
195, *ill.* 328; cyclones, xvi, 173, 175,
333; fictious brothel in, 297; fire of
1861, xii, 49, 49n1, 64, 77, 128–29;
finances and conditions (1870s),
82–84; Greeks of, 185; and the Jazz
Age, xx; Memorial Day celebration
in, 34, 34n1; and the New Deal, xxi,
xxii, 301–2, 301n1; northerners in, xv,
xvi, 14, 47, 51, 61, 94, 98, 108, 142,
253; peculiarity of, xv, 2, 72, 127, 160,
239, 240; as picturesque, 76, 118, 127,
129, 130, 135, 153; poverty of, xvi, 55,
125, 127, 150, 167, 172, 203, 297, 299;
public schools in (1865), 27; ruins of,
ill. xxvi, 49, 50, 56, 61, 64, 65, 69, 77,
85, 131–32, 137, 175, 300, 301;
Sephardic Jews of, 240; and the stock
market crash (1929), xx, 250; tourists
and tourism, xii, xvii, xviii, xx,
xxii–xxiii, 155, 168, 182, 255, 256,

266, 291, 301–2, 341; the Navy Yard
during World War I, xviii, 210–22;
World War II, xxi, xxii. *See also*
Battery, the; Charleston earthquake
(1886); French Huguenots; historic
preservation; South Carolina Inter-
state and West Indian Exposition
Charleston Arsenal, 16–17, 33
Charleston Belt Line, 202–3
Charleston City Hall, 15, 79, 199, 199n1
Charleston Club-House, 79, 79n1
Charleston College (College of Charles-
ton), 235, 236, 238; and the Museum
of Natural History, 243n4
Charleston Country Club, 286
Charleston County Courthouse (84
Broad Street), 79
Charleston Courier, 35n2, 36, 43. See
also Charleston *News & Courier*
Charleston Custom House, 25, 25n1
*Charleston Daily Courier. See Charles-
ton Courier*
Charleston earthquake (1886), xvi, 79,
79n1, 79n2, 171, 173, 190, 202, 204,
264
Charleston Etchers Club, 154
Charleston *Evening Post*, 147n1
Charleston Guard House, 79, 79n2
Charleston Hotel, 14, 78, 78n4, 93, 125,
142, 167–68
Charleston Jail (Old City Jail), 100,
100n1, 301–2, 301n1
Charleston Knights of Columbus. *See*
Knights of Columbus
Charleston Library Society, 183, 183n2
Charleston Lunatic Asylum, 77
Charleston Market (Old Market), xxiii,
118, 135–36, 175–76, 176n1, *ill.* 192,
199, 216, 340, 342; buzzards of, 118,
135, 197, 307. *See also* Market Hall
Charleston Mercury, 3, 3n1, 31
Charleston Museum, 273n1, 290, 290n4,
291
Charleston Naval Base. *See* Charleston
Navy Yard

Nathaniel Russell House, 78, 78n3

National Association for the Advancement of Colored People (NAACP), 194

Neagle, John L., 82n1

New Deal, xxi, 301–2, 301n1; effects on racial divide, xxii

New England Freedman's Aid Society of Boston, 27n2

New South, xix, xv, 47, 93n1, 96n1, 237, 238–39, 244

Newman, Frances, 282, 282n1

Newport (R.I.), xvi, 248; and Charleston families in the 1830s, 250; African American colony in, 252–53; and Stone Villa, 252, 252n1

News & Courier. See Charleston *News & Courier*

northern war journalists, *See* Peck, Farley; Andrews, Sidney; Reid, Whitelaw; Trowbridge, John

O'Conner, Flannery, 297–98

O'Connor, Mrs. T. P. (Betty Paschal O'Connor), ix, xvii, *ill.* 178; account of, 179–91

O'Donnel House (21 King Street), xx, 226, *ill.* 246, 247; as "Mr. Parson's Mansion," 249. *See also* Pinckney, Josephine

O'Hagan, William James, 292n3

Oakhurst Plantation (Hutton Plantation, Colleton County, S.C.), 258n9

Oaks Plantation. *See* Goose Creek Club

Old and Historic District, xx

Old City Jail. *See* Charleston Jail

Old Exchange or Custom House, 62–63, 62n2, 63n1, 176n1

Old Market. *See* Charleston Market

Old Plantation, The, painting, ix, 288, 294, 294n5, *ill.* 295

Old Slave Mart, 176n1

Omar Shrine Temple, 156n1

Orangeburg, S.C., xxi, 294

Ordinance of Secession, 3, 38. *See also* secession

Orphan House. *See* Charleston Orphan House

Osceola (Indian chief), 28, 28n1, 184

Ottolengui, Rodrigues, 243, 243n6

Ottolengui family, 240

Pacific Company (phosphates). *See* phosphates

Palmer, Rev. Benjamin Morgan, 6, 6n3

Palmetto Guards, 28n1, 29

Parker, Niles G., 82n1

Parker's Ferry Plantation (Yemassee, S.C.), 315–26 *passim*

Parrott guns, 10–11, 10n2, 16, 50, 196; and the Swamp Angel, 13, 13n1, 14, 25, 43, 172

Parsons, Betty (Bierne Pierson), 247

Parsons, C. L. (justice of the Liberian Supreme Court), 104n1

Parsons, Edwin, 273n4

Parsons, Mary Battle (Mrs. Edwin), 273n4. *See* Oaks Plantation

Parsons, Schuyler Livingston, ix, xx; account of, 247–60

Patriotic Association of Colored Men, and Friends of the Martyrs, 34n1

Patterson, Col. John L., 82n1

Paul Plantation (Paul and Dalton Plantation, Green Pond, S.C.), 105n2

Pavilion Hotel, 78, 78n4, 125–26, 130

Peck, Capt. Fenn, 112

Peck, Thomas Fenn Hunt, 112

Peck, Thomas Fenn Hunt, Mrs., 112

Peck, William Farley, xi. xiii, account of, 1–21

Pennell, Joseph, 153

Peterkin, Julia and *Scarlet Sister Mary,* 272; *Green Thursday* and *Black April,* 275, 275n2

Petigru, James Louis, 3, 3n2, 33, 33n1, 149, 149n1

Petigru, Jane Amelia Postell, 33, 33n1

Phillips, John, Esq., 40n1

phosphates, 76, 83–84, 84n1, 96, 107–8, 108n1, 112, 134, 331

South Carolina (*continued*)
as "petrel state," 90–92; poor whites
in, 27, 65, 244n1; State Assembly and
voting (1878), 79, 90–91, 101, 102;
state government, state debt of (1878),
and the black vote in, xxii, 90–91,
102; white supremacy in, 90, 101n2,
306–7, 306n1. *See also* secession;
Reconstruction; miscegenation
Southern Literary Renaissance, 271
Spanish-American War, 142n1
Spartanburg, S.C., 83; and Methodists,
238
Stagg, Hunter, of *The Reviewer*, 271, 272
Standard Oil Company, 286, 287
Stansbury, Mary Anna Phinney and
"How He Saved St. Michael's,"
174n1.
Star of the West, 3–5, 4n2
State Street, *ill.* 152
Stein, Gertrude, 272, 315
Stephens, Alexander Hamilton, 31, 31n4
Stevens, Clement Hoffman, 5, 5n1
Stiles Point Plantation, 100–101, 100n3
Stone Villa (Newport, R.I.). *See*
Middleton family.
Stono Company. *See* phosphates.
Stowe, Harriet Beecher, and *Uncle Tom's
Cabin*, 40n2, 293, 342
Straus, Nathan, 301, 301n1
street vendors: xviii, 117–18, 169,
170–71
Stuart, Gilbert and the Lansdowne
portrait, 200, 200n1
Sullivan's Island, S.C., 4, 6, 7, 29, 64,
134–35, 137, 190, 294. *See also* Fort
Moultrie; Moultrie House
Summerville, S.C., 135, 142, 184, 184n1.
See also Arden, Elizabeth; Pine Forest
Inn; Pinehurst Tea Plantation
Sumner, Sen. Charles, 142n2
Swamp Angel Battery. *See* Parrott guns
Széchenyi, Count László, 254, 254n1
Széchenyi, Countess László (Gladys
Vanderbilt), 254n1

taverns, 30
Thackeray, William Makepeace, 149–50,
149n2, 187, 240
Thaw, Harry Kendall, 253n1
Theus, Jeremiah, 290, 290n2
Thompson, Hugh Smith, 145, 145n3
Tillman, Benjamin Ryan, 143–45, 143n1,
143n2, 238
Tillman, James Hammond, 145, 145n1
Tilney, Dr. Fred, 249, 249n1
Timrod, Henry, 239–40, 239n3
Tolbert, Daniel Frank, 104n1
Tolbert, William R., Jr.,
Tourgée, Albion, 111–12
tourism and tourists. *See* Charleston,
tourism and tourists
Trenholm, Charles Louis, 293n1
Trenholm, Col. William Lee, 93, 93n1
Trenholm, George A., 32, 32n3, 93n1
Trenholm, Portia Burden, 288, 293,
293n1. *See Legareville, South
Carolina* painting
Trescot, William Henry, 241, 241n1,
242
Trescot family, 240
Trowbridge, John T., xiii
Trumbull, John, 199–200, 199n1, 200n1
Twig, Edward. *See* Coleman, Richard
Tyler, President John, 71n3

Uncle Tom's Cabin. See Stowe, Harriet
Beecher
Underground Railroad, 1
Union code of signals, 12
Union prisoners, 18–19, 34n1
Union troops, 6, 8–9, 10, 14, 20, 21
Unitarian Church, 204, 204n1
upstate, S.C., xix, 143, 145, 238, 279;
antagonism with the lowcountry,
307, 331; blacks from, 94, 98, 107;
cotton grown in, 98; cotton mills and
industrial development in, xix; Louis
Wright's response to Ludwig Lewisohn's description of, 237; black and
white workers at the Navy Yard from,

CPSIA information can be obtained
at www.ICGtesting.com
Printed in the USA
BVHW030947030219
539310BV00002B/3/P